Ednan Aslan · Marcia Hermansen (Eds.)

Islam and Citizenship Education

In Cooperation with Minela Salkic Joldo

Springer VS

Editors
Ednan Aslan
University of Vienna, Austria

Marcia Hermansen
Loyola University Chicago, USA

Wiener Beiträge zur Islamforschung
ISBN 978-3-658-08602-2   ISBN 978-3-658-08603-9 (eBook)
DOI 10.1007/978-3-658-08603-9

Library of Congress Control Number: 2014958971

Springer VS
© Springer Fachmedien Wiesbaden 2015

Springer VS is a brand of Springer Fachmedien Wiesbaden
Springer Fachmedien Wiesbaden is part of Springer Science+Business Media
(www.springer.com)

Wiener Beiträge zur Islamforschung

Herausgegeben von
E. Aslan, Wien, Österreich

Die Buchreihe „Wiener Beiträge zur Islamforschung" beschäftigt sich mit interdis-
ziplinären Studien aus den Fachbereich der Islamischen Theologie und Religions-
pädagogik sowie der Religionswissenschaft und Philosophie. Die Forschungs-
schwerpunkte des Herausgebers, Professor Ednan Aslan, liegen auf Themen wie
Islam in Europa, der Theorie der islamischen Erziehung in Europa sowie Fragen
zu Muslime an öffentlichen Schulen und Islamischer Theologie mit europäischer
Prägung.

Herausgegeben von
Ednan Aslan
Institut für Islamische Studien
Universität Wien
Wien, Österreich

Table of Contents

Section Two   The Balkans and the Middle East

Appendix   Messages of Felicitation

Foreword

Ednan Aslan

This fifth volume of the "Wiener Islamic Studies" series is the result of a conference bearing the same title held in Tirana, Albania in October, 2013. The interesting contributions by participants from twenty different countries investigate the intersection of religiosity and citizenship from various religious and cultural perspectives with the main focus centering on the situation of Muslims and citizenship education in Europe. The participants draw attention not only to perceived areas of conflict between Muslim religious identity and practice and Western societies, but also to the ways religion, in particular Islam, can contribute to the promotion of citizenship education.

Understanding citizenship education in secular societies from the perspective of religion poses a challenge to Muslims, particularly to those who are living in Europe and seeking to protect and perpetuate their religious identity within a pluralistic society. Within these societies Muslims are confronted with questions unfamiliar to them based on their histories and backgrounds. It is therefore not always easy for them to understand and respond appropriately. Under these circumstances Muslims feel that they have only one alternative, namely to isolate themselves from society and, within this isolation, to live a life that is artificial and distant from reality.

Such patterns of living, which are observable in many parts of Europe, have inevitably pushed Muslims to the margins of societies. This causes a multitude of problems, particularly for the younger generation, which is not quite sure whether to regard the country where they are living as home or whether to continue to dream of a country where they will ultimately never live and would probably not even aspire to inhabit. Not being able to get situated and settle down, which is a prerequisite for perceiving oneself as an equal citizen, leads many to invent an overrated and idealized home country that is waiting for them. In this way, many opportunities, which could offer the means for transforming young Muslims into mature, independent and responsible citizens, are disregarded or never realized. The resulting anxiety and doubt causes them to remain within their collective group, which, through its characteristics, creates a barrier to and inhibits a healthy socialization process.

Under these circumstances, religion, which should in fact make life simpler, instead makes daily existence more difficult. Young people are overburdened with contradictions, rendering the process of exploring the means to feel at home in Europe extremely difficult. Consequently, religion blocks rather than facilitates this process. One reason for this blockage is that the media emphasizes the potential for conflict inherent in all religions, rather than their even greater potential to promote peace and understanding.

Fostering open dialogue from within the midst of society constitutes a healthy approach for resolving this dilemma, and religious education could serve as a suitable topic for that dialogue. Islam, like other religions, could contribute toward integrating Muslim children and young adults into their new environment. It could assist in cultivating their self-perception as part of society and in stimulating their developing capacities for assuming responsibilities accordingly, thus diminishing and eventually eliminating their feeling of being strangers in Europe. The religious education of Muslim children and young adults could play a vital role in this regard.

The scholarly contributors to this volume investigate various means to stimulate and facilitate reflection on new social relations while clarifying the contradictions between religious and social affiliation from different perspectives and experiences. They explore hindrances whose removal could enable Muslim children and youth to pursue equal participation in political and social life, and the ways that education could faciliate this process. By focusing specifically on citizenship education, and the place of Islam within it, their research contributes toward the development of an educational project that could enlighten Muslim children and youth regarding their rights and obligations, prepare them to assume civic responsibilities, and make active and conscious participation in social processes more readily accessible to them without relinquishing their faith and religious practice. Thus, this new volume of the "Wiener Islamic Studies" series contributes significantly toward enabling Muslims to develop a new sense of belonging and self-perception in Europe that would strengthen their capacity for social and political participation while simultaneously creating a role and space for their religious identity.

I would hereby like to express my heartfelt thanks to all colleagues whose involvement made this book possible. In addition, it is important to emphasize that this international conference could not have succeeded without the willingness of various agencies and organizations to promote it. In this regard, I would like to express my deepest gratitude to the Austrian Foreign Ministry, the Austrian Embassy in Tirana and the Austrian Cultural Association for their generous financial support. Furthermore, my thanks also go out to our partner universities, the University of Tirana and Beder University, for their tireless commitment to the management of crucial organizational tasks. To my assistant Minela Salkic-Joldo I am indebted for her significant contributions to the production of this volume. Last but not least, I am sincerely grateful to my colleague Marcia Hermansen of Loyola University Chicago for her role as co-editor of the volume.

Introduction to the Volume and its Contents

Marcia Hermansen

The collection of papers that you have before you represents a broad collaboration of scholars and practitioners from multiple disciplines whose chapters address the theme of religion and citizenship education. These diverse studies are based on communications initially presented at a conference on citizenship, education and Islam convened in Tirana, Albania in November, 2013 by the Faculty of Philosophy and Education, Department of Education, University of Vienna, the University of Tirana, and Bedër University.

The participants, drawn from diverse European, North American, and Middle Eastern academic and governmental institutions, focus in their contributions to this volume on themes related to both citizenship and religion, especially in predominantly secular and plural societies.

A particular theme of the volume, given the interests of the Vienna University Institute for Islamic Education, a major organizer and sponsor of the conference through its Director, Dr. Ednan Aslan, is the position of Muslims and Islamic education within many of these societies, and how diverse aspects of state educational systems can support integrated yet plural civil societies and the incorporation of religious and ethnic minorities as full citizens.

These papers therefore provide a valuable baseline assessment of contemporary situations and their historical contexts across a range of diverse social and political systems. Not all chapters included in this collection focus on Muslims or Islamic education. A number of contributions consider other immigrant communities, for example, Doron Kiesel's chapter on new Russian Jewish immigrants in Germany and M. Scharer's Christian theological meditation on the nature of "citizenship" with illustrations from the Austrian context.

Two contributors from North America, HyeRan Kim-Cragg, and Eileen Daly, provide further comparative perspectives by drawing primarily on Christian views and practices that negotiate religious ideals and contemporary concepts of citizenship.

The volume's introductory section presents Islamic historical and theological parameters for initiating a discussion of religion, citizenship and civic education.

Dr. Ednan Aslan inaugurates the volume through outlining the historical background of the concept of Islam/state relations by explaining some of the tensions that have emerged between the political order and idealized religious formulations of the basis for human cooperation, not only with modernity, but also during earlier periods of Islamic history. In fact, the question of whether Islam, or at least the system of Islamic law, can function in a modern state is currently under intense discussion. First of all we must examine the roots of the modern state both historically and philosophically, and whether a shared rationality that supports a pluralistic consensus on basic human values—the basis of modern civil systems in most nations states, at least in the West, can be compatible with a system that holds God as sovereign and all human activities to be subsumed under ethical codes inscribed in revealed sources.

In his chapter, Muslim theologian Zeki Saritoprak bears in mind, in particular, the situation in many Western societies where Muslims are immigrant minority populations. The state here is often concerned with issues of their loyalty, participation and integration.

Drawing on the Qur'an, Prophetic traditions (hadith) and historical examples, Saritoprak lays the foundation of an Islamic theology of immigration as a positive religious imperative that can overcome alienation and provide transformative potential, not only for the immigrants themselves, but also through their positive contributions to their new homeland. The title of this chapter, "Migration, Feelings of Belonging to a Land, and the Universality of Islam" summarizes his argument that Muslims can feel a sense of belonging and participation anywhere in the world and that there is nothing inherently xenophobic in the Islamic tradition.

The topic of citizenship education and Islam can be approached from diverse perspectives. A number of contributions to this volume take a curricular approach, summarizing the major themes and learning objectives that either constitute one component of state mandated curricula or the educational materials designed by Muslim religious communities themselves in order to see how these align with the basic values of citizenship.

Other contributions give more consideration to theoretical aspects of the management of citizenship and religious identity, for example Nielsen and Alexander.

Still others push us to consider categories such as "belonging" on the basis of the experience of minorities and immigrants themselves (Allenbach).

A number of contributors express concern that excessive pluralism in citizenship education may ultimately erode the teaching of shared values. These include, for example, Eileen Daly's chapter on citizenship education in the United States and Dmitry Shmonin's Russian perspective.

Introduction and Overview of the Volume's Contents

The chapters in this volume on Islam, Muslims and Citizenship Education are organized into four regional sections, preceded by the two more general or theological introductions to the topic. The appendix presents messages of felicitation by two supporters of this project: László Andor, European Union Commissioner for Employment, Social Affairs and Inclusion and Ayhan Tekineş, Dean of the Faculty of Humanities, Bedër University, Tirana.

The first regional section of the volume contains eight diverse Western European Case Studies.

Jørgen S. Nielsen's chapter on "Citizenship Education in Multicultural Societies" has a much broader scope than developments in the author's native Denmark. Nielsen initially alerts us to global shifts from a previous era of nation building and educating to inculcate shared narratives of common identity to the more recent emergence of new and contested forms of collective participation concerned primarily with citizens' relations to a state. He cites, for example, the Arab Spring as one instance of such transformations, along with the rise of nostalgic and "hardline" nationalisms in both Eastern and Western Europe. Indeed, civics education has shifted to citizenship education, and its parameters are under redefinition. Thus choices are being made in educational policy about whether to inscribe fixed narratives of history that constitute a "nation" or to envision active citizenship as a renewed social contract that is constantly in process.

This chapter is followed by three distinct contributions to this topic drawing on Austrian perspectives. In the first, Matthias Scharer in "Citizenship from an Austrian Christian-theological perspective" cites the early (2-3rd century) Christian "Epistle to Diognetus" which proclaims, "Their existence is on earth, but their citizenship is in heaven". The challenges and paradox of belonging to both the earthly and spiritual realms are then examined through the theory and practice of Communicative Theology (CT). This process/method grew out of the Theme-centered Interaction (TCI) approach to group work developed by psychotherapist Ruth Cohn and the author notes that Austrian, German, American, Canadian, Croatian and Indian theologians are constructively exploring its theological implications. Scharer therefore presents a brief introduction to CT as related to citizenship, followed by a discussion of three recent historical contexts of citizenship in Austrian history: Austrofascism, National Socialism (Nazism) and post-Second World War Austria. The main theme of the contribution is how pragmatic historical realities have challenged and continue to challenge the ideal of "heavenly" citizenship for the Catholic Church. Scharer therefore concludes with the relevance of "The Letter of Diognetus" in the light of Communicative Theology, to evaluating the role of Christians and the church today. The theological assertion that true citizenship for Christians is in heaven does not have to imply an apolitical Christianity. Rather the true Christian must engage the moral and spiritual demands of his or her worldly context and be deeply involved in the very real struggles of citizenship regarding inclusion and exclusion.

In "The Contribution of Islamic Religious Education to Citizenship Education in Austria", Zekirija Sejdini, from his perspective as an official in charge of education in Islamic religious schools, gives us an introduction to the Muslim community in Austria and the way in which values of citizenship are embedded in the curriculum of Islamic schools and demonstrated to be in harmony with Islamic religious teachings. The main curricular focus is on shared values of human rights, pluralism, freedom of expression, religious freedom, interreligious dialogue, democracy, and integration/belonging. Examples from the instructional program for various grades are provided, concluding with the observation that curricular materials alone cannot deliver the message unless the teachers who impart these teachings also model such values.

In "Citizenship-Education and Islam Project: A Report (Austria)" researcher Nadire Mustafi reports on the project "Islam and Citizenship-Education" whose aim is to show Muslim youth how to to participate in the Austrian society in ways consistent with their religious beliefs. The three stages of the project, which is still in progress, involve creating curricular materials, training teachers to deliver them, and assessing the results. Successfully integrating Muslims into Austrian society is a primary project goal and therefore this research is strongly supported by the Austrian government and its institutions.

An ethnographic or sociological approach to Muslims in Switzerland is taken by Brigit Allenbach in, "To be Muslim and Swiss: Children of Muslim Immigrants From South East Europe and the Politics of Belonging".

This chapter is based on interview and survey research on young Muslims and the "politics of belonging" in Switzerland. Interviews and activity logs provide insights into the everyday lives of the sons and daughters of Muslim immigrants and what it means for them to be both Muslim and Swiss. The data indicate that school, professional qualification and a broad range of recreational activities have priority in the everyday lives of these young people who may practice religion in many and varied ways.

This study challenges the culturalist approach that sets the West against Islam by demonstrating how the multiple belonging of young Muslims in Switzerland counters a hegemonic and dichotomist view of 'us versus them'. The importance for citizenship education is that such education needs to take into account multiple dimensions of belonging in the experiences and worldviews of Muslim children and youth.

Siebren Miedema advocates pluralistic education that creates a space where diverse worldviews can be discussed in an open and dialogical way in "Learning to Live with Different Worldviews in The Netherlands". The pedagogical philosophy of such pluralistic schools would take religious personhood seriously as part of identity formation, along with other diverse components. Miedema reminds us that in a secular age 'worldview' rather than 'religion' may be the more general and generous way to frame the diversity that should be a component of citizenship education. Three concrete examples from the Netherlands of 'good practice' in teaching and learning to live with different worldviews are presented in this chapter including an interreligious school; a joint venture among the State, an Islamic and a Christian elementary school; and a group of ten Islamic elementary schools named SIMON schools located in the central and eastern part of the Netherlands.

In his study of developments in "Islamic Education in Spain" Juan Ferreiro Galguera gives us a portrait of how Muslims figure in the demographics of the country, and how their religious education in public schools is framed by a tradition of Spanish state legislation regulating and guaranteeing the provision of religious education to disparate minority groups.

Muslims, Islam and citizenship are covered in the Spanish educational system through teaching Islam in state schools, as well as through being addressed as part of the subjects "citizenship and human rights" and the "history of religions". Practical cases are cited to illustrate the interface of Islamic identity with citizenship practices in Spain including current cases of hijab bans in certain schools and Muslim based activism towards promoting engagement with Spanish civil society.

In "Patterns of Integration of Jewish Migrants from the Former Soviet Union in Germany" Doron Kiesel analyzes an instance of migration of new immigrants into an existing minority community (Jews in Germany) that challenges some of the conventional assumptions regarding immigrants and religion. Using analytic tools from the sociology of migration and Jewish contemporary history, Kiesel considers Jewish immigration from the former Soviet Union between the years

1990-2006, outlining the individual and social effects on the immigrants and their integration into Jewish communities in the Federal Republic of Germany.

As a number of previous studies have already shown, what is known to apply generally to migration differs considerably in the case of these Jewish migrants, so that the overall validity of some basic hypotheses is called into question. In the case of Russian Jewish immigrants, integration into Jewish communities in Germany leads to the adoption of much more traditional models of identity. In addition, the level of education of these migrants is unlike that of any other group that has migrated to the Federal Republic of Germany since most have academic training and were socio-professionally recognised in their society of origin. At the same time, their *Jewish identity* can seldom be described in religious terms, since they were socialized in a society that rejected all ethno-religious allegiances. The resultant largely secular civil identity does not, therefore, sit easily with the definition of Jewish life that have become established in Germany.

The Jewish community in Germany is changing dramatically in its ethno-cultural composition, and is obliged to integrate the migrants, not only into German society but also into the local Jewish community. The understandable issues of adjustment on the part of Jews coming from the former Soviet Union are sometimes wrongly interpreted by the German Jewish communities as a lack of interest in Jewishness, and these issues are further exacerbated by the rise in xenophobic utterances and the public expression of extreme right-wing views in parts of the Federal Republic of Germany.

Section Two's chapters on Bulgaria, Romania, and Macedonia survey minority Muslim populations in these countries who comprise long term inhabitants as well as more recent immigrants.

Rositsa Atanasova begins her study, "Citizenship Education and Muslims in Bulgaria", by tracing the structure of current citizenship education in Bulgaria. Citizenship education became a statutory subject in 2000 as a component of the cultural and educational subject area "Social Sciences and Citizenship Education." The transition to democracy in Bulgaria has necessitated a fresh conceptualization of the relationship between the individual and the state. Therefore citizenship education is integrated in the curriculum as an interdisciplinary field, which, depending on the grade level, is taught within other subjects with the aim of developing the necessary attitudes and skills for responsible participation in public life.

The latter part of the paper examines the current Bulgarian curriculum with regard to inclusive citizenship and seeks to evaluate the extent to which it traces an identity that is no longer conceived in purely ethnic terms. This entails a shift away from the traditional narrow model of conceptualizing national identity towards a more inclusive one that would allow minority groups, including Muslims, to feel a greater sense of belonging to their country of citizenship in order to partake more fully in civic life.

"Civil Education and Religion in Macedonia" by Muhammed Ali examines this newly introduced subject in primary education. The main aims of this subject are imparting concepts of human rights and freedoms, such as are embodied in the Universal Declaration and European Convention for human rights, opening a discussion about civil freedoms and duties in modern Macedonian society, studying the EU and its values, and introducing the democratic organization of Macedonian society.

At the same time, including religion related subjects (ethics, ethics of religions, introduction to religions) in the Macedonian primary schools also contributes to the strengthening and affirmation of democratic values. Educating youth about universal ethics, as well as inculcating positive attitudes and behaviour towards fellow citizens, the society and the country are only a small portion of the contents of the above-mentioned subjects that promotet the development of civil society and civic integration. The chapter also surveys contributions of the main Islamic institutions in Macedonia to civic integration including the activities of the IRC (Islamic Religious Community) which oversees mosques, the Isa Beg Madrasa (a high school) and the Faculty of Islamic Studies which trains Islamic scholars.

Islamic education in Romania is treated by Laurenţiu D. Tănase in "Religious Education, European Citizenship and Religious Pluralism". Noting that 2013 was the "year of the European citizen", Tănase makes important observations regarding the civic educational process in nations such as Romania that aspire to move towards the values envisioned as essential for a European democracy built upon social functionality based on pluralism. Within this process, education in religious studies can play an important role in the transmission of general human values such as tolerance and justice.

While Muslims constitute only a small 0.33% element of the Romanian population, the presence of Islam is one of the components of the religious landscape. With a historical existence of more than 500 years, the Romanian Muslim community developed from an ethnic core of Turkish origin. More recently, a Tatar ethnic expression, mainly from Crimea, has been added as a consequence of migration. After surveying the religious curriculum for Romanian state schools, Tănase discusses elements of the Islamic religious education curriculum that is provided by mandate to Muslim minority students, demonstrating that it is congruent with the aims of education for active and engaged citizenship and the embrace of pluralism.

Two Turkish contributors to this collection offer curricular and theoretical perspectives on Islam and citizenship in Turkey from the Republic period up to the present. The case of Turkey, while a Muslim majority nation, highlights tensions between religion as defined in traditional textual and pedagogical perspectives and its integration into a curriculum for forming citizens of a modern secular state.

Mustafa Köylü's chapter, "Religion and Citizenship Education: The Case of Turkey" presents a brief history of religious education in Turkey, and examines its present situation, including a discussion of religion textbooks in use and some of their characteristics. Turkish textbooks were revised in 2005 and, given Turkish aspirations to join the EU, principles of religious tolerance and freedom are increasingly accentuated in the curriculum. This chapter concludes with a more detailed discussion of the citizenship and human rights education offered at the 8th grade level as part of primary education which includes elements such as materials on other religions and the compatibility of Islam with democratic principles.

Selahattin Turan in "Citizenship Education In Turkey: A Critical View" offers a theoretical consideration of the multiple elements that have challenged formulating and implementing a model of universal citizenship in Turkey. In Republican Turkey, the perception of secularism derived from the French Revolution created an atmosphere where religion was strongly opposed by the religion of the state. In Turkey, secularism was used in order to exercise power over religion through the state, to decrease the effect of religion on society, and to limit religion's areas of activity rather than merely separating religious and state affairs while guaranteeing the religious and philosophical beliefs of individuals and groups. The enactment of the Law on the Unification of Education in 1924, either closed and banned religious educational institutions or brought them under state control.

After assessing antecedents to modern ideals of Turkish citizenship drawn from the Islamic heritage (*umma*) and the Ottoman experience (*millet*), Turan traces state definitions of modern Turkish citizenship articulated in successive constitutions since the proclamation of the Turkish Republic from the 1920s until 1960. The basis of such citizenship is an ethic of secular duty based on the assumption that a secular individual will be a good and dutiful person.

Turan further outlines the historical reasons for the neglect of citizenship education in modern Turkey. He concludes that citizenship education remained at a rhetorical level imposed by the state but which was not reflected in the behaviors and attitudes of individuals. All sections of society, both secular and pious, tried to use schools and citizenship education as tools to legitimize and sustain their own ideologies and concepts of sovereignty rather than for training good citizens. The effort of Turkey to become a member of the European Union over the last quarter of century has led to the transformation of the dilemma of secular citizenship education versus religious citizenship education into discussions of European citizenship versus Turkish citizenship. For these reasons disputes over citizenship education in Turkey are likely to continue.

Hanan Alexander offers extensive theoretical and philosophical background for thinking through the implications of educational formation in "Citizenship Education in Diverse Democracies: How Thick or Thin? How Maximal or Minimal?" Education is an important context for public dialogue among competing comprehensive goods concerning which beliefs and values to hold in common as part of what Alexander designates as "ethical discourse".

Alexander holds that in the absence of a neutral view from nowhere, only exposure to alternative perspectives can make possible the sort of critical attitude required of democratic citizens. In addition to exposure to rival traditions, maximal citizenship education in diverse democracies also requires initiation into an agreed upon set of thick common values that have emerged from extended dialogue over time, perhaps even generations, which can facilitate coexistence among these very competing views. Beyond initiation into a thick comprehensive tradition of primary identity and exposure to rival perspectives, pedagogies of difference also require education in thick shared values across difference that foster the capacity to navigate disagreement respectfully and seek common ground among competing points of view. These discussions ideally should occur both in private religious schools and in state schools.

One form of initiating such dialogue is curricular incorporation of exposure to competing comprehensive traditions, such as religious students being exposed to science, Jewish students being exposed to Islam or Christianity, or teaching and learning about both Zionist and Palestinian narratives concerning the establishment of the State of Israel.

Section Three of our volume gathers three chapters on Eastern Europe and Russia. The two chapters treating Muslim Tatars in Poland (Nalborczyk) and Russia (Almazova) trace the history of state accommodations for religious education among these populations.

"To Raise Good Muslims and Good Citizens – The Goals of Religious and Cultural Education for Polish Tatars in the 20th Century" by Agata S. Nalborczyk treats the Polish Tatar community between 1918 and 1939. Nalborczyk describes how when Poland regained independence in 1918 after 123 years of foreign rule, Muslim Tatars as rightful citizens became engaged in working for the good of the reborn motherland. This work involved activities geared towards raising new generations of young Tatars in a spirit of patriotism and service to the country, i.e. as loyal and aware citizens of the Polish state.

To realise that goal, between 1918 and 1939 Polish Muslim Tatars tried to create a new model of upbringing and education by combining Islamic religious knowledge with Tatar history and Polish cultural values and they promulgated these concepts through organizations and publications that are documented in this chapter.

In "Intellectual Contributions of Muslim scholars in the Volga-Ural region within the context of the development of Islamic ideological currents" Leyla Almazova examines evolving debates about religious interpretation among Volga-Ural Muslims over the past century. These local Tatars adopt positions common to other global Muslim contexts of that era, such as Traditionalism, Islamic Reformism, Islamic Fundamentalism and Islamic Liberalism.

Almazova then surveys the role of Islam in Tartaristan in the new post-Soviet era including state interventions and regulation, religious leadership, educational institutions, and emergent ideological currents.

Russian Orthodox theologian and educator Dmitry Shmonin in "Citizenship Education in Russia: Between 'Patriotism' and 'Spirituality'" notes that at the end of the 20th century the process of distancing from Soviet ideology dominated public education in Russia. This, in turn, inculcated ideals of individualism as well as "freedom" from traditional moral values and obligations to society. Meanwhile, the increasing influence of religion (both Orthodoxy and Islam) led to religious education being introduced, for example, through a special course "Introduction to Religious Cultures and Secular Ethics" explaining basic traditional values. This cause was incorporated into the middle school curriculum (2009-2012).

Subsequently, a new Russian federal 'Law on Education' (2013) has proclaimed citizenship and patriotism as basic principles of education while adding a new synthetic intercultural course "Principles of spiritual and moral culture of the peoples of Russia" to the curriculum. Such initiatives will require new ways to integrate ethnic and Muslim religious traditions while incorporating contemporary democratic ideals of citizenship education.

The final North American regional section of our volume offers two Christian perspectives on religion and citizenship education from the United States and Canada.

Eileen Daily, in her chapter, "Education for Citizenship in Public and Catholic Schools in the United States" initially observes that citizenship education in public schools in the United States is not centrally mandated or controlled. Instead, each state sets its own priorities and outcomes for citizenship education. Based on several statistical reports and surveys regarding citizenship education attitudes in public and private (Catholic) schools in the U.S., Daily concludes that this topic is not effectively or coherently presented.

While the founders of the United States considered the goal of education to be a "coherent worldview for a shared understanding of the common good and the values necessary for democracy", the authors of *High Schools, Civics, and Citizenship* (2010) note that with the shift in emphasis in public education in recent decades; the primary aim of education is more for "personal and professional advancement". This conflicts, for example, with Catholic Social Teaching that emphasizes individual responsibilities at least as much as rights.

One possible reason that citizenship education is no longer effective is that American schools have not educated for a common worldview since the early 1960s. The good side of this is that formerly marginalized groups are not forced to adopt the majority's worldview. However, such pluralism also comes at a price. With no common worldview, there is no common language for concepts such as justice and the common good. Each of the religious traditions has deep roots for those concepts. In concluding Daily rhetorically poses the question will the United States be able to embrace its pluralism and tap into the deep roots of its values so that its democracy will work in the future?

In her chapter, "Contributions of Religions for Citizenship Education in Canada: A Christian Religious Educator's Perspective", theologian HyeRan Kim-Cragg attempts to make the connection between two crucial factors in identity: religion and citizenship. Limiting its scope to Canadian contexts, the chapter first describes the past and current reality of Canadian policy and society, critically analyzing the official government policy of multiculturalism. Against this background Cragg raises issues of identity, belonging, and migration, while examining "Orientalizing" representations of immigrants that lead to exclusion, discrimination and minoritization. The chapter concludes by suggesting ways in which religion, and in particular Christian faith and practice, can make positive contributions to the understanding of citizenship education.

Citizenship Education and Islam

Ednan Aslan

The Muslim presence in Europe today is undoubtedly a challenge for local European societies. The growing number of mosques in cities and Muslim students at public schools, and the ongoing disruptions and violence in Muslim countries, augment existing fear and prejudice towards Muslims and call into question the compatibility of Muslim perspectives with European values. All this leads to an interrogation as to whether Muslims can really identify as citizens of European countries.

To answer this question it is necessary to explain the relationship between citizens and the state in the course of Islamic history, so that the presence of Muslims as citizens in Europe can be better understood and an informed debate can be conducted regarding this issue.

Islam and Citizenship

The terms "state", "nationality", or "citizenship", have not had a long history among Muslims, because the Qur'an defines Muslims as *khulafa* (governors or vicegerents) of God on earth and commissions them to be a community with a task for humankind.

> "You are the best community (*umma*) produced [as an example] for humanity. You enjoin what is right and forbid what is wrong and believe in Allah." (Qur'an, 3:110)

The implementation of this role knows no geographical or ethnic boundaries. Thus, the *umma,* as the real community of Muslims, is at home and in the service of God everywhere,

> "The polity or community over which this [Muslim] sovereign rules is the *umma,* the single universal Islamic community embracing all the lands in which Muslim rule is established and Islamic law prevails." (Lewis, 1988, 32)

This terminology is also found in the Constitution of Medina, which was ratified by Prophet Muhammed and had its descent from there: "... They are one community to the exclusion of [other] people." (Wellhausen, 1889, 94)

Despite this divine mandate, Muslim scholars in the lands conquered by Islamic forces were nonetheless forced to deal with the status of both Muslim and non-Muslim citizens residing in Muslim territories from the initial phases of Islamic history.

In the early decades of Islamic history, the inhabitants of the Muslim regions were identified by terms such as *"Ahl dar al-Islam"* (People of the Islamic territory) and the inhabitants of non-Muslim areas were defined as *"Ahl dar al-kufr."* (People of the land of unbelief). Later on, this terminology was replaced by other expressions, such as *tabi'yat* or *jinsiyyat* (ethnic or national belonging*)* or expanded in other ways to indicate nations with whom Muslims had treaties, for example. (Topcuoglu, 2012) Thus, citizens residing within and outside of Muslim territories were defined not by their ethnicity, but rather according to their religious affiliations and according to this might be required to indicate their identiy in visible or official ways.

The Arabic term *watan* (homeland), which in the early days of Islam described emotional and imagined geographical affiliations of Muslims, only in the 19th century, under the influence of the Western powers, came to designate the current political locations of Muslims within certain physical borders and this came to prevail throughout in the entire Muslim world:

> In modern times a new word entered the political vocabulary and is now almost universal... It is the Arabic term *watan,* with its phonetic variations and equivalents in the other languages of Islam. In classical usage, *watan* means 'one's place of birth or residence' ... The new meaning dates from the last years of the eighteenth century, and can be traced to foreign influence.(Lewis, 1988, 40)

It was not until the 18th century that one encounters in Muslim regions the use of a term equivalent to "state" in the modern sense, which defines the political affiliation of Muslims in accordance with their nationalities within certain geographical areas.

Thus, it should be noted that Muslims have not had a long tradition of employing terms such as fatherland, citizen, or nationality and still find it very difficult to identify themselves as citizens of a particular country without reference to ethnic and religious affiliation. This problem also characterizes the current affiliational conflicts, not only of Muslims living in Europe, but also of those residing in Muslim majority countries, since the relationship between the rulers of Muslim regions of the past and the political leadership of the current Muslim majority states with the inhabitants of many European countries have been and remain strained by conflicts and tension.

State and Citizen Relationships in Muslim Majority Countries

Immediately after the death of the Prophet Muhammad, Muslims were primarily engaged in establishing and perpetuating an Islamic society that emulated his model. Some pre-Islamic traditions quickly returned and caused several rebellions and divisions, deepening the chasm between rulers and ruled (Akbulut, 1992, 97).

Thus, a tradition of mistrust has characterized the entire history of Islamic states up to the present. In not a single contemporary Muslim country has there been a relaxed relationship between the government and the people. Even in a secularized country such as Turkey, the atmosphere continues to be characterized by recriminations, accusations, and threats. Due to this tension between state and citizen, political theory as a branch of Islamic theology regarded the state as a threat to a highly idealized Islamic community, as it emerged at the periphery of the state (Ibn Hazm, n. d., 45).

On the other hand, the state recognized that it had to take this theological counterweight seriously and tried either to maintain control over religion or to fight the religious authorities and their supporters. No religious authority has had a chance to survive without acknowledging the theological legitimacy of the state. In Islamic history, there are countless examples of such struggles between the religious authorities and the state. It is no coincidence that the most important founders of the Sunni law schools were either murdered or had to spend most of their lives in prison.

Shi'a Islam has known nothing but persecution and expulsion by most pre-modern state powers. In fact, the state persecuted or murdered eleven out of twelve of the Shi'i Imams. Even the Prophet's grandson, Husayn, (did) not avoid being murdered.

Muslims in Europe and Their Relationship to the State

Although the history of Islam is older than the history of Muslim migration to Europe, Islam is perceived as always having been an immigrant religion. That the history of Islam in Skopje is older than the history of Islam in Istanbul is only hesitantly noted.

Perceptions of the Muslim presence in Western Europe are primary shaped by three cultures of the Islamic world. North African Islam shapes the French perception of Islam, Turkish Islam that of Germans, and finally Pakistani Islam that of the British. Even if more recent immigrations have caused different shifts in these Muslim landscapes, the Muslim presence is mainly marked by these three immigrant groups.

It, therefore, makes sense to describe the state-citizen relationship from the experiences of these three ethnic groups, so that the debate about the European presence of Muslims is more factually oriented.

The largest proportion of Muslims in Europe lives in France. These Muslims originated primarily from North Africa and actually arrived in Europe as French citizens due to the history of the French colonial presence in the Maghreb. Their experience with democratic values in their own countries was based on the suppression and double standards of French colonial strategies. The emergence of North Africa from colonial occupation neither favored enlightened thinking nor promoted a connection to the modern world. Modernization, which was implemented only at the material level, did not produce an organic transition to modernity. It merely maintained patriarchal structures in a modernized form.

Muslim immigrants from the Maghreb arrived in France from North Africa with this experience and tried to build an identity on the fringes of society. Through the process of creating this identity at different levels of society they learned that as Arabs they are not really welcome in France. In the ghettos of the big cities, these Muslim immigrants sought an identity that was located somewhere between tradition and modernity.

The Turks who came to Germany arrived with their experience of undemocratic conditions that meant nothing more to them than oppression, displacement, and torture. It is worth noting that these Turkish migrants ultimately connected all of these bitter experiences with Europe and its values because dictatorships at home were generously supported by the Western powers. The state meant nothing more than a religious and cultural threat to these people.

Pakistani Muslims came to the UK with similar experiences. Since its founding in 1947, Pakistan has served as a laboratory for the creation of an Islamic state and the testing ground of an ideal Muslim society. The founders of this country wanted to build a society according to the example of the Prophet Muhammed and create paradisiacal conditions on earth. Pakistan's experience with democracy went hand in hand with a certain self-evident connection of religion and politics since the ideologues of that state saw no contradiction between Islam and democracy. Maudoodi's struggle from 1938 to 1947 was directed precisely against the more secular understanding of the country's founder Jinnah, because he saw in it a deviation from the Islamic principle of the state and therefore he declared Jinnah to be a traitor to Islam (Al-e Ahmad, 1982, 264).

The attempted synthesis between Islam and democracy was doomed to failure from the outset because the young Pakistani state was overwhelmed by this synthesis. According to Newman, this dream of a synthesis has remained the cardinal problem for Pakistani Muslims (Newman, 1986, 152).

This ideal of a synthesis between Islam and democracy still exists in Pakistan. However, the failure of many civilian governments in favor of military rule demonstrates the highly problematic relationship between the state and the citizens of that country, which is largely based on mutual distrust and accusations.

While disappointment in their political situation was only one reason for the emigration of Pakistani Muslims to England, the experience of failed democracy has significantly colored the Pakistani Muslim immigrants expectations of the state.

In summary, developing a new relationship to democracy and civic awareness in Europe out of these three different negative experiences will be a challenging, yet necessary process in establishing the future of Muslims in Europe.

Muslims and Values

"Values" mean "objectives that ultimately guide action," in other words, that which the society considers to be absolute and worth striving for. The various definitions of "values" do not differ significantly from one another. Values are defined by Meulemann as "ideas of that which is desirable," by which he does not mean individuals' ideas, but rather ideas that society agrees should be perceived as values. From these different definitions, we see that values are specified by the society and that the people view them as "desirable" and aspire to them. (Meulemann, 1996, 26).

If one follows the definition of values as being objectives to which people aspire, it may be noted that the two concepts of "dignity (Würde)" and "values (Werte)" not only have the same etymology, but also aim at the same goal. Tiedemann says that "[h]e who is worthy ...will have value assigned to him" (Tiedemann, 2007,

217), but also "what" is worthy receives value and becomes perceived as a value by the society.

European Values

Europe should be understood not only as an economic community, but also as a community of shared values because a community without values has no worth:

ARTICLE I-2: The Union's values
The Union is founded on the values of respect for human dignity, freedom, democracy, equality, and rule of law and respect for human rights, including the rights of persons belonging to minorities. These values are common to the Member States in a society in which pluralism, non-discrimination, tolerance, justice, solidarity and equality between women and men prevail (Charter of Fundamental Rights of the European Union, 2000).

According to a Eurobarometer survey from 2010, 38% of the respondents cited "human rights" and "democracy" as the most important values of Europe. 35% of the respondents opted for "peace." This was followed by the values of "rule of law," "solidarity", "respect for other cultures", as well as "respect for human life." The values of "equality," "freedom of the individual," "tolerance," "self-realization," and "religion" were chosen as values that best represent the EU for significantly less than one seventh of the population of the 27 EU states. (European Union, 2008; 2011)

In addition, religious communities and churches in Europe see no contradiction between European and religious values:

Many national curricula in religious education in Europe promote multiculturalism and acceptance of diversity and these are related to democratic values, solidarity, tolerance and anti-racist education and citizenship education. .. The aim of religious education is to create the context to develop respect for and recognition of religious and ideological diversity (Williams et al., 2008).

Even if in practice we still have many obstacles to its implementation, Europe recognizes the diversity of cultures and religions and is committed to the protection of this diversity:

The Union contributes to the preservation and to the development of common values while respecting the diversity of the cultures and traditions of the peoples of
Europe as well as the national identities of the Member States and the organization
of their public authorities at national, regional, and local levels; it seeks to promote
balanced and sustainable development and ensures free movement of persons,
goods, services, and capital, and the freedom of establishment (Charter of Fundamental Rights of the European Union, 2000, II).

Muslims and European Values

Although immigrating to non-Muslim lands is viewed as undesireable from the
perspective of Islamic theology, Muslims, for whom a life in their countries after
liberation from colonialism did not seem possible for economic, social, or political reasons, saw themselves as more or less forced to emigrate to non-Muslim
countries. Thus, proud Muslims came to Europe not without a certain bitterness
regarding their perceived inferiority firmly resolved not to establish themselves
there permanently.

The hope of returning to the homeland yielded more and more to the reality
of everyday life, which inevitably resulted in a softening of time-honored ways of
thinking. Gradually, the comfortable and reliable structures of a societal order
based on social and democratic justice as well as the political stability in Europe,
were perceived as highly esteemed values, which original, Islamic homelands
could not offer:

> In many European countries, nationalist tendencies have become stronger in recent
> years. At the same time Europe's Muslims are striving to be seen as equal citizens. In
> France, two-thirds of Muslims have French passports, and they are standing up for
> their rights and obligations. The same applies in England and Germany. These new
> citizens can more easily make friends with the idea of an international (European)
> identity than with that of a single nation state because of their life and family his-
> tories. Owing to the circumstances, Muslim immigrants are more likely to become
> Europeans than members of a nation state. Furthermore, Islam became a European
> religion long ago (Ramadan, 200, 211).

Since the beginning of the labor migrations of the 1960s, Muslims have been
confronted with experiences that they are unfamiliar with in their countries of
origin. The new challenges facing immigrants in Europe consist, in particular, of
proving themselves as a minority in a pluralistic society, participating in it, and
identifying themselves as part of that society.

By contrast, in the history of Islam, there existed different models of society in which different cultures and religions lived together as minorities, under rules that were legitimized by Islam. There were also theological concepts through which the temporary stay of Muslims in a society not shaped by Islam was governed.

Remaining permanently and making a new home in a pluralistic society shaped by Christianity presents Islamic theology with a new situation. For classical jurisprudence this circumstance threatens above all, an assimilation that could endanger the future of Muslims. This argues that inner peace can only be achieved through a holistic Islamic way of life in a pure Islamic society, since otherwise the individual Muslim's conscience would be overburdened with too many compromises.

Today, European Muslims live in societies that no longer derive their worldviews, dynamics, and consequently rules from faith, and therefore they are called upon to interpret their religion accordingly. This presupposes an intensive process of discussion that deals with nothing less than giving religion a new meaning in their lives. Living in the various European countries, Islamic theologians felt compelled to look beyond their traditional frameworks and to address questions that had no place within their own history.

Thus, the 'ulama gradually began to detach themselves from their traditional way of dealing with the Qur'an and to critically question their sacred texts in light of the diverse living conditions of Muslims in Europe. The recognition of religious pluralism as the norm and the perception of religion as "a discursive object" may be considered significant moments in the redefinition of Muslims' own theology against this social background.

The fact that the Muslim community is committed to a pluralistic Austrian society and that it is turning this commitment into its basis for action can be judged as one outcome of this theological process:

> The Islamic community considers serving as valuable partners to be a central task of Muslims living in Austria. This entails preserving their Muslim identity in minority situations, while simultaneously perceiving themselves as anchored in the Austrian democratic pluralistic society. In this way, we are trying to promote the idea of integration through participation (IGGiÖ, 2013).

A leading figure in this process was undoubtedly the European Muslim intellectual Smail Balic. To his credit, in addition to his intellectual contributions to the European version of Islam, is the establishment of the IGGiÖ in the 1970s. He was a staunchly secular Muslim thinker who looked for the roots of this new theology in Europe and sought to clarify the contradictions between Islam and secularism. According to him, the model in Bosnia-Herzegovina demonstrates that a European version of Islam is possible and this model generates no contradiction between a state and Islam. (Balic, 2001, 72)

The intense encounters with European culture and religion in the wake of the global developments of the recent past lent additional momentum to the preoccupation with religious pluralism in Islam. The problem of the relationships among religions was no longer portrayed as an abstract theological construct that emerged from scholars' understanding of the world, but rather as the concrete task of every believer – in the sense that it now aims at critically examining one's own theological notions about the position of Christians and Jews in Islam.

A leading role in this critical analysis of classical Islamic theology has been taken up by Muslim theologians and intellectuals residing in the West. They raised the perfectly legitimate question as to whether the representation of Jews and Christians in the Qur'an could be uncritically accepted, and whether this representation adequately describes Jews and Christians today and has universal validity for all eternity.

One of the main exponents of this debate is Seyyed Hussein Nasr, a Muslim thinker who lives in the US. He compared the truth claims of diverse religions with different self-contained solar systems that exist in the same universe:

> In fact, if there is one really new and significant dimension to the religious and spiritual life of man today, it is this presence of other worlds of sacred form and meaning not as archaeological or historical facts and phenomena but as religious reality. It is this necessity of living within one solar system and abiding by its laws yet knowing that there are other solar systems and even, by participation, coming to know something of their rhythms and harmonies, thereby gaining a vision of the haunting beauty of each one as a planetary system which is *the* planetary system for those living within it. It is to be illuminated by the Sun of one's own planetary system and still to come to know through the remarkable power of intelligence, to know by anticipation and without 'being there' that each solar system has its own sun, which again is both a sun and *the* Sun, for how can the sun which rises every morning and illuminates our world be other than *the* Sun itself? (Nasr, 1989, 252).

According to Nasr, the truth is indeed absolute and irrefutable. However, the form and language in which it reveals itself may be different and even exhibit contradictions. The words with which the truth is brought closer to the people must build on their respective cultural system of standards – precisely because it is not standardization, but rather variety that is self evident, and even corresponds to the nature of creation, and that likewise develops into increasingly complex diversity. (Ibid. 250-254)

However, what unifies all religions – beyond the diversity of individual theologies – is the promise of transcendental salvation. Discerning this fundamental unit and tolerating it is only possible for those who have attained spiritual maturity. To them there is only one God who has revealed himself in a variety of cultures in the context of diverse historical events in manifold ways. And this unity may not be destroyed by any external differences. The people who are guided through the sun of their prophets are on the right path and will not be sad (Aslan, 2000, 17-30). As Nasr suggests, they have their permanent place, their orientation in life – just as the planets of the solar system are held in their orbits through the law of gravity, which operates by way of the gravitational force of the sun.

The position advocated by Nasr is shared by contemporary theologians and the former President of the Office of Religious Affairs of Turkey, Suleyman Ateş, who also argues that the mercy and justice of God are offered to all people. (Ateş, 1989) Another Turkish theologian, Fethullah Gülen, denies the liability of any negative Qur'anic depictions of Jews and Christians by pointing to the historicity of the Qur'an (Gülen, 2012a).

In a newspaper interview, Gülen, now an immigrant living in the US, explained why he would like to understand the classic position of Islam with respect to Christians and Jews as no longer current under contemporary circumstances:

> Aspects of pluralism and acceptance of others include the equality of men before the law and freedom of religion, education, and religious instruction. These principles apply as long as they do not reduce the rights of others. If some verses in the blessed Qur'an seem contrary at first glance, one must examine the causes behind the revelation of these verses appropriately in each individual context. It is crucial that these verses are not generalized and directed against the individuals and groups, but against their attitudes and behaviors. The Islamic religion did not construct its relationship with Christians, Jews, and polytheists on the basis of differences in belief, but rather with regard to their attitudes and behaviors. The Qur'an and Sunnah already drafted the principles of coexistence. (Gülen, 2012b)

Thus while people or theologians in Muslim majority countries will probably be engaged in a discourse on religious pluralism in Islam among themselves as Muslims for a long time to come, those Muslims who live in predominantly Christian, pluralistic, and secular countries are faced with the task of making their living situations compatible with conditions that differ fundamentally from those in their home countries.

Structural Adaptation of Islam to Society

Among Muslims living in the West, a unified interest in the recognition of Islam as a public corporation, which includes legal equality with other religions, can be observed. Thus, the Islamic religion certainly cannot help but change in the direction of an ecclesiastical structure that is essentially alien to it. This will require creating new organizational structures, decision-making processes, and organs and agencies equipped to make independent and binding decisions about teaching and discipline (Köhler, 2013). This will further accelerate the secularization process of Islam and will be an opportunity for Islamic theology to disengage from the authority of its jurists and to move to the center of society.

In the new environment, not only are the personal experiences of people changing, but also Islamic theology, which is faced with completely new facts. This has an impact on the relationship between state and religion and opens up a new field of action for Islamic theology:

> Simultaneously, it is true [...] that, sociologically, we are witnessing a progressive Europeanisation of Islam in its new context (and not a so-called 'Islamization of Europe,' as is so readily claimed, ideologically, in today's political debate). The conference participants explicitly welcomed the gradual inculturation of Islam in Europe as follows: "'Cultural and theological initiatives,'" as expressions of what has been described as a "theology of inculturation," are being followed with great interest, as they allow for and encourage processes of positive participation in the cultural and social life of Europe in a pluralistic context that is open to inter-religious and intercultural dialogue (Legrand, 2011).

Meanwhile, organizations that already, or would like to represent the interests of Muslims have been formed in many European countries. They are recommended to the state as contacts in such matters as the establishment of Islamic theological faculties, the designation of religious holidays, and other religious issues, and as representatives on various committees. This is another step toward convergence with distinctly secular structures in Europe:

> Whether German citizens or not, Muslims, who are represented in the Central Council, affirm therefore the constitutionally guaranteed, power-sharing, and democratic order of the Federal Republic of Germany, including the multi-party system, active and passive voting rights for women, and freedom of religion. Thus, they also accept the right to change religions and to have a different or no religion. The Qur'an prohibits any use of violence or compulsion in matters of faith (ZRD, 2009).

To the extent to which Islamic theology is moving into the center of society, European features, which also imply an open-minded attitude towards social tasks, are increasingly coming to the fore. In this process, European values are taking on more and more weight in the education of Muslim children in Europe.

> In the context of issues concerning Islam in Europe, pupils in the 9th grade should learn that Islam and democracy are not contradictory to each other, but rather meet and overlap in so many points. Additionally, the pupils should be motivated to take an interest in political contexts and to understand them. In this context, the key dimensions of democracy are discussed intensively and references to Islam are clarified. Pupils should perceive the need to be active members of society and the need for political participation. Separation of powers, pluralism, freedom of speech, freedom of the press, freedom of religion, and free, independent and secret elections are issues that should be handled in this context (Lehrpläne der IGGiÖ in Österreich (Islamic curriculum in Austria) 2014).

For example, in Islamic Studies textbooks for Muslim pupils in Germany and Austria, agreement between European and Islamic values is repeatedly placed in the foreground (Vgl. Lehrpläne von Bayern, 2013).

What does it mean to be a citizen of a European state?

With the promulgation of human and civil rights in 1789, the modern citizen was born. Citizenship is, however, not an invention of modern times. We find the idea that the members of a community should be associated with obligations for the first time in the city states of ancient Greece (Mackert, 1999, 16-18). Political participation in society was at that time awarded only to free men who were at the top of the hierarchy, and women, slaves, artisans, foreigners, and others were excluded.

Modern citizenship as we know it today is connected to the emergence of the modern nation state and excludes no member with citizen status, and theoretically all citizens are equal before the law. According to Holz, (Holz, 2000, 7) citizenship is the "modern form of the social positioning of people according to political affiliation." In this sense, Lister assigns this membership an emotional dimension and describes citizenship as a "feeling of belonging" (Lister, 2007, 9).

While Holz and Lister consider "belonging" to be an important part of citizenship, Mackert (Ibid., 25) asserts that rights and obligations are more important, and accordingly define citizenship "as a bundle of rights and obligations that bestow a formal, legal identity on the individual."

Through the European Union, the understanding of citizenship was further developed and freed from its territorial moorings to allow for the emergence of a new sense of belonging in Europe through which people can identify themselves with their own ethnic affiliation as citizens of Europe.

To enhance this identification with Europe, the European Union is promoting active European citizenship. Active citizenship refers to a form of participation in civil society and in social, economic and political life, which is characterized by mutual respect and non-violence, and is in accordance with human rights and democracy:

> Active citizenship is a term used within European policy making to denote particular forms of participation, which should be promoted within Europe in order to ensure the continuation of participatory and representative democracy, to reduce the gap between citizens and governing institutions and to enhance social cohesion. In the European context, Active Citizenship, in terms of education and training, can be traced back to the European Commissioner on Education, Research and the Sciences in 1998, Edith Cresson. She explained that Active Citizenship was when the citizens of Europe could be both 'the architects of and actors in their own lives' (Hoskins & Mascherinin, 2008).

Thus, people in Europe have the task of shaping the future of Europe. Today, Muslims as a part of Europe also have the task of making their contribution to the future of Europe. Now we have to deal with the question of whether Muslims can really identify with Europe.

European Identity and Muslims

European cultural identity is often defined with recourse to Christianity, although the EU, as a community of values, prefers no specific religious orientation and is therefore not religiously affiliated. Accordingly, European identity draws its cultural and ethical character from that religion and thus Christianity shapes Europe's ethical and cultural property.

After recent events in Greece, Portugal, and Italy in particular, it is clear that the European Union is actually lacking profound, identity-building resources such as language, a common flag, and perhaps even more so a soccer team, through which the people in Europe could self-identify, with their minds and hearts, and thus feel connected, since a collective identity presupposes empathy as the basis for solidarity and loyalty.

The fledgling European identity seems unable to compete with existing and well-known objects of identity, such as nation or region. This identity, which still needs to grow in Europe, is challenged by the benefit-oriented components of European identity. According to the Eurobarometer survey, Europe's net contributors identify themselves less with Europe than those who are net recipients. In any case, the benefit-oriented identity of Europeans is more well developed than the emotional identity. Nonetheless, it should be noted that European identity is very sensitive to political, economic, and other influences and needs to be more carefully examined.

The largest component of Muslim identity in Europe is characterized by migration. The traditions of immigrant parents shape the religious and national identity of Muslims in Europe. The cultures of the mosques in Europe, which are variously shaped by ethnic backgrounds, and to some extent religion, demonstrate how diverse Muslim identities can be.

If Muslims repeatedly articulate their disadvantages regarding civil rights from the perspective of their migration experience, the self-evidence of the alienation of Islam and the Muslim presence from Europe will never be questioned. It is much easier for Muslims to identify with Europe as new citizens of European countries than to identify with belonging to any particular nationality of Europe.

An empirical study conducted among Muslims in Austria demonstrates that, even if one would rather not notice it, a wide segment of Muslims is increasingly adapting to European conditions and is situated in a very well developed secularization process:

> Media tags are therefore repeatedly taken up, criticized, or reinterpreted by the interviewees, including such terms as normality, integration, and freedom. New terms are introduced by them to replace the old, including such concepts as respect, social responsibility, and 'peaceful coexistence.' From the interviews a critical attitude was clearly evident as well as a distancing from rigid conceptions and the politicization of religion. Rather self-determined, emancipated attitudes critical of religion, and an extensive secularization of religious attitudes and practices, were found, which contradict the widespread image of an archaic Islam in Austrian society (Aslan et al., 2014, 47).

This development in Europe, in contrast to public debates about Islam, corresponds to the essential fact that Muslims identify more and more with Europe. Islam enables people to make sense of their lives. However to situate this meaning-making geographically would result in a misunderstanding of Islam. A Muslim can fashion his relationship with God anywhere and always, exactly as he understands and interprets it. There is no law in Europe that would deny Muslims this freedom. This freedom is even much more protected there than in many Muslim majority countries, where religiosity is prescribed by the state. The contradictions between religion and secular society are not issues that are specific to Islam and occupy only Muslims, but are rather problems that affect all religions in Europe equally.

The mismatch between public representation and concrete everyday reality was frequently mentioned in the interviews. In this connection, it was particularly noticeable that the majorities of the interviewees emphasized their sense of belonging to Austria, and simply regarded themselves as Muslim Austrians, but were constantly confronted with the fact that this normality was questioned. Their reference to "normal" worldly life, to the social environment, was repeatedly highlighted by the interviews, even by very religiously oriented persons. That one does not drink alcohol, does not eat pork, prays regularly, and dresses decently does not necessarily point to a fundamental difference from the rest of society, as expressed for example by a young woman from Carinthia:

> Yes, well I love to read about Islam and to learn new things, but I love to shop, like any other girl. I wear a headscarf, but you can also wear it fashionably. It does not mean that I have to go around wearing short skirts. Then I like to undertake things with friends, I like to go for a drink or to simply go for a stroll in the city or I just chill in front of my computer and get bored. I love to go to the library, ... what else do I love to do? (Ibid, 46).

In the research group "Citizenship Education and Islam," Muslim children in Islamic schools were asked whether they see Austria as their home or whether they see a contradiction between Islam and life in Austria? The majority of the Muslim children can identify with life in Austria:

> I've lived here for fifteen years and of course I think of it as my home. When I am in Turkey, one feels at a disadvantage there, when one, there they say then, that I am a foreigner there, because I was born here and because my language doesn't fit with the right language (Unpublished Interviews, 2014a).

With this attitude, Muslim children do not ignore their migration related issues, but they do not call into question the future of Islam in Europe.

> I: What would you change if you were a politician or chancellor or president? Would that which what you would change be that which you would do better? Not that you would do it now but rather that you would try? P: Yes.

I: Would you try something else to improve something, to structure it more pleasantly, or is that your main concern? That's precarious, I might add. (...)

P: That one way and the other, the laws so that one does not feel discriminated against as a Muslim. For instance with the headscarf, that is just such a thing. And if I'm the right president here, then I will make sure that the people who live here do not feel disadvantaged (Ibid.).

Um, yes, I think it's just, it's just the way that it (...) Wait, I think, for example, in contrast to very many other foreigners, that Austria is just the same my country. That I, because I was born here, and I already also feel like an Austrian as well as a Turk (Ibid.).

Numerous imams from the research group "Imams in Austria" reported that they see no contradiction between European and Islamic values :

I think that every people and every state has its own culture. They have their own procedures, their peculiarities, they have their own values, which we imams who come here and should respect all people. We offer Austrians many thanks, much respect, they have accepted Islam here. This is the first country in Western Europe, which recognized Islam. And I and, of course, all Bosnians, all Muslims from different regions are grateful to them. And why would you not appreciate that? Why should you not respect it? Why not respect their customs ? Of course, without neglecting one's own in the process. Why do we not demonstrate true integration? Of course we are against assimilation (Unpublished Interviews, 2014b).

On the other hand, the existing conflicts that have arisen out of the Muslim presence in European societies should not be disregarded. In spite of these conflicts, the future of Islam in Europe is not called into question by the vast majority of Muslims living in Europe. With this willingness to integrate, Muslims display good potential for acquiring a new awareness of citizenship in European countries.

Concluding Remarks

Muslims in Europe came to Europe from different cultures and encountered the existing social values from the perspective of their own experiences. Now a new generation of Muslims in Europe who have their own experiences with European democracy and have developed a critical loyalty to democratic states is maturing. This generation actually sees fewer and fewer contradictions between their faith and European values.

The genuine task of politics and the media, as well as the representatives of the religions, would be to work to ensure that the different cultures and religions find their place in the European community of values and identify themselves with it.

Out of the European project, there has emerged a new citizenship, which affirms the diversity of cultures and religions and faces its responsibility towards the state.

EU values ensure the future of religions. By endorsing this view, one also affirms the fact that Islam can only develop an identity in Europe on this basis. Now Muslims need time to discern in their own discourse the position of these values in their own theology and history, so that they no longer perceive them as foreign bodies. To achieve this goal, Muslims need an increase in democracy and experiences with democracy to be able to think freely and without suspicion and to express themselves.

As part of this process Muslims in Europe should be willing to do their share in coming to understand and appreciate their new contexts. Western Europe, for its part, must also be prepared not to perceive Muslims as an archaic and alien burden.

Ultimately an engaged citizenship that arises on this basis is to be regarded as an asset to the future of Europe.

References

Al-e Ahmad, J. A. (1982). *Gharbzadegi*. Lexington KY: Mazda Publishers.

Akbulut, A. (1992). *Sahabe devri siyasi hadiselerinin kelami problemlere Etkileri*. Istanbul: Jalal Birlesik Yayinlari

Aslan, A. (2000). "Dini Cogulculuk Problemine Yeni Bir Yaklasim" [Eine neue Betrachtung der religiösen Pluralität]. *Islami Arastirmalar Dergisi* 4, (17-30).

Aslan, E., Yildiz, E. & Kolb, J. (2014). *Muslimische Alltagspraktiken in Österreich*. From: https://iis.univie.ac.at/fileadmin/user_upload /p_iis/muslimische_alltagspraxis_in_ oesterreich. projektbericht.pdf (Accessed April 14, 2014).

Ateş, S. (1989). *Cennet kimsenin tekelinde degildir*. [No one has a monopoly on Paradise]. In: *Islami Arastirmalar, Journal of Islamic Research*. (7-24).

Balic, S. (2001). *Islam für Europa. Neue Perspektiven einer alten Religion*. Köln-Weimar-Wien.

Charter of Fundamental Rights of the European Union. *Preamble*. In: *Official Journal of the European Communities*. From: http://www.europarl.europa.eu/charter/pdf/text_en.pdf (Accessed December 18, 2000).

Europäische Kommission. (November 2008). *Eurobarometer 69: 1 Values of Europeans*.

Europäische Kommission. (February 2011). *Eurobarometer 74: Die öffentliche Meinung in der Europäischen Union*.

Gülen, F. (2012a). *Kuran'da Yahudiler ver Hiristiyanlar* [Juden und Christen im Koran]. From: http://tr.fgulen.com/content/view/11224/3%20%28 (Accessed November 20, 2006; December 05, 2012).

Gülen, F. (2012b). Interview "Islam und Moderne stehen nicht im Widerspruch". *Frankfurtter Allgemeine Zeitung*. (Accessed December 06, 2012.).

Holz, K. (2000). *Staatsbürgerschaft: Soziale Differnzierung und politische Inklusion*. Wiesbaden: Westdeutscher Verlag.

Hoskins, B. L. & Mascherinin, M. (2008). *Measuring Active Citizenship through the Development of a Composite Indicator*. In: Scences+Business Media. Springer: Published online: 12 July 2008.

Ibn Hazm, Abu Muhammad b. Ahmad ben Said Al-Andulusi. [n.d.]. *Al-Muhalla bi'l Asar*. Beirut.

IGGiÖ. *Leitbild*. (2013). From: http://www.derislam.at/?c=content&cssid=IG-Gi%D6&navid=10&par=0 (Accessed January 18, 2013).

Köhler, A. A. (2013). *Die strukturelle Assimilation des Islam in Deutschland*. From: http://islam.de/2579.php (Accessed January 18, 2013).

Lewis, B. (1988). *The Political Language of Islam*. Chicago: University of Chicago Press.

Legrand, V. (14. 09 2011). *Islam in Europa und Islamophobie. Treffen des Rates der Europäischen Bischofskonferenzen* (CCEE). From: http://www.comece.org/europeinfos/de/archiv/ausgabe141/article/4171.html (Accessed January 02, 2013).

Lehrpläne der IGGiÖ in Österreich. From: http://www.schulamt-islam.at/index.php?option=com_content &view=article&id=22&Itemid=34 (Accessed April 14, 2014).

Lehrpläne von Bayern. From: http://www.izir.de/images/docs/ Islam unterricht_HS.pdf (Accessed October 14, 2013).

Lister, R. (2007). *Gendering Citizenship in Western Europe. New challenges for citizenship research in a cross-national context*. Bristol: The Policy Press.

Mackert, J. (1999). *Kampf um Zugehörigkeit: Nationale Staatsbürgerschaft als Modus sozialer Schliessung.* Opladen: Westdeutscher Verlag.

Meulemann, H. (1996). *Werte und Wertewandel. Zur Identität einer geteilten und wieder vereinten Nation.* Weinheim u.a.: Juventa-Verlag.

Nasr, S. H. (1989). *Knowledge and the Sacred.* Albany New York: State University of New York Press

Newman, K. J. (1986). *Pakistan unter Ayub Khan und Zia-ul-Haq.* Köln: Weltforum Verlag.

Nicht veröffentlichte Interviews mit den muslimischen Privatschulen in Wien. From: http://citizenshipeducation. univie.ac.at/ (Accessed April 21, 2014).

Nicht veröffentlichte Interviews der Forschungsgruppe "Imame in Östereich". From: http://imameoesterreich.univie.ac.at/ (Accessed May 04, 2014b).

Ramadan, T. (2001). *Muslime in Europa.* Marburg, Germany: MSV.

Tiedemann, B. (2007). *Menschenwürde als Rechtsbegriff: eine philosophische Klärung.* Berlin: BWV.

Topcuoglu, A.A. (2012). "Modern hukuk ve Islam'da vatandaslik kavraminin hukuki temeli". In: *Gazi Üniversitesi Hukuk Fakültesi Dergisi* C. XVI, Y. 2012, No. 3.

Wellhausen, J. (1889). *Skizzen und Vorarbeiten.* Berlin: Georg Reimer.

Williams, K., Hinge, H. & Persson, B. L. (2008). *Religion and Citizenship Education in Europe.* London: CICE.

ZRD. *www.islam.de.* (15.09.2009). From: http://zentralrat.de/3035.php (Accessed January 10, 2013).

Migration, Feelings of Belonging to a Land, and the Universality of Islam

Zeki Saritoprak

According to Islamic theology, human beings are natural immigrants and migration is viewed positively in a variety of circumstances. There are many verses in the Qur'an praising those who migrate. Qur'an 2: 218 says, "Those who believed and migrated and struggled in the way of God are those who are hopeful of the mercy of God. God is Forgiving and Merciful." Another verse says, "Those who have migrated…surely I will forgive their sins" (Qur'an, 3:195). A common element in these verses is the combining of faith and migration. One verse asks those who were persecuted yet did not migrate: "Wasn't the land of God large enough that you could have migrated?" (Qur'an, 4:97). As part of the same narrative, the Qur'an actually encourages believers to migrate and states that those who chose to migrate when they are oppressed will find success: "Those who are migrating in the way of God will find refuge and prosperity" (Qur'an, 4:100).

Migration was an important aspect of the early development of Islam and some scholars argue that this is an important example of Islamic non-violence. From the beginning of the revelation of the Qur'an, the Prophet and his community faced persecution from the other residents of Mecca. In approximately 617 CE, the sixth year of his prophethood, about eighty-three members of Muhammad's community, both male and female, under the leadership of the Prophet's cousin Ja'far bin Abu Talib, left the city of Mecca for Abyssinia. Though the Prophet himself remained in Mecca, he asked his cousin to lead this group of new converts because they came from marginalized social classes and thus faced severe persecution. In addition to being the first major Muslim migration, this is also one of the earliest encounters between Muslims and Christians and many important contemporary lessons are drawn from it.[1] Abyssinia was a Christian kingdom, which Muhammad thought would be a safe refuge for his followers. The Abyssinian king received the Muslim immigrants and although he also received a delegation of Meccan leaders who wished him to return the migrants, the King and the Abyssinian religious hierarchy were convinced that the Muslim immigrants were innocent and thus the King did not return them to Mecca.[2] In the Qur'an, we find references to this event and upon the death of the Abyssinian king, known as the Negus, the Prophet performed a funeral prayer in absentia for him.

The persecution of the infant Muslim community did not stop with this migration, and soon the Prophet himself felt threatened. Hence, several years after the first migration, the largest and most important migration in the history of Islam, the migration of the Prophet from the city of Mecca to the town of Yathrib, which later will be called Medina or the City of the Prophet, took place. This migration is called the Hijra, simply the Arabic word for migration, and marks the beginning of the Islamic calendar.[3] Prior to the Hijra, the Prophet and the Muslims were singled out for persecution by the elite in the city of Mecca. The wealthy merchants of Mecca imposed a severe economic boycott against the Prophet and his followers for three years. It is believed that the boycott caused starvation within the Muslim community including the death of the Prophet's wife, Khadija. The Prophet called the year of her death "the year of grief (*huzn*)." Despite the terrible conditions facing the Muslim community, migration was not an easy choice. The Prophet loved his hometown and when he needed to leave, he turned back to the city of Mecca and said, "O Mecca! I know you are the most blessed (*khayr*) of the lands of God and the most beloved land of God to me. If I were not forced to leave,

---

1   For an examination of this event in light of Christian-Muslim relations see, Zeki Saritoprak, "Said Nursi on Muslim–Christian Relations Leading to World Peace," *Islam and Christian–Muslim Relations*, Vol. 19, No. 1 (January 2008) (25–37).

2   The famous Muslim historian and Qur'an commentator Ibn Kathir gives the fullest known narration of this story noting important individuals who participated in this migration including the third caliph, Uthman bin Affan. According to Ibn Kathir, the Abyssinian King, the Negus, listened to Muslim delegation and said, "You are welcome and the one from whom you came is also welcome. I believe that he is God's messenger. He is the one that I found in the Gospel. Jesus gave good news of him. Live in Abyssinia wherever you want. If I was not the King, I would be willing to carry the sandals of the Prophet." When he died, the Prophet was in Medina and he said to his companions, "Your brother Ashama (Negus) died in Abyssinia" and he asked them to have a funeral prayer for him. (See Ismail Ibn Kathir, *Al-Sira al-Nabawiyya*, Volume 2, ed. Mustafa Abd al-Wahid, Beirut: Dar al-Ma'rifa, 1976, 5-60)

3   A year in the Islamic calendar is noted as xx AH or x years after the Hijra. 1 AH corresponds to 622/3 CE.

I would never have left you" (Ibn Kathir, 1976, 285). It is also narrated that the Prophet said the following prayer while he migrated: "Lord, you have taken me away from the most beloved city to me. Take me to the most beloved city to You" (Ibn Kathir, 1976, 284).

Migrating to Yathrib was not the Prophet's first choice, but in what is considered a miracle, the people of Yathrib came to him to request that he migrate to their town. They wanted the Prophet to come to their town in order to stop its ongoing tribal warfare. Muhammad's peace-making skills prompted the people of this city to go to him with such a request. To avoid the watchful eye of their persecutors, the Prophet asked his companions to migrate surreptitiously. Eventually he and Abu Bakr, his close friend who would later become the first caliph in Islam, migrated under great risk of being attacked or killed. A skilled tracker was offered one hundred camels if he could find Muhammad and his friend and lead the Meccan leaders to them, but this failed.

This painful migration was in the month of July under the full heat of the Arabian sun. After arriving in the multicultural and multi-religious city of Yathrib, the first thing the Prophet did was to establish the foundations for an interconnected society where people could live peacefully with one another, including developing a constitution, known as the Medina Charter, which gave protections to all inhabitants no matter what their religious affiliation. It is worth noting, the population of the city was primarily made up of Arab polytheists and members of Jewish tribes, with the Muslim arrivals making up no more fifteen percent of the newly renamed city of Medina's population.

Because of the haste of their migration from Mecca, the Muslim migrants, or *Muhajirun* (s. *muhajir*), were financially weak and devoid of possessions. The wisdom of the Prophet was used to solve the problems of poverty and weakness. Though small in number, there were Muslim citizens in Medina prior to the coming of the immigrants. In order to integrate the immigrants with the local Muslims, the Prophet declared a relationship of "brotherhood" to exist between each immigrant and a local Muslim. These Medinan Muslims are called the *Ansar*, or "helpers" and he asked the local Muslims to help the immigrants such that according to Muslim tradition, the Prophet named one person from the *Ansar* and one from the *Muhajirun* and declared them to be brothers and sisters. This historical tie of symbolic brotherhood in Islam is called *muakhat*. Both groups of Muslims, the *Muhajirun* and the *Ansar* are the subjects of praise in the Qur'an. In speaking of these people, the Qur'an says the following:

The men who stayed in their own city (Medina) and embraced Islam before them loved those who have sought refuge with them. They do not covet what they are given but rather prefer (their brothers and sisters) above themselves although they are in need. Those who preserve themselves from their own greed shall surely prosper. (Qur'an, 59:9)

The *Ansar* shared their money and their farms with their brothers and sisters to such an extent that the immigrant Muslims received legal rights from the inheritance of their *Ansar* brothers. When one of the *Ansar* died, his *Muhajirun* brother would be among his heirs. Some of the immigrants were very honorable and did not want to ask for help. Instead of asking for assistance they would say, "show me the way to the marketplace." It is believed that one of the prominent companions of the Prophet, Abd al-Rahman bin 'Awf, who asked his *Ansar* brother, Sa'd bin al-Rabi, to show him the way to the market, became one of the wealthiest inhabitants of the city of Medina (Ibn Kathir, 1967, 224).

The brotherhood that the Prophet declared brought prosperity and solidarity to the entire community, (only) not; despite the challenges he faced in integrating the two groups. Prior to the migration, the Muslims had come from warring factions, particularly from the *'Aws* and *Khazraj* tribes. There is a reference to this in the Qur'an when it says: "Remember when you were enemies. God has united your hearts and through His grace you have become brothers" (Qur'an, 3:103). After the migration, it took five months for the Prophet to get to know the whole community and the declaration of brotherhood between the members of the new community was not done randomly. The Prophet looked at their characteristics, their spiritual compatibilities and even their tastes and then declared brotherhood between individual *Ansar* and *Muhajirun*. The cooperation between the *Ansar* and the *Muhajirun* was not limited to the material; it was also spiritual. For example, the Companions from each group would listen to the Prophet in turn so that no one would miss what the Prophet said. This also helped to create a warm environment for the immigrants and strengthened Muslim society. Despite the hierarchical nature of Arab society, the Prophet was able to create a fully inclusive community, into which even marginalized groups such as blacks and women were integrated.

There are also important hadiths that relate to the Hijra specifically and the concept of migration more broadly. One is of particular note and it explains that intention is most important when someone migrates: "For the one whose (intent in) migration was for Allah and His Messenger, his migration was for Allah and His Messenger; and for the one whose migration was to achieve some worldly benefit or to take a woman in marriage, his migration was for that for which he migrated" (al-Bukhari, 1990, 41). The Prophet indicates that migration for world-ly things is not as ideal as migration for the sake of God and His Messenger and suggests that the intent of the immigrant should be pure.

Migrating, leaving the original land in which a person grew up and relocating to another land, can be emotionally difficult. Therefore, balancing love of the old and the new lands is important. While there are people who migrate to a new land and consider the new land as their home, it is more likely that people who migrate will throughout their lives long for their original homeland. For Muslims, this emotional difficulty can be overcome by examining the theological and mystical dimensions of their faith.

To begin with, it is important to examine a well-known tradition which says that "love of country is part of faith"[4] which is often used today to argue that all Muslim believers must love their native country. How are we to understand this tradition in light of Islamic support for migration? The simplest answer is that in Islamic teaching, the real country is the country of the afterlife; a country with no end or borders. Additionally, when Muslims consider this idea, they should not see a contradiction since loving one (country) does not imply hatred for another (country). One Muslim scholar interpreted this statement by saying that a true believer should build his country with wholesome actions and beautiful things (al-Shafi'i, 2004, 37). Some people have even argued that the country in question is the original country of human beings in which Adam and Eve lived, paradise. However it is interpreted, this "hadith" should not be considered to be in conflict with the Prophetic encouragement to migration.

In Islam, the entire world belongs to God. A hadith says, "God has made the entire face of the earth as a mosque for me and its soil as pure."[5] Every part of earth is the property of God and is beautiful. Because of this, early Muslims did not hesitate to migrate from their own lands to other lands. Although some Islamic legal scholars divided the world into the land of faith or Islam and the land of disbelief, in today's conditions that categorization seems no longer to be valid. Arguably, if Muslims are able to practice their religion in Western countries where they are a small minority, and are unable to practice their religion in the country of their birth, then the former is much more the land of Islam than the latter. Islam looks

---

4 It is debatable whether or not this is a reliable hadith, but even those who find it unreliable as a hadith still consider the meaning to be true. See, 'Ali bin Sutlan Muhammad al-Qari, *Mirqat al-Mafatih Sharh Mishkat al-Masabih*, Beirut: Dar al-Fikr, 2002, vol 3, 1158.

5 An additional understanding of this hadith is that the whole face of the earth was made ritually pure and available as a place of worship or as a mosque. Al-Bukhari, *al-Sahih*, "al-Tayammum," 1.

at the land from a universal perspective and does not discriminate on the basis of location. A story from my own immigrant experience, I feel, sheds light on what I have said about the universality of Islam.

While I was a professor in a small town in the American state of Georgia, one of my students asked me if I felt I was in a foreign land and missed my native country of Turkey. I told him that initially I had felt this way, until one night when I looked at the sky and saw that the same stars I was seeing there, I had seen in Turkey; I saw the same moon and sun as well. In the morning, as the sun rose, I noticed that it had the same beauty as when I would watch the sun come over the hill near my house in Istanbul. Then I looked at my students and realized that they were just like my students in Turkey. They had come from different places to this one place for the sake of learning. After that, I looked at our planet in a more holistic way.

Of course feelings of belonging to the land where you are born or where you grew up are important, but these are not an essential part of the Islamic faith. Shortly after the establishment of the Turkish Republic, an exiled Turkish Islamic scholar said: "If the mercy of the Most Merciful (God) is your companion, everyone is friendly and everything is good. If the mercy of God is not your companion, everything is a burden on the heart and everyone becomes like an enemy" (Nursi, 1976, 477).

Because the Prophet Muhammad, the greatest example for Muslims, migrated and he followed all earlier prophets in this tradition of migration, Muslims should find no difficulty migrating from one place to another. The Qur'an features many stories of the migrations of the prophets, the first of which was Adam's migration from heaven to earth. According to the Qur'anic narrative Adam was in paradise and due to the Divine will, he was expelled from paradise and sent to the earth where he became the first immigrant. It should be noted that Adam sought God's forgiveness which was granted. Further, this was God's plan for had Adam not immigrated to earth, there would have been no chain of prophets, including the Seal of the Prophets, Muhammad. The Qur'anic narratives of Abraham, Lot, Jonah, Jacob and Moses all contain migrations. By considering this encompassing picture of migration one can see the universal dimension of the Islamic understanding of migration.

In the Islamic tradition, life on earth is but one stage in every human's journey. There is a famous hadith in which the Prophet encapsulates this idea. In it, he compares himself to a traveler resting under the shade of a tree before continuing on his journey. The hadith goes as a follows. While the Prophet was sitting on a mat, Umar visited him and said to the Prophet that the Prophet should have a comfortable bed, instead of sleeping on a mat. The Prophet responded: "I don't have anything to do with this world. My story is like a rider in a desert who takes shade under a tree for a certain moment and then departs from there" (al-Tirmidhi, 1975, 44).

The permanence of migration is echoed in another hadith that mentions how "migration will never come to end until repentance comes to an end. Repentance will never come to an end until the end of the world" (al-Tayalisi, n.d. 2). This hadith indicates that migration is a part of every human's journey on earth and will continue as long as life on earth continues. In other words, migration will never come to an end until the end of time. As migration is a part of human nature, people should develop institutions to deal with this. From a religious perspective, there will be religious migration throughout human history. This migration can be undertaken to escape religious persecution or to spread the Divine message. The other aspect of the hadith is that migration is a human phenomenon and will continue and therefore humanity should be aware of this and make all efforts to prevent possible calamities and to help with the difficult situations faced by immigrants. [6]

The encouragement that Islam gives to Muslims to offer charity constitutes a remarkable resource for modern aid organizations who deal with the problems of immigrants. The Qur'anic language of charity encompasses every aspect of life, from financial support and education to simple kindness and portions of *zakat*, the compulsory charity that is one of the five pillars of Islam, are given to those who are in poverty as well as travellers who are unable to pay their expenses. The reward that the Qur'an promises for those who help travellers is not limited to this world, but includes the afterlife as well. A prominent saying of the Prophet articulates the idea that anyone who removes the grief of a brother or sister, God will remove his or her grief in the afterlife. Such grief is a common experience for many migrants thus as this hadith indicates, Islam provides encouragement to those who help immigrants in bettering their conditions.

Throughout the history of Islam, there have been many examples of kindness and generosity towards immigrants. Bilal Habashi, a black African slave, was an immigrant in Mecca and considered a second-class human being in the period

---

6   For instance, the Turkish Muslim organization known as Kimse Yok Mu, literally "Is Anybody There?" which in the Turkish context is equivalent to "help," assists immigrants and refugees from around the world. Recently, the organization has been active in providing relief aid to the Syrian refugees in southern Turkey who lack many basic necessities, while suffering through severe winter conditions. See Sevgi Akarcesmet, "Kimse Yok Mu reaches out to Syrians in joint project with UNHCR," *Today's Zaman*, 9 Feb 2014. See also İlkay Gocmen, "56 TIR 'Kimse Yok Mu' diyen Suriyeliler için yola çıktı," *Zaman*, 19 Feb 2014.

prior to Islam. Abu Bakr rescued him from that situation by paying the ransom for his freedom. After he was freed, he became the first muezzin (prayer caller) in Islam. As mentioned above, the Qur'an speaks of the *Ansar*, and hence of all people who are generous, in a highly positive manner: "They do not covet what they are given but rather prefer (their brothers and sisters) above themselves although they are in need." (Qur'an, 59:9). Al-Tabari (d. 923 C.E), commenting on this verse in his *tafsir*, narrates the following story that is understood to have taken place in Medina and was the occasion for the verse's revelation. A hungry *muhajir* came to the Prophet as a guest. Since the Prophet did not have any food to provide, he asked if anyone else could host the *muhajir*. One of the *Ansar*, Abu Talha, took the man to his home. Though his family was poor and they only had enough food for one person, he advised his wife to honor the Prophet's guest. Abu Talha dimmed the lights and put his children to bed. He and his wife decided that they would pretend to eat, so that there would be food for their guest (al-Tabari, 2000, 285).

Considering the relationship between Europe and its Muslim immigrants, it is clear that Muslims constitute a significant proportion of new Europeans and will continue to do so for the foreseeable future. These immigrants come not only from Muslim majority countries within Europe like Albania and Bosnia, but also from many different parts of the Islamic world, Turkey, the Arab world, sub-Saharan Africa, and the Indian subcontinent being the most prominent. By the second and third generation, European Muslims tend to consider themselves European and they have generally been integrated into the host society to the extent that some have lost their religious identities. If the Islamic model of migration and the universality of Islam are well understood by Muslim immigrants, they could become an engine of development for Europe because the idea of God's ownership of all lands gives Muslims the belief that all countries are God's country whether the place of their birth or not. If they feel alienated in Europe due to discrimination, racism, or social ostracism, European Muslims will become an obstacle to, rather than an engine of development. Therefore policy makers and administrators should find ways to make Muslims, who, according to the Pew Research Forum, number roughly 45 million in Europe, feel at home (Pew Research Religion and Public Life Project, 2011). There is no way to remove all Muslims from Europe, but there is a way to make Muslims feel more comfortable in their European environment and become fruitful citizens, socially and economically. In this regard, Europeans can take lessons from America where Muslims feel much more comfortable, not because America has solved all of its immigration problems, but because America is open to immigration and works to integrate immigrants into society. If Europeans can develop similar institutions, Europe can become a better place for all immigrants.

Islam provides an important historical and ideological foundation for a society composed of immigrants and nonimmigrants. The practice of the Prophet of Islam gives important examples of creating harmony between the various segments of society and can be used as a model for dealing with immigration today. Muslim immigrants are ultimately capable of providing a source of economic strength and social harmony. Such harmony in Europe is important not only for Europe, but for the entire world.

References

Akarcesmet, S. "Kimse Yok Mu reaches out to Syrians in joint project with UHCR." *Today's Zaman*, (9 Feb 2014).

al-Bukhari, Abu 'Abdillah Muhammad bin Isma'il. (1990). *Al-Sahih*. Edited by Mustafa Dayb al-Bugha. Damascus: Dar Ibn Kathir.

Gocmen, İlkay. "56 TIR 'Kimse Yok Mu' diyen Suriyeliler için yola çıktı." Zaman, (19 Feb. 2014).

Ibn Kathir, Ismail. (1976). *Al-Sira Al-Nabawiyya*. Edited by Mustafa Abd al-Wahid. Beirut: Dar al-Ma'rifa.

Muhammad 'Ali Ibn Muhammad Ibn 'Allan. (2004). *Dalil al-Falihin li Turuq Riyad al-Salihin*. Beirut: Dar al-Ma'rifa. Nursi, Bediüzzaman Said. (1976). *Mektubat*. Istanbul. Sozler Yayinevi.

Pew Research Religion and Public Life Project. *"The Future of the Global Muslim Population: Regional Europe."* From: http://www.pewforum.org/2011/01/27/future-of-the-global-muslim-population-regional-europe/. (Accessed January 27, 2011).

al-Qari, 'Ali bin Sutlan Muhammad. (2002). *Mirqat al-Mafatih Sharh Mishkat al-Masabih*. Beirut: Dar al-Fikr.

Saritoprak, Z. "Said Nursi on Muslim–Christian Relations Leading to World Peace."*Islam and Christian–Muslim Relations*, Vol. 19, No. 1 (25–37). (January 2008).

al-Tabari, Muhammad bin Jarir. (2000). *Jami' al-Bayan 'an Tafsir Ay al-Qur'an*. Beirut: Mu'assasat al-Risalah.

al-Tayalisi, Sulaiman bin Abi Dawud. (n.d.) *Al-Musnad*. Beirut: Dar al-Ma'rifa.

al-Tirmidhi, Abu 'Isa Muhammad bin 'Isa bin Sawra. (1975). *Al-Jami' al-Sahih*. Edited by Ibrahim 'Atwa 'Awad. Cairo: Maktabat Mustafa al-Babi al-Halabi.

Section One

Western European Cases

Citizenship Education in Multicultural Societies

Jørgen S. Nielsen

The challenge to 'citizenship' in the Arab world

The events of the last three years in the Arab world, what used to be called rather optimistically the 'Arab spring', have focused on diverse issues in different countries but one of the common elements to them all has been the struggle to define some form of collective belonging to a nation, often expressed in the term *muwatana*. This Arabic word is most often translated into English as 'citizenship', an idea which had been thought to have become the defining dimension of the new nations arising out of the collapse of the Ottoman empire at the end of the first world war.

In the 1980s a number of widely-read Islamic intellectuals, especially in Egypt, individuals who were associated with the moderate end of the spectrum of the Muslim Brotherhood tradition, engaged in arguments for citizenship. In 1985 the journalist and commentator Fahmy Howeidi argued that the struggle for independence against the colonial powers was one in which all sections of the population participated, Coptic Christians as well as Muslims. The status of *dhimmi* was therefore no longer relevant, however useful it may have been in a certain historical period. This shared commitment to the Egyptian nation made people of all communities common citizens (Howeidi, 1985).

Echoing this argument, Muhammad Salim al-'Awwa asserts that the modern state represents a new kind of Islamic sovereignty to which much of traditional law cannot apply. Reasoning based on first principles (*ijtihad*) must be used to deduce a new system. The modern Muslim state is the result of a common struggle for independence and nation building in which the Muslim majority and the non-Muslim minority have shared. In this way it differs sharply from the early

Muslim state that was based on conquest. In this situation it is the duty of the Muslim majority to concentrate on applying the principles established by God and the Prophet rather than stubbornly insisting on applying outdated and inappropriate rules. The discourse in this approach has changed from one of contract (*'aqd*) to one of constitution (*dustur*) and from *dhimmah* to citizenship (*muwatanah*) (Al-'Awwa, 1989, 257-63).[7]

The background for these and similar writings during the latter third of the 20th century was growing support for religious forms of expression, which found a place also in politics, reviving many of the Islamic forms of categorisation which observers thought had disappeared. Helped along by the Iranian revolution of 1979, the world was again increasingly divided into *dar al-harb* and *dar al-islam*. And non-Muslim religious minorities were once again being described as *dhimmis*, protected communities.

The revival of 'citizenship' in Europe

This increase in the references to citizenship in the Arab world accompanies similar developments in Europe. When I was in high school in Copenhagen in the 1960s it was a natural state of affairs, which nobody gave any deep thought to, that our general studies courses included dimensions of what was sometimes called 'civics' in English. These modules were about the country's constitution, how local and national government worked, the role and mechanics of elections, and how parliament and the government resulted from elections. They also dealt with some of the country's international relationships, the UN, and the European Convention on Human Rights.

To the extent that anyone talked about it, the tradition of civics was about duties: to family, to community, to country. In some countries, especially in Eastern Europe and in the Arab world, it was quite ideological in character: here it was often a question of creating a cohesive sense of nationhood were none existed or where it was very weak. Where it was less ideological, it was often assumed that the teaching of language, literature, history, etc. would subliminally form a nation-oriented consciousness from which a sense of citizenship (whatever that meant, we didn't talk about it) might flow. Most people of my generation will remember aspects of this from their school days.

---

7   Fahmy Howeidi has recently reasserted his views in the face of the incidents of sectarian violence that have increased through the Egyptian unrest since 2011.

But in recent years we have seen much more deliberate and objective-oriented developments of 'citizenship education'. In some countries the use of the local equivalent to 'citizen' (Danish *borger* or *medborger*; German *Mitbürger*) has become much more prevalent since the 1990s, now used in a sense which is reminiscent of the *citoyen* of the French Revolution or even the 'comrade' of the Communist tradition.

At the same time a steadily growing number of countries in Western Europe have introduced 'citizenship' tests as part of the process by which foreigners acquire the nationality of their new country of residence. The pressure for such measures grew markedly after the terrorist attacks on the US of 11 September 2001. The murder of Theo van Gogh in Amsterdam in 2004 and the train bombing in Madrid in 2005 increased pressure for policy measures to strengthen the integration of immigrants, especially those of Muslim heritage (Joppke, 2007, 1-22). Such measures tended to take two forms. The simplest was to introduce stricter requirements on people seeking permanent residence or wanting to change nationality. More complicated was the introduction of citizenship education.

In the United Kingdom, then Home Secretary David Blunket, introduced such a test requirement in the Nationality, Immigration and Asylum Act 2002. First applied to people seeking UK nationality in late 2007, it was subsequently also applied to foreigners seeking permanent residence. Entitled the 'Life in the United Kingdom' test, the intention of the computerized test was to assess the applicant's knowledge of life in the UK (Government Digital Service). In November 2007 Red Squirrel publishing, which produces study guides for people preparing for the UK test, conducted a large survey on Facebook. Only 14% of UK citizens passed, less than a number of other nationalities. The participants in this survey had not prepared for the test; when applicants prepared the average pass rate is around 70% (Red Squirrel Publishing).

In the Netherlands a 'civic integration examination' was introduced at the beginning of 2007 that included a language element and a series of questions about Dutch history and society. Denmark introduced a similar test requirement in May 2007. This also focused on factual knowledge about Danish history and society (Humanity In Action Inc.). The test has been made gradually more difficult so as to reduce the pass rate under pressure from the political right wing. However, trials conducted by newspapers have consistently shown that Danish citizens have a surprisingly high failure rate (The Copenhagen Post). Increasingly, these tests must be passed before the person concerned can obtain an entry visa for permanent residence (Government of the Netherlands).

The growing explicit focus on citizenship indicates that it is a concept which is no longer taken for granted, that it is a contested field – why else pay so much attention to it? It seems obvious that the introduction of citizenship tests is, at least partially, a response to the popular pressures to 'do something' after the terrorist attacks at the beginning of the century – the dates of the legislation alone are an indicator of this. But the growing focus on citizenship as a part of the political discourse predates 9/11. That date may have become an icon for many of the changes which we have experienced recently, but the end of the Cold War and the dismantling of the Iron Curtain were the substantial turning points.

In the period after 1945, it was as if Europe had found a degree of equilibrium, if not stability, after what amounted to centuries of uncertainty characterised by wars of religion, dynasties, classes, and national ambitions. In the east, societies and economies and conflicts of nationality, religion and class had been subjugated to the dream of the solidarity of the proletariat. In the west, the nation states had found their fulfilment within agreed borders under the guidance of social capitalism and liberal democracy. But by the 1990s both of these settlements were being challenged. In the west immigration and the consequent growth of ethnic and cultural pluralism had moved to the centre of the political and cultural world, symbolically expressed in the 'affairs' of 1990: the protests against the publication of Salman Rushdie's *The Satanic Verses* in Britain and the first 'head scarves affair' in France. In the east it turned out that the national conflicts of the period before 1914 had not disappeared but only been suppressed: in fact, appeals to atavistic national feelings were a common refuge for communist leaders seeking to survive the decline and fall of the single-party security state. The wars around the breakup of Yugoslavia were only the most extreme expression of this.

This gradual departure from the known and assured state of affairs has meant that there has been a degree of convergence between the eastern and western parts of Europe. Following the fall of Communism, many eastern European countries too have begun to experience immigration from parts of the Muslim world. At the same time, the existing structures of religious authority, previously strictly controlled, have lost their monopolies and found themselves having to deal with contesting claims to correct belief and practice.[8] They have become more directly exposed to the forces of globalisation and the regional supra-national governance of the European Union, NATO, the Council of Europe, and the OSCE (Organisation for Security and Cooperation in Europe). Overall, the whole European subcontinent has had to face the challenges of the relationships between ethnicity, religion, language, law, nationality, and citizenship.

---

8   Details of the various country situations are summarised in the relevant country chapters of Jørgen S. Nielsen *et al* (eds.), *Yearbook of Muslims in Europe*, vol.5 (Leiden: Brill, 2013).

Finding refuge in nostalgia

This is becoming particularly clear in popular responses to these challenges coming especially from the nationalist right-wing.[9] In Denmark the events of 9/11 legitimised an open shift from a general political concern with immigration, which during the 1990s had underpinned a gradual tightening of immigration rules in a country which hitherto had had one of the most liberal regimes in Euriope, to an explicit targeting of Muslims and Islam. It happened that the country held a general election a couple of months after 9/11, and the right-wing Danish People's Party (DPP) adopted a programme explicitly framed to be against Muslims. The subsequent installation of a right-of centre minority coalition government, whose parliamentary majority was assured by the DPP, enabled a yet more aggressive tightening of immigration rules as well as regular amendments to social policy aimed at curtailing life styles commonly associated in the public mind with Muslims: having many children, regulating internal community social order, polygamy, arranged and forced marriages, importing unsuitable spouses, to mention just some examples.

The DPP became a trendsetter in Scandinavia. Similar parties in Sweden (the Sweden Democrats) and Norway (Progress Party) achieved growing electoral success in the first decade of the present century. Elections in both countries early in the present decade led to the Sweden Democrats becoming a supporting party for a right-of-centre minority coalition, and the Progress Party to become part of the Norwegian government in 2013.

This Scandinavian trend was often associated with the rise of Geert Wilders and his Party for Freedom (PVV) in the Netherlands. Common to all of them is a combination of strong positions against Islam and immigration, associated with sympathy for Israel, and support for conservative social values and strong social welfare.

In other countries, the growth of forms of hardline nationalism, which can be characterised as nostalgic, can be traced back to the appearance of the Front National in France in the early 1970s under the leadership of Jean-Marie Le Pen. Under his leadership the party adopted a marked anti-Semitic stance as well as anti-immigrant platform. In the last dozen years – Jean-Marie Le Pen was succeeded as leader in 2011 by his daughter Marine – the former has been marginalized, while the anti-Islam stance has been strengthened. Through roughly the

---

9   For a critical discussion of this terminology in a Danish context, see Mark Sedgwick, 'Something Varied in the State of Denmark: Neo-nationalism, Anti-Islamic Activism, and Street-level Thuggery,' *Politics, Religion and Ideology*, vol. 14 (2013), pp.208-233.

same period, Jörg Haider had pushed the Austrian Freedom Party towards the nationalist right. In 2000 the party was the first such to enter a governing coalition, much to the consternation of EU partners.

Since the 1990s, in fact, no country in the European Union has not experienced the growth of such political movements. Characterised by many as 'populist', they tend to have in common a strong anti-immigration stance that in some cases, at least in their extreme factions, support expulsion of certain immigrant and ethnic minority groups. While some have a history of anti-Semitism, and in some instances active flirtations with fascist and national-socialist ideas, they have steadily strengthened their anti-Islamic focus (Hungary's Jobbik is apparently an exception to this). All have a very strong, sometimes aggressive nationalist focus. A few appear to have factions that tend to cross the border into violence.

What does all this have to do with the theme of this volume? Firstly, these movements are a response to the changing nature of society within existing state boundaries. The impact of non-European immigration into western European countries since 1945 alone has served to make the changing population structures in the big cities visible. As they have settled, the changing image of the urban space, with minority ethnic food and clothing outlets and, above all, new 'strange' places of worship, have unsettled the existing populations both physically and mentally. Schools and other community institutions in the affected areas are no longer as they were. These changes have combined with a growing sense of distance and, indeed, alienation of the local from the larger world 'out there.' This has been exacerbated by the growing public role of the European Union, especially after the introduction of the single market that has necessitated a high degree of product regulation across borders. Further globalisation of the world economy has sharpened awareness of the influence of factors beyond local control, whether commodity prices such as oil or the growing economic power of countries like China. Those sections of society that feel left out of these developments are – understandably – prone to respond by turning inwards.

Secondly, in such responses appeals to a mythological history of the nation may be alluring: 'Victorian values' was the phrase used by Mrs Thatcher. Characteristic of all of these movements is their perception of a time when the nation was stable and coherent, comfortable within itself. In the case of larger nations, such as Britain, France and, more recently, Russia, such nostalgia is tinged also with memory, usually 'false' memory, of empire. Whether this empire was imagined to be benevolent or civilizing is of little matter. Such imagined history is then pushed further askew by positing it as the final and closing phase of the making of the nation that is being defended. This becomes visible in ever more obsessive discussions about 'values', values which are selectively mobilised. The built environment is imagined to have developed a particular national character, in which minarets are a much more threatening element than modern brutalist glass and concrete office blocks. Head-scarved women refusing to shake hands is somehow threatening, while the Indian greeting of hands held together in front of the chest is cute and exotic. *Laïcité* entails that to rest a political argument in the French National Assembly on the Bible is unacceptable, but this did not stop deputies suddenly becoming experts in Qur'an interpretation when they discussed the banning of the *burqa*. Muslim objections to same-sex marriage in Denmark were evidence of their failure to integrate, but the same was not suggested of the 40% of priests who were opposed. One can go on.

Thirdly, and consequently, these movements are challenging existing institutions, and above all the educational system. European government and private institutions have been surprisingly flexible in making space for the cultures and religions of immigrant communities – never enough, of course, for the community representatives themselves nor as seen from the perspectives of anti-racist and other similar activists. Institutions were never going to satisfy all parties. They had to manoeuver and negotiate among competing claims in ways which would never satisfy everyone but which hopefully would not alienate the main stakeholders. In different countries, various paths through this maze have been found so, again, a common description of the European situation is not possible. But the new nationalisms are not characterised by a willingness to enter into the compromises that have traditionally kept politics and government moving.

Countries of Eastern Europe were thought to be different. Yes, they experienced the revival of the national and linguistic conflicts that had not been settled before dictatorships took over in the middle of the twentieth century. But so far they were still dealing with native populations, whether they were Tatars in the Belarus, Lithuania, Poland triangle or Slavic speakers in the Balkans, or, for that matter, ethnic Turks in Bulgaria, Greece or parts of former Yugoslavia. This did not make it any easier, especially not in the bloody break-up of Yugoslavia, except that there the outcome partly served to separate some of the conflicts behind new borders (others clearly remain). However, I suggest that the rise of the new contests about national identity in the west have been exported to the eastern part of the European subcontinent. It is a nostalgic imagination of a presumed nationhood that underpins the propaganda and appeal of movements like Jobbik in Hungary, Golden Dawn in Greece, and Ataka in Bulgaria.

What role for citizenship education?

At first sight, one might think that citizenship education must obviously be a major factor in solving these tensions. It seems clear that when a sense of national cohesion and collective solidarity is breaking down, schools must be one of the main locations for creating that solidarity and cohesion. Of course, there is also an element of self-delusion in this dream. First,it overrates what can be achieved in school. In Britain where anti-racist and multicultural approaches to education have been practiced, or at least widely attempted, for many decades, educators are the first to accept that the home environment often undermines their best efforts. Secondly, it ignores that education has often itself been a driver of national and social division. Even in the absence of schools formally separated on the basis of religion, ethnicity, region, language or class – something which exists in most countries in one form or another – schools will be thus distinguished simply by the social environment in which they are located: the catchment area is a major determinant of the character of a school.

Given all of this, there remains some degree of educational influence on the way children grow up and society is formed. Education as social and national engineering was a major factor in creating cohesion and a sense of shared nationhood in countries like France, Italy, Germany and the Nordic countries – in different ways and with different degrees of success, certainly, but universal literacy was a formative driver of the emergence of national languages in many of these (Anderson, 2006).

If we are going to call for expanded citizenship education, we must be clear about what is meant, and essentially there is a choice between two routes:

1. One option is to go the way of social engineering for national cohesion, what one might call the nation-building route. At first sight this looks attractive: it aims at strengthening cohesion within the national boundaries, and surely that cohesion is what is missing in our plural societies. The problem is that it almost by definition must create and strengthen minority feelings, be they linguistic, ethnic or religious. This is especially the implication of those citizenship tests. Their starting point is what constituted the nation before the recent immigrants arrived, particularly unhelpful when those immigrants have come from areas that were under the colonial rule of the country of settlement. This approach implies exclusion rather than inclusion. In that this approach also implies the dominance of an imaginary national history, a mythological approach to history; it also legitimises the closing down of a dialogue within

society about collective identity.[10] Ultimately it is an approach that is more easily associated with authoritarianism than liberal democracy.

2. The other option is to move to an approach where process is the most important factor. The various constituent communities, or for that matter individuals, of a national population may vary widely in their views on particular issues, their points of departure may be fundamentally different, but they can function in a shared space due to a common understanding of how to do so.[11] Basically this approach requires a common understanding that the public space is a space of negotiation and give and take. This is uncomfortable for people and movements with absolute convictions that their views on an issue – and only their views – are correct and legitimate. This applies also to dominant groups, be they population groups or political movements, and this includes the state. The government or state that imposes a form of citizenship education, that dictates what constitutes citizenship, is inevitably going to provoke opposition and will have no hope of creating the nation that they professedly want to create.

A term that has been widely used in recent years is 'active citizenship'. In the balance between individual rights and responsibilities in society, the feeling has been that the rights part were becoming dominant, so 'active citizenship' is posited as a rebalancing between the two. It is suggested that it might find expression in volunteering, membership in civil associations, and the like (Wikipedia). Described in this way it is not all that helpful in this discussion. But understood in its full sense, the concept implies an obligation also on the state, even though those government leaders who have adopted this position may not have paid much attention to that. It implies a form of a renewed social contract. Why should individuals put themselves forward as active citizens if the state does not reciprocate by engaging in a permanent dialogue with the citizens about society, culture, economic and political processes and institutions? Only in this kind of environment does the status of citizen, and with that the role of citizenship education, begin to make sense. Otherwise it regresses to where it started, namely teaching about the myths and facts, which students must absorb and regurgitate on appropriate occasions, and the inculcation of respect (and obedience?) towards parents, elders, leaders and traditions.

---

10 For a Bulgarian example of this approach, see Evelina Kelbecheva, (2012) 'The short history of Bulgaria for export', in Jørgen Nielsen (ed.), *Religion, Ethnicity and Contested Nationhood in the Former Ottoman Space* (233-247). Leiden: Brill.

11 This is central to the political philosophy of John Rawls (1993) in his *Political Liberalism*, New York: Columbia University Press.

References

Anderson, B. (2006). *Imagined Communities: Reflections on the Origin and Spread of Nationalism.* (revised ed.). London: Verso.

Al-'Awwa, M. S. (1989). *Fi al-Nizam al-Siyasi li'l-Dawlah al-Islamiyyah.* Cairo: Dar al-Shuruq.

Government Digital Service. From: https://www.gov.uk/life-in-the-uk-test (Accessed February 12, 2014).

Government of the Netherlands. From: http://www.government.nl/issues/integration (Accessed February 12, 2014).

Howeidi, F. (1985). *Muwatinun, La Dhimmiyun.* Cairo: Dar al-Shuruq.

Humanity In Action Inc. From: http://www.humanityinaction.org/knowledgebase/143-becoming-a-dane-can-danish-ness-be-tested (Accessed February 12, 2014).

Joppke, C. (2007). 'Beyond national models: Civic integration policies for immigrants in Western Europe', *West European Politics.* vol.30, no.1, (1-22).

Kelbecheva, E. (2012) *'The short history of Bulgaria for export'.* In: Nielsen J. (ed.) *Religion, Ethnicity and Contested Nationhood in the Former Ottoman Space.* (233-247). Leiden: Brill.

Nielsen, J. S. et al (Eds.) (2013). *Yearbook of Muslims in Europe.* vol. 5, Leiden: Brill.

Rawls, J. (1993). *Political Liberalism.* New York: Columbia University Press.

Red Squirrel Publishing. From: http://lifeintheuk.net/index.php/news/polish_score_top_marks_in_britishness_test/, (Accessed February 12, 2014).

Sedgwick, M. (2013). 'Something Varied in the State of Denmark: Neo-nationalism, Anti-Islamic Activism, and Street-level Thuggery'. *Politics, Religion and Ideology.* vol. 14, (208-233).

The Copenhagen Post. From: http://cphpost.dk/news/new-citizenship-tests-still-not-ready.4662.html (Accessed February 12, 2014).

Wikipedia. From: http://en.wikipedia.org/wiki/Active_citizenship, (Accessed February 17, 2014).

Citizenship from an Austrian Christian Theological perspective

Matthias Scharer

"Their existence is on earth, but their citizenship is in heaven" (Letter to Diognetus)

Communicative Theology as related to citizenship

If you Google "Citizenship in Austria", you will find a huge number of references nearly all of which are definitions of citizenship in Austrian law. Can a legal definition encompass all of what citizenship in Austria means? I know a lot of people who are citizens of Austria by law but they are not by mentality. Citizenship in Austria cannot be defined as a "cold" term. Rather it is a "hot" metaphor that can be appropriated by everybody. Having this in mind, we will interrogate how Communicative Theology can lead us to a deeper understanding of citizenship from a theological perspective.

What is Communicative Theology?

In brief "Communicative theology is theology done in and from a living process of communication" (Scharer & Hilberath, 2003, 15). When we speak about "living processes", we address living communication processes. The term "living communication" evokes Ruth C. Cohn's concept of "living learning" (Cohn, 1971, 245), which is in contrast to "dead learning" (Scharer & Hilberath, 2008).

Ruth Cohn was born in 1912 in Berlin. As a Jew, she emigrated from the Nazi terror initially to Switzerland and then, to the U.S. (Cohn & Farau, 2008, 222-225). Her understanding of "living learning" is a response to inhumanity. "Dead learning" takes a very limited stance or is often just a sham communication: 'something', a task, a learning object, a content, a piece of tradition– as a quasi-neutral object, as matters devoid of personal reference without considering the dynamics in (learning) groups and independently of contexts in which learning process-es are communicated. "Dead Learning", according to Cohn, mainly occurs at universities and schools. It is dry knowledge, as an anonymous product, isolated from its background without personal reference. Dead Learning is distant from any real social context and lacks an anthropological or ethical basis (Matzdorf & Cohn, 1992).

Not only is it characteristic of dead learning but also it is part of human com-munication. Single-line transfer distinguishes the multi-dimensional informa-tion and increasingly intimate human communication. Therefore, it makes sense not only to speak of living and dead learning, but also to equally distinguish "liv-ing communication" from "dead communication" (Hilberath & Scharer, 2012, 63-111). Citizenship can be communicated as a "dead object" within the legal system or as an existential theme. As an existential theme it includes:

- The "I" of everyone as an autonomous-interdependent subject: Who am I as a citizen or without citizenship? What are my personal experiences with cit-izenship?
- The "We", which expresses the dynamics of groups/communities. Who is in-cluded or excluded from the "We" of citizenship? The "We" does not have in-strumental significance.
- The "It", as the thing or concern which the interaction revolves around: It is citizenship as a subject of discourse.
- The "Globe", which represents the temporal and the social context, encom-passes the three dimensions by way of an equilateral triangle within a sphere (for example, citizenship exists in different historical situations).

The value reference is most clearly expressed in the "axioms" of TCI,[12] which formulate the "irreducible" of the TCI approach and contain "elements of faith" (Cohn, 1974, 215). Due to the limited space that I have, I can only show the figure for the whole approach with some of the different aspects.

---

12 TCI (**Theme-centered interaction**) is a concept and a method for working in groups aimed at social learning and development of the person. TCI was developed by the psy-choanalyst and psychologist Ruth Cohn. The diagrams in this chapter, for example, are based on TCI concepts.

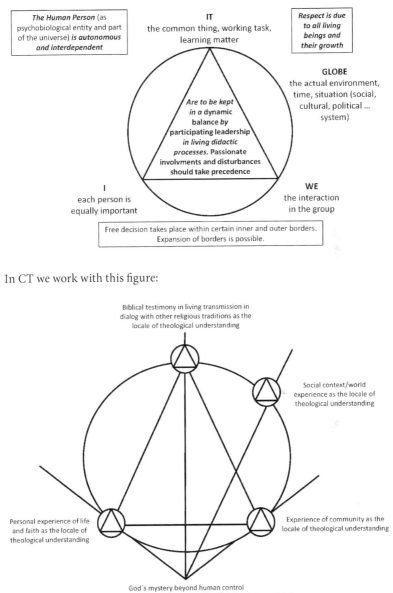

The Human Person (as psychobiological entity and part of the universe) *is autonomous and interdependent*

IT
the common thing, working task, learning matter

Respect is due to all living beings and their growth

GLOBE
the actual environment, time, situation (social, cultural, political ... system)

Are to be kept in a **dynamic balance** *by* **participating leadership** *in* **living didactic** *processes.* Passionate **involvments and disturbances should take precedence**

I
each person is equally important

WE
the interaction in the group

Free decision takes place within certain inner and outer borders. Expansion of borders is possible.

In CT we work with this figure:

Biblical testimony in living transmission in dialog with other religious traditions as the locale of theological understanding

Social context/world experience as the locale of theological understanding

Personal experience of life and faith as the locale of theological understanding

Experience of community as the locale of theological understanding

God´s mystery beyond human control
God´s revelation in creation, history etc. (for Christians in Jesus Christ)

This figure reminds us of the "I", the "We", the "It" and the "Globe" of R. Cohn's triangle in the sphere. But in CT the figure is open. The human aspects of every form of communication are transcended from God's mystery and revelation. Before I explain this more precisely, I have to refer to another factor of CT: In a communicative culture of theologizing, we oscillate between:

- The level of immediate involvement
- The level of experience and primary interpretation
- The level of scientific reflection

as the following graph illustrates.

Levels and dimensions of CT

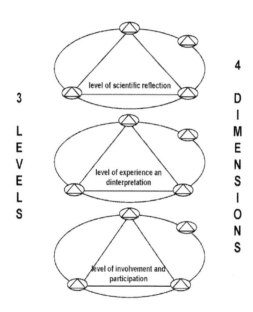

It's not only the oscillation through the levels that is typical of CT. In addition, we find a Dynamic Balance, either a correlation or abduction between different dimensions.

If we relate (Foster, 2007) our question to a theological understanding of "citizenship" we could write the secular term in the middle of the triangle in the sphere. In CT, a new meaning is formed: Citizenship becomes a metaphor for a "good life" for every human being.

Since early Christianity, citizenship for Christians has been based on controversial experiences. A very impressive full example of the struggle between Christian and non-Christian understandings is in the "Letter to Diognetus" (Foster, 2007). This letter was written at the end of the second, or the beginning of the third century. A Roman citizen who is not a Christian asks his Christian friend: "What is typical for a Christian?" The Christian friend answers:

> Christians are not distinguished from the rest of mankind, either in locality or in speech or in customs; for they dwell not somewhere in cities of their own. They neither use a different language, nor practice an extraordinary kind of life. They don't possess any invention discovered by ingenious men and are not masters of any human dogma.
> While they dwell in cities of Greeks and barbarians and follow the native customs in dress, food and lifestyle, the constitution of their own citizenship, which they set forth, is marvelous and confessedly contradicts expectations.
> They dwell in their own countries, but only as sojourners; they bear their share in all things as citizens, and they endure all hardships as strangers. Every foreign country is a fatherland to them, and every fatherland is foreign.
> They marry like all other men and they beget children; but they do not cast away their offspring.
> They have their meals in common, but not their wives.
> They find themselves in the flesh, and yet they live not after the flesh.
> Their existence is on earth, but their citizenship is in heaven.

Based on this text we can concretize our figure for research on citizenship in this way:

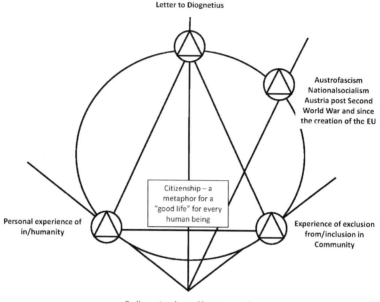

Letter to Diognetius

Austrofascism
Nationalsocialism
Austria post Second
World War and since
the creation of the EU

Citizenship – a
metaphor for a
"good life" for every
human being

Personal experience of
in/humanity

Experience of exclusion
from/inclusion in
Community

God's mystery beyond human control
God's revelation in creation, history etc. (for Christians in Jesus Christ)

Three contexts of Citizenship in Austrian history: Austrofascism, Nationalsocialism and Austria post the Second World War since the creation of the EU

As my second point I try to figure out what happens if the historical context – R. Cohn mentioned "the Globe" – changes. The context/globe touches every other dimension, "Who does not respect the Globe will be eaten by it" (R. Cohn).

Austrofascism

Austrofascism is a term which is frequently used by historians to describe the authoritarian system installed in Austria with the May Constitution of 1934. It ended with the annexing of the newly founded Federal State of Austria by Nazi Germany in 1938 (Talos & Neugebauer, 2012). Austrofascism was based on a ruling party, the Christian Social Party, with their Home Guard, the Fatherland Front, as a paramilitary militia. They were close to the Catholic Church. Ignac Seipel, a Catholic priest, was Lord Chancellor before Austrofascism expanded. Leaders of Austrofascism were Engelbert Dollfuss and, after Dollfuss' assassination, Kurt Schuschnigg. All were original politicians of the Christian Social Party, which was quickly integrated into the new movement. The Socialists, and their paramilitary militia, were more and more excluded from the movement (Wenninger & Dreidemy, 2013).

Austrofascism shows us the big problem of an excluding "We." Catholicism and the Christian Social ideas of the leading party could not prevent the practical exclusion of nearly half of the citizens. They were not excluded from citizenship legally but mentally. The Austrofascists were not Nazis but the system led to National Socialism.

Nationalsocialism

The blackest time in Austrian and German history, was that of Nationalsocialism. Adolf Hitler, the dictator, was an Austrian, born in Braunau near to my home (Zehnpfennig, 2011). He was obsessed by the idea of an Aryan Race according to which Aryans as the followers of Germaniums should be the only honored citizens. All others, especially Jews, were excluded. Jews, handicapped and resistant people were transported to be executed in special camps (Zucconi, 2011).

Close to the small town where Hitler was born in 1889, a man called Franz Jägerstätter came into the world eighteen years later (Bergmann, 1988). He was a simple man working on a small farm (Putz, 2007). Jägerstätter, as a citizen of Hitler's "Millennial Kingdom" had to serve in the military. Before he did, he had a nightmare. He saw a train, which was driving directly into Hell. The train was full of people. The simple man identified the train with the Nazi regime. He refused to join the military. To make sure of heeding the voice of his conscience he asked the religious authority what he should do: He was married and had children. The religious authority who was the bishop of Linz encouraged Jägerstätter to go to the military. He would not be responsible for Nationalsocialism. He would be responsible to his family. Jägerstätter refused and was executed (Jägerstätter, 2007).

Many years after the Second World War, Jägerstätter was honored by the Catholic Church as a holy person (Zucconi, 2011). This led to broad discussions on the meaning of citizenship under a dictatorship. Did Jägerstätter serve his citizenship well by resisting the Nazis? I remember the fury of my father who had been in Hitler's military. He argued: If people of "Greater Germany" had resisted the military they would not have done their duty as citizens. This example can make us aware of the big ideological power of a dictatorship like the Nazi regime over everyone and on the community. One of the aims of theology is to enlighten us about the nature of ideologies from wherever they come; even if they come from religious establishments.

Austria after the Second World War and since the creation of the EU

It seems as if there aren't any problems for citizenship in Austria post World War II and since the creation of the EU (Gschiegl & Ucakar, 2012). The Catholic Church learned a lot from Austrofascism and Nationalsocialism: Government and church should be in "Equidistance." This means, for example, that every Catholic should be free to follow his own political beliefs. The church is not involved in politics. Catholic priests are not allowed to get involved in parties. The prior Cardinal of Vienna demonstrated Equidistance personally: He was invited by the Socialists to give a presentation for a large audience. He did. From this time on, he was called the "Red" Cardinal. The Conservatives were very angry and intervened with the Vatican to install more conservative Bishops in Austria, and this succeeded.

In the liberal Austria of the EU, there exists a new problem, which relates to citizenship: Who maintains the newcomers, especially those from countries which are not in the EU? Austria, and also other countries in the EU, are getting more and more strict with respect to laws on immigration. More and more people are excluded from citizenship. Some weeks before Christmas 2012, some immigrants occupied a Catholic Church in Vienna. The police wanted to evacuate them by force, but the Cardinal granted them asylum. His action was clearly against the strict immigration laws of the government and EU. In this context, we can also respect the clear intervention of Pope Francis in the drama of the boat people in Lambedusa. Today the Catholic Church has the option to open up possibilities of citizenship to more people in Austria and in the EU. Christians know that citizenship is not a "cold", legal, term. It has become a metaphor for inclusion or exclusion from society.

Brief Conclusions

In the late modern context, citizenship seems to be a clear and "cold" secular term with a strict legal understanding: The decision of who gets citizenship in Austria follows strict rules. Education in citizenship is required of all students but is especially necessary for new immigrants.

When we bring citizenship into the "hermeneutic play" of TCI and CT, we learn different perspectives of citizenship. Citizenship is not only related to a subject: What is Austrian Citizenship? Citizenship includes deep biographical, interactive, contextual dimensions.

"The letter to Diognetus" written in early Christianity, shows us the metaphorical character of citizenship: "True Citizenship for Christians is in heaven." The metaphor of "Citizenship in heaven" leads us, not as Karl Marx argued, to an apolitical Christianity: True Christians only think about getting into heaven. As Latin America liberation theology shows us: Christians are deeply involved in the very real struggles of citizenship regarding inclusion and exclusion.

Bringing citizenship from some periods of Austrian history together with the "hermeneutic play" of CT shows us where there is a lack of understanding. Aspects of inhumanity and exclusion thereby come to light and are reawakened.

One of the responses of the Austrian Catholic Church to the misunderstanding of citizenship in Austrofascism and Nationalsocialism was "Equidistance". This means that the Church is not connected with a specific political party.

To live with a perspective of "citizenship in heaven" in the modern world would be acceptable, as long it does not remove us from recognizing the inhumanity of earthly political systems.

The problem of Austrian citizenship post-World War Two, and since the creation of the EU, is not the symbiosis of government and Church. It is rather the symbiosis of liberal economics and strict government laws of citizenship.

Therefore, theologians and religious people of all faiths have to open themselves up to the theological metaphor that leads us to an understanding of citizenship as the human right to a "good life" for everyone in Austria and globally.

References

Bergmann, G. (1988). *Franz Jägerstätter: Ein Leben vom Gewissen entschieden* (2 Ausg.). (A. Guillet, Eds.) Berlin: Christiana.

Cohn, R. C. (1971). Living-Learning Encounters: The Theme-Centered Interactional Method. In: Blank L., Gottsegen G., & Gottsegen M. (Eds.), *Confrontations* (245-271). New York: Macmillan and London.

Cohn, R. C. (1974). Zur Grundlage des thenezentrierten, interaktionellen Systems: Axiome, Postulate, Hilfsregeln. *Gruppendynamik*, *3*, (150-159).

Cohn, R. C., & Farau, A. (2008). *Gelebte Geschichte der Psychotherapie* (4. Auflage Ausg.). Stuttgart: Klett-Cotta.

Foster, P. (2007). "The Epistle to Diognetus. *Expository Times*, *118*, (162-168).

Gschiegl, S., & Ucakar, K. (2012). *Das politische System Österreichs und die EU* (3 Ausg.). facultas.wuv.

Hilberath, B. J., & Scharer, M. (2012). *Kommunikative Theologie: Grundlagen-Erfahrungen-Klärungen*. Ostfildern: Matthias-Grünewald.

Jägerstätter, F. (2007). *Aufzeichnungen 1941 - 1943: Der gesamte Briefwechsel mit Franziska*. (E. Putz, Eds.) Graz: Styria Premium.

Matzdorf, P., & Cohn, R. C. (1992). Das Konzept der Themenzentrierten Interaktion. In: L. C., & S. R. (Eds.), *TZI. Pädagogisch-therapeutische Gruppenarbeit nach Ruth C. Cohn* (39-92). Stuttgart: Klett-Cotta.

Putz, E. (2007). *Franz Jägerstätter - Martyr: A Shinig Example in Cark Times*. (S. L. Episcopal Chair of the Diocese of Linz, Eds., & C. L. Danner, Übers.) Franz Steinmassl.

Scharer, M., & Hilberath, B. J. (2003). *Kommunikative Theologie. Eine Grundlegung* (2 Ausg., Bd. 1). Mainz: Matthias-Grünewald-Verlag.

Scharer, M., & Hilberath, B. J. (2008). *The Practice of Communicative Theology. Introduction to a New Theological Culture*. New York: The Crossroad Publishing Company.

Talos, E., & Neugebauer, W. (Eds.). (2012). *Austrofaschismus. Politi - Ökonomie - Kultur 1933 - 1938*. Wien: Lit Verlag.

Wenninger, F., & Dreidemy, L. (Eds.). (2013). *Das Dollfuß/Schuschnigg-Regime 1933-1938. Vermessungen eines Forschungsfeldes*. Wien: Böhlau.

Zehnpfennig, B. (2011). *Adolf Hitler: Mein Kampf. Studienkommentar*. Stuttgart: UTB.

Zucconi, C. G. (2011). *Christus oder Hitler?: Das Leben des seligen Franz Jägerstätter*. Würzburg. Echter.

The Contribution of Islamic Religious Education to Citizenship Education in Austria

Zekirija Sejdini

Regarding the subject of citizenship education and the Islamic religion in Austria, my research concerns the possible benefits of Islamic religious education in Austria for citizenship education. Certainly, my role as an official in charge of education in Islamic religious schools has contributed to my perspective on this topic, but the real reason why I chose this subject in particular, is that the Islamic religious education constitutes an interface between the state and Islamic religious community. In addition, it is one of the most important areas through which the Islamic Religious Community can impact the largest population of Muslims.

In order to provide an overview, I will briefly survey the situation of Muslims in Austria and give some information about the legal status of the Islamic religion there. In the main body of this chapter, I will analyze the curriculum for Islamic religious education in Austrian public schools in order to interrogate whether the current curriculum contributes to citizenship education. After all, the lessons in this curriculum are paid for by the state of Austria where the members of the Islamic community are the largest ethnic and religious minority in the country.

Islam in Austria

Initially I will present some figures on religious affiliation in Austria, while omitting consideration of the historical development of these demographics.

Since religious affiliation has not been surveyed since 2001, all statistics regarding religion in Austria are based on various estimates. According to recent calculations, there are 515,914 Muslims living in Austria, who comprise about 6.2% of the total population (Marik-Lebeck, 2010, 7). Muslims have enjoyed legal recognition since 1912.[13] This unique recognition in Europe was the legal basis for the institutional recognition of Muslims in Austria to receive the full recognition of Islam as a public corporation in 1979. Through the recognition of the Islamic community, the opportunity arose to offer religious instruction in public schools.

Religious education is a compulsory elementary school subject and can be chosen for one subject of the high school exam. In order to ensure religious freedom, it is possible to unsubscribe from the religious education within the first five days at the beginning of the school year. The normal amount of religious education lessons is two hours per week. The adoption of the curricula, examination and supervision of religious instruction are regulated by the particular religious community. The salary of the teachers is paid by the ministry in charge (The Federal Law of 13 July 1949). After institutional recognition in 1979, it took three years for Islamic religious education to be initiated as a subject during school year 1982/83.

Curriculum of Islamic religious education and Citizenship Education

In order to quantify the potential contribution of Islamic religious education to citizenship education in Austria, an analysis of the curriculum is reasonable, because this approach seems to be the only possible way to gain objective information. At the same time, it shouldn't be forgotten that this is not the primary task of religious instruction and the definitions of citizenship couldn't be more diverse. Therefore I decided to concentrate on some major points, which occur to some extent in all definitions of citizenship, and to evaluate their consideration in the curriculum.

First of all, I will provide an overview of the topics that are covered in every school grade. These are:

1. Living and understanding Islam
2. Sources of Islam
3. Living together
4. Islamic art, culture and science
5. Islam in Austria and Europe

---

13 Act of 15 July 1912 on the recognition of the followers of Islam according to the Hanafi rite as a religious society, RGBl 1912/159.

6. Stories
7. Current topic[14]

Common points that I could gather from varying definitions of citizenship, and which seem to be important in our context, are the following:

1. Human rights/human dignity
2. Pluralism
3. Freedom of expression
4. Freedom of faith / interreligious dialogue
5. Democracy
6. Integration/Belonging

It should not be overlooked that I couldn't take into account all of these points nor could the points mentioned always be distinguished from each other. I will also indicate the school grade in which the contents are specified, so as to provide a general view as to which contents are taught in which school grade.

Because the curriculum for Islamic religious instruction is not published in printed form, and the edition published in the Federal Gazette of the Federal Ministry for Education, Arts and Culture curriculum has no page numbers, I will quote the paginated version of the curriculum, which is on the official site of the Office of Education of the Religious Community in Austria.

I would like to start with the topic *human rights* and *human dignity*, as it is the foundation of membership in a society.

Human rights/ Human dignity

The curriculum already takes human rights into account during the first grade of primary school. Referring to the life of the prophet Muhammad, an orphan, pupils should already learn in the first grade that the future prospects of a person are not previously determined (Overall curriculum Part 1, 36). Furthermore, the necessity of helping other people should be conveyed in primary school. In the third grade of primary school the pupils should understand that all people are equal and that the value of a human being cannot be reduced to his external features

---

14 Topic Overview 1 class. (n.d.). Retrieved January 30, 2014 from Official Web site of the Office of Education of the Islamic Religious Community in Austria: http://schulamt-is-lam.at/images/stories/lehrplaene/klasse1.pdf

(Overall curriculum Part 1, 48) and this is a point which affects human dignity as the foundation of human rights as well. In this context, pupils in the fourth and fifth grades should develop excellent skills in interaction with others, learn to feel responsible for their actions, and they should work actively towards solidarity and peaceful coexistence (Overall curriculum Part 1, 56).

In the seventh grade, the prophetic tradition *"The best of you is the one that is most useful to people"* has priority in the curriculum. In this way, willingness to help and sacrifice should be strenghtened. Pupils should learn that racism and excessive nationalism are rejected from the Islamic perspective. Referring to the Qur'an it should be ascertained, that Satan was the first racist in history, because he considered himself to be better than human beings due to his being created out of fire, rather than earth, as humans were (Overall curriculum Part 1, 76).

In the 10th school grade the curriculum provides an intensive study of the dignity of human beings, which is discussed from the points of view of different religions as well as the secular point of view. Based on inviolable human dignity the pupils should be able to recognize all forms of discrimination and firmly reject them (Overall curriculum Part 2, 179-180).

In order to theologically justify the aforementioned principles, pupils of the 12th and last grade are introduced to the aims (maqasid) of Islamic religious regulations as formulated by Imam Ishaq al-Shatibi, in his work *al-Muwafaqat* as being:

- Protection of life
- Protection of human dignity
- Protecetion of the intellect
- Protection of human assets
- Protection of human civilization (Overall curriculum Part 2, 191).

Pluralism

Ethnic and religious diversity should be considered as enrichment as early as the first grade, which encourages pupils to live in peace and solidarity despite their differences. At the same time, they should also be taught that belonging to a certain family or nation cannot be seen as an advantage over other people. Diversity of any kind should not prevent the pupils of a school class from seeing themselves as a community (Overall curriculum Part 1, 34). The curriculum of the 6th grade conveys that any existing differences between individuals don't necessarily lead to conflicts on one or both sides, or even to rejection (Overall curriculum Part 1,

69). Therefore, anti-Semitism and xenophobia must be rejected and this is theo-logically justified in the 7th grade. Based on the special protection of religion in Austria, the pupils should become aware of all aspects of discrimination (Overall curriculum Part 1, 73).

In the 8th grade, pupils should learn how to decenter "the self" and give more space to other people and through practical exercises they ought to achieve more awareness about the similarities between the four Sunni schools in Islam. Differ-ences from Shi'a law will also be studied in this school year (Overall curriculum Part 1, 78).

Freedom of expression

By the first grade pupils should learn respectful social interaction with other opinions and also how to present their own opinion in a polite and thoughtful manner without hurting anybody. This can mean both gentle demeanor, as well as avoiding pretention and arrogance, says the curiculum of the second school grade (Overall curriculum Part 1, 34). In the fourth grade pupils are taught not to interfere in someone's affairs and to establish clear limits in respecting someone else's privacy (Overall curriculum Part 1, 56).

How a respectful interaction should look is taught in the eighth grade. In this two components are particulary important: the art of listening and having em-pathy, so that they are able to understand others (Overall curriculum Part 1, 80). In order to emphasize the importance of freedom of expression in the 12th grade, pupils learn that Islamic scholars and scientists have always dealt with disagree-ments and that tolerating diversity of opinions has a long tradition in Islam (Over-all curriculum Part 2, 188).

Freedom of religion / interreligious dialogue

Pupils in the third grade should be empowered to allow others their own opinions and religious preferences and they should recognize that faith and belief can only come from within a person. The curriculum furthermore states that religion aris-es from personal inner belief and conviction, and that people base responsibility for their own lives on this conviction. Accordingly, the slogan of this school year is: *I believe in what I want and so do you!* This statement surely corresponds with the Qur'an (Overall curriculum Part 1, 48).

In the 4th grade the pupils should experience respectful and appreciative exchanges on religious matters with children of other religions, in order to identify similarities despite the differences. They should also experience how enriching it is to participate in life together with others. By this means, the pupils should learn that peaceful coexistence is only possible through mutual respect and recognition. Offering congratulations on the religious holidays of other faiths should help to put theory into practice (Overall curriculum Part 1, 59).

After emphasizing the importance of mutual recognition, the curriculum of the 5th grade requires that pupils should be capable of dealing with other people's beliefs, their values and religious beliefs. Therefore, it is proposed that in this school grade, the religious holidays of Jews, Christians and Buddhists should be studied so as to know more about them (Overall curriculum Part 1, 64).

In the 7th grade, pupils should develop familiarity with the Gospel and the Torah, and with the houses of worship of other religious communities. Another aim is to visit representatives of other religious communities in order to talk to them in open exchanges.

In the 8th grade pupils should become better acquainted with the perspective of other religions and learn how to respect them. This should deepen the perspective of the pupils from a superficial appreciation of visible differences to a deeper spiritual and content-based level of recognizing similarities.

In the 11th grade eight principles of the Qur'an for peaceful coexistence of religions should be presented. These principles are:

- Commitment to mutual knowledge and exchange (Q 49:13).
- Invitation to performing good deeds (Q 3:104).
- Wisdom and good advice (Q 16:125; 14:46).
- Speaking kindly and behaving pleasantly (Q 3:159; 60:8).
- Emphasizing similarities (Q 3:64; 29:46).
- Observe limits- never offend (Q 4:140; 6:68, 108).
- Freedom of choice (Q 18:29).
- No compulsion in religion - everyone should follow his or her own path (Q 2:139,256; 10:99; 21:107-109) (Overall curriculum Part 2, 186).

This should empower pupils to play an important role in peaceful coexistence. Ultimately, the important insights for religious freedom and the emphasis on inter-religious dialogue, as well as the global ethic for world religions and world peace of Professor Hans Küng should be analyzed in the 12th grade (Overall curriculum Part 2, 193).

Democracy

According to the curriculum, pupils by the second grade of primary school should be able to act and to think independently in order to strengthen responsibility and reject blind obedience. The own group membership should be questioned, as well (Overall curriculum Part 1, 44).

In the context of issues concerning Islam in Europe, pupils in the 9th grade should learn that Islam and democracy are not only not contradictory to each other, but rather meet and overlap on so many points. Additionally, pupils should be motivated to take an interest in politics and to understand them. In this context, the key dimensions of democracy are discussed intensively and references to Islam are clarified. Pupils should perceive the need to be active members of society and the need for political participation. Separation of powers, pluralism, freedom of speech, freedom of the press, freedom of religion, free, independent and secret elections are issues that should be handled in this context (Overall curriculum Part 1, 91).

In the 11th grade, pupils should deal with the issue of fundamentalism. They should deal with reasons for the spread of radical ideas and be able to argue based on Islamic sources that any fanaticism must be rejected in all its forms, and that it doesn't solve, but rather causes problems. Pupils at this grade level should also be able to detect possible signs of radicalization. To facilitate the detection of radicalization, the curriculum provides a definition of what is meant by the radicalization of people: namely, when someone is forcing other people to follow his path, if he allows only one understanding of religion and only one form of the implementation of religion, and if he declares others, who think differently than him, to be unbelievers and boycotts them, he is classified as radical (Overall curriculum Part 2, 189).

Integration or the sense of belonging

In the area of all of the responsibilities of Islamic religious education that I mentioned previously, there is another truly significant element– facilitating integration, or in other words: imparting a sense of belonging. This is of great importance in cases of cultural, ethnic and religious minorities. A great number of European Muslims are not only religious, but also cultural and ethnic minorities in Europe. This reinforces their isolation and increases the need for an intensive discussion about their new home, so that identification with it can take place. The attention that this issue is given in the curriculum shows the importance of religion in this area, which is also recognized by the Muslim community.

In order to enable the pupils to identify with their new home country, by the third grade they should already be affirmed as being part of Austrian society. They should be encouraged to recognize Austria as their homeland and to feel Austrian. In the 4th grade, pupils should understand that there is no contradiction between their being Muslims and their devotion to Austria. In the subsequent 5th grade, pupils should not only learn that there is no contradiction between being Muslim and their commitment to Austria and Europe, but rather that it is an opportunity and a duty for Muslims in Austria and in Europe to reconcile these identities, just as the Muslims in other countries reconcile their religious and national identities (Overall curriculum Part 1, 59). Through the integration of Muslims in society, pupils should recognize how self-evidently Islam can be lived out in Austria. They should concentrate on areas with a lot of catching-up to do and see how important it is that Muslims not only concentrate on their own needs and facilities, but also make a constructive contribution to the whole society (Overall curriculum Part 1, 71). Austrian Muslim personalities such as Muhammad Asad and Karl Eduard Hammerschmidt should be presented as Muslim role models who have achieved great recognition in their particular areas of achievement. This should also be understood as a sign that it is possible to be a practicing Muslim and to be successful at work at the same time.

In order to strengthen the affiliation, pupils should be taught the legal regulations which must be observed and followed in Austria in the 8th grade. Pupils should reflect on what contribution they can make to the society they live in and what they could accomplish out of their religiosity or even what they must accomplish! Based on the desirable characteristic of being a pillar of the society you live in, pupils should be encouraged to accept the Austrian-Islamic identity and to feel at home in Austria, regardless of their actual citizenship. Only through their orientation towards Austria, can they become responsible members of society and function as part of it (Overall curriculum Part 1, 82).

Another objective is that pupils will perceive and discuss the importance of the Islamic religious community for Austrian Muslims and its unique position in Europe and in the international sphere. In addition to the structure of the Islamic Religious Community in Austria (IGGiÖ), possible future perspectives should be shown to the pupils. They should ask themselves what would be desirable for the development of the Muslim community in Austria (Overall curriculum Part 2, 183).

In the final school grade, pupils should think about where the Muslims in Austria would be without the Islamic Religious Community and in what situation they would be at the moment. Looking at cases beyond Austria could certainly be useful in answering this question. Pupils should be able to understand the pathbreaking Austrian Imam conferences and their summary documents. These documents summarize in a few pages the baseline of Muslim in Europe and also facilitate an overview of controversial issues for students (Overall curriculum Part 2, 194).

Conclusion

The analysis of the curriculum for Islamic religious education in Austrian schools clearly demonstrates that it considers almost all of the key points that are of crucial importance for building a spiritual home for Muslims in Austria and that it tries to support their identification with the new home country through Islamic theological arguments.

However, it remains open whether teachers are able to effectively communicate the prescribed contents to pupils in a satisfactory manner and which measures can be taken in order to disprove theological positions that are contrary to the contents of this curriculum.

References

Act of 15 July 1912 on the recognition of the followers of Islam according to the Hanafi rite as a religious society. (RGBl 1912/159).

Marik-Lebeck, S. (2010). *Die muslimische Bevölkerung Österreichs: Bestand und Veränderung 2001-2009.* In: Janda, A. & Vogl, M. (Eds.). Islam in Österreich. (7). Wien: Österreichscher Integrationsfonds.

Overall curriculum Part 1. From: Official Web site of the Office of Education of the Islamic Religious Community in Austria: http://schulamt-islam.at/images/stories/lehrplaene/gesamt_1-99.pdf (Accessed January 30, 2014).

Overall curriculum Part 2. From: Official Web site of the Office of Education of the Islamic Religious Community in Austria: http://schulamt-islam.at/images/stories/lehrplaene/gesamt_100-195.pdf (Accessed January 30, 2014).

The Federal Law of 13 July 1949 concerning religious instruction in schools. (RelUG; BGBl.190/1949).

Topic Overview 1 class. (n.d.). From: Official Web site of the Office of Education of the Islamic Religious Community in Austria: http://schulamt-islam.at/images/stories/lehrplaene/klasse1.pdf (Accessed January 30, 2014).

Citizenship-Education and Islam

The Austrian Situation

Nadire Mustafi

The growing number of Muslim children in Austria is a particular challenge for the Austrian education system. Quite often children with a migrant background – especially Muslim children and youth – are either excluded or they isolate themselves. Such experiences make it difficult for these children to identify with the norms and values of the country in which they live. Often teachers are overwhelmed because they are not sufficiently familiar with the children's cultural and religious backgrounds. To avoid potential disadvantages, many parents choose Islamic private schools for their children, exacerbating the children's isolation from the larger society, and their access to the pluralistic and democratic values of the indigenous population. Thus, it is crucial to create opportunities within Austria's educational system that enable the participation of Muslim youth in shaping the future of the nation. The main objective of the project *Islam and Citizenship-Education* is to model for Muslim youth ways to participate individually within Austrian society without it affecting their religious beliefs. Not only would Muslim children be prepared for equal social and political participation, but their teachers and educators would be also. Additionally, fear of contact would be eliminated and engagement with democracy as a lifestyle would be enhanced. Values such as self- and co-determination, solidarity, cooperation, fairness, and tolerance are the core principles of the project. In three steps, project partners will be identified, from among private and public schools, and will receive instruction in offering a comprehensive curriculum created by specialists.

The Current Situation in Austria

The great social diversity that currently exists in Austria is a tremendous challenge, not only at the institutional level of society (particularly in the educational system), but also in interpersonal relationships. Due to lack of background information, many people are overwhelmed with this diversity and instead of intercultural understanding and mutual acceptance, prejudice and intolerance arises.

Public discourse and media reporting are mostly counterproductive in this situation as they often create and promote negative stereotypes. A clear example is the federal party leader of the right-wing populist Freedom Party of Austria, Heinz-Christian Strache, repeatedly creating and utilizing anti-Islamic slogans within his election advertisements. In 2006, before the general election he caused a great stir with the slogan *"Daham statt Islam"* (*home instead of Islam*). President Heinz Fischer responded critically, denouncing that *"people of other religions and nationality"* have been painted as enemies (Pajevic, 2006). Another example is the promulgation of incorrect opinions, for example, that liberal democratic values are incompatible with those of Islam, in order to stigmatize Muslims (2010). However, one-sided reporting or politically motivated discourses are not the only factor to blame. Muslims themselves sometimes lack knowledge about their own religious values and norms; such knowledge could support intra-Muslim discourse and provide counter-evidence to such opinions. Coles notes that many Muslims are often confused regarding the task of such discussions, i.e. how they should form their own opinions regarding their identity, the role of religious practice in everyday life, and citizenship (Coles, 2010, 3).

The term *Citizenship* has been retained in German usage, since it describes in detail what is meant and it is derived from the Latin *civitas*. In English, it is often used in conjunction with active involvement, participation, and commitment and comprises the ideal of active citizenship (Coles, 2010, 5). The term citizenship-education is defined as raising the consciousness of democracy among the citizens of a country. It is a broad term whose interpretive framework is far-reaching. Basically citizenship-education can be understood as a range of general political socializations, which include all the "conscious and unconscious learning processes that characterize politically relevant personality traits, knowledge, feelings and values, attitudes and behavioral patterns" (Ackermann, 1999, 185). Political socialization inevitably takes place at all levels where socialization agencies are operative, such as the family or school, and represents a life-long ongoing process (Pelinka, 1979, 41).

Because of distorted media reporting on Islam and Muslims on the one hand and a lack of attention to these topics within the Muslim community on the other hand, Muslim children and young people often have difficulty identifying with the country in which they live. A consequence is that they hardly participate in the local society. A survey has shown that the greater the lack of opportunities for immigrants, the less respondents feel integrated, with the response among religious and politically oriented Muslims being particularly pronounced (GfK-Austria GmbH, 2009, 30). The educational institutions of Austrian society, in particular, have the ability to make a significant contribution to better integrating the diverse population since it is precisely within these institutions that the greatest diversity exists. If students of different religious or cultural backgrounds meet in school, this situation offers an opportunity to learn strategies that optimize coexistence. It is important to note that 40% of Austrians see "big problems", and 52% "some problems" in the educational arena, while only 6% see "no problems" (GfK-Austria GmbH, 2009, 77).

The project "Islam and Citizenship-Education" starts exactly at this problematic site through a holistic approach geared to make a significant educational contribution to the quality of life of both the cultural majority and the Muslim minority in Austria. Its objective is to take Muslim youth, in terms of their religious background, seriously and to offer them both factual content as well as a personal and emotional engagement with the question of what constitutes authentic participation in Austrian society. To be Muslim and Austrian at the same time requires a learning process, which is not just about knowledge, but attitudes as well. Through citizenship-education, young people can learn about and engage in peaceful and democratic coexistence.

The causes of current problem areas and conflicts were elicited with the cooperation of public-state schools and other madrasahs, and Islamic private schools. One area of exploration during the initial stage of the research stage examined whether education affects the integration of young people and whether concrete citizenship-education can enhance the sense of belonging. The questions of whether the loss of commitment to religion is constructed as a social condition and whether both Islamic and democratic values can be taught simultaneously in schools and mosques may be answered through this project.

Current Status of Research

A good example of such a study is the research project entitled "Islam and Citizenship Education", which was conducted over three years in the UK. The project, launched by Maurice Irfan Coles, was funded by the UK government, and consisted of cooperation among various Muslim communities, imams, scholars, government officials, teachers, students, and parents. Priorities such as "democracy, justice, law and order," "rights and responsibilities", "identity and diversity," and "skills for the practice of citizenship" formed the core of the project. The ICE Project Team from the UK constructed a model for citizenship based on the principles of BIRR (Belonging, Interacting, Rights and Responsibilities) (Coles, 2010, 16).

Islam and the Citizenship Project at the University of Vienna

Inspired and animated by the UK project, the research project in Austria will provide an opportunity for young Muslims to understand and experience democracy as a form of life, resulting in a reduced fear of contact with the rest of Austrian culture and society. The participants will be Muslim youth and children aged 10-18, and they will be prepared for equal socio-political participation in social life. Teachers and educators will be sensitized to stress important and relevant aspects of citizenship-education to Muslim children. Teachers and educators will also provide them with opportunities to practice self-determination, participation, cooperation and solidarity, as provided for in the Austrian curriculum of civic education (BMUKK, 2014).

Grounded in a holistic approach to education, the focus of this research is the interaction between schools and mosques with the involvement of families in the educational process. On the one hand, it confronts the "inner" disunity of Muslim students. On the other hand, it promises to have a more lasting effect.

Theoretical Principles of the Research and Research Objectives

At this point, the importance of social cohesion in a society should be mentioned. It is essential to measure "social capital" as part of this project since social capital is the effective binding force of social networks and social systems and the social capital of the community contributes to its success (Knack & Keefer, 1997). Around the beginning of the new millennium, the World Bank and the Organization for Economic Co-operation and Development conducted a program known as "Measuring Social Capital," which served to make economically effective social forces measurable. Based on this finding, the research's focus was first directed toward the measurement of social capital among Muslim participants.

In the pluralistic society of Austria, democracy is of great importance and should be highly valued. The pupils are adolescents, who should continue and maintain the potential of democracy as a way of life. The Islam and Citizenship-Education project's first objective is the goal of understanding democracy. Experts will participate in the research in order to build on these strengths and suggest solutions for conflicts.

Methodological Approach

The project is divided into three phases, through which the objectives are to be reached.

Spectrum of the Schools Involved

At the outset, project partners from public schools, Islamic private schools, mosques, and madrasahs should be identified and recruited. As this project targets children and adolescents aged 10-18 years, only secondary schools and general secondary schools are suitable for participation. In the madrasahs and mosques children usually are taught in groups and not in classes. Therefore only children from 10 to 18 years of age attending mosques rather than the whole cohort will be involved in the research.

First, social capital will be measured by quantitative research methods. In this regard the staff of the Islam and Citizenship-Education project developed a questionnaire with the help of the social scientific study society, SWS-Rundschau, which has already been distributed in our partner schools and filled in by the pupils during one of their lessons. Through the survey of social capital on the basis of qualitative research methods, we should be able to respond specifically to areas of interpersonal or intercultural conflict and to explore the causes.

Exploratory Stage of the Research

Subsequently, conflicts that may arise between teachers and pupils during the course of teaching events, will be explored. Even those conflicts that might arise between classmates are highly relevant for this research project. Therefore, it will be very interesting to observe specific settings inside and outside the classroom. Various environments and contexts, such as diverse subjects, different teaching procedures, breaks, afternoon care, etc., will provide opportunities for observation. Aside from participant observations, qualitative interviews with teachers, students, parents, and group discussions will be organized. Field-induced conflicts will also be analyzed by the project team as part of the qualitative research phase.

Transferring the Empirical Data into Practice

After the collection and analysis, a group of experts consisting of educators, theologians, and other scholars, will try to develop a curriculum and appropriate teaching approaches in an open process, so as to make an educational contribution to improving the current situation.

In the second stage, teachers in the participating institutions will be trained in accordance with the relevant curriculum, in order to integrate its content into their teaching units. Based on this, observations on whether the implementation of content is possible as well as its effectiveness will be made.

During the last phase, the documents should be made available for all those who want to teach using these concepts. Therefore, these will be posted online. Finally evaluation in the classroom setting will take place, to perform follow up assessments of project results.

Initial Stage of the Research

The project team carried out some investigations in relation to the current civic education lessons that have been implemented in schools. The results of these studies were based on the principles of adoption and statements from the relevant ministries. They also considered the curriculum of civic education, teacher training, and input from other stakeholders in relation to civic education (BMUKK, 2014).

In another further stage of the project, the project team met in advance with specialists, sociologists, and educators to establish a common approach. After contacting the participating schools and mosques, an informational session was organized. Teachers who wanted to participate in this project were invited. Representatives of two Islamic private schools in addition to teachers at a public school in Vienna and a secondary school in Lower Austria were present.

In the final section of this chapter, a few key organizations which are relevant for citizenship-education in Austria are listed. First, the Federal Ministry for Education, Arts and Culture (BMUKK) – Department of Political Education, Environmental Education and Consumer Education – should be mentioned. These provide information on projects, materials, service facilities, and training events for school education. Furthermore they participate in an international collaboration with the Education for Democratic Citizenship program of Europe and the German Federal Agency for Civic Education. Topics such as civic education, European political education, education for sustainable development and environmental education, business education and consumer education, transportation education – mobility and road safety, European and international cooperation, teacher training, and participation in curricula are discussed by this ministry.

The next important organization is the Forum for Civic Education. As an interface between academic research and education, the forum creates teaching materials in collaboration with teachers, such as informational materials about civic education. Their Project Exchange provides examples of teaching, project ideas, and methodological-didactic support to those who need them (Forum Politische Bildung).

Centre Polis is the central educational service institution for civic education in school. The center supports teachers in the implementation of civic education, human rights education, business education, and consumer education through lessons made available to the teachers. It acts as an information platform and helpline, and creates new materials for teaching (Zentrum polis).

Furthermore, Teacher Training Colleges cover areas of civic education, human rights education and intercultural learning.

The focus of the work of the Federal Agency for Civic Education is the promotion of consciousness about democracy and political participation. Through their events and materials they focus on current and historical issues.

Nevertheless, it can be noted that in Austria no other projects like the Islam and Citizenship-Education study have taken place in schools. Indeed, diverse group projects were carried out in certain classes, which were, however, 'general' in terms of intercultural learning and not directly focused on Muslim students.

We therefore consider that this project, and its results, will render an important contribution to the field of education in promoting the integration and participation of Muslims in Austrian society.

References

Ackermann, P. (1999). *Politische Bildung*. In: Dagmar, R. & Weißno G. (eds.) Lexikon der politischen Bildung. Didaktik und Schule. Schwalbach/Ts.: Wochenschau-Verl.

BMUKK. *Bundesgesetzblatt für die Republik Österreich* - BGBl Nr.II 290/2008. From: http://www.bmukk.gv.at/medienpool/17041/lp_vs_hs_ahs_nov_08.pdf. (Accessed December 16, 2014).

BMUKK. *Curriculum for Civic Education*. From: http://www.bmukk.gv.at/medienpool/11857/lp_neu_ahs_05.pdf. (Accessed Februry 16, 2014).

BMUKK. *Grundsatzerlass*. From: http://www.bmukk.gv.at/medienpool/15683/pb_grundsatzerlass.pdf. (Accessed Februry 16, 2014).

BMUKK. *Lehrpläne der AHS Unterstufe*. From: http://www.bmukk.gv.at/medienpool/786/ahs11.pdf. (Accessed February 16, 2014).

Coles, M. I. (2010). *When hope and history rhyme*. Islam, citizenship and education: building Akhlaq, Adhab and Tahdhib; a discussion paper. (Leicester): Islam & Citizenship Education Project.

Forum Politische Bildung: From: http://www.politischebildung.com/?Sel=23 . (Accessed February 16, 2014).

GfK-Austria GmbH. (2009). *Integration in Österreich. Einstellungen, Orientierungen, und Erfahrungen*. From: http://www.bmi.gv.at/cms/BMI_Service/Integrationsstudie.pdf. (Accessed February 16, 2014).

IMAS International GmbH. (2010). *DER ISLAM IN DEN AUGEN DER BEVÖLKERUNG*. IMAS-Report. From: http://www.imas.at/images/imas-report/2010/06-2010.pdf (Accessed February 16, 2014).

Knack, S., & Keefer, P. (1997). *Does Social Capital Have an Economic Payoff? A Cross-Country Investigation*. The Quarterly Journal of Economics, 112(4), 1251-1288. doi: 10.1162/003355300555475

Pajevic, A. (2006). *Daham statt Islam*. Der Tagesspiegel. From: http://www.tagesspiegel.de/politik/international/oesterreich-daham-statt-islam/757274.html. (Accessed February 15, 2014).

Pelinka, A. (1979). *Zur Strategie der politischen Bildung in Österreich*. ÖZP 1979/1, 67-90.

Zentrum polis. From: http://www.politik-lernen.at/ (Accessed 16, 2014).

To be Muslim and Swiss

Children of Muslim Immigrants from South East Europe and the Politics of Belonging[15]

Brigit Allenbach

Introduction

Recently Annalisa Frisina has outlined two dominant frames (Goffman, 1974) concerning the role of Muslims in Europe's multicultural states. On one hand, we have the security frame – Muslims are subject to broad suspicions of terrorism. On the other hand, there is the culturalist frame – Islam is portrayed as the religious and cultural opposite of the West, both are seen as uniform blocks existing outside of history (Frisina, 2010, 560). Talal Asad has emphasized this second frame by characterising Europe as a narrative that excludes Islam, with liberal and reactionary political voices largely coinciding in this regard (Asad, 2003, 164). Since the ban on minarets – introduced by way of a referendum in November 2009 – the crescendo of anti-Islamic voices in Switzerland can't be ignored. Pimarily responsible in the process is the SVP (Swiss People's Party), who even added a section about religion in their party platform, entitled "Our Values are Challenged."[16] We have pointed out elsewhere the extent to which this debate is dominated by a mono-identity discourse, i. e. Muslims are essentially Muslims (cf. Allenbach & Sökefeld, 2010). Since other affiliations and identifications are not represented, differences among Muslims and similarities with non-Muslims are kept largely hidden. This chapter draws attention to the children of Muslim immigrants, growing up in Switzerland, and to their sense of *multiple belonging*.

---

15 This chapter was first published in German in *Tsantsa*, the journal of the Swiss Ethnological Society (cf. Allenbach 2012). For this English translation the text was slightly revised by the author.

16 See the SVP Party program 2011-2015, accessible at www.svp.ch.

It aims to investigate the negotiation of belonging as an active process. What affiliations and identifications are important? What role do family and peer relationships play? Can the effects of Islamophobic discourse be discovered in interviews with Muslim teenagers?

This chapter is based on my research on migration and religion in the National Research Programme "Religions, the State, and Society" (NRP, 58).[17] Children and young people were involved in various fields of action as part of the investigation. In the first phase of the project, we conducted group discussions on the topic of religion in intermediate and advanced level schools. During a second stage, the goal was to investigate the significance of religion for the children of immigrants in the "action arena of the family." Following the research activities in class, we sent a letter to parents via school teachers, announcing that we would like to get to know a child's family in order to learn more about the situation of immigrant families and the importance of religion in their everyday lives. However, only a few contacts emerged from this strategy. Therefore, we recruited young people ourselves, in particular with the help of religious and cultural associations.

In the second phase of the project the target groups were restricted to families from South Asia and South East Europe. This author interviewed mostly "Secondos"[18] of age 11 to 18 from South East Europe. The main objective of the project was to include children and young people of different faiths and from religious and non-religious families in the study in order to encompass the broadest possible spectrum of "lived religion" (cf. McGuire, 2008).[19] Since children and youth are dependent, to a large extent, on adults, we usually also had contact with parents of the respondents and/or adult members of the cultural or religious associations that were involved. Informal discussions and participant observation were an important part of the study (visiting families at home, attending events, etc.).

The first three sections of this chapter present (1) the theoretical framework, as well as (2) the background information on immigration from South East Europe

---

17 The project "Migration and religion and how these are perceived by children and young people in Switzerland" was financed by the Swiss National Science Foundation (see Allenbach, Herzig & Müller, 2010; Müller, 2013). Additional data were collected as part of a project funded by the Jacobs Foundation Fellowship at the University of Zurich.

18 A Swiss neologism coined by film director Samir in *Babylon 2* naming the second generation (D'Amato, 2010, 178).

19 "Lived religion" encompasses more than the requirements of religious institutions on religiosity. The concept of the American anthropologist of religion Meredith McGuire (2008) provides a basis for the ethnographic study of religious practice and the subjective importance of religion. The interwoven quality of religion and culture, as it presents itself in everyday life, is central.

and (3) situation of second-generation Muslim immigrants as a religious minority in Switzerland. The fourth and fifth sections discuss (4) methodological considerations and illustrate (5) the field access by means of examples. In this regard, the way 11-to-15-year-olds dealt with the researcher and her project must be taken in account. The sixth section presents (6) the young people's portrayals of Ramadan in Switzerland. The conclusion (7) links the ethnographic case studies with the theory of the "politics of belonging". It is suggested that to situate young people in terms of their belonging to a religious minority, and the related attribution of being "strangers", is highly questionable, since it does not do justice to the multiple belongings of the children of Muslim immigrants.

Politics of Belonging

Children, as citizens, enjoy special protection and certain rights. Recent research emphasizes the changed relationship between citizens and the nation-state resulting from transnationalism and globalization. In the following discussion, I rely mainly on the theory of "politics of belonging", as it has been formulated by John Crowley (1999) and Nira Yuval-Davis et al. (2006; see also Yuval-Davis, 2011). In short, it is an attempt to provide a basis for a *thick description* of the institutional and discursive processes associated with migration and integration from a comparative perspective (Crowley, 1999, 22-23).

Following Yuval-Davis et al. (2006) the central notions are "citizenship", "identity" and "belonging". Citizenship is defined referencing the British sociologist Thomas H. Marshall as "(...) full membership in a community with all its rights and obligations" (Yuval-Davies et al, 2006, 2). This definition does not limit citizenship to nationality, but also refers more generally to the possibilities of participation in "(...) all kinds of polities from local to global" (ibid.). Whereas citizenship underlines the participatory dimension of belonging, however, the notion of identity relates to the ways in which people define themselves and others. Therefore, identities can best be examined in the light of people's stories (narratives) about who they are:

> These narratives are contested, fluid and constantly changing, but are clustered around some hegemonic constructions of boundaries between "self" and "other" and between "us" and "them" and are closely related to political processes (ibid.).

The notion of belonging implies emotional attachment to something, and includes, for example, the feeling of being at home and feeling safe and in good hands (ibid.). "Politics of belonging" refers to political projects or processes "(...) aimed at constructing belonging to a particular collectivity or collectivities which themselves are being constructed in these projects in very specific ways" (ibid., 3). In fact, boundary making plays a decisive role in politics of belonging discourses. An example is the campaign in the run-up to the vote against minarets in Switzerland. Presumably, the anti-Islamic propaganda caused more harm to Muslims than the ban on building minarets itself. In summary, the notion of belonging is an alternative to the concept of identity, overloaded with meanings. Belonging includes a wide range of identifications and attributions, which are each embedded in specific contexts and power relations (cf. Brubaker, 2007; Anthias, 2009).

The Second Generation From South East Europe in Switzerland

In 2006, there were approximately 333,000 people from the successor states of Yugoslavia in Switzerland (Kämpf, 2008, 96). The number of those who have been naturalized, together with the number of refugees, yields the estimate of around half a million immigrants from the former Yugoslavia, which corresponds to about 7% of the resident population of Switzerland. Families coming from the successor states of Yugoslavia are very heterogeneous with regard to religious affiliation – primarily Muslims (mainly from Kosovo, Macedonia, Bosnia, and Herzegovina), Roman Catholic, and Serbian Orthodox Christians, and a relatively high proportion of people who have no religious affiliation or provide no information in that regard (see Allenbach, 2011). In many families, there are members with different religious affiliations.

In 2012, there were about 440,000 Muslims living in Switzerland, corresponding to 5.5 % of the Swiss population. Most of them are migrants, who had taken residence in Switzerland with their families since the late 1970s. They originate mainly from the Balkans and Turkey. About one third of all Muslims living in Switzerland have Swiss citizenship. The proportion of young Muslims (under 25 years) is high and amounts to approximately 40% (EKM, 2010, 8). It should be noted that the majority of Muslims in Switzerland are either non-believers or not practicing (ibid., 14).[20] Werner Schiffauer made the following observations in the context of his investigations of the Muslim diaspora in Germany: Second-generation Muslims must find their own way, depending on where they live and work. For young Muslims in European countries open to immigration, this task is cur-

---

20 For more details, see Schweizerischer Bundesrat (2013); Endres et al. (2013); Lathion and Tunger-Zanetti (2013).

rently particularly complicated (Schiffauer 2004, 354). Two factors are significant: First, not only the host society, but also the first generation of immigrants, construct the opposition of Islam and Europe as a relationship between self and other. Second, it's about power relations and not about relations among equals. Long-time residents are more powerful; newcomers, who are fighting for a place for their religion, are, therefore, in a structurally disadvantaged position compared to the placeholders, who define the conditions for that approval (ibid.). Today a conscious turn to Islam by choice is evident among the second generation in European countries open to immigrants. According to Schiffauer (2004, 357), there are no systematic studies on this topic because it is much more difficult to investigate this individually defined Muslim way of life than communal or revolutionary Islam. This gap cannot be closed by the present contribution. However, it is important to understand that in this study the category "Muslim" does not refer to a group of people with common characteristics, but rather to the vast majority of "ordinary Muslims" (EKM, 2010) who are largely invisible to the public. Muslim youths actively participate in Swiss youth culture. Ironically the Swiss *word of the year* for 2009 was "minaret ban," whereas the Swiss "*youth word of the year*" was a Balkan slang phrase created by a 21-year-old "secondo" from Macedonia, that goes as follows: "S Beschte wos je hets gits!" meaning "the best that has ever been" (Wikipedia, 2011).

Ethnographic Fieldwork and Teenagers

The most important finding of the latest social scientific research on childhood is the abandonment of the idea that children are passive recipients of culture and socialization with only marginal participation in social change (Caputo, 1995, 22). Methodically, similar questions arise in research on teenagers as with any social scientific investigation: "(...) [W]hat is important is that the particular methods chosen (...) are appropriate for the people involved in the study, its social and cultural context, and the kinds of research questions being posed" (Christensen & James, 2000, 2). Therefore, reflection on the asymmetrical relationship between the researcher and the researched is central to ethnographic research on childhood. Judith Okely puts it succinctly: "Social research is always about social relationships" (1992, cited in ibid., 5). In her classic introduction to ethnographic fieldwork, Rosalie H. Wax (1971, 9-10) discusses the importance of the age, gender and social status of the researcher to field access. As a means of introducing some of the challenges, she reports on her own attempt to conduct interviews with Native Americans in their teens. It turned out that the girls were more willing to complete questionnaires in writing than to talk to "strangers", which in this case applied to Wax's research assistants, who were themselves "young" Native Americans. Since they were college graduates, the social distance between them and the local young people was great. It is not surprising that the informal discussions between the research assistants and the teenagers were the most interesting element of the research. These informal discussions arose only when the assistants were given opportunities to accompany the teenagers during their daily activities.

Within the parameters of the NRP 58 project, opportunities for researchers to participate in the young people's activities were limited, not solely on the basis of the age, gender and social status of the researchers. The role of religion in the everyday life of the young people also needs to be taken into account. Apart from religious instruction and religious festivals – outside of the private area – the young people's activities were hardly ever connected with religion. [21] In order to record their activities, at least selectively, in addition to semi-structured interviews and group discussions, activity logs were used. What was to be included in the activity logs was explained on a flyer as follows: Over a seven-day period, the young people were to record: What they do and with whom, how long the activities last, and where the activities take place (school, leisure, family, etc.). Although these activity logs cannot replace participation in the the young people's activities, they offer the possibility of learning more about their various worlds. It should be noted here, however, that it was not easy to persuade the young people to get involved. In contrast to the world of the school where the teacher issued orders to their charges, the researchers had to rely on the goodwill of the young people.

Ethnographic Fieldwork and "Lived Religion"

The aim of the following examples is to integrate the access to the field and field research as practice into the analysis. The point is to examine how the researched deal with the researcher and her concerns in order to give them an active role in the interpretation of the project. It will be shown that reflection on research practices enable a better understanding of the social context of those under inves-

---

21 At the time of the research there were no Muslim youth organizations in Switzerland. In the mosque associations I was familiar with, the activities of the young people were very limited and rather informal. In terms of age, the organizations of Muslim students at universities did not correspond to the target group of our research (see Endres et al., 2013).

tigation. In this way, the motives behind their willingness, as well as their refusal to cooperate, can be brought into view.

Ariana and Dafina[22]

My contact with the family of Ariana (12) and Dafina (11) was arranged by the Albanian Women's Association, after I had repeatedly participated in women's meetings. Ariana and Dafina received me with their mother in the living room and we chatted excitedly. The family has lived in Switzerland for 21 years and is naturalized. I learned that they celebrate all religious festivals, not only Bayram,[23] but also Christmas and New Year. Ariana (12) said: "We have many similar holidays. You have, for example, Mother's Day – as far as I know, in May, we celebrate Mother's Day on the 8th of March." It turned out that the female members of the family make a pilgrimage with their girlfriends to a women's disco in an Albanian club on the occasion of International Women's Day. Some time later, when I called to schedule an interview, Dafina told me that she had decided to stop participating in the project. She justified her decision with the fact that her family did not go to the mosque. She believes in God and prays at night before sleeping, but she no longer wanted to participate, she explained.

Dafina's cancellation can be understood as an indication that she has very little interest in the subject of religion and that she lacks the motivation to participate. The statement that her family does not go to the mosque pointed to the internal differentiation among Muslim families.

Fatima

My contact with Fatima (15) was arranged by a volunteer working for Caritas, who sometimes helps Fatima with her homework. On the phone, I learned that Fatima's parents were Albanians from Macedonia and very religious. Fatima's father came to Switzerland as a seasonal worker 25 years ago. When Fatima was

---

22 To protect the anonymity of the persons represented here, the names were changed and other details were partially altered. I edited the quotes to make them linguistically accurate and as reader friendly as possible.

23 In Turkish "bayram" means holiday or festival. It refers to the two major Islamic festivals (Eids): The Festival of Sweets, which celebrates the end of Ramadan, and the Festival of Sacrifice, which takes place 70 days later.

three months old, the family moved to Switzerland, and they were recently naturalized. Fatima was against tape recording, therefore, the following excerpts are
based on a memory protocol. She told me that she had been attending Qur'an
lessons in the mosque on weekends until recently. Since she has finished reading
the entire Qur'an, she no longer goes to the mosque, except during the month of
Ramadan, when events are held specifically for women.

One of Fatima's hobbies is playing basketball. She recently won a competition.
Fatima dreams of one day wearing a headscarf: "I am sure that I will one day wear
a headscarf, but I do not know exactly when ... maybe when I am married, perhaps
at the birth of my first child ...", she explained, and her husband would also have
to accept this. She admires women in her circle of acquaintances that are a little
older and wear a headscarf. Fatima knows that with a headscarf she would have
many disadvantages in finding an apprenticeship in Switzerland. She told me that
her teacher has a negative attitude towards Muslims: "He does not understand
Islam and sometimes makes funny remarks. He says that he would tolerate no girl
wearing a headscarf in his class!"

Fatima created an activity log from the 19/10/2009 to 25/10/2009. At that time,
she was in tenth grade and looking for an apprenticeship:

Monday: I got up at six o'clock, had breakfast, and got ready for school. (...). In the
evening, I did my homework and went to sleep after that.

Tuesday: Since school was out already at three o'clock today, I went with my colleague to the city to look for boots and found a few nice ones, but had no money. At
5 pm, I was at home. Because I had no homework, I read five pages of the Qur'an.
When I had finished reading the Qur'an, I prayed with my mother. After that we
had something to eat.

Wednesday: I went to school, like every day, with my colleague. I was finished at
four, but stayed on and wrote an application. At 6:20 pm, I arrived at home. After
dinner I watched a movie then I still had to do homework.

Thursday: In the lunch break, I went to eat kebab with a few colleagues. Then I
went, like every Thursday, to the [Project for young people who are looking for an
apprenticeship]. I wrote five applications for hairdresser positions. At 3 pm, I had
finished this and met my mother in town and we went to buy the boots together. At
home, I helped my mother with the cooking. After that I studied for the exam on
Friday and went to bed.

Fridays I can sleep until nine o'clock. I do not have school until 9:45. At 12:30, I
had lunch. At school we have a kiosk, where you can buy something to eat. I bought
a hotdog. I was at school until four. With my colleague, I went into town to buy
a birthday present for my cousin. It didn't take us long to find something. In the

evening I went for a drink (with my colleagues and the birthday child). We stayed out until 9:30 then we went home. At home I watched a movie and went to sleep after that.

Saturday: I slept in until 11 o'clock. My cousin called and asked me if I would go with him into town to shop a little. I bought two pair of pants and a scarf. At 5 pm, I went home. I had something to eat, and then I went to my cousin's house. We stayed awake until three in the morning.

Sunday: At noon we got up and had something to eat. Then we went for a walk with a couple of small children. At 4 pm, I went home. We had guests until 9 pm and then I went to sleep.

It is apparent that "religion" takes only a little time in Fatima's weekly schedule. Many of her activities correspond to those of young people from families who do not practice Islam. School and training, hobbies, and sometimes sports are of central importance to young people, and female adolescents also help with household tasks and looking after small children. In their leisure time, watching movies, shopping, celebrating colleagues' birthdays and spending the night in the homes of their peers on weekends are common among the young people.

Isa

I met Isa in May 2008, while I was doing fieldwork at his school. He was then 12 years old. His parents are from Kosovo. Within the framework of interviews in pairs, he presented himself as a devout Muslim, who strictly adheres to religious standards. A couple of weeks later, within the framework of an ethnographic interview at Isa's home, he and his elder sister emphasized that religion is hardly ever an issue in their everyday life. In the context of peer group discussions at school, Isa said that living as a Muslim in Switzerland has become commonplace since many Muslims live there. In the familial realm, he stressed that he was born in Switzerland and that he feels like a Swiss citizen (see also Allenbach und Herzig, 2010).

Isa said that he likes living in Switzerland: "Nearly everything, it is clean, no war…, I was born here, I call myself a Swiss citizen, too." What Isa does not like about Switzerland he articulated as follows:

When Albanians act badly, it is published in the newspaper (…). Albanians and Serbs are always guilty (…), Swiss people are always against foreigners (…). Actually this is not so much the case at school (…). Among children it doesn't matter where somebody comes from.

Isa logged his activities from 28/12/2009 to 01/01/2010:

On Monday I woke up very late. At 2 pm I went with my friend to the city. We got money from our parents, and I bought a pullover sweater. Later we went to have something to eat. When I got home, my brother challenged me to a video game. Before I went to sleep, I read (...) half an hour

Tuesday: As always, I got up very late. Today was not such a special day, I read and studied a bit for school. In the evening I visited my cousin, and we watched a movie. The film was called "Blow." It was about a drug dealer.

Wednesday: My cousin spent the night with me and as planned we went to the indoor pool. We met several colleagues who also happened to be there. Then we also made the acquaintance of some girls. They were very nice, and we exchanged phone numbers.

On Thursday [New Year] I spent the whole day at home and watched TV. In the evening, my sister and her husband came to our house to celebrate. My mother cooked a very nice meal for us. [As every year] we watched a funny video of a comedian from Kosovo together. Shortly before midnight we got our glasses ready. Since I do not drink alcohol, I filled my glass with water. After twelve o'clock, we set off our fireworks. Then my brother and I went out [we rented a room and had a free night with some boys].

On Friday, nothing was going on because I came home at about nine in the morning and slept all day.

In December 2009, Isa described to me how he had been experiencing the vote on the ban on new minarets:

They are free to decide, the Swiss citizens are deciding, the majority wins, you can't do anything about that (...). A vote is a vote, he who gains more people, just wins. That's simple. (...) But I believe that the posters were exaggerated... They could have said: "We don't want minarets!" That would have been enough, without hanging up the posters. Have you seen the posters? Stop minarets and so on. That was unnecessary! We were annoyed about it. The posters were put up on every corner..., up front over there, everywhere..., the posters were excessive!

Isa's comment on the vote illustrates the impact of the ban on minarets on boundary-making processes between "us" and "them." On the posters, the minarets were represented as missiles. Equating Islam with terrorism in this manner was harshly criticized in Switzerland, and Isa adopted this critique. By contrast, he was unable to object to the culturalist framework that sets the West against Islam. Probably Isa's profile in the school context can be interpreted in that way. When he portrayed himself as a Muslim believer, he himself was evoking the culturalist framework. The categorization of specific rules and attitudes that are not relevant in Isa's everyday life as Islamic illustrates that he can express his Muslim belonging only by othering himself, that is, by being "different" and "foreign."

I suppose that the research on religion had inspired Isa to invent himself as a Muslim. Obviously, Isa has his own view about the study. An e-mail sent to me by Isa's teacher afterwards can be seen as a clue for understanding his self-expression in the classroom, "(…) great, that it went so well, Isa said, it was very exciting." He said he had not known that some children in the class have no religion."

It seems that Isa knows only categories such as "Muslims," "Christians" or "Jews," which are general religious denominations. Because he feels that he belongs to the category "Muslims," he probably wished to show that he knew the basics of the Muslim faith, for example praying five times a day and attending the Friday prayer in the mosque.

Interestingly, the process of othering (Fabian, 1993) was in this case produced by the research itself. It can be said that the research about religion and religious belonging is actively taking part in the construction of Islam as the religion of the "others." Even if it was not intentional, it does not change the reality. Instead, it shows that unintended effects of the study have to be taken into account in order to understand the field data.

Ramadan in Switzerland

Depending on the context, not all religions are equally present and visible. This is evident in an excerpt from an interview with Lule (23). She is studying chemistry and lives with peers in an apartment in the city during the week, and spends the weekend with her family in a rural community, often together with her boyfriend, who is also Albanian from Macedonia. Lule describes herself as a "believer, but not religious." Religion is indeed important to her family, so her father sometimes goes to the mosque in the evening during Ramadan. He does this even though he is not actually a believer. Although her mother, who stems from a strict religious family, is a believer, she does not go along with everything, because, as Lule puts it, "She has a mind of her own." To the question of what religion means to her, she replied:

> Religion is something that is always a little present for me (...) for example, on television or in the newspapers... Lately it seems that a lot of what one reads is a little anti-Islamic. Then you feel really directly affected. But on the other hand, it is something that is not actually there, not really, (...) how should I put it? An example

would be Christmas here in Switzerland, you notice it, you see it everywhere, it is Christmas, you feel so truly connected to it. And for Muslims, it is difficult to feel truly connected to religion, if you do not get to really feel it. To me it is always a little bit there but yet not. (...) If you were, for example, in Macedonia, and it was Bayram, then everyone would be celebrating Bayram and then you can really feel it.

Her description makes clear to what extent the meaning of religion is context specific. It depends on where one lives as a Muslim. Following the sociologist of religion Gustavo Benavides (1998), we can say that our attention should not be directed at the creed itself, but at its position in a specific societal constellation.

Fasting during the month of Ramadan is a good example of Islam as a "modern" religion which forces individuals to take their own positions. Zaïda (17) – who, at the age of two, fled with her mother from Bosnia to Switzerland – related how she fasts:

When one does Ramadan here, (...) in my class there is also an Egyptian girl who fasts, and there is only she and I together (...). But prayer is actually also part of Ramadan, but you have no way of praying. If you work (...), you can perhaps not even do Ramadan because it is [too] tiring. And also the holiday, here most have to work on the holiday (...). You have to find a way, if you want to fast, you're on your own. (...) Fortunately, I find that it is not so hard. But the beauty of it [would be] actually the mood and that everyone can then eat together and so on ... That is not possible during the week, at my house I am then the only one who fasts. It's a little lonely, so it's not so bad, but...

Zaïda began to be interested in Islam and her Bosnian origin at the age of 15. Fasting allows her to express concretely this belonging. Something similar happened to her friend Zlata (17), whose parents are also from Bosnia:

My parents do not want me to fast during Ramadan, when I go to school. They say: This is not good for you. You will not be able to do it. You have to go to school, you have to work! It was my choice (...) and they suggested that I at least limit my fasting to weekends.

Lule (23) fasts only when she has no lectures and no exams. When asked why she fasts, she replied:

(...) I think it's a good thing, because one goes through with something that other people in this world are doing (...). Actually, the fact that it's meant to cleanse the body comes from Islam. But to me that's less central than the humility ... that you just go through with this humility; that you learn to deal with the fact that you can't have anything from early morning until evening. This is what it mainly means to me. That's why I do it, when I don't have anything big to focus on at the university.

Lule does not fast because Muslims have to fast, or because her family has always fasted. On the contrary, she fasts because it is a good thing. The idea that fasting is supposed to be cleansing does not mean much to her. Instead, she formulated a rationale for fasting that even non-Muslims can comprehend.

These examples can only hint at the extent to which the meaning of Islam as a religion and a way of life is renegotiated in a perpetual process of complex interactions between immigrants and host society. These second-generation students are living Islam in a new way and do not accept simple traditions that their parents may have once embraced.

Conclusion

In conclusion I would like to emphasize the following points: Firstly, there are many possible ways of orienting one's life as a young Muslim in Switzerland. I suggest that placing greater emphasis on the multiple ways of belonging found among young Muslims in Switzerland can help call into question the widespread tendency to put forward a hegemonic and dichotomizing view of Muslim and non-Muslim Swiss citizens as fitting into the two categories of "them" and "us." Given the increasing significance of the politics of belonging in terms of religion, it should be the task of citizenship education to highlight these multiple dimensions of belonging among children and young people.

Secondly, the examples described above provide insight into the many possible configurations of how Islam is lived in Switzerland. Like the families of Dafina and Isa, most families do not regularly go to the mosque. But that, in itself, says nothing about whether they believe and how they practice Islam. The prayer in the mosque is not obligatory for Muslims. One can just as well pray at home. The examples of Lule, Zaïda and Zlata show that young people do not necessarily get to know the Islamic traditions in the family, but rather begin to deal with their Muslim affiliation on their own during adolescence. In the process, relationships with peers of the same ethnic origin play an important role. Thirdly, while equating Islam with terrorism is implausible, the culturalist frame, which posits Islam as the cultural and religious opposite of the West, seems difficult to refute. However, in my view, the problem lies not in children and young people knowing too little about their religion. Nor does it lie in the rather superfluous knowledge about religious diversity. Pseudo-knowledge concerning religious minorities only becomes problematic when it is combined with the notion that religious affiliation determines the essence of the person. Such an ideology can be defined as a form of cultural racism (Miles, 1999). Educational settings in public schools could be adjusted to avoid intensifying this mechanism. Islam, and every other system of belief, is lived in very different ways. Addressing this complexity remains a huge challenge to citizenship education in Europe's multicultural states and beyond.

References

Allenbach, B. (2012). Bairam, Balkanslang, Basketball…: Die vielfältigen Zugehörigkeiten von muslimischen Jugendlichen in der Schweiz. *Tsantsa* 17, (86-95).

Allenbach, B. (2011). Made in Switzerland: Politik der Zugehörigkeit und Religion am Beispiel von Secondos aus Südosteuropa. In: Allenbach, B., Goel, U., Hummrich, M. & Weissköppel, C. (Eds.). *Jugend, Migration und Religion. Interdisziplinäre Perspektiven.* (199–224). Zürich/Baden-Baden: Pano/Nomos.

Allenbach, B., & Herzig, P. (2010). Der Islam aus der Sicht von Kindern und Jugendlichen. In: Allenbach, B., & Sökefeld, M. (Eds.). *Muslime in der Schweiz.* (296–330). Zürich: Seismo.

Allenbach, B., Herzig, P., & Müller, M. (2010). *Schlussbericht Migration und Religion: Perspektiven von Kindern und Jugendlichen in der Schweiz.* Bern: Nationales Forschungsprogramm NFP 58. From: www.nfp58.ch/files/downloads/SB_Giordano.pdf. (Accessed January 20, 2014).

Allenbach, B., & Sökefeld, M. (2010). Einleitung. In: Allenbach, B., & Sökefeld, M. (Eds.). *Muslime in der Schweiz.* (9–40). Zürich: Seismo.

Anthias, F. (2009). Translocational belonging, identity and generation: Questions and problems in migration and ethnic studies. *Finnish Journal of Ethnicity and Migration* 4(1), (6–15).

Asad, T. (2003). *Formations of the Secular. Christianity, Islam, Modernity.* Stanford: Stanford University Press.

Barth, F. (1994). Enduring and emerging issues in the analysis of ethnicity. In: Vermeulen, H., & Govers, C. (Eds.). *The anthropology of ethnicity: Beyond "Ethnic Groups and Boundaries.* (11–32). Amsterdam: Het Spinhuis.

Benavides, G. (1998). Modernity. In: Taylor, M. C. (Ed.). *Critical terms for religious studies.* (186-204). Chicago: University of Chicago Press.

Brubaker, R. (2007). *Ethnizität ohne Gruppen.* Hamburg: Hamburger Edition.

Caputo, V. (1995). Anthropology's silent "others": A consideration of some conceptual and methodological issues for the study of youth and children's cultures. In: Amit-Talai, V., & Wulff, H. (Eds.). *Youth culture: A cross-cultural perspective.* (19–42). London: Routledge.

Christensen, P., & James, A. (2000). Introduction: Researching children and childhood: Cultures of communication. In: Christensen, P., James, A. (Eds.). *Research with children: Perspectives and practices* (1–8). London: Falmer Press.

Crowley, J. (1999). The politics of belonging: Some theoretical considerations. In: Geddes, A., & Favell, A. (Eds.). *The politics of belonging: Migrants and minorities in contemporary Europe.* (15–41). Aldershot: Ashgate.

D'Amato, G. (2010). Die Secondos – Von „tickenden Zeitbomben" zu „Overperformern". In: Ritter, C., Muri, G., & Rogger, B. (Eds.). *Magische Ambivalenz. Identität und Visualität im transkulturellen Raum* (178–185). Zürich: Diaphanes.

EKM Eidgenössische Kommission für Migrationsfragten (2010). *Muslime in der Schweiz. Identitätsprofile, Erwartungen und Einstellungen. Eine Studie der Forschungsgruppe „Islam in der Schweiz" (GRIS).* Bern: EKM.

Endres, J., Tunger-Zanetti, A., Behloul, S., & Baumann, M. (2013). *Jung, muslimisch, schweizerisch. Muslimische Jugendgruppen, islamische Lebensführung und Schweizer*

Gesellschaft. Ein Forschungsbericht Luzern: Universität Luzern, Zentrum für Religionsforschung.

Fabian, J. (1993). Präsenz und Repräsentation. Die Anderen und das anthropologische
Schreiben. In: Berg, E., & Fuchs, M. (Eds.). *Kultur, soziale Praxis, Text. Die Krise der
ethnographischen Repräsentation* (335–364) Frankfurt/Main: Suhrkamp.

Frisina, A. (2010). Young Muslims' everyday tactics and strategies: Resisting Islamophobia,
negotiating Italianness, becoming citizens. *Journal of Intercultural Studies*. 31 (557–572).

Goffman, E. (1974). *Frame analysis: An essay on the organization of experience.* New York:
Harper and Row.

Kämpf, Ph. (2008). *Die „Jugo-Schweiz": Klischees, Provokationen, Visionen.* Zürich: Rüegger.

McGuire, M. B. (2008). *Lived religion: Faith and practice in everyday life.* New York: Oxford
University Press.

Lathion, St., & Tunger-Zanetti, A. (2013). Switzerland. In *Yearbook of Muslims in Europe,
vol. 5* (pp. 633–647). Leiden: Brill.

Miles, R. (1992). Einwanderung nach Grossbritannien – eine historische Betrachtung. In:
Institut für Migrations- und Rassismusforschung (Ed.) *Rassismus und Migration in Europa.* (268–270). Hamburg: Argument.

Müller, M. (2013). *Migration und Religion: Junge hinduistische und muslimische Männer in
der Schweiz.* Wiesbaden: Springer VS.

Schiffauer, W. (2004). Vom Exil- zum Diaspora-Islam. Muslimische Identitäten in Europa.
Soziale Welt 55(4), (347–368).

Schweizerischer Bundesrat (2013). *Bericht des Bundesrates über die Situation der Muslime in der Schweiz.* From: http://www.ejpd.admin.ch/content/dam/data/pressemittei-
lung/2013/2013-05-08/ber-d.pdf. (Accessed January 20, 2014).

Wax, R. H. (1971). *Doing fieldwork: Warnings and advice.* Chicago: The University of Chicago Press.

Wikipedia (2011). Wort des Jahres. From: http://de.wikipedia.org/wiki/Wort_des_Jahres.
(Accessed July 28, 2012).

Yuval-Davis, N. (2011). *The politics of belonging. Intersectional contestations.* London: Sage.

Yuval-Davis, N., Kannabiran, K., & Vieten, U. M. (2006). Introduction: Situating contemporary politics of belonging. In: Yuval-Davis, N., Kannabiran, K., & Vieten, U. M. (Eds.).
Situating contemporary politics of belonging. (1-14). London: Sage.

Learning to Live with Different Worldviews in The Netherlands

Siebren Miedema

Introduction

What is the pedagogical aim of a school being an educational institution? In my view, the answer to this question is crucial and decisive. For me that aim is embracing the identity formation of students, their personhood, and that is why we should be aware of fostering and hindering factors with respect to teachers as persons and professionals, the circumstances, pedagogical and didactical arrangements in the school, policies of the government, et cetera.

In dealing with religious education, and in line with the aim of holistic personhood formation formulated above, the question could also be posed: What is the impact of the schools' role in terms of the selected subject-matter and of the arrangement of pedagogical relations and situations by the professionals on personal identity construction, and more specifically on religious identity development–the formation of religious personhood on the part of students?

The tragic events of 9/11 in New York and, the murder of Theo van Gogh in Amsterdam by a radical Muslim in November 2004, have tremendously affected the debates on the place and role of religion in society and education. These events have confirmed my view that education and, in particular, schools in the Netherlands, in Europe (cf. Jackson et al., 2007), and worldwide could and should really make a difference precisely through the way they are dealing with religious diversity. Schools could foster religious citizenship education in which encounter and dialogue have a prominent place and by which students can learn to live together while being different in terms of social, cultural or religious background.

However, the parties are divided on the issue as to whether religion should be an integral part of the public domain or restricted to the private domain. After

9/11 the non-practicing Jewish mayor of the city of Amsterdam, Job Cohen, called on people not to underestimate the binding role of religion and to give more attention to it in the public domain, because "if we want to keep the dialogue between each other going, then we also need to take into account the religious infrastructure. Without mosques, temples, churches and synagogues we will not succeed" (Cohen, 2002). The Leiden University professor of law, Paul Cliteur, took an opposite stance in a plea for the strict separation of church and state, religion and state. In his view, religion should not belong to the public domain, because morality is sufficient here. For Cliteur, France should be the guiding example of how to deal with these issues, thus in the Netherlands we should follow the French principle and practices of laïcité (Cliteur, 2006).

In the remainder of this chapter I will, following Charles Taylor, first point to the new religious landscape of the secular age. Then, I will argue for the use of "worldview" instead of "religion" because of the former's stronger emphasis on diversity and inclusivity. Favoring Job Cohen's approach, I will then outline a plea for a combination of citizenship education that would include religious or worldview education. I combine this with the plea that the state should take the political-pedagogical responsibility for stimulating the policy and practice in schools of fostering religious or worldview citizenship education as an integral component of citizenship education. Governments should hereby abstain from any preference for a particular worldview or religion, but should guarantee the political constellation in which religious or worldview citizenship education can flourish for the benefit of children and young people, the students in the schools. This would provide students with the opportunity to experience, be confronted by and become acquainted with other students' religious and worldview background, ideas, experiences, and practices already in the embryonic or mini society of the school as John Dewey has so adequately stated. Seeing the impact of the religious domain on political, cultural and economic areas, students can also benefit from such experiences and insights when they encounter religious "others" in society at large. Such practices might bring about mutual respect and understanding, thereby stimulating the development of the personal religious or worldview identity formation of students. Thus, the pedagogical and political, as well as the theological or religious studies perspectives can and should adequately meet here in fostering learning to live with different religions and worldviews.

Religion/Worldview in the Secular Age

Charles Taylor (Taylor, 2007) has pointed to the secular age in a very particular sense with a focus on the conditions of belief. This form of secularity focuses on:

> a move from a society where belief in God is unchallenged and indeed, unproblematic, to one in which it is understood to be one option among others, and frequently not the easiest to embrace. (…) Secularity in this sense is a matter of the whole context of understanding (i.e. matters explicitly formulated by almost everyone, such as the plurality of options, and some which form the implicit, largely unfocussed background of this experience and this search) in which our moral, spiritual or religious experience and search takes place. (Taylor, 2007, 3)

At this juncture educators and religious instructors have to face this challenge explicitly from the aim of the religious identity formation of pupils. It is my contention that, here, we need to reflect anew on the different modes of exploration, commitment, and participation that might result from religious or worldview education in schools, but also distinguish more adequately between belief, faith, and worldview if we want to do justice to what Taylor has convincingly characterized as "options."

That is one of the reasons why, pedagogically speaking, I prefer to use the concept "worldview" over "religion". "Religion" is, in my conceptualization, a sub-concept of "worldview", and I define "worldview" as the system, which is always subject to changes, of implicit and explicit views, feelings and attitudes of an individual in relation to human life. "Views, feelings and attitudes in relation to human life" can refer to everything with which people can be occupied and consider important. In empirical research with students we use a short "stipulative definition", namely, "A worldview is the way one looks at life" (Bertram-Troost, De Roos & Miedema, 2006).

Using the concept of "worldview" may help avoid strong and aversive secularist approaches against religion, which want to leave religion and religious education out of the curriculum of the school completely (the Cliteur approach). Everyone has at least a personal worldview that may or may not be directly influenced by an organized or established worldview or religious tradition. And, in line with the approach of Cohen, this personal worldview, with its existential layers, should pedagogically be taken into account as we have claimed elsewhere (Van der Kooij, De Ruyter & Miedema, 2013). The concept "worldview" can also prevent exclusivist claims leading, for example, to preferential argumentation for paying attention only to one religion, for instance Christianity, or even to preferring teaching and learning about a particular worldview or religion. Both cases can be interpreted as universalistic worldview or religious claims against, for instance, the universal claim in human rights of self-development and self-appropriation. A thick conception of worldview education includes teaching and learning about and from worldviews, and this, in contrast to a thin conception, is merely teaching and learning about worldviews.

Citizenship Education and Worldview Education

The late Terrence McLaughlin wrote that it is important to remember that "citizenship" and "education for citizenship" are not abstract notions, but rather require a concrete specification in relation to a particular society (McLaughlin, 1992, 241; see Miedema & Ter Avest, 2011 *in extenso* on McLaughlin's approach). McLaughlin's plea is for a interpretation of citizenship education characterized by an emphasis on active learning and inclusion, interactivity, that is values-based and process led, while allowing students to develop and articulate their own views and to engage in debate. That view is fully compatible with the religious and worldview education we outlined earlier, when the aim no longer will be teaching and learning of a religion or worldview, but rather combining teaching and learning about religions with teaching and learning from religions and worldviews. This will enable students to develop their own point of view in matters of religion and worldview in the context of plurality via encounter and dialogue.

In that article McLaughlin introduced an ideal-typical distinction of what he called a "maximal interpretation of education for citizenship" in contrast to a "minimal interpretation of education for citizenship" (McLaughlin, 1992). McLaughlin, himself, interpreted these distinctions in terms of contrasting interpretations on the continuum of the very concept of "democratic citizenship." It was his aim "to offer a substantial notion of 'education for citizenship' in the context of the diversity of a pluralistic democratic society"; a notion " 'thick' or substantial enough to satisfy the communal demands of citizenship, yet compatible with liberal demands concerning the development of critical rationality by citizens and satisfaction of the demands of justice relating to diversity" (McLaughlin, 1992, 235). Such a society, according to McLaughlin, should seek to find a balance between social and cultural diversity with cohesion. This could have been said in the first decade of the twenty-first century.

His elaboration of minimal and maximal approaches runs as follows. In the minimal approach to citizenship and education for citizenship the subject is presented in a purely knowledge-based way and with a particular civics-related content to be transmitted in a formal and didactic manner. The identity conferred on an individual in this conception of citizenship is merely seen in formal, legal and juridical terms. In schools, the development of the students' broad critical reflection and understanding is neither stimulated nor fostered. A maximal conceptualization of citizenship and education for citizenship, however, is characterized by an emphasis on active learning and inclusion, is interactive, values-based, and process led, allowing students to develop and articulate their own opinions and engage in debate. The individual's identity in this conception of citizenship is dynamic, instead of static, and a matter for continuing debate and redefinition. Maximal conceptions of citizenship education "require a considerable degree of explicit understanding of democratic principles, values and procedures on the part of the citizen, together with the dispositions and capacities required for participation in democratic citizenship generously conceived" (McLaughlin, 1992, 237).

McLaughlin observed that the minimal interpretation is open to various objections. The most notable is "that it may involve merely an unreflective socialization into the political and social *status quo*, and is therefore inadequate on educational, as well as on other, grounds" (McLaughlin 1992, 238). That is why he was in favor of more maximal conceptions of education for citizenship, because these require "a much fuller educational program, in which the development of a broad critical understanding and a much more extensive range of dispositions and virtues in the light of a general liberal and political education are seen as crucial" (McLaughlin 1992, 238). But he was not blind to objections against the maximalist interpretation either, because such interpretations "are in danger of presupposing a substantive set of 'public virtues', which may exceed the principled consensus that exists or can be achieved" (McLaughlin, 1992, 241).

Although religious/worldview education is not the same as citizenship education, there are fruitful possibilities and, in my opinion, also the need to further link these two fields. McLaughlin's preference for a maximalist interpretation of education for citizenship may be helpful here, because he points to the necessity of full educational programs in which the development of a broad critical understanding and a much more extensive range of dispositions and virtues in the light of a general liberal and political education are seen as crucial. His view on education for citizenship offers the possibility to include religious and worldview education as part of such educational programs and makes it even fuller in combining democratic education for citizenship and religious and worldview education in schools. It is my contention that this combination could adequately be termed "religious or worldview citizenship education." This is fully combinable with what I have claimed elsewhere to be the aim of education in schools, namely that every child and youngster in every school should be able to develop her or his personal identity or personhood (Wardekker & Miedema, 2001). Religious edification (*Bildung*) is interpreted, then, as an integral part of an embracing concept of personal identity development. An embracing concept of citizenship education should imply, then, that religious and worldview education and development is an inclusive part of citizenship education. It should form a structural and necessary element of all citizenship education in all schools, thus including common or state schools as well as denominational schools, based on a transformative pedagogy stressing the agency and authorship of students. In all cases, the aim is the students' responsible self-determination regarding religious/worldview.

It is widely recognized that citizenship education is the responsibility of each country's government in liberal-democratic societies. And if a government should take the responsibility for an inclusive concept of education for citizenship seriously, it means that without any preference per se on the side of the government itself for a particular worldview or religion, each government could take the political-pedagogical responsibility to stimulate the policy and practice in schools of supporting religious or worldview education as part of an integral citizenship education (cf. Doedens & Weisse, 1997; Knauth, 2007; Miedema & Bertram-Troost, 2008). In that way, the state can support democratic citizenship and religious, worldview education definitively combined in schools as religious or worldview citizenship education.

Following the train of thought of the philosopher and pedagogue John Dewey (Dewey, 1897/1972; 1916), it is, pedagogically speaking and from a societal perspective, desirable that students, already in the embryonic society of the school, experience or be confronted by and should become acquainted with other children's religious backgrounds, ideas, experiences and practices. Seeing the impact of the religious domain on political, cultural, and economic areas they can also benefit from such experiences and insights when they encounter religious "others" in society at large. Thus, from a societal as well as pedagogical point of view, all schools should be obliged to foster a religious and/or worldview dimension to citizenship, and thereby bring about mutual respect and understanding that may stimulate the development of the personal religious identity formation of children and youngsters in school life (Miedema, 2006).

Promising Practices

Examples of good practices of learning to live with different worldviews in the Netherlands are the so-called *co-operation schools*. These are schools of different religious and/or worldview profiles that work together. Such forms of cooperation might also be inspirational for forms of education and schooling elsewhere in the world.

One example in the Netherlands, as it was practiced for ten years, is the one and only interreligious primary school we have had, the Juliana van Stolberg Primary School (Ter Avest, 2003; 2009). In a similar way this is still concretized and practiced in the state of Hamburg in Germany (Doedens & Weisse, 1997). The use of such an approach holds when the aim of religious/worldview education is no longer either the teaching and learning of a particular religion nor exclusively consists of mere teaching and learning *about* religions or worldviews. Rather, when educating about religions/worldviews, this will be conceptualized as a function of teaching and learning *from* religions, that is enabling students to develop their own point of view in matters of religion(s) and worldview(s) in the context of plurality and to develop their own personal religious/worldview identity (Jackson, 1997; Wardekker & Miedema, 2001). Unfortunately, the Juliana van Stolberg School – which was the only interreligious school in the Netherlands recognized officially by the Dutch government and bringing students from Christian and Islamic traditions together - was forced to cease operations in 2003. The reason for this was that Christian parents no longer sent their children to the school. The school gradually became in practice a "black", Islamic school, and that was, of course, not what the participants initially had in mind when founding this school.

Elsewhere we have extensively dealt with the promising co-operation between schools of different denominations in the Bijlmer district in the south-east part of the city of Amsterdam (Miedema & Ter Avest, 2011). Here three primary schools belonging to different denominations - that is a state school (*Bijlmerhorst* school), an Islamic school (the *As-Soeffah* school) and an open Christian school (*De Polsstok*) - practice what they preach and preach what they practice: living together in difference. In these three schools, the population of teachers, as well as those of students and parents, represent different nationalities and a variety of religious commitments. The pedagogical approach used here is termed the "Bijlmer Conversations", emphasizing the need to continuously draw each other into the conversation. Although the teachers play a central role in the "Bijlmer Conversations", the focus is on the needs of the student who is raised and who will also live in a multicultural and multi-religious society.

The three elementary schools in Bijlmer have made a decision for close co-operation, because the problematic situation of most of the students in this poorer area of Amsterdam – where more than seventy different national and over twenty denominational backgrounds are represented – was and is perceived by the Principals of these three schools as a shared problem, and this forms the main focus of their pedagogical task. In the meetings of the teams, the above mentioned "Bijlmer Conversations", the officials from the three school (individually and jointly) develop their own way of responding to the diversity of their student population and the complexity of the acculturation and adjustment of the students. The voice of the teacher, the variety of sources of inspiration, the voice of the student, the need of the students to be equipped to live alongside one another in the multicultural and multi-religious society, are combined in the pedagogical approach of "learning in difference" of the "Bijlmer Conversations." The different pedagogical strategies of each of the three teams are rooted in the personal, whether religious or secular, worldviews of the members of the team. Religion(s) is/are seen as something you have to know about and that you can learn from, provided that there is a certain sensibility towards, and recognition of, situations and *experiences of awe*; practices that render speechless. Diversity in religious and secular worldviews is seen as a given, societal fact, and challenge rather than a problem. Creating social cohesion as a network of teachers and parents from different cultural and religious backgrounds is seen as a challenge. For the creation of such networks each of the partners is of equal importance, or to put it differently: each of the schools is not able to develop solely its own identity without the contrasting or confronting encounters with the other schools. The slogan of the schools is: *The Plural of Togetherness is Future.* The schools' characteristic approach to difference is cemented in classroom activities stimulating the development of social competencies, and is related to the respectful encounter of students of different religious backgrounds. Respect and tolerance are main foci of citizenship education in this case.

Such forms of co-operation could be, and possibly are, realized on a local level in a lot of other countries too, while retaining separate school management and budgetary responsibilities or in the form of a complete joint venture. However, the prerequisite for such practices of cooperative teaching and learning in the school setting is that both the participating denominational schools as well as the common or state schools interpret religious and/or worldview education as an integral part of an embracing concept of personal identity development, and combine this with a transformative pedagogy that stresses the agency and authorship of the students (Miedema, 2000).

Another promising practice that I would like to mention here are the so-called SIMON schools. Since 9/11 Islamic schools as one branch of denominational schools in the Netherlands have had to face a lot of societal and governmental criticism, and as it turned out, both on the basis of reports of the Inspectorate of Education and reports of the National Security Service, the criticism was in nearly 95% of cases always wrong (see *in extenso* Miedema, 2003). At the moment we have 48 Islamic elementary schools and 1 Islamic secondary school in the Netherlands.

The SIMON schools are 10 Islamic elementary schools in the center and in the eastern part of our country. They have joined forces and want to serve both the students and society and want to show their responsibility by giving open accounts of their pedagogical and didactical, as well as of their religious views, on the identity conception of their schools in theory and practice. These schools conquer segregation by positioning themselves in the midst of Dutch society. They have an open admittance policy for students from different sub-denominations of Islam as well as for non-Muslim students. From these non-Muslim students respect is presupposed for the particular religious identity of the schools. The aim of the schools is the holistic identity formation and development of the students from a developmental educational approach in line with Vygotskian and neo-Vygotskian theoretical and practical conceptualizations. The application policy regarding teachers is that they desire to have 50% of teachers committed to the Islamic religious tradition and 50% non-Muslim teachers representing diverse other religions or worldviews while these teachers respect the special religious identity profile of the schools. The pedagogical underpinning for the 50/50 % is that this mixture of teachers offers the students a rich array of different and differing views/commitments in terms of knowledge, insights, expertise, dialogue, and encounter vis á vis religions and worldviews (Aktaran, 2012; Miedema, 2012).

Conclusions

Most countries nowadays have populations representing a lot of differences, including differences in worldview or religion, and they need to try and live peacefully together. This will not happen automatically, but should be learned in families, in schools, and in other societal sites and this will create lifelong challenges. This is what citizenship education is about, what values education is about, and what worldview education is about.

"Citizenship" and "education for citizenship" are not abstract notions, but require concrete specification in relation to a particular society. The same prevails when we add "religious or worldview education" to these two terms. How specific or diverse particular societies are from a religious or worldview perspective, I have learned as a member of a consortium of academic philosophers of education and religious educators during the project *Religion in Education: A contribution to Dialogue or a factor of Conflict in transforming societies of European countries* (REDCo). This project was funded by the European Commission for three years (2006-2009) and carried out by research teams from eight countries across Europe: Estonia, Norway, Spain, France, the Netherlands, Germany, England, Russia (Jackson *et al.*, 2007; Miedema, 2007; Knauth *et al.*, 2008; Valk *et al.*, 2009). Being able to adequately understand a particular niche from a religious or worldview point of view in respect to education presupposes knowledge of and insight into historical, political, educational, theological, economical, and cultural antecedents. It has made me aware, as well, of the historically constructed particularity of the arrangements in my own country; arrangements constructed, not fallen from heaven, and therefore changeable!

Outcomes of empirical research projects in the Netherlands, and also from this REDCo-project, has shown that students really want to learn from, and are interested in, the worldviews and religions of their fellow students. They are also in favor of schools where they can encounter a diversity of worldviews and religions among teachers and students. Dialogue and encounter are important to them, and it is their view that knowing more about other religions and worldviews and meeting peers and adults representing other religions and worldviews can diminish fear and anxiety about otherness, difference or strangeness. It is their contention, as well, that worldview education as part of citizenship education in school is of great value and can prepare them to learn to live peacefully together at early stages in the embryonic society of the school, but also later on in society at large.

References

Aktaran, E. (2012). *Worden wie je bent. Kaders voor identiteitsbeleid op de Simon scholen* [Becoming who you are. Frameworks for identity policy at the SIMON schools]. Leusden: SIMON.

Bertram-Troost, G.D., de Roos, S.A. & Miedema, S. (2006). Religious identity development of adolescents in religiously affiliated schools: A theoretical foundation for empirical research. *Journal of Beliefs and Values. 27*, (303-314).

Cliteur, P. (2006). Zin en onzin van levensbeschouwelijke vorming [Meaning and nonsense about religious education]. In: S. Miedema (Eds.). *Religie in het onderwijs. Zekerheden en onzekerheden van levensbeschouwelijke vorming* [Religion in education. Certainties and uncertainties of religious education] (33-54). Zoetermeer: Meinema.

Cohen, J. (2002). Zoals het nu gaat, zo kan het niet langer [The current situation should not continue]. *NRC/HB*, January 4.

Dewey, J. (1897/1972). My Pedagogic Creed. In: J.A. Boydston (Eds.), *John Dewey. The Early Works. Volume 5.* (84-95). Carbondale and Edwardsville: Southern Illinois University Press.

Dewey, J. (1916). *Democracy and Education. An Introduction to the Philosophy of Education.* New York : The Free Press.

Doedens, F. & Weisse, W. (Eds.) (1997). *Religionsunterricht für alle. Hamburger Perspektiven zur Religionsdidaktik* [Religious education for all. Perspectives on the didactics of religion from Hamburg]. Münster/New York/München/Berlin: Waxmann.

Jackson, R. (1997). *Religious education: an interpretive approach.* London: Hodder and Stoughton.

Jackson, R., Miedema, S., Weisse, W. & Willaime, J.P. (Eds.). *Religion and Education in Europe. Developments, Contexts and Debates.* Münster/New York/München/Berlin: Waxmann.

Knauth, T. (2007). Religious Education in Germany – a contribution to dialogue or conflict? Historical and contextual analysis of the developments since the 1960s. In: Jackson, R., Miedema, S., Weisse W. & Willaime, J.P. (Eds.), *Religion and Education in Europe. Developments, Contexts and Debates* (243-265). Münster/New York/München/Berlin: Waxmann.

Knauth, T., Jozsa, D-P., Bertram-Troost, G. & Ipgrave, J. (Eds.) (2008). *Encountering Religious Pluralism in School and Society. A Qualitative Study of Teenage Perspectives in Europe.* Münster/New York/München/Berlin: Waxmann.

McLaughlin, T.H. (1992). Citizenship, Diversity and Education : A Philosophical Perspective. *Journal of Moral Education, 21*, (235-250).

Miedema, S. (2000). The Need for Multi-Religious Schools. *Religious Education. 95*, (285-298).

Miedema, S. (2003). *De onmogelijke mogelijkheid van levensbeschouwelijke opvoeding* [The impossible possibility of worldview education]. Amsterdam: VU University Press.

Miedema, S. (2006). Educating for Religious Citizenship. Religious Education as Identity Formation. In: De Souza, M., Engebretson, K., Durka ,G., Jackson, R. & McGrady, A. (Eds.) *International Handbook of the Religious, Spiritual and Moral Dimensions of Education. Vol. I and II.* (965-974). Dordrecht: Springer.

Miedema, S. (2007). Contexts, Debates and Perspectives of Religion in Education in Europe. A Comparative Analysis. In: Jackson, R., S. Miedema, W. Weisse & J.P. Willaime

(Eds.), *Religion and Education in Europe. Developments, Contexts and Debates.* (267-283). Münster/New York/München/Berlin: Waxmann.

Miedema, S. (2012). *Levensbeschouwelijke vorming in een (post-)seculiere tijd* [Worldview education in a (post-)secular age]. Amsterdam: VU University Press.

Miedema, S., & Bertram-Troost, G.D. (2008). Democratic Citizenship and Religious Education: Challenges and Perspectives for Schools in the Netherlands. *British Journal of Religious Education. 30*, (123-132).

Miedema, S. & ter Avest, I. (2011). In the Flow to Maximal Interreligious Citizenship Education. *Religious Education. 106*, (410-424).

Taylor, Ch. (2007). *A Secular Age.* Cambridge, MA/London, England: The Belknap Press of Harvard University Press.

Ter Avest, I. (2003). *Kinderen en God, verteld in verhalen* [Children and God, told in Stories]. Zoetermeer: Boekencentrum.

Ter Avest, I. (2009). Dutch children and their 'God': the development of the 'God' concept among indigenous and immigrant children in the Netherlands. *British Journal of Religious Education. 31*, (251-262).

Valk, P., Bertram-Troost, G., Friederici, M. & Béraud, C. (Eds.) (2009). *Teenagers' Perspectives on the Role of Religion in their Lives, Schools and Societies. A European Quantitative Study.* Münster/New York/München/Berlin: Waxmann.

Van der Kooij, J.C. , de Ruyter, D.J. & Miedema S. (2013). "Worldview": the meaning of the concept and the impact on Religious Education. *Religious Education. 108*, (210-228).

Wardekker, W.L. & Miedema, S. (2001). Identity, Cultural Change and Religious. Education. *British Journal of Religious Education. 2*, (76-87).

Islamic Education in Spain

Juan Ferreiro Galguera

Demographic Profile of Muslims In Spain: Figures

According to an official census, in 2013 Spain had a population of 47.1 million inhabitants.[24] Most of them (41,539,400) are Spanish citizens, but a small number (5,520,133) are foreigners (11.7%: 5% of which are EU citizens (2,352,978.). Romania is the country from which most immigrants come (796,576). The second on the list is Morocco (710,041). Among the countries with Muslim backgrounds, the second (but 19th on the general list) is Pakistan (80,714). Other Muslim countries from which immigrants come are Senegal (63,760) and Algeria (63,969).

We cannot provide an official number of Muslims in Spain. The Spanish census (the last one was in 2011) doesn't ask citizens about religious affiliation. It would be not only very interesting but also legally possible to ask this, because the Constitution only forbids forcing people to indicate their religion, not asking about religion (art. 16.2: *No one may be compelled to make statements about his/ her ideology, religion, or beliefs*). In my opinion it would be very useful if the census could ask that question of citizens. In any case, estimates say that there are approximately 1.4 million Muslims in Spain (2.5 % of the population: 30% of them are Spanish Muslims and 70% are immigrants). They mainly live in Catalonia, Andalusia and Madrid.

---

24 47,095,533 inhabitants, according to the January 1, 2014 statistics preview of the continuous census.

The Legal Status Of Islam in Spain

The Spanish Constitution recognizes in article 16[25] the fundamental right of religious freedom, not only for individuals, but also for groups and communities. The only limits to manifestations of religious freedom (whether of individuals or groups) are those necessary for the maintenance of public order that is protected by the law. The Religious Freedom Act 7/1980 implements this fundamental right and also the legal concept of public order. When speaking about the limits of religious freedom this act enshrines two kinds of limits: religious freedom shall respect, both the fundamental rights of others and the Public Order. According to the law, this legal concept (public order) has three dimensions: public security, public health, and public morality.

According to the Constitution of 1978 (art. 16.3),[26] the relationship between the public powers and denominations may be implemented in a metaphorical area formed by two coordinates: the principle of a non-confessional State (*laicidad o aconfesionalidad*) and the principle of cooperation. In other worlds, all relations between public powers and denominations should respect those two principles. The principle of the non-confessional state is based on two pillars: separation between church and State and neutrality of the State regarding religious affairs. With regard to the principle of cooperation, the Constitution gives two mandates to the public authorities: to take into account the religious beliefs of the Spanish population and to maintain the resulting relations of cooperation with the Catholic Church and other denominations.

The Constitution does not state how relations of cooperation between the State and religious denominations should be developed. However, the Parliament "answered" that open question at two different moments. First, five days after the Constitution was implemented (January 3rd, 1979), when the State signed four Cooperation Agreements with the Holy See. Second, when the constitutional mandate of cooperation was implemented by the above mentioned Religious Freedom Act of 1980.

---

25 Art. 16.1:

1. Freedom of ideology, religion and worship of individuals and communities is guaranteed, with no other restriction on their expression than may be necessary to maintain public order as protected by law.

26 3. No religion shall have a state character. The public authorities shall take into account the religious beliefs of Spanish society and shall consequently maintain appropriate cooperative relations with the Catholic Church and other confessions.

So, we can distinguish among four types of religions from a legal perspective. In other words, denominations in Spain adopt one of these four legal forms:

1. Non-registered religious entities:
Religious entities need not to register in order to be entitled to religious freedom. The Constitution guarantees the fundamental right of religious freedom to all religious communities, whatever legal form they adopt, without other limitation than respect for fundamental rights of others and public order. The Religious Freedom Act refers in article 2 to several manifestations of religious freedom of individuals and communities; among others,[27] the rights of religious groups to impart religious teaching.
Registering in the Register of Religious Entities (RRE) is not the only way for a religious group to become a legal entity. Another possibility for religious entities is opting to constitute an association under the Law of Associations[28]. In this case, if they opt to be a civil association, they can enroll either in the National Registry of Associations in the Ministry of the Interior (if their sphere of activity is within the whole country) or in any of the registers of associations existing in each of the 17 Autonomous Communities in Spain, as long as the sphere of the association's activity is located within only one of those Autonomous Communities. In any case, intervention or approval by a public authority is not necessary for a group to be entitled to the fundamental right of religious freedom.

2. Religious entities enrolled in the Register of Religious Entities (hereinafter RRE).
As we have just said, to be entitled to religious freedom, religious groups do not need to adopt any special legal form. Nevertheless, they do have the option to enroll in a special nation-wide register: Register of Religious Entities (RRE), which is under the responsibility of the Ministry of Justice. Once they are registered, religious groups are guaranteed legal representation as religious entities.

---

27 Other manifestations expressly enshrined in the art. 2 or religious freedom act: to hold worship celebrations, commemorate feast days, celebrate marriage rites, establish places of worship, appoint and train ministers of the cult, spread the group's creed, maintain relations with their own organizations and with other religious denominations, and provide religious assistance in public institutions (Army, prisons, hospitals, etc.)

28 In this case, the requirements would be to submit an agreement between at least three individuals and also a charter (in a public or private document) approving the organization and operation of the association Organic Law 1/2002, March 22th, on the right of Association.

Registration shall be made by a written request sent by anyone representing that religious entity. This application must be accompanied by a reliable document containing notice of the foundation or establishment of the organization in Spain, as well as the following information:
a) the entity's name (which appropriately distinguishes it from any other religious group) and its address; b) Declaration of religious purposes which cannot go beyond the limits established in the Religious Freedom Act, which includes respect for the fundamental rights of others and public order; c) Rules of procedure for the organization and its representative bodies, including their powers and requisites for a valid designation.

Religious entities can enroll in that Register, provided they fulfill the requirements described above, once verified by the public authority (General Department of International Cooperation and Relations with denominations). The most controversial of those requirements is the declaration of religious purposes. According to the Spanish Constitutional Court, the Administration should not assess religious purposes. Thus, registration can only be refused if the aforementioned requirements are not met by the religious group or if it is legally proven (for example by a legal sentence) that this group uses activities or methods for illegal targets or goals.

The immediate effects of registry in the RRE are:
• Those entities fully enjoy fully legal personality as religious groups,
• They can organize themselves with complete autonomy (a democratic organization is not compulsory for religious entities, as it is in regular associations),[29]
• They are able to include clauses safeguarding religious identity (particularly important in matters of labor relations), and exemption for ministers of cult from the requirement to have a residence permit in order to reside in Spain.
3. Religious groups registered in the RRE which have being classified as "deeply or firmly rooted" according to their domain and followers.
   According to article 7 of the Religious Freedom Act of 1980, the State may establish Cooperation Agreements with those registered religious entities that, due to their domain or number of followers, have obtained the classification of a "deeply rooted" (*notorio arraigo*) denomination. If the Advisory Commission for Religious Freedoms grants a registered religious group the "deeply rooted" designation, two main further legal effects accrue: the right to have a

---

29 Article 2.5 of the Organic Law 1/2002, March 22nd, on the right of Association: "Internal organization and functioning process of associations must be democratic, fully respecting pluralism…"

representative in the Advisory Commission of Religious Freedom and the possibility of reaching a Cooperation Agreement with the State. Islam received the classification of a "deeply rooted" denomination by the Advisory Commission for Religious Freedoms in 1989.

4. Registered "deeply rooted" entities that have signed a Cooperation Agreements with the State[30]

   Only deeply rooted entities have the possibility of signing Cooperation Agreements with the State. At this point, we may distinguish between the four cooperation agreements signed by the State with Catholic Church, on the one hand, and cooperation agreements signed by the State with the official bodies of Protestants, Jews and Muslims on the other.

Cooperation Agreements with Catholic Church:

The Holy See reached four specific Cooperation Agreements with the Spanish State in 1979, five days after the Constitution came into force; before the Religious Freedom Act of 1980 was even projected. These Agreements, which have a legal status of International Treaties,[31] contain more privileges than those reached by the Protestants, Muslims and Jews in 1992. Among others, the Agreement on Educational and Cultural Affairs foresees an educational system in which teaching of the Catholic religion must be compulsorily offered by all public schools (and also private schools funded by State "concertados") although it is voluntary for the students.

---

30 Since 1992 four other denominations have obtained the "deeply rooted" legal status: the Church of Jesus Christ of Latter Day Saints (Mormons) in 2003, the Jehovah's Witnesses in 2006, Buddhism in 2007, and the Orthodox Churches in 2010. But so far these groups have not signed a Cooperation Agreement with the State.

31 As the Holy See is legally considered a State, these Cooperation Agreements have the legal form of international treaties. So, according to the Constitution, their provisions cannot be repealed, amended or suspended by internal laws, but only "in the manner provided for in the treaties themselves or in accordance with the general rules of international law" (art. 96.1).

Cooperation Agreements with Islam, Judaism and Protestantism

Once the respective Federations that represented Muslims, Protestants and Jews received their "deeply rooted" status from the Advising Council for Religious Freedom, those three denominations negotiated three different but extremely similar Cooperation Agreements with the State that, once reached, were passed as laws in the Parliament (Law 26 of November 10th 1992 as the Cooperation Agreement between the Spanish State and the Islamic commission of Spain).[32] Among other special rights enshrined in the Cooperation Agreements are both spiritual guidance in public establishments or the right of parents to demand religious education for their children in public schools

The benefits of the Agreements only affect those religious communities that belong to the representative bodies that have signed those Agreements with the State. Regarding Islam, this includes those religious entities that belong to the representative body of Islam in Spain: the Islamic Commission of Spain (CIE).

Muslims in School

According to the law[33] education in primary and secondary school is compulsory (from 6 to 16 years old).

There are three types of schools in Spain: public schools, which are financed entirely by the State; private schools, financed by private entities, and "colegios concertados", which are private schools with partial funding from the State.

There are about 250,000 Muslims students in the Spanish school system, and practically all of them attend public schools. There is only one private Islamic

---

32 The other two are, **Law 24/1992, of 10 November 1992, whereby the cooperation agreement between the Spanish state and the Federation of Evangelical Religious Entities of Spain is approved and Law 25/1992, of 10 November 1992, whereby the cooperation agreement between the Spanish state and the federation of Israelite communities of Spain is approved.** As those denomination are not organized as an State (like the Catholic Church) the Cooperation Agreements they have signed with the State doesn't have the legal form of international treaties, but ordinary laws, which, according with art. 96 of the Spanish Constitution, can be repealed, suspended or amended by subsequent, ordinary laws.

33 Until December 9th 2013, the law of education in force was LOE (Organic Law 2/2006 of May 3th on Education). It has been modified by the Organic Law 8/2013 of December 9th for the Improvement of the Educational System, which is now in force. Nevertheless, the new regulation needs to be implemented by Royal Decree.

School. That school is located within the Mosque Omar, one of two mosques in Madrid. This mosque, known as M-30 Mosque,[34] is governed by the Islamic Cultural Centre (financed by Saudi Arabia). The school within it is a foreign school. Students that attend that educational center are basically children of diplomats from Muslim countries.

Regarding "*centros concertados*" (private schools with their own ideology and partially funded by the State), the fact is that there is not any Muslim school of this kind. Most of them are Catholic schools. There are even three Protestants and three Jewish schools of this type, but no Muslim school. Therefore, almost 100% of Muslim students attend public or state schools, financed entirely by the State, where education is free.

Impact of Education on the Integration Process

I would define the Spanish model of integration as a model of "*convivencia*" [coexistence]. When I was at the Ministry of Justice[35] one of my duties was being a member of the staff of a public foundation attached to the ministry called "*Pluralismo y Convivencia.*" Whenever I had to present that foundation in seminars or meetings abroad I always had some difficulty with translating the title of the foundation. Not with the first word "pluralism" which is very easy to translate (pluralism –in English; pluralisme –in French) but with the term "*convivencia.*" In France they usually use the term "cohabitation"; in English there is the term "coexistence". But, in fact, I didn't feel myself comfortable with any of these two terms. Because "*convivir*" is not exactly "cohabiter" nor "coexist". *Convivir* means "*vivir con*": "to live with"…living together all mixed, all together, sharing not only rights and duties, but much more: the whole existence… living together. That's why I always referred to that foundation as "Pluralism and Living Together", an expression that reflects the spirit of our policy of integration: integration as living together.

---

34 After the name of the highway that passes nearby.

35 I was deputy director of coordination and promotion of religious freedom, under the Ministry of Justice from 2006-2010.

Teaching of Islam in Public Schools: Religious Integration

In Spain, denominations which have signed Cooperation Agreements with the State (Catholic Church,[36] Protestants, Judaism and Islam)[37] are entitled to teach their religion in public schools.[38]

---

36 Art. II of the agreement of January 3th 1979, between the Spanish State and the Holy See, concerning education and cultural affairs: *"Educational plans at the levels of pre-school, Elementary School (EGB) and High School (BUP) and technical colleges for students of the corresponding ages, shall include the teaching of the Catholic Religion in all Educational Centers, in conditions equal to those of the basic subjects. Out of respect for freedom of conscience, this religious education shall not be obligatory for all students. However, the right to receive it is guaranteed. Academic authorities shall adopt the necessary means so that receiving or not receiving religious instruction shall not suppose any discrimination at the school. At the teaching levels previously named, the corresponding academic authorities shall allow the Ecclesiastical Hierarchy to establish, under the specific conditions agreed upon, other complementary activities of training and religious attendance."*

37 Article 10 of the **Law 26/1992, of 10 November 1992, whereby the Cooperation Agreement between the Spanish State and the Islamic Commission of Spain (art. 10 of the Cooperation Agreement with protestants and Jewish is almost identical):** 1. In compliance with the provisions of Article 27.3 of the Constitution and Organic Law 8 of 3 July 1985 concerning the right to education, and Organic Law 1 of 3 October 1990 on the general regulation of the educational system, Muslim pupils, their parents and school governing entities shall be entitled, at their request, to exercise the right of Muslim pupils to receive Islamic religious education at preschool, primary and secondary level in public schools and state-subsidized private schools, provided this is not in contradiction with the ideological nature of the private school in question. 2. Islamic religious education shall be dispensed by teachers appointed by the communities that are members of the Islamic Commission of Spain, with the agreement of the federation to which they belong. 3. The contents of Islamic religious education and the corresponding textbooks shall be provided by the respective communities, with the agreement of the Islamic Commission of Spain. 4. Public schools and state–subsidized private schools, as referred to in paragraph 1 of this Article, shall provide suitable premises for dispensing the religious education to which pupils are entitled by law, without detriment to academic activities. 5. The Islamic Commission of Spain and its member communities may organize religious teaching courses at public universities, using the premises and resources they dispose of to this end, with the agreement of the academic authorities. 6. The Islamic Commission of Spain and its member communities may establish and run preschool, primary and secondary schools, and Islamic universities and training centers, subject to the laws in force in this respect.

38 As we have said, Jews are also entitled according to their Cooperation Agreement. But they didn't want to implement it since they did not sign the decree which implements this right (Norm of Ministry of Presidency of April 26th 1996), they do not teach the Jewish faith in State schools.

Thus Muslim students can receive Islamic education in public school. Teachers are appointed by the representative bodies of Islam but their salary is paid by the State as long as the group of students that have asked for Islamic lessons is composed of 10 or more students. Nowadays there are only 45 teachers of Islam in Spain. It is not a large number if we compare it with the Catholic Church: nowadays there are more than 10,600 teachers of Catholicism all around the country.

Education for Citizenship and Human Rights

It is important for all students (regardless of religion) to learn about the scope of human rights, and the meaning of democratic values. Until now, this subject was mandatory in Primary and Secondary Education. As long as this subject was established by that law, the Catholic Church, or at least its hierarchy, alongside parents' groups, not only organized several demonstrations against it but also some parents raised several conscience objections to that subject. Ultimately, those conscience objections were rejected by judges.

The new Law of Education (Organic Law 8/2013 of December 9th for the Improvement of the Educational System –LOMCE[39]), the so-called "Wert" Law (named after the minister of education) abolishes this subject matter. According to the Preamble, the goal of this Law is that "Civic Constitutional Education" be taught as a cross curricular subject

There was another subject that was very positive for the objective of integration: "History of Religions", where religion was taught not from a theological, but from an academic point of view. As religious education is optional, history of religions, which offers elementary knowledge about the principles of the main religions rooted in our society, was one of the alternatives to religious education in Secondary School. We will not go more deeply into the structure and organization of this course because it has been suspended by the Act now in force. According to the LOMCE, the alternative to religious education will be "Social and Civic Values", in primary grades, and "Ethical Values" in secondary grades.

---

39 Ley Orgánica para la Mejora de la Calidad Educativa (LOMCE).

Some Exceptional Problems of Muslim Integration: Students Wearing Hijab in State Schools

At least for the media, the main problem of integrating Muslim students in public schools was caused by the use of *hijab* within state facilities. Those events occurred about two years ago in three Spanish public Schools (Madrid, Arteixo, Burgos). Even if that issue is now before the court (the case is waiting adjudication by the Supreme Court) in my opinion the legal solution is clear. According to our Constitution, our Religious Freedom Act, our Constitutional Court and even the European Court of Human Rights, wearing a *hijab* is considered without any doubt a manifestation of religious freedom, which is a fundamental right. Everybody knows that none of the fundamental rights is absolute. They all have limits. But those limits should be expressly described in the law. According to the Law (Religious Freedom Organic Act of 1980) there are two limits to religious freedom:

- fundamental rights of others and
- public order, which is a legal concept comprised by three elements: public moral, public health and public security.

If a student decides to wear *hijab* in public school, she is not attempting to violate the human rights of others, nor is she acting against the public order. It could be so if there was a law forbidding the use of symbols (public security can include legal security, obeying the established laws) for example, an act that bans the students from wearing clothes or symbols which obviously show religious membership, as there is in France (Law of March 15th 2004). But in Spain there is no such law. There were some internal regulations in some public schools that banned the use of hats or similar clothing on the head. Not only are school internal regulations not the proper means to regulate fundamental rights, but also, they didn't take into account that wearing a *hijab* in not like wearing a hat or body piercing because it is clearly a display of religious freedom. And, as we have just said, that display is not forbidden by the Organic Law of Religious Freedom of 1980 in force. So, the only legal way to ban that manifestation of religious freedom would be through an organic act (amending the current one or elaborating a new one), in any case, never through the internal regulations of a public school, which are not passed by the Parliament but only by the representatives of the teachers, parents and students of that school. Clearly democracy does not require us to regulate, and so limit, a fundamental right.

Challenges of Integration

We are living in an era of crisis. Not only economic, but also moral. Our societies are characterized by an increasing individualism, a lack of participation in civic issues, a lack of solidarity, in sum, a lack of a solid sense of community: the group, if any, ends at the family. In modern European cities, even in Spain, we have lost the concept of the "village square" as a place for congregation, a place where citizens can gather to talk and share daily experiences without being expressly invited. The Internet has made it even more difficult to restore that part of community spirit. Of course this is not a problem of Muslims alone, but of the whole society, in our multi-confessional collectivity. Imparting subjects at school like civic education and the like are of course important for the task of integration. But the goal of recovering from individualism and slowly recovering the sense of civil community is above all a challenge, not only for politicians, but for the society as a whole.

In this volume where we focus on a part of society (students, and more concretely, Muslim students) it is very important to take into account and to underline that Islam has some values that we are losing in Europe. In all countries of the EU we can observe how some groups of European Muslims are still preserving some of those communitarian values: the importance of the family, of hospitality, of solidarity...

European Muslim students should play an important role in this decisive task of shaping and preserving these values of participation, democracy, and closeness (proximity). An important path towards it could be, of course, engaging in politics. We have very close to us the example of Egypt, where the youth played a decisive role in the so called "Arab Spring", even if they are now suffering oppression, after the military ousted the elected president, Mohamed Morsi... (oppression that we hope is just temporary).

In Europe we have a crisis of democracy. We need to improve our democracy. Youth and Muslim youth will have much to contribute in this regard.

An Example of Good Practice

One example of a good practice in Spain is *Achime*[40] (Spanish Muslim Girls' Association), a pioneering national youth organization, focused on Muslim girls. They are a completely independent institution, created by young active women to help and support their fellow sisters.

Their mission is, according to them, to embrace their Spanish-Muslim identity and engage in active participation in all different fields of our society, proving that being Spanish/European while preserving their religious values is possible. Another goal is to empower Muslim girls and make them aware of their important role within Spanish society. In addition, they aim to promote interfaith dialogue in order to attain a deeper understanding of our rich diversity. Finally, they try to raise awareness about negative developments affecting Spanish youth, and to find solutions for them.

Their work aims to develop equally the three basic dimensions of every human being: body, mind and soul. According to the first, and as an example, they have organized an *Eid al-Adha* celebration at an Adventure Park and several women's races. Some other recent activities were a conference about the right to wear *hijab*, a workshop about rhetoric and body-language, and a photography contest. Referring to the soul, they have organized a volunteer project in *Ramadan* (working with sick children and the elderly population) and they have also celebrated *qiyam*, a voluntary night prayer. Their goal is organizing at least three activities per month, one for each dimension (mind, soul, body). These are simple things but with perseverance and determination, step by step, with a feminine spirit of happiness, equality, and democracy they work toward pure integration.

---

40 Asociación de Chicas Musulmanas de España. www.asociacionachime.com. Facebook. com/asoc.achime

References

Act 26 of November 10th 1992 whereby the Cooperation Agreement between the Spanish State and the Islamic commission of Spain.

Comisión Islámica de España-CIE-[Islamic Commission of Spain]. From: http://muslim. multiplexor.es/promo/cie.htm. (Accessed January 17, 2011).

Cooperation Agreement of January 3th 1979. Between the Spanish State and the Holy See, concerning education and cultural affairs (International Treaty).

Ferreiro, J. (2010). "Financing of Minority Religious Societies". In: Michaela Moravčíková (ed.) *Financing of churches and religious societies.* (195-209). Bratislava: Institute for State-Churches Relations.

Ferreiro, J. (2011) "Islamic religious education in Spain". In: Aslan E. (ed.) *Islamic Textbooks and curricula in Europe.* (237-250). Peter Lang: Frankfurt am Main.

Ministerio del Interior [Ministry of the Interior]. From: http://www.mir.es/. (Accessed February 2, 2014).

Observatorio del Pluralismo religioso en España. From: http://www.observatorioreligion. es/directorio-lugares-de-culto/ (Accessed February 3 2014).

Organic Act 1/2002. March 22nd, on the right of Association.

Organic Act 2/2006 of Education of May 3th.

Organic Act 8/2013 for the Improvement of the Educational System, of December 9th.

Registro de Entidades Religiosas del Minisaterio de Justicia. From: http://maper.mjusticia. gob.es/Maper/RER.action#bloqueBuscadorProcesos (Accessed February 3, 2014).

Spanish Constitution 1978.

Patterns of Integration of Jewish Migrants from the Former Soviet Union in Germany

Doron Kiesel

Unlike the migrant communities in Germany that are familiar and have been thoroughly described in the past, Jewish immigrants from the former Soviet Union are generally vocationally qualified when they arrive and possess considerable awareness of the demands of industrialized societies. While these migrants may associate settling in the Federal Republic above all with the hope of earning a secure living – in terms of social recognition and money they are having a crucial influence on the future of existing, unstable Jewish communities.

What is unusual about them is their highly secular, modernized identity, which owes little to religion and culture, making it difficult for them to fit into the model of identity developed by the Jewish communities in Germany, and hence with what is expected of Jewish immigrants. The existing Jewish communities welcome and support immigration, since this should help to make them more stable. Furthermore, an increase in numbers should lend legitimacy to Jewish life in Germany, both within the country and in the international context. However, these communities are interested not merely in quantitative expansion; rather they expect immigration to lead to a considerable strengthening of the community in a religious and cultural sense.

Theoretical Framework for Migration

Immigration to Germany by Jews from the former USSR accords at first sight exactly with the developments thoroughly described and analysed in studies of migration theory. These argue that migratory movements became larger in both quantitative and qualitative terms in the wake of industrialization, the spread of technology and urbanization, and the creation of nation-states (Treibel, 1999; Joppke, 1999; Kymlica, 2001; Heckmann, 1992). Migration in all its forms, whether forced or voluntary, was and is therefore a structural feature of modernization and of its economic and social implications. The modern regions and societies where goods and services are produced by a constantly growing proportion of the population, that is literate and increasingly trained in science and technology, are therefore also the targets of current migratory flows. Hence, integrating immigrants means fitting them into a modern society that is mobile, both geographically and socially, in which the importance of family ties is diminishing, public life is highly bureaucratized, and government and politics have a high capacity for control. The opposite pole, which is the starting point for migration, is therefore an under industrialized, traditional and comparatively closed society.

Migration theories assume that migration has a number of causes. Some migrants seek to improve their socio-occupational status, and act according to the principle of economic rationalism, based on a knowledge of finance and demography (Langenheder, 1968; Esser, 1980; Feithen, 1985).

The combined influence of factors, in both the region of origin and the destination region, is described as the "pull-push model" (Lee, 1972). The key pull-push factor is an imbalance in the labour market (Künne, 1979). This states that the situation in the labour market in the home region does not match the expectations of the migrant, while social advancement appears to be possible in the destination region. Another factor in migration is the information hypothesis (migrant-stock variable). This says that the networks of personal relationships (Faist, 1997) and channels of information between those who have already migrated and those who may migrate have a crucial impact on the decision to migrate.

According to the classic study by Shmuel Noah Eisenstadt on "The Absorption of Immigrants" (1954), migration occurs when a society is unable to fulfill the expectations of its members. The first stage in a migratory movement is initial motivation, which is rooted in the living conditions in the society of origin. Eisenstadt distinguishes five main social areas in which a "feeling of frustration and inadequacy; lack of gratification" may provide the stimulus to migrate: the physical survival of the migrant and his family are no longer guaranteed; the institutional structure can no longer guarantee the material goals; friction in the area of political ideology; absence of identification and solidarity with the goals or members of the society; individual expectations of life cannot be fulfilled."

The area to which this initial motivation relates continues to influence the further migration process, determining the direction and the willingness to accept changes.

A number of migration theory studies (Esser 1989; Ronzani 1980) demonstrate that it is not only economic differences that lead to migration. In fact, it is more often the comparative social situation that leads to the decision to migrate. The individual feels disadvantaged by comparison with real or imaginary groups in the region of origin or the destination region. The reason for migration is usually not solely political, religio-ethnic, or financial, but stems from a combination of causes, motivations and circumstances. Furthermore, individual, group and chain migration overlap when it comes to actual migratory events. Every migratory flow has various phases, each of them with a heterogeneous composition of migrants, and each acquires its own particular dynamic. Migration not only implies movement in the geographical sense, i.e. people moving from one place to another. Migration also leads to far-reaching social changes:

- for the individuals concerned, in terms of their orientation, behaviour and social context;
- for the groups concerned, either groups to which the migrant has belonged, still belongs or feels a sense of belonging, or groups which the migrant encounters on arrival;
- for the host society, and
- for the abandoned society.

As a number of previous studies have already shown, what is known to apply generally to migration differs considerably in the case of Jewish migrants, so that the overall validity of the basic hypotheses is called into question. By contrast to the perception of migration as a process of fast-track individual modernization (Inkeles, 1984), clear structures are discernible which would seem to overturn these assumptions: in the case of Jewish migrants, integration into Jewish communities in Germany leads to the adoption of much more traditional models of identity. The level of education of the migrants is consistently unlike that of any other group that has migrated to the Federal Republic. Most of the migrants have academic training and were socio-professionally recognised in their society of origin. At the same time, their *Jewish identity* can seldom be described in religious terms, since they were socialized in a society that rejected all ethno-religious allegiance. The resultant very largely secular civil identity does not, therefore, sit easily with the patterns of definition of Jewish life that have become established in Germany.

Jewish Immigration from the Former Soviet Union

The theoretical analyses of migration in the context of German society all look at the integration of migrants from economically and infrastructurally underdeveloped societies. The consequence of this is that the host society reacts socially, educationally and culturally to immigrants lacking a modern outlook and places them under pressure to modernize and assimilate.

The very different social and cultural status of the Jewish migrants from the former USSR, therefore, conflicts with the points of view and approaches familiar from migration theory and policy in the integration of the target group. This mismatch between the respective expectations of host society and migrants makes it appreciably harder for them to become integrated into the Jewish communities in particular, since these anticipate that a quantitative increase will also strengthen what they regard as *Jewish life*. In re-establishing and stabilizing Jewish life in Germany after the Holocaust, Jewish communities have faced the task of finding their own social and religious profile within society as a whole. The models of Jewish life in Germany worked out to date are currently in competition with the perceptions of the immigrants.

The Jewish communities in post-war Germany were for the most part founded by Holocaust survivors, so-called "displaced persons", largely from the countries of Eastern Europe. The overall numbers of the Jewish communities, heavily weighted towards the older age range, had remained relatively constant for 45 years, being increased by a number of returnees and immigrants who arrived in waves, initially from Eastern Europe, and then also from Israel and other countries in the Middle East, and counterbalanced by a simultaneous tendency for their children's generation to emigrate. In sharp contrast to this picture, however, a dramatic development has occurred since the early 1990s that provokes completely new questions: the Jewish communities are growing quite substantially in numbers. The expanded Jewish religious communities which have grown to several times their accustomed size (approx. 30,000 long-standing members until 1989 and now approx. 110,000 registered members of the communities, including 90,000 new migrants, according to the statistics of the Central Welfare Agency of Jews in Germany) are facing huge changes. The Jewish community in Germany is changing dramatically in its ethno-cultural composition, and is obliged to integrate the migrants not only into German society but also into the local Jewish community.

The reason for this development was the political end of the USSR as a relatively closed state system, and the consequent opportunity to leave the successor states. Among the Jewish population in the former Soviet Union, the desire to emigrate to another country varied greatly, depending on political factors and other circumstances. The latent Anti-Semitism that had always existed in the Soviet population was stirred up by nationalist parties and the Russian Orthodox Church after the collapse. At the same time, an economic meltdown and closure of many state institutions, particularly in the infrastructure, academic and cultural sectors, have led to a rapid escalation in the number of highly qualified people being unemployed. Since the Jewish population was overrepresented statistically in the elite despite restrictive measures, it suffered particularly severely from this development. The lack of suitable economic prospects, and frequently indeed of any, was, therefore, added to the political reasons for the emigration of highly qualified people who were unemployed. Migrants' main destination countries have been Israel, the United States and Germany. Israel is well ahead, with about 1,000,000 immigrants, while around 220,000 Jewish migrants have so far settled in Germany. The precondition for approval of an application to immigrate into Germany as a quota refugee is proof of membership of the Jewish community in the country of· origin, and this is provided by the ethnic status stated in the identity papers issued by the countries of origin. As refugees, Jewish migrants to Germany are awarded special status: this includes permission to work and a basic living allowance subject to social security legislation. Assistance is also offered with integration.

From the point of view of the Jewish communities in Germany, fundamental structural problems arise at once. These are generally marked by a lively resurgence of the debate about the nature of Jewish community life, and ultimately also about models of Jewish identity. At a structural level, the large numbers of migrants encounter very weak infrastructures within the communities, particularly in the smaller communities, in such areas as religious teaching and social support. Even in the few large communities such as Berlin, Frankfurt am Main and Munich, existing institutions that are of importance to migrants, such as social services departments, advice and counseling services, kindergartens, schools and youth centres, are generally overwhelmed by the additional demand, since the scale and design of these institutions were based on the structural, social, financial and cultural needs and potential of the previously existing communities.

However, even the kinds of activities offered by existing Jewish institutions are scarcely suited to the demands of communities that have changed in structure and size, so that there is increasingly a need to redefine what the institutions are expected to do. Migrants' psychological and social problems require institutions with adequate support capacity, as well as a high degree of professional expertise in dealing with cultural differences and the difficulties and crises that arise from these, tasks which the Jewish communities undertake in addition to state resources, but which they can only handle by investing considerable energy.

This structural change is further driven by intense concern over the nature of Jewish community life, and hence over whether immigrants are to be assimilated into existing models, or shared patterns of identity need to be worked out afresh. The institutions of the Jewish communities are *Jewish* in the sense that they regard themselves as representing, creating and having the duty to preserve Jewish identity. By far the greatest proportion of the immigrants from the states of the Commonwealth of Independent States (CIS), however, demonstrate a Jewish identity that is, from the point of view of the models that apply to the German-Jewish communities, at best very weak. Because of the absence of Jewish institutions in the former USSR, the immigrants have few points of contact with Jewish religion, religious laws, tradition and culture. The problems that arise from this fact are, from the standpoint of the host communities, reflected in various ways:

- religious deficits;
- lack of Jewish identity;
- problems fitting into the receiving Jewish communities and the host society.

The areas of friction between members of the receiving communities and the migrants can be arranged systematically in five categories:

- widely varying individual outlooks among the two groups
- communication problems and language barriers;
- feelings of estrangement and rejection by established members of the community;
- the well-established shared experience among members of the host communities in tension with the specific narratives of the migrants;
- the organizational principle of *uniting the community* with the aim of subordinating differing religious outlooks to an understanding of religiosity expressed in an orthodox manner is undermined by Jewish immigration, because new religious outlooks are being formed.

Cultural Contacts and Cultural Conflicts between Jewish Immigrants and Jewish Communities

This problem concerns changes within the Jewish communities brought about by immigration, and immigrants' views of those communities. Besides an analysis of structural changes due to increasing and changing needs that have already been mentioned, we shall also look in particular at the process of negotiating Jewish identity and the Jewish sense of community.

Jewish immigration will be considered from the perspective of selected Jewish communities, in which both long established members and immigrants take joint responsibility for shaping the life of the community, in the context of general questions raised by migration theory and integration theory. In addition to common features, differences from other migratory movements into Germany will be explored, although it is already apparent that the migration theory perception of migration – as a process of acquiring a stake in society through rapid modernization – is turned completely upside down: the negotiations between the two groups seem to be hampered in particular by the fact that it is not a traditional society that is being integrated into a modern society, but that in this case modern views are expected ultimately to be revised in line with traditional models such as ethnicity and religion. Contrary to the usual assumption that the relationship between immigrants and host group always represents the integration of a minority into a majority, the indicators in this case are totally different: the high number of Jewish migrants, in most cases, exceeds the number of members of the relevant communities, sometimes quite substantially. This calls into question approaches to integration and participation that are based on migration theory.

These huge changes are affecting Jewish communities in Germany at a time when the lengthy and painful process of finding a legitimate basis for Jewish life in the *country of the perpetrators* is gradually becoming more settled. The post-war communities found themselves at first having to build up again from scratch, by a series of small steps, and now they are to a critical degree in a similar situation once more. Besides the need to create a basis for survival after 1945, the Jewish communities were forced to redefine their perception of Jewish life under their peculiar circumstances, as they were unwilling and unable for various reasons to build on the destroyed tradition of German Jewry. Instead of carefully distancing themselves from their surroundings, as they did particularly in the early years after the Holocaust, a Jewish self-awareness has now developed of being a cultural community with a history defined by the shared experience of the destruction of European Jewry. This has meant adopting the model of a *united community,* which regards Orthodoxy and its models of religious interpretation as its shared standpoint, especially in relation to its institutions, and as an assurance of Jewish identity. However, although individual attitudes and personal religious practice are often completely different, a secular lifestyle is perceived as a dereliction, and the community has therefore preserved its ties to religion. The constant tension is mitigated by the perception of Jewish identity as a widely differing sense of cultural belonging with a particular relationship to the state of Israel. This is based on an awareness both of the shared experience of the Holocaust and of the specific situation of life in post-war Germany.

These models of identity came into being through a process of highly contentious negotiation between members of postwar communities from cultural traditions that were very different, even while being Jewish. The identity of the Jewish community in Germany, which is still unstable and precarious, is now under great strain, if only on account of the number of immigrants to be integrated because the Russian immigrants bring with them completely different ways of looking at questions of Jewish identity. Since they come from a communist society opposed to religion, in which even non-religious Jewish community life was impossible, the perceptions of Jewish identity agreed upon in Germany are largely alien to them: the highly negative connotation of religion that they have internalized makes it difficult for them to identify with the key attitude of the German Jewish communities, which rises above ideology. The considerable reservations of the well-established Jewish population towards Orthodox lifestyles and religious rituals, which might provide a point of contact, does little to alter this situation since the immigrants take a totally different view of their own culture in the second area of relevance, cultural orientation, and primarily adopt a Russian nationalist view which completely ignores ethnic features such as a distinct Jewish culture. It is problematic even to see themselves as a Jewish community in Germany with strong ties to the state of Israel: this is highly contentious, since Israel ought to be the *true* destination for anyone emigrating as a Jew. They are, thus, additionally faced with the question of the legitimacy of living as Jews in Germany, while shared experience of the Holocaust provides little point of contact with the lives of Jews who have been living in Germany, at least among the younger generation. They tend to focus rather on the experience of repression under Stalinism and on migration. Here too, expectations do not coincide: although immigrants are received in a particular way because they are *Jewish* refugees, the Jewish communities expect them to occupy the kind of marginalized social situation that they have just fled. Their understandable reservations, which are sometimes wrongly interpreted by the communities as a lack of interest in Jewishness, are strengthened by the rise in xenophobic utterances and the public expression of extreme right-wing views in parts of the Federal Republic of Germany.

References

Bade, K. & Troen, I. (Eds.) (1993). *Zuwanderung und Eingliederung von deutschen und Juden aus der früheren Sowjetunion in Deutschland und Israel.* Bonn: Bundeszentrale für politische Bildung.

Bade, K. (2000). *Europa in Bewegung. Migration vom späten 18. Jahrhundert bis zur Gegenwart.* Munich: C.H. Beck Verlag.

Bar-Yosef, R. (Ed.) (1990). *Family-Absorption-Work. Selected Issues in the Analysis of the Israeli Society.* Jerusalem: The Hebrew University, Department of Sociology.

Bukow, W.D. & Llaryora, R. (1988). *Mitbürger aus der Fremde. Soziogenese ethnischer Minoritäten.* Opladen: Westdeutscher Verlag.

Bukow, W.-D., Nikodem, C., Schulze, E. & Yildiz, E. (Eds.) (2001). *Auf dem Weg zur Stadtgesellschaft. Die multikulturelle Stadt zwischen globaler Neuorientierung Restauration.* Opladen: Leske & Budrich.

Bukow, W.-D. (1993). *Leben in der multikulturellen Gesellschaft. Die Entstehung kleiner Unternehmer und der Umgang mit ethnischen Minderheiten.* Opladen: Westdeutscher Verlag.

Diehm, I. & Radtke, F.O. (1999). *Erziehung und Migration.* Stuttgart: Kohlhammer.

Eisenstadt, S. N. (1987). *Die Transformation der israelischen Gesellschaft.* Frankfurt am Main: Suhrkamp.

Elwert, G. (1990). *Nationalismus und Ethnizität. Über die Bildung von Wir-Gruppen.* Berlin.

Eppenstein, T. (2004). *Einfalt der Vielfalt? Interkulturelle pädagogische Kompetenz in der Migrationsgesellschaft.* Frankfurt am Main: Cooperative Verlag.

Esser, H. (1980). *Aspekte der Wanderungssoziologie. Assimilation und Integration von Wandern, ethnischen Gruppen und Minderheiten.* Darmstadt: Luchterhand.

Faist, T. (1997). *Migration und Transfer sozialen Kapitals.* In: Pries, L. *Transnationale Migration.* Baden-Baden: Nomos-Verlag.

Fechler, B., Kößler, G. & Liebertz-Groß, T. (Eds.) (2000). *Erziehung nach Auschwitz" in der multikulturellen Gesellschaft.* Weinheim: Juventa Verlag.

Feithen, R. (1985). *Arbeitskräftewanderungen in der Europäischen Gemeinschaft.* Frankfurt am Main, New York: Campus-Verlag.

Gotzmann, A. (2002). *Eigenheit und Einheit. Modernisierungsdiskurse des deutschen Judentums der Emanzipationszeit.* (Studies in European Judaism, Vol. 2). Leiden, Boston: Brill.

Gotzmann, A. (2001). *Pluralismus als Gefahr? Jüdische Perspektiven.* In: Malik, J., Rüpke, J. & Makrides, V. (Eds.) *Pluralismus in der europäischen Religionsgeschichte. Religionswissen schaftliche Antrittsvorlesungen.* (35-52). (Europ. Religionsgeschichte, 1). Marburg: Diagonal-Verlag.

Gutmann, A. (Ed.) (1993). *Multikulturalismus und die Politik der Anerkennung.* Frankfurt am Main: Fischer Taschenbuch.

Hacohen, D. (Ed.) (1998). *Ingathering of Exiles. Aliya to the Land of Israel. Myth and Reality.* Jerusalem: The Zalman Shazar Center for Jewish History.

Heckmann, F. (1992). *Ethnische Minderheiten, Volk und Nation.* Stuttgart: F. Enke.

Herbert, U. (2001). *Geschichte der Ausländerpolitik in Deutschland.* Munich: C.H. Beck Verlag.

Hess, R. (2000). *Juedische Existenz in Deutschland heute*: *Probleme des Wandels der juedischen Gemeinden in der Bundes republik Deutschland infolge der Zuwanderung russischer Juden nach 1989*. Berlin.

Hutchinson, J. & Smith, A.D. (Eds.) (1996). *Ethnicity*. Oxford: University Press.

Joppke, C. (1999). *Immigration and the Nation-State*. Oxford: University Press.

Kiesel, D. (1996). *Das Dilemma der Differenz. Zur Kritik des Kulturalismus in der interkulturellen Pädagogik*. Frankfurt am Main: Cooperative Verlag.

Kiesel, D., Messerschmidt, A. & Scherr, A. (Eds.) (1998). *Die Erfindung der Fremdheit. Zur Kontroverse um Gleichheit und Differenz im Sozialstaat*. Frankfurt am Main: Brandes und Apsel.

Koopmans, R. & Slatham, P. (Eds.) (2000). *Challenging Immigration and Ethnic Relations*. Oxford: University Press.

Künne, W. (1979). *Die Außenwanderung jugoslawischer Arbeitskräfte*. Königstein, Ts. : Hanstein.

Kymlicka, W. & Norman, W. (Eds.) (2000). *Citizenship in Diverse Societies*. Oxford: Universuty Press.

Kymlicka, W. (2000). *Politics in the Vernacular. Nationalism, Multiculturalism and Citizenship*. Oxford: University Press.

Langenheder, W. (1968). *Ansatz zu einer allgemeinen Verhaltenstheorie in den Sozialwissenschaften. Dargestellt und überprüft an Ergebnissen empirischer Untersuchungen über Ursachen von Wanderungen*. Cologne, Opladen: Westdeutscher Verlag.

Lee, E. (1972). *Eine Theorie der Wanderung*. In: Szell, G. *Regionale Mobilität*. Munich: Nymphenburger Verlagshaus.

Mautner, M., Sagi, A. & Shamir, R. (Eds.) (1998). *Multiculturalism in a Democratic and Jewish State*. Tel Aviv: Ramot.

Müller-Schneider, T. (2000). *Zuwanderung in westlichen Gesellschaften*. Opladen: Leske & Budrich.

Peres, Y. (1985). *Ethnic Relations in Israel*. Tel Aviv: Sifriyat Hapoalim.

Schoeps, J., Jasper, W. & Vogt, B. (1996). *Russische Juden in Deutschland. Integration und Selbstbehauptung in einem fremden Land*. Weinheim: Beltz, Athenäum.

Schoeps, J., Jasper, W. & Vogt, B. (1999). *Ein neues Judentum in Deutschland? Fremd und Eigenbilder der russischjüdischen Einwanderer*. Potsdam: Verlag für Berlin-Brandenburg.

Spülbeck, S. (1997). *Ordnung und Angst. Russische Juden aus der. Sicht eines ostdeutschen Dorfes nach der Wende*. Frankfurt am Main, New York: Campus.

Stromberg, C. (2001). *Akkulturation russischer Juden in Deutschland und Israel: Wertekongruenz und Wohlbefinden*. Lengerich: Pabst.

Todorov, T. (1996). *Abenteuer des Zusammenlebens. Versuch einer allgemeinen Anthropologie*. Berlin: Wagenbach.

Treibel, A. (1999). *Migration in modernen Gesellschaften*. Weinheim: Juventa.

Section Two

The Balkans and the Middle East

Citizenship Education and Muslims in Bulgaria

Rositsa Atanasova

The transition to democracy in Bulgaria necessitated a fresh re-conceptualiza-
tion of the relationship between the individual and the state. Citizenship education became a statutory subject in the curriculum in Bulgarian schools relatively
recently. It is integrated in the curriculum as an interdisciplinary field, which,
depending on the class level, is taught within other subjects with the aim of developing citizen attitudes and skills for responsible participation in public life. The
basic presumption of the current system is that citizenship provides a common
denominator of identity within which an accommodation of individual differences is possible. This paper begins by tracing the general structure of citizenship
education in Bulgaria. I then explore some of the modules, which are of particular
relevance to the Muslim minority in Bulgaria and to the development of an inclusive model of citizenship. I will ultimately assess the progress that has been made
in that direction and the challenges that remain.

In 2000 Order No. 2 on Curriculum Content was promulgated on the basis of
the Law on National Education. It provides the current legal basis for citizenship
education in the Bulgarian educational system. The Order contains the national
educational standards (NES), which outlines the structure of citizenship education
and constitutes the foundation for curricula in the various subjects through which
citizenship education is taught. Citizenship education forms part of the cultural
and educational field "Social Sciences and Citizenship Education." However, it is
not a freestanding discipline. Rather, it is integrated in the curriculum as an interdisciplinary inquiry, which is taught through the medium of these other subjects.
These subjects vary from one educational level to another, but in so far as they are
mandatory for all students in a particular grade, they are taught through the same
curriculum in the Islamic religious schools alongside specialized subjects.

The cultural and educational field "Social Sciences and Citizenship Education" consists of different subjects depending on the educational level. Thus, in primary school the two subjects are "Homeland" and "Man and Society" and it is through them that citizenship education is taught. In middle school, in turn, citizenship education is taught through the medium of "History and Civilization" and "Geography and Economics". In high school, citizenship education is taught through the subjects of the so-called philosophical cycle – "Psychology and Logic", "Ethics and Law" and "Philosophy". Only in the final 11th grade of high school is citizenship education conveyed as a separate, integrated topic called "the world and the individual."

The structure of citizenship education in Bulgaria has been the subject of debate (Paideia Foundation). The proponents of citizenship education as a separate subject have argued that such an approach would result in a more holistic and systematic curriculum. According to this view, the teaching of citizenship education as a freestanding discipline would avoid the confusion of introducing the same concept differently depending on the varying methodology and context of the subject. The proponents of an interdisciplinary approach, on the other hand, have argued that the very nature of citizenship education is interdisciplinary and therefore such an approach is most true to the nature of the subject. The interdisciplinary approach further ensures the effective linkages among the various subjects as well as the overall integration of the "Social Sciences and Citizenship Education Field." Currently, the Bulgarian educational system adopts an interdisciplinary approach to citizenship education. The "World and the Individual" (Ministry of Education and Science) is the only free standing citizenship education course in the curriculum. However, it is not meant to constitute a separate theoretical course on citizenship education. Rather, it is envisioned as an opportunity for students to apply in practice the citizenship competencies they have learned through the other subjects.

The current structure of citizenship education as defined by Order No. 2 is not without problems. One of the most significant challenges is that the national educational standards still provide a more theoretical framework of competences without focusing sufficiently on imparting practical skills. Significantly, "passive verbs" feature prominently in the language used to render the national educational standards. Students are meant to "know", "describe", "define" or "enumerate" pieces of information as opposed to analytically approaching a case study. The negative effect of this pedagogical approach is further strengthened by the content-heavy nature of the subjects, which reveal the lack of clarity or pragmatism regarding the skills and knowledge that need to be mastered at each level. The combined effect of these elements is that no space is left in the curriculum to focus on developing citizenship consciousness and conduct.

The persistence of traditional educational practices further aggravates the situation. There is still an excessive focus on lecturing and passive reproduction in the Bulgarian classroom. The 2009 PISA study revealed that the Bulgarian educational system still lays undue emphasis on memorization at the expense of analytical skills (PISA, 2009). These indicators show the need for all teachers of the social sciences to undergo the requisite training but no uniform program has been advanced to that end until now.[41]

These findings served as an impetus behind the currently contemplated reform of the national educational standards and the related curricula under a Ministry of Education project entitled "For Better Education."[42] The national educational standards proposed with regard to the subject "The World and the Individual", which may now alternatively be called expressly "Citizenship education", display a departure from the old format. The language that defines the knowledge, skills and relationships to be acquired in the various areas of competency is much more active, interactive and analytical. In addition, each area cross-references the eight key competencies that it seeks to develop from the European Reference Framework, which was adopted in 2006, along with a ninth national competency on skills aimed at sustainable development and a healthy way of life. These changes are further reflected in the respective curricula. The model curriculum for "The World and the Individual" explicitly states that testing content should form 40% of the final grade, whereas 60% should be allocated to other forms of participation such as project and portfolio work as well as solving practical cases.

It is instructive to compare how the old national educational standards fare against the new and how they translate to the respective curricula in the area of competency within "The World and the Individual", which is of direct concern to the Muslim minority, namely "National identity and difference in society".

The current version of the standards as listed in Order No. 2 envisions that students should (Order No. 2 on Curricular Content, 2000, 66):

---

41 Sofia University has launched a Master's program for history teachers called "Citizenship education through teaching History and Civilization". While the initiative is laudable, the number of graduates is small and the impact is therefore limited. The description and the curriculum of the degree are available at: http://www.clio.uni-sofia. bg/bg/m-go_hist.pdf

42 The new national educational standards (NES) and the curricula based on them under the project "For Better Education" are available in a zip file at: http://www.mon. bg/?go=page&pageId=13&subpageId=177

1. **Distinguish** the main social groups and communities and comments on their interests and problems.
2. **Explain** the role of language, religion, traditions in social affiliation and differences in society.
3. **Understand** the sources of tension between the various ethnic and religious communities.
4. **Know** the national ideals, traditions, and values and identify Bulgaria's place in world culture.

In contrast, the model national standards in the same area of competency suggest that students are meant to (Ministry of Education and Science):

1. **Demonstrate** the ability to communicate constructively in diverse settings and situations.
2. **Realize** the necessity to counter violence and strive to solve conflict situations in a constructive way.
3. **Analyze** European culture and values and give examples for inter-penetration and cultural influences.
4. **Be conscious** of his/her European identity and the rights and responsibilities of European citizenship.

In what follows we will compare how these standards translate into the expected results listed under the same area of competency in the respective curricula. The current curriculum for "The world and the individual" enumerates the following expected results (Ministry of Education and Science):

1. **Explain** the role of cultural heritage and religion for the formation of the ethnic communities in Bulgaria.
2. **Compare** the role of cultural heritage and religion for the formation of the ethnic and religious minorities in Bulgaria.
3. **Know** the role played by the different cultural traditions in the historical development of ideas about United Europe.

The model curriculum for "The world and the individual", on the other hand, envisions the following expected results. Students will be expected to develop a portfolio (either digital or on paper) that relates to at least one component from the following list (Ministry of Education and Science):

1. **Description and analysis of personal experiences** related to difference and tolerance.
2. **Initiatives/projects for interaction** between the different communities.
3. **Participation in events**
4. **Case studies from historical experience** or the present that illustrate inter-penetration and cultural interaction of local, national or European importance.
5. **Discernment of identity and difference problems** of significance to the local community, Bulgaria, Europe, and the world.
6. **Well-structured and argued demands addressed to the relevant institutions and communities** that seek to facilitate the resolution of the problems.

The change in language and structure clearly demonstrate a shift towards tolerance as practice, rather than as a theoretical construct.

One of the subjects where the challenges of teaching citizenship education in Bulgaria most surface is History and Civilization. Isov has explored the troubled relationship with the period of Ottoman rule that has traditionally plagued history instruction in Bulgarian schools. His study reveals that historically the model of Bulgarian national identity has been largely ethnic-centered to the exclusion of minority identities (Isov, 2005). Isov sees the solution of the problem in the advancement of an inclusive model of citizenship through the chronological localization of historical events (Isov, 2005, 185) and the demythologizing of the historical narrative. The model of citizenship that he advocates is civic or political in nature and aims to accommodate religious or political diversity (Isov, 2005, 246).

In what follows I will explore how the current history curricula for the 5th and 6th grades fare when measured against the two strands of the inclusive citizenship model that Isov advocates, namely the chronological localization of events and its political or civic nature. History is taught for the first time as an independent subject in the 5th grade, which covers the period from ancient times to pre-independence. In 6th grade the material spans Bulgarian history from the proclamation of independence to the contemporary period. The two years thus form a coherent whole and constitute the history course for the middle school.

The preamble to the 5th grade curriculum (Ministry of Education and Science) aims to outline the general approach to the subject and the respective goals. An attempt is evident to emphasize the social at the expense of political history. The goal here is to teach individual activity as a basic citizenship value. The territorial definition of the Bulgarian community is further emphasized, thus marking a shift away from an ethnic-centered definition. Presenting change as a fundamental characteristic of past and present periods and mobility as a necessity in a constantly changing world further effectuates this shift. Yet another goal is to highlight the frequent contacts between Bulgarians and other peoples. In this way Bulgarian identity is presented as traditionally European and the societal and personal struggle for integration is commended.

Table 1 *Chronological localization of events, Examples, Grade 5* (Ministry of Education and Science)

Standard	Themes	Basic Concepts
Describes the changes in Bulgarian society after the Christening and the Ottoman conquest (NES Reference: Traces and explains migration in Bulgaria and the world)	The concept of statehood on Bulgarian territory: - Slavs and Bulgarians before statehood - formation and development of the Bulgarian state - the changing civic life of Bulgarians in the Middle Ages - Byzantium and Bulgarian statehood - The Ottoman Empire and the place of Bulgarians within it	State: - Khandom - Kingdom - Empire Ruler: - khan - prince - tsar - king - emperor - sultan

Table 1 presents some examples from the 5th grade history curriculum where the chronological localization of events is attempted through the positioning of traditionally controversial themes and concepts into a coherent and neutral conceptual matrix. The relevant national educational standard here envisions that the student should be able to trace and explain migration in Bulgaria and the world. This is the general standard, which is found in Order No.2 and which relates to the fulfillment of citizenship education criteria. This general standard is deployed in the context of the history curriculum by requiring the student to describe the changes in Bulgarian society after Christianization and the Ottoman conquest. Thus, the Ottoman conquest, which has traditionally been presented emotively as the breakdown of Bulgarian statehood, is conceived here rather as a change in the political and social order parallel to Christianization. The parallel is highly significant due to the unique place that the conversion to Christianity has in the traditional articulation of Bulgarian identity. In the contemporary approach, as the themes section highlights, the concept of statehood on Bulgarian territory is not a fixed entity but rather varies across historical periods and this variation is presented as a natural historical process. The concepts section further emphasizes

this chronological localization by listing empire along with khandom and king-dom and sultan along with khan and tsar.

Table 2   *Chronological localization of events, Examples, Grade 6* (Ministry of Education and Science)

Standard	Themes
- Establishes the anachronism between the Revival period and the present in Bulgaria and the world. - Establishes commonalities and differences between social changes in Bulgaria and Europe during the 18th-19th century.	- Distinguishes the attitude of Bulgarians of the Revival period towards the Empire and the other ethnic communities within it. - Appreciates coexistence between different communities as a virtue. (NES Reference: Determines the importance of equality, security and tolerance for the social life of the country)

Table 2 shows a further example of the chronological localization of events, this time from grade 6 in the context of the so-called Revival period and post-independence.

The relevant national educational standard here requires students to appreciate and determine the importance of equality, security and tolerance for the social life of the country. This standard translates into the specific history curriculum standard of being able to establish the anachronism between the Revival period and the present in Bulgaria and the world. Thus, the Revival period and the present are explicitly dissociated as distinct and unrelated historical periods, in terms, in particular, as the themes section reveals, of the attitude of Bulgarians towards the Empire and the other ethnic communities within it. The bottom line is that the student should be able through this exploration to appreciate coexistence between the different communities in the contemporary Bulgarian state as a virtue.

We shall now explore how the current history curricula compare against the second strand of Isov's inclusive citizenship model, namely the establishment of civic or political model of citizenship that is not ethnic-centered and thus accommodates ethnic and religious diversity. *Table 3* presents the particular themes and standards in the 6th grade history curriculum with relation to the national educational standard that requires students to distinguish ethnic, religious and linguistic belonging to a community (Ministry of Education and Science). The focal point here is the emphasis on the distinction between state and religious holidays. Students are invited to explore the ethnic and religious diversity of Bulgarian society in the 19th-20th century and link it to the present by presenting the history of a holiday particular to the community to which the student belongs. The themes in relation to these standards seek to foster understanding in students of the positive role of cohabitation between the different linguistic and religious groups as well as understanding and acceptance of the challenges of cohabitation.

Table 3   Civic or Political Model of Citizenship, Examples, Grade 6

Standard	Theme
Determines belonging to a community on the basis of linguistic and religious differences. (NES Reference: Distinguishes ethnic, religious and linguistic belonging to a community) - Distinguishes religious from state holidays and explains their meaning. - Presents the history of a holiday, particular to the community to which the student belongs. - Establishes the ethnic and religious diversity of Bulgarian society in the 19th-20th century	- Understands the positive role of coexistence between the different linguistic and religious communities. - Understands and accepts difference and the challenges of coexistence. (NES Reference: Determines the importance of equality, security and tolerance for the social life of the country)

Table 4   *Civic or Political Model of Citizenship, Examples, Grade 6 (* Ministry of Education and Science)

Standard
Recognizes the Constitution as the fundamental legal norm in the Republic of Bulgaria and the basic rights and responsibilities of Bulgarian citizens: Knows the basic rights and responsibilities of Bulgarian citizens according to the Tarnovo Constitution.   Knows the basic rights and responsibilities of Bulgarian citizens according to the 1991 Constitution of the Republic of Bulgaria.   (NES Reference: Recognizes the Constitution of the Republic of Bulgaria as the fundamental legal norm)

The establishment of an inclusive citizenship model requires the recognition of a fundamental legal norm that recognizes and accommodates religious, ethnic or linguistic difference, yet remains the common denominator of citizenship irrespective of them. Thus a shared sense of belonging could be fostered on the basis of common rights and responsibilities irrespective of minority identity but not to its expense. *Table 4* exemplifies how the history curriculum posits the Constitution of the Republic of Bulgaria as such a fundamental legal norm and the respective national educational standard requires students to recognize the Constitution as this normative bedrock. The idea is that minority identity is vital but could not be the basis of an inclusive citizenship model because it is in its very nature divisive when based solely on religious, ethnic or linguistic affiliation. In contrast, a civic or political model of citizenship could foster a shared sense of belonging for members of different minority groups when it is based on shared rights and responsibilities.

These are just a few examples of how the history curricula have adapted to propagate a more inclusive citizenship model. Difficulties certainly remain. The national educational standards and respective subject curricula constitute ideal types that often diverge largely from the social reality. The legacy of the traditional presentation of national identity is enduring and shapes widely popular discourse and attitudes with regard to the different minorities within the contemporary Bulgarian state. Unfortunately, this tendency is also attributed to teachers. Their personal biases and dispositions tend to color the way they present the material despite the clear guidance of the national educational standards and the new approach evident in the curricula. The Ministry of Education has, however, been diligent in sanctioning any behavior or discourse that deviates from the accepted norm. A further difficulty is presented by the curricula themselves. They present a genuine attempt to break with the past but might prove a little too ambitious given the target age group and the complexity of the matter. The term Bulgarian, for example, remains ambivalent. In the historical context as well as nowadays it usually refers to ethnic Bulgarians who are understood to be Christian. The same term however now inevitably designates a Bulgarian citizen. The difficulty remains for minority members to adopt the term in reference to citizenship given its persistent connotations.

Despite the fact that the examined curricula constitute ideal types, they are nonetheless indicative of significant changes in a productive direction. Most importantly, they indicate and effectuate a change in discourse, which in time will gain prominence. In addition, the relationship between the citizen and the state is still in flux in post-communist Bulgaria. This means that the very concept of citizenship is still new and is being infused with meaning at present, thus leaving ample space for minority members to become part of this articulation as it is crafted. It is important to note, that unlike many other European states, Bulgaria does not constitute an immigrant context. In other words, members of the linguistic, religious and ethnic minorities do not have to inscribe themselves into a fully constituted model of citizenship but can rather call on a cultural and territorial sense of belonging and look to the common past for successful models of coexistence and tolerance. Lastly, the rise of shared European identity has varied the flatness of the identity relief by showing that it is not incompatible to hold and live multiple identities at the same time. Thus, it should not be incompatible to be both Muslim and a Bulgarian citizen in a European as well as global reality of multiple belongings.

In conclusion, it is evident that citizenship education is effecting a significant change in Bulgarian education in terms of both teaching practices and course content. As the cited examples demonstrate, there is a marked shift away from the traditional narrow model of conceptualizing national identity towards a more inclusive one that would allow minority groups to feel a greater sense of belonging to their country of citizenship and partake more fully in civic life. The greatest challenges remain the prevailing nationalistic discourse that stems from tradition as well as the general unpreparedness of teachers of the various subjects through which citizenship education is taught to tackle this sensitive yet vital subject matter. The overall picture, however, calls for cautious optimism. The change in discourse is already tangible and one can reasonably hope that it is only a matter of time that the same can be said of societal attitudes.

References

Balkanski, P. & Zahariev. Z. (1998). *Vavedenie v grazhdanskoto obrazovanie* [*Introduction to Citizenship Education*]. Sofia: Laska.

Ivanov, I. (2000). *Vaprosi na grazhdanskoto obrazovanie* [*Questions of Citizenship education*]. Shumen: Aksisos.

Ivanov, I. (2000). *Grazhdansko obrazovanie i interkulturno obrazovanie* [*Citizenship education and intercultural education*]. *Paper presented at the Intercultural Communication and Civic Society Conference*. Sofia, Bulgaria.

Isov, M. (2005). *Nai-razlichniat sased: Obrazat na osmantsite (turtsite) i Osmanskata imperia (Turtsia) v uchebnitsite po istoria vav vtorata polovina na 20ti vek* [*The Most Different Neighbor: the Image of Ottomans (Turks) and the Ottoman Empire (Turkey) in Bulgarian History Textbooks in the Second Half of the 20ᵗʰ Century*]. Sofia: IMIR.

Ministry of Education and Sinece. From: http://www.mon.bg/?go=page&pageId=1&subpageId=25 (Accessed February 11, 2014).

Ministry of Education and Science. From: http://www.mon.bg/?go=page&pageId=1&subpageId=28 (Accessed February 12, 2014).

Ministry of Education and Science. From: http://www.mon.bg/?go=page&pageId=13&subpageId=177 (Accessed February 12, 2014).

Organization for Economic Co-operation and Development (OECD). From: http://www.oecd.org/pisa/pisaproducts/46619703.pdf (Accessed February 12, 2014).

Paideia Foundation. From: http://www.paideiafoundation.org/ssp.php?page=18 (Accessed February 10, 2014)

Valchev, R. (2004). *Interaktivni metodi i grazhdansko obrazovanie* [*Interactive methods and citizenship education*]. Sofia: Open Education Center.

Valchev, R. (2005). *Kniga za uchidelya* [*A Handbook for the Teacher*]. Sofia: Open Education Center.

Valchev, R. (UNESCO) (2006). *Education, Intercultural Dialogue and the Development of Democratic Attitudes: the Reality and Perspectives - the perspectives from South-Eastern Europe, Dialogue among Civilizations*. Paris.

Religious Education, European Citizenship and Religious Pluralism

Islamic Education – The Case of Romania

Laurenţiu D. Tănase

Romania is a European country with a Christian-Orthodox religious majority and a religiosity that is actively present in the public sphere, a reflection of its lower degree of secularization compared with that of the advanced secularized space of Western European societies, as well as most of Central Europe. The evolution and development of contemporary Romanian society, especially in the last two decades, is generating a re-thinking of the entire socio-political and economic systems of the country. The institutional and legislative changes that came along with Romania's integration into the Euro-Atlantic sphere, especially after Romania joined the North-Atlantic Treaty Organization (NATO) in 2004 and the European Union (EU) in 2007, had a decisive influence on the functional democratic development of Romanian society.

Social and institutional changes were encountered by all structural components of Romania's contemporary society; changes that were and still remain dependant on European institutional benchmarks, both from the political and economic points of view, as well as from the legislative perspective.

Construction of European citizenship is one of the challenges that Romania (and of course all other countries in the EU), currently faces. Religious denominations can play a significant role in the formation of a European citizenship that is inclusive of religious pluralism.

Priests, pastors, imams, and rabbis can contribute substantially, via their attitude, toward the development of a European consciousness and citizenship, as well as to the consolidation of a pluralistic society that shows tolerance toward religious diversity.

In particular, through preaching and religion classes, they can contribute to the formation of favourable attitudes towards pluralism and European citizenship. We contend that the European Union project cannot be successful unless the religious and moral values of all religions are appreciated.

Religious education

The importance of education in modern society is, generally speaking, considerable. Only by having a high-performance educational system are we able to understand the fast-paced changes that are taking place around us, and make sense of the profound meaning of life. Education can provide the necessary means for the promotion of moral and cultural values and for the protection of the historical and cultural richness of minorities living alongside different majority groups.

Through education we can avoid religious extremism and curtail disrespect for human rights and fundamental freedoms. Education represents an essential concern of the socio-cultural, economic, and political establishment of the modern European sphere. Contemporary European education contributes to social balance, as well as to the protection and promotion of the cultural values achieved through the course of history. All of the above-mentioned reasons legitimize the search for the most appropriate cultural patterns that are to be promoted by education in order to avoid cultural imbalances, extremism, and conflicting situations.

From the religious point of view, there has always been a strong connection between ethnic and cultural-religious identities, especially when we talk about minority groups. Unfortunately, this ethno-religious identity hallmark, excessively used in politics, has often represented the grounds for disputes and conflicts. Because of this, it is important to learn, through education, about the ethnic, religious, and cultural specificities of the diverse populations comprising modern European society. In the context of contemporary realities, knowledge of and cultural dialogue with European Islam becomes a priority.

It needs to be underlined that the establishment of the European Muslim communities, especially in Western Europe, has occurred through immigration over the last century. Only in the Balkans and South-Eastern Europe, more than in any other European region, do we find native Muslim communities of different ethnic identities, the main one being Turkish. This community is reflective of the political and military influences of the Ottoman Empire.

European Citizenship - Religious Pluralism

As many know, 2013 was the European Year of Citizens dedicated to the rights of EU citizenship. The conference in Tirana on which this volume is based was an expression of this political and juridical goal. European citizenship has a strong "supranational character, which is one of the basic principles of contemporary society and of democratic regimes" (Mazilu, 2006). It symbolises, at the ideal level, a communion of objectives and means that exist among the member countries of the European Union. In order to build a European citizenship we have to get over the rivalries of local or national cultures in order to create a civic European culture (Mazilu, 2006).

Contemporary European democracy is defined through social functionality based on pluralism. When we take economic, cultural, political, or religious pluralism into account, it is apparent how pluralism ensures social equilibrium and represents juridical protection amidst contemporary social competition.

In the domain of religious life, religious pluralism defines the plural religious structure of modern democratic societies and constitutes an important component of the functioning of contemporary society.

In a context of religious pluralism, religious power within society or, to be more precise, within the relationship between the state and the church, is not held by one church or one religion only. The existence of religious pluralism entails that religious power is distributed according to certain criteria related to historic existence, cultural visibility, or to numeric representation among competitive groups.

Therefore, in order to be able to speak about the existence of religious pluralism, we need to take into account the idea of religious competition. However, in order for religious competition not to turn into an open conflict, an appropriate judicial frame is necessary so as to allow for a functional competition. In this context, we can define religious pluralism as a form of expression of dialogue and reciprocal respect among religious actors.

The juxtaposition of the diverse religious cultures within the same society contributes to the relativisation of the "truth" of each of them and, consequently, to the standardization of religions, which, as of that moment, will find them exposed to the preferences of consumers and confronted with the logic of a free and highly competitive market (Berger, 1971, 214-233).

The loss of a monopoly within society by traditional institutionalised religions is a socio-structural process that modifies the social status of religion (Luckmann, 2003, 281). A common expression in studies addressing this phenomenon is: *free market religious pluralism*. If we use this concept as a starting point, we can construct a pertinent analysis and a full discourse about contemporary religious marketing, seen as a free and competitive form of the expression of religious plural-ism.

When religious pluralism is respected it can provide evidence of sound civic education, which, at the level of the realities of the European Union is called *European citizenship*. As with any act of knowledge, European citizenship and plu-ralism are aspects of society that are developed and learned through a sustained educational process. Within that process, religious studies can play an important role in the transmission of general human values such as *tolerance and justice*. Awareness and understanding of these principles in the specific contexts of reli-gious pluralism and of free competition in the domain of the symbolic religious products are necessary, but are, at the same time, a challenge for both politicians and religious leaders.

Within the EU, we hear, more and more often, reference to Muslim commu-nities during discussions on the failure of multiculturalism. Islam in Europe is growing, statistically speaking, and represents one of the main challenges for the social and economic balance of the European sphere in the short, medium, and long terms.

The more non-Muslim communities knows about Islam, the easier it will be to accept it and ensure acceptance of religious pluralism in Europe. Terrorism, polygamy, fanaticism and women deprived of their fundamental rights represent just a few of the clichés and misconceptions regarding Islam held by people be-longing to different religions. To overcome these clichés, a common effort is nec-essary to improve communication, education, and mutual confidence.

The Muslim Religion in Romania

In Romania the presence of Islam is one of the components of the religious land-scape. With a historical existence of more than 500 years, the Romanian Muslim community developed from an ethnic core of Turkish origin. Starting with the 19th century, and accelerating in the 20th century, a Tatar ethnic expression, main-ly from Crimea, has been added as a consequence of migration.

Although today there are small Turk-Tatar Muslim communities in all the re-gions and cities of Romania, the most significant presence is in Dobrogea region. The Muslim community is organised as a *Muftiate*, with the centre in the city of Constanta, located in the South-East of Romania. The *Muftiate* is an important and representative institution of the Islamic Denomination in Romania. The Ta-tars in Dobrogea speak a specific language of the Turkic family of languages and practice the Muslim religion as *Sunnis* (Osman, 2007). By analysing the statistics, we notice the important relationship between the Muslim religion and ethnic affiliation.

The relationship between the Muslim minority in Dobrogea and the Romanian Christian Orthodox majority (but also with other minorities: Roman-Catholic, Jewish, Greek-Orthodox) has never encountered social tensions based on religious disagreements or disputes that generated violent conflicts. It might be argued that such a relationship expresses the logic of a pluralistic construction of society on the religious level, characterized by the specific criteria of competition and free market. Because of that, this kind of inter-religious and inter-cultural peaceful coexistence could represent a case study and also a successful model to be followed in the modern European sphere.

The Muslim community in Romania represents a *minority* among the other cults and religions. Romania is a Christian Orthodox country where, as of 2011, 86% of the 19 million people are Orthodox. According to the last National Census (2011), the Muslim community does not exceed 0.33 % of the population, which corresponds to 62,882 Muslims, belonging to different nationalities. Moreover, statistics about the Romanian people's interest in religious institutions and practices demonstrate that the population has a very high degree of confidence in the churches (as denominations). In fact, Romania and Poland have the greatest degree of religiosity among the former Communist countries in the Central and South-Eastern Europe (Tanase, 2008, 256-266).

If we compare the data from the national censuses of 1992, 2002, and 2011, we observe the configuration of the religious life at present and its dynamics, as well as the numerical difference expressed in percentages between the majority Orthodox religion and the other religious minorities.

Concerning the configuration of the Romanian religious life after 1989, the year of the fall of the communist regime, for a population of approximately 20 million inhabitants, we have the following chart.

T.1. ROMANIA - the religious distribution of population
Comparative interpretation between the Censuses of 1992, 2002 and 2011

Religion - Confession	1992		2002		Differences 1992 to 2002	
	Census	Percentage %	Census	Percentage %		
TOTAL	22,810,035	100.00%	21,680,974	100.00%	Number	-1,129,061
					Percentage %	-4.95%
Orthodox	19,802,389	86.81%	18,817,975	86.79%	Number	-984,414
					Percentage %	-4.97%
Roman - Catholic	1,161,942	5.09%	1,026,429	4./3%	Number	-135,513
					Percentage %	-11.66%
Greek - Catholic	223,327	0.98%	191,556	0.88%	Number	-31,771
					Percentage %	-14.23%
Reformed	802,454	3.52%	701,077	3.23%	Number	-101,377
					Percentage %	-12.63%
Pentecostal	220,824	0.97%	324,462	1.50%	Number	103,638
					Percentage %	46.93%
Baptist	109,462	0.48%	126,639	0.58%	Number	17,177
					Percentage %	15.69%
Adventist of the Seventh Day	77,546	0.34%	93,670	0.43%	Number	16,124
					Percentage %	20.79%
Unitarian	76,708	0.34%	66,944	0.31%	Number	-9,764
					Percentage %	-12.73%
Muslim	55,928	0.25%	67,257	0.31%	Number	11,329
					Percentage %	20.26%
Evangelical Christians	49,963	0.22%	62,654	0.29%	Number	12,691
					Percentage %	25.40%
Old Rite Christians	28,141	0.12%	38,147	0.18%	Number	10,006
					Percentage %	35.56%
Lutheran church (secui)	21,221	0.09%	27,112	0.13%	Number	5,891
					Percentage %	27.76%
Evangelical Church C.A. (sași)	39,119	0.17%	8,716	0.04%	Number	-30,403
					Percentage %	-77.72%
Jews	9,670	0.04%	6,057	0.03%	Number	-3,613
					Percentage %	-37.36%
Other Religions	56,329	0.25%	89,196	0.41%	Number	32,867
					Percentage %	58.35%
No Religion	24,314	0.11%	12,825	0.06%	Number	-11,489
					Percentage %	-47.25%
Atheists	10,331	0.05%	8,524	0.04%	Number	-1,807
					Percentage %	-17.49%
Undeclared Religion	8,139	0.04%	11,734	0.05%	Number	3,595
					Percentage %	44.17%
Jehovah's Witnesses	0	0.00%	0	0.00%	Number	0
					Percentage %	0.00%
Other religions, no religion, undeclared religion = NMR	88,782	0.39%	113,755	0.52%	Number	24,973
					Percentage %	28.13%

2011 Census	Percentage %	Differences 2002 to 2011		Differences 1992 to 2011	
19,043,767	100.00%	Number -2,637,207	Percentage % -12.16%	Number -3,766,268	Percentage % -16.51%
16,367,267	85.95%	Number -2,450,708	Percentage % -13.02%	Number -3,435,122	Percentage % -17.35%
869,246	4.56%	Number -157,183	Percentage % -15.31%	Number -292,696	Percentage % -25.19%
160,275	0.84%	Number -31,281	Percentage % -16.33%	Number -63,052	Percentage % -28.23%
600,970	3.16%	Number -100,107	Percentage % -14.28%	Number -201,484	Percentage % -25.11%
367,938	1.93%	Number 43,476	Percentage % 13.40%	Number 147,114	Percentage % 66.62%
118,003	0.62%	Number -8,636	Percentage % -6.82%	Number 8,541	Percentage % 7.80%
85,902	0.45%	Number -7,768	Percentage % -8.29%	Number 8,356	Percentage % 10.78%
57,558	0.30%	Number -9,386	Percentage % -14.02%	Number -19,150	Percentage % -24.96%
62,882	0.33%	Number -4,375	Percentage % -6.50%	Number 6,954	Percentage % 12.43%
60,924	0.32%	Number -1,730	Percentage % -2.76%	Number 10,961	Percentage % 21.94%
32,055	0.17%	Number -6,092	Percentage % -15.97%	Number 3,914	Percentage % 13.91%
20,580	0.11%	Number -6,532	Percentage % -24.09%	Number -641	Percentage % -3.02%
6,990	0.04%	Number -1,726	Percentage % -19.80%	Number -32,129	Percentage % -82.13%
3,823	0.02%	Number -2,234	Percentage % -36.88%	Number -5,847	Percentage % -60.47%
22,518 (cu MJ 74,328)	0.12%	Number -66,678	Percentage % -74.75%	Number -33,811	Percentage % -60.02%
23,918	0.13%	Number 11,093	Percentage % 86.50%	Number -396	Percentage % -1.63%
21,196	0.11%	Number 12,672	Percentage % 148.66%	Number 10,865	Percentage % 105.17%
84,753	0.45%	Number 73,019	Percentage % 622.29%	Number 76,614	Percentage % 941.32%
51,810	0.27%	Number 51,810	Percentage % 0.00%	Number 51,810	Percentage % 100.00%
131,189	0.69%	Number 17,434	Percentage % 15.33%	Number 42,407	Percentage % 47.77%

Source: L.D.T. – Comparative table on the data base of the 1992 Census, C.N.S., Bucharest, 1995, 296; the 2002 Census, I.N.S., vol. I, Bucharest, 2003, 802-803, and the 2011 Census, - http://www.recensamantromania.ro (Accessed September 03, 2013).

As one can observe in the table above, the traditional Churches (Orthodox, Catholic, Greek-Catholic, and Protestant) recorded a decrease in the number of believers during the 20 years between the three censuses. At the same time, the Neo-Protestant Churches (Adventist, Baptist, and Pentecostal) and the *Muslim community* recorded an important increase. Numerous factors have contributed to this demographic shift. Overall, Romania recorded a decrease in the number of inhabitants, caused in large part by a decrease in the birth-rate and the aging of the population, but also due to massive emigration to other countries of the European Union for economic reasons. The immigration rate was even greater after 2003, when the conditions for obtaining an exit visa became more flexible.

It is interesting that in all other ethnic communities, except for Muslims, the number of members has decreased by over 5% in 20 years, with most emigrating to European countries with which they have a common culture and language, such as Hungary, Austria, or Germany. In addition, others immigrated to other countries of Europe or to America in the pursuit of more attractive economic conditions and a higher standard of living.

The number of ethnic Turks in Romania increased by 7.6% (almost 2,266 people), over the last ten years. The primary reasons for this increase include the development of economic relationships with Turkey and the development of the Romanian economy, which favoured the immigration of Turkish businessmen to Romania (Tanase, 2008, 163-164).

In most cases, Muslim Turks marry women belonging to the Muslim community, but also may marry Christian-Orthodox Romanians who embrace Islam through marriage.[43] This situation somehow explains the 12% increase in the number of Muslim believers in Romania during the last 20 years, but it is not the only explanation. Also contributing are people Muslims coming from countries other than Turkey such as Syria, Saudi Arabia, Jordan, Iran, Egypt, Palestine, Pakistan, etc.

They are mostly businessmen or former students at Romanian universities who decided after graduation not to return to their home countries. Only a few of them are professionals. Instead, most of them are developing commercial *import-export* businesses, operating their own restaurants, or selling oriental merchandise. Apart from the Turk-Tatars, there are also Muslims within the Albanian community.

---

43 Interview with Mr. Yusuf Murat, the Grand Mufti of the Muslim Cult, in Romania, at the Centre of the Mufti in Constanta, February 14, 2008.

Islamic Religious Education in Romanian State Schools

Romania is one of the European countries with a state school system. The main responsibility for organising and coordinating state education in Romania rests upon the Ministry of National Education. State education is compulsory and free and includes religious education, which is predominantly confessional.

The Ministry of National Education collaborates with the Churches and religious denominations on developing the themes to be addressed (the specialised curriculum), on approving textbooks, and on training and selecting teachers. Teaching religion has constituted a real challenge both for the religious denominations and for the Romanian school system subsequent to the fall of the totalitarian political communist regime in 1989.

The new context required trained teachers of religion and new appropriate curricula paired with proper textbooks. Additionally, studies of the Psychology of Religion, methodologies of teaching religion and school guides for assessment were developed (Timis, 2006, 41). The Ministry of National Education, for no charge, provides the curricula and textbooks used for teaching in the mother-tongues of minorities. Since the ethnic component is strongly interconnected with the Muslim religious component, the teachers that teach Turkish language usually also teach the Islamic religion.

The presence of religion in state schools responds to a social reality, both Romanian and European, a social reality that is characterized by vast religious, ethnic, and cultural diversity. In the opinion of the governmental representatives, the objectives of religious education allow "learning about one's own religious identity and overcoming prejudice, as well as favouring the manifestation of tolerance and respect towards other beliefs and convictions" (Horga, 2006, 26).

Within the state education in Romania, all traditional churches and all recognised religious denominations have the right to teach their own religions. This approach involves an important confessional feature. The curricula include general outcomes and specific objectives that all sects have in common. However, at the level of the themes that are actually taught, the different sects use different approaches, the content being organised around their teaching: catechism, the history of the group, traditions, and specific religious practices, all with a practical and applied side and exercised in ritual contexts. Apart from these topics specific to each religious group, students in high school also study intercultural and inter-religious themes under the rubric of the History of Religions or Christian Morality (Horga, 2006, 35).

Education in the State School System
for the Muslim Turk-Tatar Community

For the minority community of the Muslim Turk-Tatars, mother-tongue teaching (Turkish and Tatar) relates to the teaching of Islam, as it is also taught in their own language. More precisely, the teacher that teaches the Turkish language usually teaches Islam to the same children (Interview with Ms. Ene Ulgean). The geographical representation of the Turk-Tatar communities in Romania is specific to Dobrogea and to the South-Eastern part of Romania, where we find instruction in these mother tongues in localities such as: Constanta, Medgidia, Cobadin, Mangalia, Valu lui Traian, Fântâna Mare, Tuzla, Castelu, Basarabi, Tulcea, Eforie Sud, București (Department for interethnic relations, 2006, 46-47).

The general outcome for the teaching of Islam in Romanian state schools is to "form the student's personality in accordance with religious values, by integrating this knowledge in developing a moral-religious attitude and by applying Islamic teachings in personal life as well as in the life of the community" (Curriculum for Grade 1, 2004). The aim of teaching religion is to "offer students the possibility of learning and understanding the principal characteristics of their own religious confession" (Curriculum for Grade 1, 2004).

After a thorough analysis of the curricula and while trying to find common elements between the primary, middle, and high school materials, we have identified the following educational outcomes:

Table 1 Comparative table with the reference educational outcomes for the main educational levels

Educational outcomes by Grade Level	Primary school (Grades 1 through 4)	Middle school (Grades 5 through 8)	High school (Grades 9 through 12)
Educational outcomes	- learning about and loving God/Allah, as the fundament of man's fulfilment; - showing knowledge of and using appropriately language in the sphere of religious values; - showing knowledge of Koranic teachings, of religious traditions and of the history of the Islamic Religion; - developing Muslim virtues and consolidating moral-religious behaviour; - **inculcating attitudes of acceptance, understanding, and respect towards people of other beliefs and convictions.**	- showing knowledge of and understanding religion as the fundament of existence; - showing knowledge of the main principles of the Koran and putting them into practice in daily life; - educating with a view to achieving spiritual purity and moral correctness in accordance with the Islamic commandments; - **showing knowledge of and appropriately using language in showing tolerance towards people of other beliefs and convictions.**	- defining the specifics of their own faith, - appropriate usage of concepts specific to the Turk – Tatar Islamic culture and civilisation in various communicative contexts, - integrating religious values, and traditions and secular customs in the structure of their own attitudes and behaviour; - applying Muslim teachings in personal life as well as in community life; - correlating religious knowledge with knowledge acquired in a transdisciplinary manner.

Sources: *The Religion Curricula for Grades 1 through 12*, Ministry of Education, Research and Youth.[44]

From the comparative table above, we can observe that the objectives include an emphasis on *educating with a view to a tolerant and respectful attitude towards*

---

44 The Curricula for Muslim Religion were kindly offered to us to study by Mr. Vasile TIMIS, General Inspector for Religion in the Ministry of Education and Research and by Mr. Yusuf Murat, the Great Mufti of the Muslim Cult in Romania

people of other religious beliefs and convictions. A total of 10% to 15% of the themes of study for grades 1 through 4 are organised toward inculcating this trait in the student's character. For example, the first themes of study for second grade include the following topics:

- People live in communities
- People have different religions
- People practice their own religion
- We should respect the beliefs and traditions of others

In middle school, thematic interest in the inculcation of a tolerant and pluralistic spirit increases to almost 20% to 25%. In Grade 5 the curriculum includes general notions about religions and the relation between religion and morality, with specific aspects regarding commitments towards oneself and towards the society. Apart from this general information about religions, there is a distinct chapter of study entitled: *Tolerance toward people of other religions and convictions*, featuring the following topics:

- Showing tolerance
- What tolerance means
- What peaceful coexistence means
- How to show respect towards other's beliefs
- How to behave with neighbours, colleagues and relatives

In Grade 6 the preoccupation with cultivating *attitudes toward people and society* is structured in three important directions:

a) Freedom of conscience
b) Love and respect
   • toward human beings,
   • toward nature
   • toward moral laws
   • toward teachings
c) Non-conflictual behaviour

In Grades 7 and 8, interest in cultivating a civic and tolerant spirit decreases, while specific aspects of the Islamic religion are emphasized:

- Faith in Allah
- Faith in angels
- Faith in Holy Books and the Koran
- Faith in Prophets
- Faith in the Day of Judgment
- Ceremonies and traditions specific to the Islamic Religion
- Religious days, months and nights
- Norms of behaviour for the Muslim believer
- Concepts of Islamic history

The curriculum for high school is more attentively structured toward developing and cultivating a tolerant and pluralistic spirit. The themes of study regarding the History of Religions and general knowledge from the domain of the religious life constitute 40% to 60% of the curriculum. The main topics include:

a) The concept of religion; religion and humankind
  • The definition of religion
  • Opinions regarding the origin of religions
  • People's need for religion
  • The importance of religion from the individual as well as from the social point of view
b) Main religions of the world and their particularities
  • Hinduism, Buddhism, Confucianism, Judaism, Christianity
  • Islam
c) Religion, science and education
  • The religion – science relationship
  • Religion and education
  • The universal importance of education in general, and of religious education in particular

The curriculum for Grades 11 and 12 continues to include the study of the main religions. The interest in religious pluralism is maintained by the introduction of aspects regarding contemporary social issues:

- Christianity and the problems of the contemporary world,
- Changes in the contemporary world,
- Correct answers to the real questions of the present world.

Conclusions

Apart from the state system that supports the teaching of religion to students belonging to the Muslim Turk-Tatar community, there are no other forms of Islamic education in Romania, either funded by the state or privately, that are structured upon methodological principles and pedagogic standards.

An exception is the study of the Koran. Lessons are periodically offered by different organizations and non-governmental associations of the Muslim community that emerged in the wake of post-1990 emigration. These differ from the situation in the autochthonous ethnic Turk-Tatar community. Generally, these classes take place on weekends and are attended by a small number of students. Their goal is to familiarize Muslim children with the contents and the study of the Holy Book of Islam.

The Turk-Tatar Muslim community, completely different from the Romanian Christian majority in some respects, represents a cultural and religious richness for Romania. The resulting interreligious dialogue and religious education represent essential components of diverse ethnic identity in modern society, especially in the context of globalisation.

Within modern Europe, it is mandatory to be better acquainted with the characteristics that define specific minority communities. Such acquaintance improves understanding and communication regarding the political attitudes and values that the majority of the population wishes to promote in order to ensure the social equilibrium and cultural dialogue which should ideally characterize democratic pluralism and European citizenship.

References

Berger, P. (1971). *La religion dans la conscience moderne*. Paris: Le Centurion.

Bunescu, G. (2004). *Antologia Legilor Învăţământului din România [Anthology of the Laws of Education in Romania]*. Bucureşti: The Institute of Educational Sciences.

Constituţia României. (2003). *[Constitution of Romania]*. Monitorul Oficial.

Curriculum for Grade 1-12. (2007). *Religion*. Bucharest: The Ministry of Education, Research and Youth.

Department for interethnic relations. (2006). *Panorama invatamantului minoritatilor naţionale din Romania in perioada 2003 - 2006, Departamentul pentru relatii inter-etnice*. Bucureşti: Coresi.

Enache, S. (Ed.). (2007). *Educaţia religioasa in şcolile publice*. Targu-Mureş: Pro-Europa.

Garlan, M. A. (2007). *Ethnopsihologii minoritare in spatiul dobrogean*. Iasi: Lumen.

Horga, I. (2006). *Religious Education- European approaches and tendencies*. In: Lemeni, A. & Dedu, B. *Învăţământul religios şi teologic în România [The Religious and Theological Education in Romania]*. Sibiu: TechnoMedia.

Ibran, N. (2007). *Musulmanii din Romania [Muslims in Romania]*. Constanta: Golden Publishing House.

Iordachescu, N. (2006). *Masuri legislative referitoare la educatia religioasa si la predarea Religiei dupa 1989 [Legislative measures regarding the Theological education and teaching of Religion after 1989]*. In: Lemeni, A. and Dedu, B. *Învăţământul religios şi teologic în România [The Religious and Theological Education in Romania]*. Sibiu: TechnoMedia.

Luckman, T. (2003). "Transformations of Religion and Morality in Modern Europe". In: *Social Compass*, vol. 50 (3), 215-285

Mazilu, R. (April 9, 2006). "cetatenia europeana". In: rev. *Cadran politic – revista de analiza si informare politica*. From: www.cadranpolitic.ro (Accessed October 17, 2013).

Moravcikova, M. & Lojda, M. (Eds.). (2005). *Islam in Europe*. Bratislava.

Osman, N. S. (2007). *Tatars from Dobrogea*. In: *Karadeniz [The Black Sea]*, the Tatar comunity newspaper, no. 177/December.

Tanase, L. D. (2008). *Pluralisation religieuse et société en Roumanie*. Bern: Peter Lang.

Tanase, L. D. (2009). "Study regarding the Muslim community and the Islamic education in Romania". In: Aslan, E. (Ed.) *Islamic education in Europe*. (367-402). Bölau: Wien.

Timis, V. (2006). "Religious Education within the Curricular area of Man and Society". In: Lemeni, A. & Dedu, B. *The Religious and Theological Education in Romania*. Sibiu: TechnoMedia.

Qualitative research, the area of Dobrudja, south-east of Romania
Interview *(convorbire)*, with Ms Ene Ulgean – School Inspector, Turk – Tatar minorities, at the Muslim Collegium of Medgidia. (13.02.2008).

Interview *(convorbire)*, with Mr Yusuf Murat – Great Mufti of Muslims in Romania, at the centre of the Muftyat in Constanta (2008, 2009, 2010, 2013).

Curriculum for Grade 1, approved by the order of the Ministry of Education and Research, no 5350/ 22.11.2004.

Websites: *with useful information for the research of the Muslim Turko-Tatar community in Romania:*

www.culte.ro – *State Secretariat for the Religious Affaires* - Governmental organism within the Ministry of Culture and Cults, (*Secretariatul de Stat pentru Culte* – Organism guvernamental în componenţa Ministerului Culturii şi Cultelor).

www.dri.gov.ro – the *Department of inter-ethnic relationships (DIR)* is a governmental institution founded in 2001 and its aim is '*to be one of the main factors to promote good inter-ethnic relations, pluralism and diversity*.' The department is subordinated to the Prime Minister and is coordinated by a Secretary of State.

www.edu.ro – *Ministry of National Education, Research and Youth, (Ministerul Educaţiei Nationale).*

www.muftiyat.ro – the official website of the Mufti at of the Muslim community in Romania

www.tatar.ro – the official website of the Tatar community in Romania

www.udtr.ro – Romanian, Democratic Turkish Union.

Civil Education and Religion in Macedonia

Muhamed Ali

Civic education is one of the newly introduced subjects being taught as part of Macedonian primary and high school education. The main aim of this subject is to introduce students to concepts of human rights and freedoms, the Universal Declaration and European Conventions for human rights, and to initiate discussions around civic freedoms and duties in modern Macedonian society by studying the EU and its values, as well as the introduction of democracy to Macedonian society. At the same time, including subjects related to religion for example: ethics; religious ethics; introduction to World Religions in Macedonian primary schools is contributing to strengthening and affirming democratic values. Universal ethics, codes of state behaviour towards citizens, the society and the country are only a small part of the contents of the above-mentioned subjects that contribute toward developing civic society and promoting civic integration. The role of Islamic institutions in Macedonia must not be forgotten, as they are considered to be an important segment receiving the values derived from civic education.

Civic education in public schools in Macedonia

In the recent period (since 2008-2009), the Republic of Macedonia[45] has taken significant steps towards introducing cultural and civic educational values. In this direction, it introduced new subjects in the educational system, such as the

---

45 The name "Macedonia" originates from the old Greek or old Macedonian name Μακεδονία (*Makedonía*). The name was initially used for the Macedonian Empire, and then for the Roman province *Macedonia*, the Byzantine theme *Macedonia* and

subjects of civic education, ethics, religious ethics and introduction to religions. Through the introduction of these subjects in the curriculum of primary and high schools in the Republic of Macedonia, the government intends to equip new generations with the knowledge and skills necessary to live in a pluralistic civic society, as well as to be future citizens of the European Union.

The subject of civic education is one of the latest subjects to be introduced in the primary and high school education system in the Republic of Macedonia. This subject is being taught in years VII and VIII, respectively, and since 2009/2010 in years VIII and IX, for one academic hour per week or 36 academic hours per academic year. In order to attain the intended goals, the teaching of this subject is being carried out, both individually and in groups, with teachers using a sophisticated methodology in accordance with contemporary educational principles. The subject civic culture (education) in grade VII (in the new educational system it is year VIII) is strongly connected with other subjects in primary education such as history, the culture of European civilisation, etc. This subject aims to teach pupils to:

---

nowadays for the Macedonian region and the country Macedonia. The Republic of Macedonia is situated in the Balkan Peninsula. The country is one of the successors of former Yugoslavia and claimed its independence from it in 1991. The Republic of Macedonia occupies approximately 38% of the total surface of the Macedonian region. Geographically, the country is bordered by Serbia and Kosovo to the North, Bulgaria, to the East, Greece to the South and Albania to the West. Macedonia is a sovereign, independent, democratic and social state. The capital is Skopje. In 1993, Macedonia became a member of the United Nations, but because of a name dispute with the Republic of Greece, it was accepted as the *Former Yugoslav Republic of Macedonia*. Macedonia is also a member of the Council of Europe. Since December 2005, Macedonia has also been a candidate to join the European Union and applied to join NATO. According to the census of 2002, the Republic of Macedonia's population of 2,071,210 and is divided as follows: Macedonians - 1,297,981 (64.18%); Albanians - 509,083 (25.17%); Turks - 77,959(3.85 %); Romas - 53,879 (2.66%); Serbs - 35,939 (1.78 %): Bosnians - 17,018 (0.84%): Vlachos - 9,695 or 0,48 %, others -20,993 or 1,04%. It should be mentioned that besides its multicultural character, this country also has a multi-religious character, as Christians, Muslims, Jews and members of other religions live here. The constitution of the Republic of Macedonia offers free and obligatory primary, secondary and high school education. Primary and secondary school lasts for 9 years, while the high school for four years (or three, dependably on the school). In all other higher education, the Bologna system is applied, as there are approximately 20 institutions of higher education, some of them are public and some of them are private.

1. Learn about primary human rights and understand their value
2. Learn cultural, ecological, civil, and political rights
3. Understand connections between civil rights, freedoms and obligations
4. Understand the term "responsibility" and how to differentiate among various responsibilities towards oneself, the family, and the state of Macedonia
5. Develop skills in order to recognize cases in society where human rights are violated and democratic values are not respected
6. Understand the right to diversity and develop feeling of tolerance towards members of other civilizations and cultures
7. Learn the meaning of concepts like equality, diversity, justice, authority, property, privacy, intimacy
8. Knowing how and why human rights should be defended
9. Learn about democracy and a citizen's role in it
10. Learn about the role of citizens and civic organizations in the Republic of Macedonia
11. Learn about the foundation, role and institutions of the EU (Ugrinoski, 2009, 5-6).

On the other hand, the subject civic culture (education) of year VIII (in the new educational system it is year IX) is being taught for 1 academic hour per week, respectively 36 academic hours per academic year. This subject aims to prepare pupils to:

1. Learn what is meant by the term "power"
2. Differentiate between executive, juridical and legislative power
3. Know the primary competencies of power bearers in the Republic of Macedonia
4. Know about the forms of citizens' participation in public life
5. Stimulate the spread of tolerance towards different opinions
6. Form opinions about human values
7. Solve situations of conflict initiated on the basis of ethnicity, religion, etc.
8. Understand the vitality of media in modern society
9. Learn how to live in a society with various cultures
10. Establish a culture of peace (Kostovska, 2010, 81-82).

It should be highlighted that learning subjects related to religion such as introduction to religions, religious ethics and ethics in the educational system of Macedonia, result in the reinforcement and affirmation of democratic values in society. The subject "introduction to religions" is being taught in year V for two academic hours per week, for a total of 72 academic hours per year and it prepares pupils to:

1. Learn that human beings are religious beings – *homo religiosus*
2. Learn about monotheistic and prevalent religions in modern times
3. Learn the most distinctive elements of these religions
4. Learn how to respect diverse beliefs
5. Learn about the nature of different beliefs
6. Gain skills for dialogue with members of other religions
7. Learn about the role of religion in the maintenance of peace (Shotarovska, 2010, 104-105).

The subject "religious ethics" is being taught in year V for two academic hours per week. Through studying this subject, pupils will:

1. Be introduced to ethics as a topic related to goodness and morals
2. Be introduced to the elementary principles of ethics in Islam, Christianity, etc.
3. Learn that the ethics of religions obliges religious adherents to be humane and tolerant towards other religions
4. Learn tolerance and respect for different religions in Macedonia
5. Develop skills of tolerance, dialogue, and cooperation with other religious and ethnic communities (Ramadani, 2010, 111-112).

Another subject that introduces civic educational values is ethics, which is being taught in year VI. The teaching of this subject involves:

1. Learning about ethics and morals
2. Learning about general ethical values
3. Learning about moral obligations (Temkov, 2010, 68).

Also, it should be mentioned that the subject civic education is one of the latest subjects to be introduced in the high school educational system in the Republic of Macedonia. The purpose of this strategy is to provide new generations with values that are commensurate with European civil society.

We can see from the above that through introducing these subjects in primary and high school curricula of the Republic of Macedonia, an important effort is being made to raise civic awareness among new generations in Macedonia, who are expected to become citizens of the European Union in the near future.

The role of religious institutions within the IRC (Islamic Religious Community) in promoting values of civil education and culture

The role of Islamic institutions and activities within IRC in Macedonia should not be forgotten, as they represent an important segment in affirming and disseminating the values of civic education. In this context, we will mention the role of the following institutions and activities of the IRC:

The Isa Beg Madrasa (High school)[46] and Faculty of Islamic Studies[47]

It should be highlighted that inside these two very important institutions of Islamic Studies in Macedonia, subjects are taught that promote elements of civil education and culture. In this context, it is important to indicate these subjects:

---

46 The "Isa Beg Madrasa" continues the tradition of the former *madrasa* with the same name, established in the XV century, when the Ottomans came to this region. It holds the name of its founder, Isa Beg, who was the son of Ishaq Beg, the famous protector of Skopje. In the past, this *madrasa* represented the highest educational institution and was known as the most famous school in Rumelia. Since its establishment until today, this *madrasa* stopped functioning a few times because it was demolished by wars and other misfortunes. It stopped functioning for the first time in 1689, when the Austrian general, Piccolomini, and his army burned Skopje to the ground . After this demolition, the ruins of the walls of its buildings were kept until the beginning of World War II. After the Ottomans left this area, the *Isa Beg Madrasa* was rebuilt in 1932 under the initiative of religious leaders and intellectuals of that time, and in 1936, conditions were made to recommence its regular operation. At the same time, its program was reformed and it gained the status of a high school. After World War II, it stopped functioning again for a long period of time, until 1979, when the Islamic Community took a decision to rebuild it. After many vicissitudes, the new building was built and during the academic year 1984-85, educational activities began again. It is the only school of this type in the Republic of Macedonia. Retrieved 9 March 2014 from http://www.medrese-ja-isabeu.com/reth-medreses/

47 Besides the madrasa, within the IRC of Macedonia, the Faculty of Islamic Studies is also functioning as the highest religious institution in the country. The Faculty of Islamic Studies was founded in 1995 and commenced operation in 1997. This institution of higher education is conducting various studies and researches, especially in the field of Islamic studies (Retrieved 10 March 2014 from http://fshi.edu.mk/index.php?option=com_content&view=article&id=58&Itemid=64).

da'wah (propagating Islam), Islamic civilization, and *akhlaq* (Islamic moral education). Through these subjects, students learn the following:

1. Cultural similarities and differences, functions of religion in society
2. Islamic civilization and its distinctive characteristics
3. Relations of Islamic culture and civilization with other civilizations
4. Being a model of tolerance and cooperation inside the society where one lives
5. Coexistence in multicultural societies and the positive attitude of Islam towards this, Islam and tolerance, etc. (Medreseja Isa Beu, n.d.)

IRC's mosques and the mass media

Numerous activities in more than 600 registered mosques found in the territory of the Republic of Macedonia, religious and cultural articles in the cultural magazine "Hena e Re" (New Moon, it is being published in three languages) which functions as an organ of the IRC, the publications of the "Ilmije" association, as well as active participation in religious programs on various radio and TV stations are only a part of IRC's most important activities in the promotion of Islamic values which are in accordance with democratic values like tolerance and coexistence with members of other religious communities (Bashkësia Fetare Islame, n.d.).

Participation in the World Conference for Inter-Religious and Inter-Civilization Dialogue

Starting in 2007, the world conference for inter-religious and inter-civilization dialogue is being held every three years, under the organization of the Ministry of Culture and in cooperation with the Commission for relations with religious communities and religious groups, with religious communities in the Republic of Macedonia, as well as the Ministry of Foreign Affairs.

The most eminent participants on these conferences are heads of state and governments, ministers of foreign affairs, ministers of culture, directors/chairmen of commissions for relations with religious communities, religious leaders, representatives of religious communities and organizations, representatives of international organizations such as UNESCO, Alliance of civilizations, the Council of Europe, Organization of the Islamic conference, Arab league, World Council of Churches, International conference for religions of peace, International organization of Francophones, eminent experts and university lecturers, who deal with matters from religious and cultural perspectives.;

The First World Conference for Inter-Religious and Inter-Civilization Dialogue on the topic: "The contribution of religion towards peace, common respect and co-existence" was successfully held in 2007 in Ohrid. The Second World Conference for Dialogue between Religions and Civilizations was held in 2010 in Ohrid as well, on the topic "Religion and culture – unbreakable connections between people".

Both conferences involved numerous participants who included eminent religious leaders, intellectuals and politicians who deal with inter-religious and inter-cultural dialogue. Both conferences included participants from more than 50 countries and were followed by a hundred accredited journalists and reporters from both Macedonia and abroad. From these conferences, many common declarations were adopted and an international committee for organizing the next world conference was formed. The above mentioned two conferences made great contributions towards strengthening inter-religious dialogue, tolerance and affirming democratic values that play a vital role on respect between differences (Министерство за култура, 2013).

However, the third conference held in 2013 was boycotted by IRC, an act that caused a series of reactions. This action of the IRC authorities was justified by the discriminatory politics of the Macedonian government towards this institution and among other things, the following reasons were mentioned in the explanation for the boycott: 'Delay of Carshi Mosque rebuilding in Prilep, burned by Macedonian nationalists during the 2001 conflict, delay of Lazhec Mosque rebuilding, crosses painted on the Clock Tower in Manastir and Prilep, call for the restitution of IRC's nationalized land, separation of land for building an Islamic centre in Skopje, exclusion of Islamic elements in the centre of Skopje from the Skopje 2014 project and other reasons' (Bashkësia Fetare Islame, n.d.; Канал 5, n.d.; Lajm Maqedoni Vite, n.d.; Република Online, 2013).

Conclusions

Although civic education plays a vital role in the education of new generations with democratic values, nevertheless the everyday politics of political parties in Macedonia, whether the ones in power or opposition, have the biggest influence on the non-development and non-affirmation of civic cultural values. Furthermore, the unbalanced attitude of the Macedonian government towards certain religious communities in Macedonia damages the process of education and creating a positive civil culture.

The vitality of the role of religious communities in the promotion of civic educational values should not be forgotten. Coordination between institutions representing religious communities and policy makers in Macedonia regarding the development of long term strategies promoting civic culture should be one of the important aims of the relevant bodies in this multi-ethnic state.

Finally, it should be highlighted that introducing civic educational and cultural values to the citizens of a country is closely connected with the application and cultivation of these values in everyday life. Without sincere support for these values on the part of the country's policy makers, religious institutions, and media, we cannot talk about a genuine implementation of the values of civic education.

References

Bashkësia Fetare Islame. (n.d.) From http://bfi.mk/faqja/ (Retrieved 10 March 2014).

Bashkësia Fetare Islame. (n.d.) From: http://bfi.mk/faqja/?tag=bfi-bojkoton-konferencen-per%20bashkepunim-nderfetar (Retrieved 9 March 2014).

Канал 5 [Kanal 5]. (n.d.). From: http://www.kanal5.com.mk/vesti_detail.asp?ID=6457 (Retrieved 9 March 2014).

Kostovska, T.G. et.al. (2010). *Arsimi qytetar për klasën VIII.* Shkup: Ministria e Arsimit dhe Shkencës e Republikës së Maqedonisë.

Lajm Maqedoni Vite. (n.d.) From: http://lajmpress.com/lajme/maqedoni/20338.html (Retrieved 9 March 2014).

Medreseja Isa Beu. (n.d.) From: http://www.medreseja-isabeu.com/reth-medreses/ (Retrieved 9 March 2014).

Министерство за култура [Ministry of Culture]. (30.04.2013) From: http://www.kultura.gov.mk/index.php/odnosi-so-javnost/soopstenija/933-treta-svetska-konferencija-za-megjureligiski-i%20megjucivilizaciskidijalog (Retrieved 8 March 2014)

Ramadani, N. (2010). *Etika e religjioneve për klasën e pestë.* Shkup: Ministria e Arsimit dhe Shkencës e Republikës së Maqedonisë.

Република Online [Republic Online]. (08.05.2013). From: http://republika.mk/?p=64376 (Retrieved 9 March 2014).

Shotarovska, B. et.al. (2010). *Njohja me religjionet për klasën V.* Shkup: Ministria e Arsimit dhe Shkencës e Republikës së Maqedonisë.

Temkov, K. (2010). *Etika për klasën VI.* Shkup Ministria e Arsimit dhe Shkencës e Republikës së Maqedonisë.

Ugrinoski, K. et.al. (2009). *Arsimi qytetar për klasën VII në arsimin fillor tetëvjeçar.* Shkup Ministria e Arsimit dhe Shkencës e Republikës së Maqedonisë.

Religion and Citizenship Education

The Case of Turkey[48]

Mustafa Köylü

Introduction

In order to understand the present situation of religion and citizenship education in Turkey, a brief overview of the history of religious education in modern Turkey is required. One of the most controversial issues in Turkey since the establishment of the republic in 1923 has been the question of religious education. Why is this so? While several answers can be given to this question, the key to understanding the issue of religious education is the understanding of secularism in Turkey. One segment of the population argues that secularism prohibits the state from intervening in religious issues at all. Their operative definition of secularism is that the state and religious matters should be completely separated from each other. A larger segment of the population supports the opposite position. They believe that the teaching of religion must be statutory at all public and private schools, that religious men and women should be educated by the state, and that the religious needs of people should be adequately met. Because this group comprises the overwhelming Muslim majority in Turkey, the state cannot ignore the teaching of Islam in public schools.

The situation raises the following question: If the state accepts itself as a secular one, does it have any right to intervene in the religious beliefs and practices of people? While the answer to this question is still under debate, it remains a historical fact that all religious matters in Turkey have been under the control of the

---

48 An earlier verison of this chapter was presented at CIES 2006: 50th Anniversary Celebration Conference: Rethinking the Comparative, March 14-18, 2006, Honolulu, Hawaii.

state since the republic's establishment, and it seems that the state will continue to organize, teach, and administer all religious issues in the country.

There are a number of institutions that contribute to the teaching of Islam in Turkey. However, broadly speaking, we can divide these agents and institutions into four categories. The first category includes official religious education offered by the specialized religion teachers at public and private schools from fourth to the twelfth grades under the control of the Ministry of National Education. The second category consists of common or non-formal religious education offered by the Presidency of Religious Affairs through mosques, Quranic courses, and various published materials. The third category consists of the mass media, including TV channels (both private and state), newspapers, books, magazines, and communicational networks. The fourth category includes various religious groups and their activities related to the teaching of religion. While the first two categories are completely under the control of the state, the other two are mostly civic and independent religious teaching agencies. This chapter discusses the first category of religious education, official religious education offered by religion teachers at schools, as well as citizenship education.

A Short History of the Development of Religious Education in Public Schools

Many states have been established by Turkish people throughout history. The most influential and long lasting was the Ottoman Empire. Established in 1299, it collapsed in 1923. While basically an Islamic state with manifestations of Islamic faith evident in all aspects of its citizens' lives, the Ottoman state recognized different religions and did not distinguish between members of any religion on racial or religious grounds. The result was that Turks, Arabs, Kurds, and other ethnicities were treated as members of the Islamic community.

The so-called "golden age" of the Ottomans lasted from 1451 and 1566, a period that witnessed many technological, artistic, and architectural advances (Kazıcı, 1991, 217-270; Atay, 1983, 75-130). During the beginning of the seventeenth century, as a result of both internal and external factors, the Ottoman state began a long period of decline (Bilgiseven 1987, 188-198). Among the external factors was its contact with the West, particularly with France. As a result, French ideas about political and legal philosophy and the place of religion in the state began to penetrate into Turkey. Those ideas, along with growing European interference in Ottoman affairs, led Turkish intellectuals to debate what the Ottoman response to the challenge of the West should be. At this point, while some Turkish intellectuals grasped the concept of *nationalism* and argued that religion could be regarded as a matter of private belief of the individual, others held the view that *Islam* should be involved in every aspect of life and should form the foundation of the state and society. Ideas about nationalism and reducing religion to a matter of private, individual belief met with fierce resistance.

Overall, three rival remedies were suggested for the empire's ills, each offering a different basis on which unity might be achieved. In 1904, these were listed as: *Ottomanism*, a common citizenship and loyalty of all subjects of the empire without regard for religion or race, as had been the case in the past; *Islamism* (pan-Islamism), the union of all Muslim people in the world; and *Turkism* (or pan-Turkism), the unity of all people speaking the Turkish language. In the end, neither Ottomanism nor Islamism could prevail against a rising tide of nationalism, resulting in the collapse of the Ottoman Empire and leading the Turkish people to establish a new state, "a secular, democratic, and social legislative" entity called the Republic of Turkey (Norton, 1988, 390-398). Of course, this decisive change in the structure of the state affected religious life and the religious education of Turkish people, as well.

Although many reforms were actualized in the new state (Reed, 1954, 269), the most important reform was the acceptance of secularism. As Nyrop writes: "As Islam had formed the identity of the Ottoman subject and empire, so secularism would form the identity of the new Turkish man and nation" (Nyrop, 1973, 120). The Ministry of Interior at the time explained this principle as follows: "We say that...religions should stay in the internal forum (conscience) and places of worship should not be mixed with material life and worldly concerns" (Mardin, 1982, 180). With the acceptance of secularism, religion was separated from the legal, educational, and cultural life of Turkish people. The state not only declared itself to be secular, but it also took severe precautions to control and direct religious affairs and to keep them out of the political sphere. For this purpose, the Grand National Assembly (GNA) passed a criminal code in 1926, which lays down penalties for "those who, by misuse of religion, religious sentiments, or things in that area religiously considered as holy, in any way incite the people to action prejudicial to the security of the state, or form associations for this purpose...Political associations on the basis of religion and religious sentiments may not be formed (Article 163)" (Lewis, 1968, 412). As Elisabeth Ozdalga notes, Turkish secularism was concerned not only with clearing the state apparatus of religious influences, but also with restricting the influence of religion as a belief and faith system (Ozdalga, 1992, 332).

The effects of secularist reform on people were immediate. Between 1924-1937, there was a notable decline in public worship and traditional Muslim feasts and observations. While most religious specialists known as *ulema* were pensioned (Shaw-Kural, 1977, 385), the authorities imposed very immediate and strong penalties on those who did not want to accept the reforms of Atatürk (Mardin, 1982, 181). As a result of these state reforms, particularly those promoting secularism, Islam became a department of the state and the religious specialists (*ulema*) became minor religious servants (Norton, 1988, 403). In fact, the task of the state's Department of Religous Affairs was to ensure that religion was to be in the service of the state and to control all training for religious positions, as well the salaries and appointments of all religious officials. The aims of the Religious Affairs Department (Diyanet), which was set up under direct control of the prime minister in 1924, also indicated this truth.[49]

With regard to religious education in schools, one of the most important decisions – which is still operative – was the acceptance of "the Law of Unified Education" on March 3, 1924. Before the establishment of the Republic of Turkey, three kinds of education were offered to the students in the Ottoman Empire: 1) the *madrasa* curriculum, which mostly consisted of traditional Islamic courses, closing its eyes to modern developments and evaluating other approaches as disbelief (*kufr*), 2) new schools opened by some Western countries, which groomed their students in Western culture and argued that the religion of Islam was the cause of the backwardness of Ottoman Empire, and 3) "missionary" schools whose teachers were foreigners or belonged to other minority groups in the Ottoman Empire. These three institutions behaved with animosity towards each other, accusing one another of being nonreligious, bigots, or traitors (Ayhan, 1999a, 23-31; Cebeci, 1999, 227-228; Haydaroğlu, 1993, 183-212). As a result of these developments, the Law of Unified Education enacted in 1924 aimed to produce students who had similar outlooks, aims, and objectives.

The principle of secularism negatively affected religious education at schools throughout the history of republic. Although the Grand National Assembly (GNA) did not enact any detrimental decisions concerning religion courses, such courses were abolished from urban schools and later from rural schools in 1931 and 1939, respectively. Szylowicz addresses the subsequent removal of religion courses from rural schools: "There it [religion] remained a part of the curriculum though it was placed within the framework of a liberal philosophy emphasizing respect for different beliefs, avoidance of fanaticism and fatalism, and the importance of good citizenship" (Szyliowich, 1973, 202).

---

49 Its purpose was defined as follows: "To direct the affairs pertaining to the beliefs of the Muslim religion and to the foundation of worship and morals; to enlighten the population on the subject of religion; and to administer places of worship."

Thus, religion courses were absent from the general educational system of Turkey between the years 1931 and 1949 (Ayhan, 1999b, 250). However, due to the fear of spreading Communism and the increase in immoral behavior among younger generations, even some deputies of the Republic People's Party, which was and still is mostly opposed to compulsory religious education in schools began to discuss its necessity and importance. As a result of these social and psychological needs, religion courses were introduced into the fourth and fifth grades as elective courses that required parental consent in 1949.

The Minister of Education of that time explained the situation as follows:

> Those parents who did not want their children to take the religion course had to give a petition to the school's administration, but only one professor from Ankara brought me a letter concerning the religion course. I had expected that Alawi people would not make their children take this course, but all Alawi people including some Armanies from Sivas sent their children to take this course (Ayhan, 1999b, 251).

In addition to not being compulsory, the course, while part of the school program, was taught after school during the afternoon and did not affect receiving a passing grade. In addition, as Münir Koştaş points out, the course book was prepared in such a modern style that neither Meccan nor Damascene Muslims could understand it easily (Koştaş, 1999, 192-193). These developments continued in the next years of the republic, and religion courses were added to the first two years of middle school in 1956. The program was further expanded by the government to the first and second grades of high school (for an hour a week) upon receipt of thousands of letters from the population and two hundred petitions from the deputies of the GNA (Koştaş, 1999, 195). Despite the program's continuing until 1982, the students' needs for religious knowledge and practices were not adequately addressed. In fact, as Mardin states: "This instruction was seen as a thin and useless propaganda course which had been placed in the same slot as music and physical education" (Mardin, 1982, 191).

Another important decision concerning religion courses in Turkey was made in the Constitution of 1982 and remained in effect until 2007. With the acceptance of the 1982 Constitution, religion courses were made compulsory for all students from the fourth grade of primary school to the last grade of high school. Thus, two credit hours a week for the fourth to the eighth grades and one credit hour for the high school students became compulsory. This regulation applied to all private and public schools.

The Present Situation of Religious Education

Before preceding to the content of religion textbooks, it is necessary to identify the current context as well as some important features of religious education in Turkey. First, since religion courses are required at both public and private schools, there is not much debate at present concerning its legal status. Instead, discussion focuses on course content and teaching methods.

Secondly, religious instruction in Turkey does not aim to inspire in the students an identity rooted in a nation-transcending Muslim community (*umma*), as was the case in some Muslim countries (Leirvik, 224). The goal was to develop a national Turkish identity. Education in general, and religious education in particular, has traditionally been used as a tool for promoting a certain set of ideological, religious, or nationalist perspectives in many countries (Leirvik, 223). This is especially true for Turkey. When we examine the general aims of school education from primary school to the university, we clearly see this aspect of education. Law number 1739 of the Basic Law on National Education (June 14, 1973) defines the major objectives of the Turkish educational system as follows:

> Educating citizens to be aware of their duties and responsibilities towards the Government of the Turkish Republic, which is democratic, secular and social legislative government based on human rights and the basic principles explained in the initial part of the Constitution.

> Educating them to become individuals having free and scientific intellectual power, having a comprehensive philosophy of life, respectful of human rights, esteeming personality and entrepreneurship, and feeling responsible to society, constructive, creative and productive.

Supporting this building of national identity is the teaching of Kemalism and the Principles of Atatürk in every grade from the primary school to the university level. The principles of Atatürk, named after Mustafa Kemal Atatürk, the founder of the Republic of Turkey, have had a great impact on the teaching of religion. The thoughts and sayings of Atatürk are interspersed in almost all subjects, including those related to religious instruction.

Thirdly, although Muslims traditionally believe that the only true religion is Islam and that other religions (be they Judaism or Christianity) are corrupted, the religious textbooks typically display great tolerance towards other religions and their followers. There is an emphasis on freedom of religion for people of other faiths. According to Article Four of the Basic Principles of Religion Courses, those students who are Christians and Jews are not compelled to memorize the words for bearing witness to belief in Islam (There is no God, but Allah and Muhammad is His messenger) or Qur'anic verses, or required to learn information concerning practicing the five daily Islamic prayers, fasting, giving alms, and pilgrimage to Mecca. In addition, these students are not evaluated in these subjects. Their instruction about Islam is limited to some moral imperatives and general knowledge about Islam and other religions. According to another decision issued in 1990, when a Christian or Jewish student brings a document indicating that he or she is a Christian or a Jew, the student is completely exempted from studying religion in all grades. If they want to take these courses, their parents must give a petition to the school administration stating that they want their children to take these courses (Tebliğler Dergisi, 1990, 553).

Fourth, although religion courses are confessional (Islamic) in nature, there is no coercion of students regarding its practice in their daily lives. The aim of these courses is simply to give information to students about Islamic teaching and moral behavior. This approach is a result of the understanding of the concept of secularism as it applies to religious education. In fact, the aims of religion courses clearly display a focus on secularism. In the process of teaching religion it is said that the principle of secularism will always be taken into consideration. Thus, the freedom of religion, conscience, and thought will be protected (M.E.B. 2000, 93-94). The curriculum of religious courses focuses on faith, worship, and ethics and tends to ignore the social and political dimensions of Islam. This is the case not only for formal religious education, but also for all kinds of religious education in Turkey. As a whole, the Turkish textbooks for religious education serve to sanctify the nation and legitimate secularism by rationalizing Islamic precepts such as religious freedom (Günay, Güngör & Ecer, 1997, 109-156).

Religion Textbooks and Their Characteristics

There have recently been great changes in both contents and methods in the teaching of religion in Turkey. In 2005, textbooks for religious education in primary and secondary schools were revised completely from their 1992 format. The new program has two aims, one called 'general' and the other 'special.' Among the general aims, the importance of the principles of secularism and Kemalism, the unity and integrity of Turkish people, and material and spiritual values are again stressed. The special aims section contains 38 principles. These principles aim to educate students to become more tolerant of others and more open to other faiths (M.E.B. 2005a, 1-3). For example, Principle 9 states that students should recognize that various religious understandings and applications are not related to the essence of religion, but are a social reality. He/she should accept that secularism must be the guarantor of freedom of religion and conscience (Principle 31). He/She should know that Islam is the religion of peace (Principle 32) and recognize the points common among world religions (Principle 37) (M.E.B. 2005a, 3).

An interesting aspect of this reform is the influence that Turkey's candidacy to the European Union may have had on the process. While maintaining its national focus, the revised Turkish curriculum may also be seen as responding to some extent to European Union demands for multicultural education. As a result, school education aims to encourage students to increase understanding and respect among people of different religions or world views as supported by Oslo Coalition on Freedom of Religion and Belief (Jackson, 2004, 7). Although Muslims formally constitute almost 99 percent of the Turkish population, religious education provides some space for teaching about other religions and developing more tolerant attitudes towards the followers of other faiths. The next section of this chapter will discuss specific topics from the new Turkish religious education textbooks.

Islam and Peace

In the religious education textbooks, great emphasis is placed on peace. For example, under the heading "Peace at home, peace abroad," the sixth-grade textbook quotes Atatürk: "Unless we are compelled to fight against an enemy, we should strive for peace, for our ancestors lived with others peacefully through history and showed great tolerance towards their religions, languages, and customs" (M.E.B. 2005b, 55). In the section "Islam is the Religion of Love and Peace," these remarks are made:

> Islam gives a great importance to peace and love. Our religion has been sent to all humanity for living with peace, justice, and love, and acquiring the happiness of both this world and the next world. "The Muslim is a peaceful person." The source of peace and happiness is love. A verse is mentioned in relation to peace: "O ye who believe! Embrace peace whole-heartedly..." (Qur'an, 2:208).

Throughout the textbooks peace is always a focus. Based on certain Qur'an verses and Hadith, it is said that all people in the world are like the members of the same family. The father of all human beings is Adam. This statement is supported by a Qur'an verse (49:13). In addition, a *hadith* of the Prophet is mentioned: "O people! Your God is one; your father is one and the same, you are all the children of Adam" (Muslim, Hajj, 147). Thus, Islam calls for peace not only for and among

Muslims living in Turkey, but also for and among people living in other parts of the world (M.E.B. 2005b, 85-86).

The textbook also emphasizes that Islam is a universal religion that embraces all human beings regardless of their religions, nationalities, colors and languages, for Allah is the God of all creatures, and the Prophet Muhammad was sent to all human beings. Later some examples are given from Sufi sayings to indicate their tolerance, love, and respect towards others.

In the eleventh-grade religion textbooks, a whole unit, "Islam and Peace," is dedicated to peace. The unit contains five chapters: 1) Living in peace is obligatory, 2) Islam gives great importance to living in peace and unity, 3) Saving one life is like saving the lives of all of humanity, 4) Muhammad is the Prophet of Peace, and 5) Unless it is unavoidable, war is a crime against humanity.

The most important topic in this unit is the case of war. It is argued that peace is the basic rule for human beings while war is an exception. After discussing the harms of war for people and society, it is said that the main objective of Islam is to establish peace. Because of that the Qur'an commands Muhammad (and, by extension, all Muslims), "But if the enemy inclines towards peace, do thou (also) incline towards peace…" (Qur'an, 8: 61). War is unwanted and, therefore, the last remedy. Killing is absolutely forbidden by Islam. Later, the text discusses situations in which war may be permitted, such as defending the country and religion and protecting the safety of life and property. But, even in cases of war, only active combatants may be killed. Apart from unusual situations, waging war or causing war is blameworthy (Kızıler & Koçak, 2005, 78-80).

At the end of the course, the students are to have acquired the following dispositions:

- Peace is an important factor for humanity.
- Islam is the religion of peace, which students should be able to support by giving references from Qur'an verses and *hadith* reports,
- Islam gives great importance to the right to life.
- Atatürk gives importance to the issue of peace.
- As long as it is not a necessity, war is a crime against humanity (M.E.B. 2005a, 52).

The religious education textbooks also focus on the unity and integrity of Turkish citizens without taking into consideration their religion, nationality, and ethnic background. For example, in the sixth grade textbook it is said that people of various religious and ethnic backgrounds had lived for centuries in peace and unity as citizens of the Ottoman Empire. In Turkey, every citizen has equal rights and responsibilities. Every Turkish citizen has the right to property, association, accepting any religion, and freedom of thought and speech (M.E.B. 2005b, 52).

Islam and Other Religions in Religious Education Textbooks

Kaymakcan, who studies the teaching of other religions in Turkish religious education textbooks, notes that there is no separate textbook devoted to Christianity, Judaism, or any other religion. However, some discussion of world religions, including primal religions, takes place in the textbooks. Islam distinguishes between Judaism, Christianity, and other religions. The first two are accepted as divine religions while the others are defined as non-divine religions. As a result of this classification, while Judaism and Christianity are presented on the basis of Qur'an verses, the other religions are explained in a descriptive way, providing brief data about their emergence, doctrine, scripture, and worship from their own points of view without making any reference to their contemporary forms. Since they are accepted as non-divine religions from the beginning, no criticism of them from a Muslim or other perspective is apparent (Kaymakcan, 1999, 284).

As we have seen, religion courses as a whole are mostly related to the Islamic faith system and values, but other examples of teaching about other religions are present. For example, in the sixth grade there is a unit called "Let's Recognize the Sacred Books." In this unit, four great books, the Torah, Psalms of David, Gospel, and Qur'an, are examined. Definitions of the sacred books are provided, followed by some basic information. Included in the information is: All sacred books are sent by Allah. There is no difference among them in terms of their being sent by God. Mentioning some verses from the Qur'an, it states that, "The Bible was sent by God to the Children of Israel. It is the sacred book of Christians. It contains the life of Jesus Christ, various difficulties met by Jesus when he proclaimed the message of God to people, and some admonitions concerning the peace and prosperity of people. Three pages concerning the Torah, Bible and Qur'an are presented in the textbooks (M.E.B. 2005b, 95).

In addition, it is said that believing in the sacred books is one of the basic principles of Islam. Therefore, every Muslim must believe in these books without making any distinction among them, for they all were sent by God. Concerning this belief, the following Qur'an verse is mentioned: "The messenger believeth in what hath been revealed to him from his Lord, as do the men of faith, each one (of them) believeth in God, His angels, His books, and His messengers. 'We make no distinction (they say) between one and another.'" (Qur'an, 2:285). It is said that all sacred books talk about the oneness and presence of God and the necessity of praying to God. They all prescribe good behavior and prohibit all kinds of evil behavior. They all want people to live in peace, love, happiness, and brotherhood/ sisterhood. In short, it is said that all sacred books have the same messages for human beings. Later, some admonitions from these sacred books are given (M.E.B. 2005b, 91-100).

More detailed information about other religions is given in the seventh grade. In the 7th unit of the seventh grade textbook called "Living Religions and Their Common Features," there are four basic subjects. The first is a general overview of living world religions. This topic contains the Abrahamic religions (Judaism, Christianity, and Islam), Asian religions (Hinduism, Chinese, and Japanese traditions), and some traditional religions. The second covers common points regarding religion, faith, and moral principles. The third discusses environmental awareness in religion. The fourth reviews global interreligious relations. The outcomes for students of this unit are:

• He/she should recognize the major features of the world religions.
• He/she should recognize that divine religions have doctrinal, practical, and moral features,
• He/she should know the common universal values taught by divine religions.
• He/she should be able to compare the various beliefs about God, the next world, prophecy, and sacred books.
• He/she should respect the thoughts of people of different faith.
• He/she should accept that the respect for faith is a basic requirement for providing societal peace and quiet.
• He/she should recognize that interreligious relations are very important on a global scale.
• He/she should gain knowledge about the misuse of missionary activities (M.E.B. 2005a, 37).

As to the content of other religions, their belief systems, prayers, and some ethical values are mentioned without making any comparisons among them. In addition to the information, there are pictures of sacred places belonging to these religions. The focus is only on brief and concrete information; evaluations or critiques of these world religions are absent. As an illustration, the following is said about Christianity. It is one of the largest religions today, with 20 percent of the world population believing in Christ. The prophet of Christianity is Jesus. (Muslims believe that Jesus is a prophet.) Belief in the Trinity, prayers, holidays, places of prayer, the men of religion and some principles of faith are explained (M.E.B. 2005c, 105-115).

In the 8th grade, there is one more unit about other religions called "Universal admonitions of Islam and other religions." In this unit, some information concerning moral conduct is given, but without any information about the belief systems of these religions. In this context, positive behavior is identified as cleanliness, righteousness, helping each other, showing love and respect for people, kindness to animals, and protecting the environment. Negative behavior includes dangerous habits, harming others, killing, stealing, and lying.

Although the major world religions are taught in the religious education textbook, consideration must be given to whether the teachings of world religions are accurately presented. For the purposes of this chapter, Patrick Bartsch's analysis of the teaching of Christianity is utilized. Bartsch identifies six positive elements and seven negative points or omissions regarding Christianity that are presented in Turkish religious education textbooks.

He cites the following positive points:

1. In the religion textbooks, respectful language is used for describing Christianity, and Christianity, like Judaism, is depicted as a divine religion by the Qur'an.
2. Jesus Christ is presented as an important element of Christianity. He is accepted as a great prophet in the Qur'an. As a result, his teaching is very important.
3. Some information concerning the sacred books of Christianity is given. Some quotations from the Bible are presented, and the teaching of Jesus is emphasized.
4. Some important teachings of Christianity receive attention. Christian thinking about the crucifixion of Jesus and his resurrection is presented. In addition, belief in the Trinity is mentioned and this belief is indicated as being the biggest difference between Islam and Christianity.
5. The major sects of Christianity such as Catholicism, Orthodoxy, and Protestantism are indicated and some prayers and the concept of religiousness in Christianity are mentioned.
6. After giving information about Christianity, some material about missionary activities and methods is presented.

Besides these positive elements concerning the teachings of Christianity in Turkish religious education textbooks, Bartsch identifies some omissions and makes suggestions for improving it. They are as follows:

1. Very brief information about Christianity is given. Although various ideas concerning Christianity are presented, in general, the traditional Islamic con-

cepts about Christianity are dominant. Because of that many Christians think that their religion is taught improperly. Directly or indirectly, Christianity is judged negatively and depicted as irrational.

2. The identity of Jesus is depicted according to Qur'an verses. His birth is seen as a miracle, and some of his miracles and teachings are mentioned. However, all are presented from an Islamic point of view. When a Christian reads this information, he or she cannot recognize that it is Christianity. In addition, belief in the Trinity is explained not from a Christian, but instead from an Islamic perspective.

3. Regarding the sacred books of Christianity, insufficient and even incorrect information is given. In general, Muslims talk about four Gospels and claim that these books contain many historical mistakes and were chosen from among many Gospels by the Council of Nicaea in 325. Most of this information is wrong. Although much research in relation to the Gospels has been done, the results of this research are not taken into consideration in the textbooks.

4. The Trinity is interpreted incorrectly. On account of these explanations, most Muslims think that Christians believe in three gods. However, the Trinity has a very special meaning for Christians.

5. Although three important sects of Christianity (Catholicism, Protestantism and Orthodoxy) are given place, there is very limited information about them.

6. Missionary activities are represented in a very negative light. These kinds of efforts are depicted as deceiving Muslims and proclaiming Christianity. In fact, Muslims do the same thing. Everyone tries to convert other people to his/her religion. In addition, while these textbooks talk about the missionary activities of Christians, they do not talk about any useful works of Christians such as interreligious dialogue, working for poor people, global ethics, and other activities.

7. Lastly, in the textbook, only some basic information about the faith and teachings of Christianity is given. However, the teaching of Christianity may be made more vivid, realistic, and lively by listening to a Christian student or a priest in class or visiting a church. Thus, more accurate knowledge about Christianity may be acquired.

What should be done to improve the teaching of Christianity? Bartsch suggests that:

1. Christianity should not be taught from the perspective of Muslims, but from the perspective of Christian sects.

2. Some topics such as the crucifixion of Jesus, his resurrection, and the Trinity should not be taught superficially, but in theological depth.
3. The central role of Jesus Christ in Christianity should be emphasized.
4. In fact, the chapter on Christianity should be written by Christian experts and theologians from a Christian perspective. This is a better solution (see Bilgin, 2005, 334-339).

Teaching Christianity is not problematic in Turkey because the religion is accepted by the Qur'an as being divinely revealed. No Muslim can ignore this truth. However, since there is limited informaton about Christianity in the Qur'an, and the writers of the textbooks do not have enough knowledge about it, they may make some mistakes about Christianity. Therefore, as Bilgin suggests, the chapters on Christinaity may be written by those who are originally Christian or know Christianity well, or, after being written, these chapters may be reviewed and edited by Christian theologians (Bilgin, 2005, 339). In fact, by doing this, Turkish students would have a chance to learn about Christianity or other religions more accurately, and thus some prejudices and misunderstanding about religions may be prevented.

Secularism and the Freedom of Religion

One of the most important topics of focus in the religious education textbooks is secularism. Secularism is accepted as the guarantee of the freedom of religion. In the 8th grade textbook, it is said that a secular state leaves people to their own conscience, whether they believe in any religion or not. This is completely a matter of individual choice. Concerning this subject, Atatürk is quoted: "Secularism is not just the separation between religious and state matters, it also means that all Turkish citizens have the right to the freedom of belief, worship, and conscience" (M.E.B. 2005d; 94).

After giving some information about the necessity of religion in the lives of people and societies, it states that there is no compulsory religion. In order to support the idea of secularism, two verses are cited from the Qur'an: "Let there be no compulsion in religion: Truth stands out clear from error..." (Qur'an, 2:256), and "The messenger's duty is but to proclaim (the message). But Allah knoweth all that ye reveal and ye conceal" (Qur'an, 5:99). It is also argued that the prophet Muhammad never used any force against unbelievers during his lifetime. In addition to these Qur'an verses and hadiths, it is also mentioned that the freedom of religion is guaranteed by law in Article 24.

Later, the textbooks claim that Islam is also open to secularist thought. At no time in history, did Muslims interfere with the people of other faiths. According to Islam, there is no compulsion in religious matters. In Islam, tolerance, and freedom of religion and conscience are essential. (M.E.B. 2005d, 95). Thus, every Turkish citizen has the right to select his or her religion and live it accordingly. It is also stressed that secularism is not irreligiousness. The words of Atatürk are quoted about this point: "Secularism is not absolute irreligiousness, but...it provides for true development of religiousness" (M.E.B. 2005d, 95).

The subject of secularism is found in the curriculum of high schools, too. In the 9th grade textbook, there is a separate unit called "Secularism and Religion." This unit covers the following topics: 1) Religion is basically an individual concern, 2) The reasons for promoting secularism, 3) the secular state, 4) secularism guarantees freedom of religion and conscience, and 5) Atatürk's understanding of secularism. This unit also defines secularism, and advances the importance and the necessity of the secular state. It is also argued that secularism is not irreligiousness, but guarantees religious faith and practice. Later, sayings of Atatürk about this subject are cited. (İşler, 81-86).

Rights, Freedoms, and Religion

In the 10th grade text there is a unit called "Rights, freedoms and religion." There are six basic topics in this unit. These are: 1) The concept of rights and freedoms, 2) some rights, freedoms, and religion (the right to life, health, education, prayer, privacy, and economic rights; freedom of thought, and faith), 3) applied rights and freedoms, 4) some habits that restrict the expression of rights and freedoms, 5) the supremacy of law, and 6) the abuse of human rights is a great sin.

Special importance is given to the right to life. It is said that the most important and sacred right is the right to life. This right is valid for everybody without any discrimination based on religion, language, and nationality. Killing anyone is accepted as the biggest sin. Even during the time of war, there is a distinction between combatants and non-combatants. Thus, those who do not participate actively in war are excluded from fighting. At the same time, Islam forbids suicide. Again, the freedom of religion is emphasized by the title of the freedom of faith (Kızıler & Koçak, 2005, 74-90).

After teaching of this unit, it is expected that

- Students can interpret the concepts of rights and freedoms.
- Students can explain the importance of these rights and freedoms for both individuals and society.
- Students will know that Islam supports these basic human rights and freedoms and be able to give some examples from the basic Islamic sources.
- Students will know the limits of using of these rights and freedoms.
- Students will be aware of their own rights and freedoms, and when it is necessary, they will seek their own rights.
- They will respect others' rights and freedoms, etc. (M.E.B. 2005a, 12).

Citizenship and Human Rights Education

As in most countries, human rights education at the primary and secondary school levels in Turkey was not a distinct subject until 1995. In spite of this, human rights and democracy have been stressed at all educational levels since the establishment of the Republic of Turkey. The Turkish constitution states that individuals should have inviolable, inalienable fundamental rights and freedoms and educational rights and duties.

When the primary education curricula that have been operative in Turkey from the first years of Republic to the present are examined, it may be observed that the main objective of primary school is to educate students to become "good citizens." According to the Primary Education Curriculum of 1926, primary education aimed to develop students who would effectively adapt to their environment. For this reason, the curriculum adopted the "collective education" principle that would be realized through the subject "Knowledge of Life." In 1930-31, the curriculum evolved to include the subject of "Civics" in the 2nd and 3rd grades of secondary schools. This was later renamed "Civic Education," and information on the topics of human rights and democracy was added. The Curriculum of 1932 aimed at "providing the child with true basic thoughts on the rights and responsibilities of the citizens in a democratic country, to make them aware of their role in their society." In the Primary Education Curriculum of 1936, the main objective of primary education was defined as ending illiteracy and the "Civics" program of the 3rd grade continued its aim to bring up well-mannered and tolerant citizens. In the Primary Education Curriculum of 1948, four objectives were set for National Education. These were "social relations," "individual relations," "human relations," and "economic life." With their advent, the curriculum sought to train students to respect each other's rights and opinions and to obey some rules in daily life.

In addition to these school programs, a decision about teaching and interpreting the Universal Declaration of Human Rights in schools and other educational institutions and broadcasting related subjects through the radio and newspapers was made by the Cabinet on April 6, 1949. This was followed in August 1949 with the presentation of a report on "Democracy Education" by the Ministry of National Education at the Convention of 4th National Education Council. The report explained the main facts about democracy education and its objective of educating the citizens of the future. The Primary Education Curriculum of 1968 and 1988 defined one of the main objectives of the education as enabling students to live in a democratic system by emphasizing that the individual is of value.

However, the most positive steps towards Human Rights Education were taken in the 1990s. The Ministry of National Education and Ministry Responsible for Human Rights signed a protocol concerning human rights education, adopting the following provisions:

- Change Civics Education in Primary Education to "Civics and Human Rights Education"
- Insert the subject "Democracy and Human Rights" into Upper-Secondary Education Programs
- Further improve the education programs of formal and non-formal educational institutions regarding democracy and human rights
- Organize in-service training courses and workshops for all teachers of human rights

Due to these positive developments, since the academic year 1995-1996, two hours of "Civics and Human Rights Education" is taught in the 8th grade in primary education. This was followed in the 1997-1998 academic year by the implementation of Law No. 4306 on "permanent eight-year compulsory primary education," through which the course was re-designated to last one hour a week in both the 7th and 8th grades of primary schools.

The Main Objectives of this Civics and Human Rights Education Course

The major principles of this course can be summarized as follows:

- Becoming aware of people regarding human rights and their sincere wish to use and maintain them, and comprehending the reason for maintaining them, as well as knowing what, why, and how they can be maintained, may only come true through their education.
- It should be explained that the level of contemporary civilization has been achieved as the result of the efforts of humanity, and it is necessary to approach people with tenderness and respect in an unprejudiced and tolerant way.
- Awareness should be acquired in order for people to use their basic rights and freedoms completely and continually without discrimination on the basis of birth, in an indispensable, non-transferable, immune way.

In light of these principles, the general objectives of the course can be listed as follows:
-
- Providing an awareness of being human
- Emphasizing the moral dimension of human rights
- Providing awareness of citizenship
- Teaching rights acquired and responsibilities undertaken by citizenship
- Stressing the role of the individual in protecting human rights
- Informing students on the duties and responsibilities of a democratic government towards its citizens
- Providing students with the knowledge of and the ability to use basic rights and freedom as a citizen
- Emphasizing that human rights are for all people, indispensable, non-transferable, and intact, without discrimination by birth
- Stressing the necessity for the maintenance of human rights
- Emphasizing the importance of the principle "Peace in the country, peace in the world" for humanity (Kepenekçi, 2000, 16-17)

When we look at the outline of the human rights course at the 7th grade, we see the following basic topics:

- Basic principles on humanity's common heritage
- Basic principles on human rights
- Basic principles on moral and human rights

- Maintaining and advocating for human rights
- Basic principles on basic rights and freedoms

The outline of human rights course at the 8th grade is as follows:

- Basic principles on "Citizenship, Rights and Responsibilities of Citizens"
- Basic principles on "Maintenance of Human Rights"
- Problems to be confronted in the maintenance of human rights
- The role of education in maintaining and protecting human rights

In Turkey, there are other activities for promoting human rights and democracy as well. In this vein, the Ministry of National Education invites teachers to attend courses and workshops, sometimes in cooperation with other public and non-governmental organizations, to achieve the objectives of human rights education set out in these programs. The aims of all the courses and activities are to provide a better society for the citizens of Turkey in light of universal and fundamental values that have been developed in human history.

Thus far I have tried to explain the situation of religious and human rights education in Turkey. In both, Turkey has gained great experience and moved towards a more tolerant and sophisticated curriculum. However, there are some critiques and objectionable aspects, too. Two scholars have done important analyses of the content and methods of religious and human rights education.

Fatma Gök, who analyzed Turkish textbooks for civics and human rights education, critiqued the following topics: gender inequality; the concept of Turkish citizenship; prejudices and intolerance towards certain other nations and their people; exalting performing military service and dying for one's country, martyrdom, approval of violence and war under some circumstances; emphasizing the authority of the state; stressing responsibilities and duties rather than rights; basing citizenship on Turkish ethnicity; sanctifying certain authorities such as the state, constitution, and Atatürk's thought; promoting Turkish nationalism and militarism (Gök, 2003, 158-171). As a teaching method, she argues that the textbooks on human rights are mostly informative and teacher centered. She argues that they should be more student centered, and remote from any kinds of prejudices and intolerances.

The same complaints apply to the religion course. Bülent Akdağ, who examined all textbooks of religion from the perspective of human rights, critiques the following points: the emphasis on the role of the state and its sanctification; promotion of secularism; gender discrimination; limiting roles for women; placing great emphasis on Atatürk's thought in the teaching Islam; overemphasizing the teaching of Islam in the World Religions course; legitimizing the use of violence in certain conditions; defining the national values as Turkism in reference to ethnicity and Islamic identity; and using indoctrination as a teaching method (Akdağ, 2003, 240-263).

Conclusion

Turkey has a unique place among Muslim countries today. While the great majority of Turks are Muslim, the form of state is secular and democratic. Because of this, throughout the history of the republic, religious education has faced challenges. Sometimes religion courses have been electives, other times they were taken out of the curriculum altogether. However, by 1982 it was compulsory and continues to be today. During this time there have been some changes in terms of the legal position and content of this education. It is hoped that teaching religion will be better in both content and methods in the future. As for human rights education, although there are still some problems concerning its content and teaching methods, it can be said that Turkey has made positive steps in this area, as well.

References

Akdağ, B. (2003). Türkiye'de din öğretimi kitaplarında insan hakları problemleri. In: Çotuksöken B., Erzan A. & Silier O. (Eds.). *Ders Kitaplarında İnsan Hakları: Tarama Sonuçları.* (240-263). İstanbul: Tarih Vakfı.

Atay, H. (1983). *Osmanlılarda Yüksek Din Egitim.* İstanbul: Dergah.

Ayhan, H. (1999a). Cumhuriyet dönemi din eğitimine genel bir bakış. (237-254). Ankara: *Ankara Üniversitesi İlahiyat Fakültesi Dergisi.*

Ayhan. H. (1999b). *Türkiye'de Din Egitimi.* İstanbul: Ifav.

Bilgin, B (2005). Müslüman ülkelerdeki okul kitaplarında hıristiyanlık anlatımı. In: Yılmaz R. (Ed.). *Kültürel Çeşitlilik ve Din.* (331-343). Ankara: Sinemis Yayınları.

Bilgiseven, A. K. (1987). *Egitim Sosyolojisi.* İstanbul: Türk Dünyası Araştırmaları Vakfı Yayınları.

Cebeci, S. (1999). Cumhuriyet döneminde yüksek din egitimi. (227-235). Ankara: *Ankara Üniversitesi İlahiyat Fakültesi Dergisi.*

Doğan, R. (1999). *İslamcıların Eğitim ve Ogretin Görüşleri.* Ankara: Bizim Büro Basimevi

Eren, N. (1963). *Turkey Today-and Tomorrow.* New York/London: Praeger.

Gök, F. (2003). Vatandaşlık ve insan hakları eğitimi ders kitapları. In: Çotuksöken B., Erzan A. & Silier O. (Eds.) *Ders Kitaplarında İnsan Hakları: Tarama Sonuçları.* (158-171). İstanbul: Tarih Vakfı,

Gökalp, Z. (2004). *Türkleşmek, Islamlasmak, Muasırlasma.* İstanbul: Türk Klasikleri.

Gülcan, M. G. (2002). Human rights education in the Turkish educational system. *Human Rights Education and Practice in Turkey in the Process of Candidacy to the EU.* Muzaffer Dartan and Münevver Cebeci, Marmara University European Community Institute (69-81).

Günay Ü., Güngör H. & Ecer A. V. (1997). *Laiklik, Din ve Türkiye.* Ankara: Adım Yayınları.

Haydaroğlu, İ. P. (1993). *Osmanlı İmparotorluğunda Yabancı Okullar.* Ankara: Ocak Yayınları.

İşler, N. (n.d.). *Din Kültürü ve Ahlak Bilgisi Lise 1.* İstanbul: Meram Yayıncılık.

Jackson, R. (2004). Intercultural education and recent European pedagogies of religious education. *Intercultural Education.* vol. 15, no. 1, (3-14).

Kaymakcan, R. (1999). Christianity in Turkish religious education. *Islam and Christian-Muslim Relations,* vol 10, no 3, (279-293).

Kazıcı, Z. (1991). *İslam Müesseleri Tarihi.* İstanbul: Kayıhan.

Kızıler, H. & Koçak, N. (2005). *Din Kültürü ve Ahlak Bilgisi Lise 2.* Ankara: İpekyolu Yayıncılık.

Kızıler, H. & Koçak, N. (2005). *Din Kültürü ve Ahlak Bilgisi Lise 3.* Ankara: İpekyolu Yayıncılık.

Kinsbury, J. A. (1961). Turkey's new constitution. *The Muslim World.* (152-155).

Koştaş, M. (1999). Türkiye'de laikliğin gelişimi (1920'den günümüze kadar). Ankara: *Ankara Üniversitesi İlahiyat Fakültesi Dergisi.*

Leirvik, O. (2004) Religious education, communal identity and national politics in the Muslim world. *British Journal of Religious Education,* vol 26, no, 3, (223-236).

Lewis, B. (1968). *The Emergence of Modern Turkey.* 2nd. London: Oxford University Press, 1968.

Mardin, Ş. (1982). Turkey: Islam and modernization. In: Caldarola C. (ed.) *Religions and Societies: Asia and Middle East.* Berlin/New York: Mouton.

M.E.B. Komisyon. (2005a). *İlköğretim Din Kültürü ve Ahlak Bilgisi 6*, İstanbul: M.E.B.

M.E.B. Komisyon. (2005b). *İlköğretim Din Kültürü ve Ahlak Bilgisi 7*, İstanbul: M.E.B.

M.E.B. Komisyon. (2005c). *İlköğretim Din Kültürü ve Ahlak Bilgisi 8*, İstanbul: M.E.B.

M.E.B. Komisyon. (2005d). *Orta Öğretim Din Kültürü ve Ahlak Bilgisi Dersi (9. 10. 11 ve 12. sınıflar) Öğretim Programı*, İstanbul: M.E.B.

M.E.B. (1990). Tebliğler Dergisi. 553.

M.E.B. (2000). Tebliğler Dergisi. 2517.

M.E.B. Komisyon. (2000). *İlköğretim Din Kültürü ve Ahlak Bilgisi Dersi Öğretim Programı.* İstanbul: M.E.B. Yay.

Norton, J. D. (1988). The Turks and Islam. In: Sutherland S. et al (Eds.) *The World's Religions.* (390-408). Boston: G. K.: Hall and Co.

Nyrop, R. F. (1973). *Area Handbook for the Republic of Turkey.* 2nd Washington D. C.

Özdalga, E. (1992). On Islamic revivalism and radicalism in Turkey. In: Reimer J. (Ed.) *The Influence on the Frankfurt School on Contemporary Theology.* (331-342). Lewiston: The Edwin Mellen Press.

Reed, H. A. (1954). Revival of Islam in secular Turkey. *The Middle East Journal.* (267-282). vol. 8, pt 3.

Shaw S. J. & Kural E. (1977). *History of the Ottoman Empire and Modern Turkey.* vol. II, Cambridge: Cambridge University Press.

Szyliowich, J. S. (1973). *Education and Modernization in the Middle East.* Ithaca and London: Cornell University Press.

A Retrospective and Critical View of Turkish Citizenship Education

Selahattin Turan

An ideological intent has long been attributed to citizenship and citizenship education in Turkey (Çayır & Gürkaynak, 2007; Çayır, 2011; Koçal, 2012). Therefore, related concepts should be evaluated in their historical and cultural context in order to understand Turkish citizenship and citizenship education: In the ancient tradition of Turkey, the notion of *Homeland* had an identity associated with sacred connotations. Traditionally, the notion of the state such as *the eternal state* [*in Turkish, devlet-i ebed-müddet*] dominated individual and collective consciousness. In the view of the state regarding society, the understanding *"keep society alive to make the state live"* was adopted as a principle; in other words, there existed a spiritual-oral *contract* between the state and society for mutual preservation. Therefore, we are involved in the sacred whenever speaking about the *state*. In addition, the sacred attributions to these concepts of the state still persist in Turkey and *citizenship-belonging* remains a controversial issue nowadays. However, perceptions have changed over time. When discussing today's understandings of citizenship, the historical dimension of the existing situation and its undeniable relationship with other elements should be taken into consideration. The Turkish Republic is a *nation*-state which is the remnant of Ottoman Empire; therefore the situation should be analyzed starting from the Ottoman period until today. Thus, to discuss the level at which citizenship education is realized in Turkey poses distinctive problems that raise the following questions:

- How did the Ottoman Empire constitute the '*me-homeland-state*' relationship?
- What importance did the Turkish Republic give to the intellectual historicity of the state-individual-society sectors?

- Could definitions of citizenship be articulated by successive constitutions of the Turkish Republic so as to create inclusive language for all sections of society?
- Is citizenship in Turkey based on the homeland phenomenon or the state phenomenon?
- At what level does the relationship of post-republic state structuring in Turkey with various social sectors proceed?
- Are there historical circumstances that allow the building of sympathetic relationships between individuals that prioritize the references of religion and the state?
- What are the conditions and forms of the presence of the state, nation and religious community in the minds of Muslims who constitute the majority in Turkey?
- Is the privilege of benefitting from the services and opportunities administered or controlled by the state applied equally to all the segments of society?
- How do teachers providing citizenship education construct the concept of citizenship in their own intellectual world?

Turkish Citizenship in Historical and Legal Context

In order to assess the areas of tension regarding the adoption of citizenship identity in today's Turkey, the experiences in its predecessor, the Ottoman Empire, should be examined. The social order, in Ottoman times, was formed around the concept of the *nation*. 'Nation' (*millet*) [50] indicates individuals with mutual responsibilities and affiliation with a common soul and ethos. The national structuring of the Ottomans enabled both the actual and nominal presence of more than one nation or religious community (*millet*) within the body of the state. Inter-*communal* relationships were realized across a horizontal platform. A privileged community (*millet*) was out of the question but each nation/community might have had privileged persons (Ortaylı, 2009).

Since the organization of the nation's body is not based on race or state, the elements binding individuals to each other was neither *bloodline* nor *sovereignty*. The answer demanded by the question *"Which nation do you belong to?"* was not the answer to the question *"Which administration are you under?"* or *"Which race do you belong to?"*; rather *"Which religion are you a member of?"* This religious ba-

---

50 The famous Ottoman millet system accorded rights and degrees of autonomy to specific religious communities in the empire.

sis for belonging is partially valid for today's Turkey, as well. Since ethnicity is not always clear while religious belonging is determinative; the vast predominance of the Muslim population in all areas of the Ottoman social order might become a coercive element. Islam was not the sole religion in the Ottoman Empire, in some regions, Muslims were a minority. The religious composition of different regions varied over time, depending on various factors and developments. Even the same ethnic origins and religious belonging could be organized in sub-units according to differences in religious sects (Ortaylı, 2009).

In the Ottoman nation (*millet*) system, non-Muslim groups were assigned "*dhimmi*" status. *Dhimmis* (protected non-Muslims) did not need to perform military service and in return, paid a special tax called the "*jizya*." *Dhimmi* groups had their own schools, courts, and religious buildings, as well as educational and legal systems of their own. In addition, the members of *dhimmi* communities had the right to resolve their legal problems in Muslim courts. It was not uncommon in *dhimmi* communities that a criminal, judged according to their own law order, was delivered to the state courts in order for execution of the sentence (An-Na'im, 2008). Therefore, the Ottoman judicial system was related to the *millet* system. In accordance with the religious, ethnic and cultural diversity of the population, the Ottoman judicial system had a decentralized and dynamic structure. The *Millet* system, which was the guaranty of pluralism, and made state authority felt at a minimum level, started to disintegrate in the 19th century. The meaning underlying the concepts of "nation" and "nationalism" changed with the emergence of the nation-state in the 19th century and began to be used with ethnic, rather than religious, referents.

"Umma" is another concept that can be considered to parallel the nation concept in Muslim society or that can be used as the definition indicated by "Islamic nation" in later periods. The concept of "umma" not only posits belonging to the Islamic religion as the sole criteria of belonging but also declares political borders to be null and void. The verse in the Qur'an declaring that all believers are brothers (49: 10) and the hadith indicating that "a Muslim is the brother of other Muslims…" (Bukhari) have legitimized transcending borders in the minds of Muslims. The implementations of nationalism in the Ottoman Period were inspired by these sources. In the structuring of the nation in Ottoman society, the attitude of the state towards Muslim/Non-Muslim individuals or communities was tolerance, rather than conversion. This perception enabled the judiciary and educational systems to be local and autonomous. According to Ortaylı (2009), the concept of "*nation*" (*millet*) referred to religious belonging. The use of this concept with the connotation of "community, society" has evolved with the westernizing of Turkish studies in the 19th century.

The structuring of "nation" in the Ottoman society, which continued until the era of 'Tanzimat' reforms, designated not only the community to be structured but also external perspectives to be adopted. For Europe, which had become ever stronger –since the Crusades-, the Turkish issue and the Islamic issue were the same concepts bearing the same meaning, which all rested on the concept of the Ottoman Empire in addition to its caliphal power. The modern Turkish Republic, however, preferred to constitute the bonds between individuals outside of this framework (Kara, 2012).

Furthermore, the adventure of the transformation in the perceptions of "me" and "society" in Turkey has a long history. This intellectual transformation became a social transformation with the efforts for modernization in the period of Mahmud the 2nd and the Tanzimat Era in 1839. The foundation of the Turkish Republic is the most important point of transition in the efforts in this direction. Thus, the new state implemented two attractive responses in its revolutions and constitution: ignoring and controlling. These two responses can be interpreted as a result of the impulse to create and preserve the state in the chaotic environment that was undoubtedly dominant at a local and global level during this period. However, the interpretation that this motive of preservation was the only intent is naïve. The process, whose basis for legitimacy was created with the motto "to exceed the level of contemporary civilizations", was experienced as systematic social engineering. At the same time, rejecting the heritage of the Ottoman Empire was considered a principle in this process.

As a result of the attitude of ignoring the past, the legal texts created after the 1924 Constitution tried to singularize the plurality of diverse communities which had sustained their social relations within a pluralistic-diversified "nation." The concept of citizenship therefore has been defined in different ways in the Constitutions promulgated since the proclamation of the Turkish Republic.

Turkish citizenship was defined in two paragraphs in the Article 88 of 1924 Constitution based on 1921 Constitution:

> Article 88: Paragraph 1: The Turkish community is accepted as holding Turkish in citizenship regardless of religion and race. Paragraph 2: Everyone who was born as an offspring of a Turkish father in Turkey or abroad or who was born in Turkey as the offspring of a foreign father located in Turkey and is located within the borders of the motherland and officially prefers Turkishness when reaching the age of maturity or who is accepted as Turkish in compliance with Citizenship Act is Turkish. Turkish identity is rescinded under the circumstances determined by law.

Turkish citizenship was defined as follows in Article 88 after Amendment 5 of the 1924 Constitution:

Article 88. –In Turkey, everyone is called a "Turk" in terms of citizenship regardless of religion and race. Everyone who was born as an offspring of a Turkish father in Turkey or abroad or who was born in Turkey as the offspring of a foreign father located in Turkey and is located within the borders of the motherland and officially demands Turkish citizenship when reaching the age of maturity or who is accepted as Turkish in compliance with the Citizenship Act is Turkish. The loss of the designation "Turk" occurs under the circumstances determined by law.

It was defined as follows in 1961 Constitution prepared after coup d'état of 27 May, 1960:

Article 54: Everyone who is bound to the Turkish State with the bond of citizenship is Turkish. The offspring of a Turkish father or Turkish mother is Turkish. The citizenship of an offspring from a foreign father and a Turkish mother is regulated by law. Citizenship is acquired with the provisions determined by law and is lost only under the circumstances determined by law. Any Turk cannot be deprived of citizenship as long as he/she does an act in a manner incompatible with loyalty to country. Judicial remedy cannot be denied against decisions and proceedings regarding deprivation of citizenship.

Citizenship was defined as follows in the Article 66 in the Constitution of the Turkish Republic rewritten in 1981:

Article 66: Everyone who is bound to the Turkish State with the bond of citizenship is Turkish. The offspring of a Turkish father or Turkish mother is Turkish. Citizenship is acquired with the provisions determined by law and is lost only under the circumstances determined by law. Any Turk cannot be deprived of citizenship as long as he/she does not perform an act incompatible with loyalty to country. Judicial remedy cannot be denied against decisions and proceedings regarding deprivation of citizenship.

As indicated in the articles above, citizenship is not plainly defined in the Turkish Constitutions. Rather than a definition of universal citizenship, ideological definitions are predominant. According to Öğün (1997), the founders of the Republic aimed to create a new identity for "country" and "citizenship", which resulted in the emergence of a "state, political society", rather than a "founding nation" based on a cultural-historical-civil nationalism. Thus, it is known that Gökalp (1970) mentioned the concept of "Turkishness" and studied a concept of citizenship with legal-constitutional content. In addition, Öğün (1997) states that this is the continuation of the Tanzimat vision. Ottoman identity, which was formulized in the statement *'bilâ tefrik-i cins ü mezheb'* (no distinction on the basis of race or religion) by Tanzimat dignitaries, and Turkish identity, as designated by Republic, overlap with each other in terms of "political motivation." The clear difference between them is that Republicans, definitely, prefer the elimination of past hesitations and dilemmas regarding ethnic or religious identity.

In this context, the important point for our topic is the adoption of the non-religious perspective as an axis for commitment to the state while creating a new definition of "country" and "citizenship." The basis of citizenship is now an ethic of secular duty (Öğün, 1997). The legal regulations on citizenship in the Republican period are based on the assumption that *a secular individual will be a good and dutiful person*. This subject will be examined in the following pages of this article. In this sense, the historical relationship between the foundation of the "nation-state" and secularism was stated by the founders of the Republic: For the continuation of the existence of the nation, instead of bonding around religion or sect, the nation will unite its individuals in the bond of the Turkish nation (Karal, 1998; Kili, 1969).

The Republic's model of citizenship, depending on the denial of religious loyalty, is, as a romantic discourse, the remnant of affiliation (*asabiyya*),[51] and thus close to a revival of "pagan" history, similar to the basis of national identities on the part of Arabs. What is in question here is the fictionalizing of the Hegelian conceptualization of self-other as being "past/future" in a temporal dimension. The foundation of the future is thus based on political affiliation under a nation state, in which constituting "an individual without memory" is envisaged through the denial of both the Islamic and the local and distant past (Öğün, 1997: 262-63).

With the goal of "reaching the level of contemporary civilizations", Turkey went through a radical process of transformation, manifested in three basic changes: the transformation from Emperorship to a nation state, from monarchy to republic, and from theocracy to secularism. These developments represent the tip of the iceberg in manifesting radical and complex changes, and Turkey became the first Muslim country to accede to secularism (Lewis, 1993). The essence of the multifaceted dynamics of this transformation is based on the articulation of the "nation-state." Legal persons who are distinctive to modernity and the "nation" and "state" as fictional subjects constitute the basic dynamics of the passage to secularism (Gencer, 2000).

As stated earlier, the foundation of the Turkish Republic and the "nationalization/secularization" process actually began with the Tanzimat in 1839. Contrary to the traditional "nation system", based on the organization of communal elements constituting the Ottoman Empire upon the axis of religion, the 1839

---

51 The bonds of community or tribal affiliation as defined by the famous Muslim thinker, Ibn Khaldun.

Decree included the guaranty of individual rights such as life, property, honor and household given to non-Muslims as part of "*dhimmi*" status and this became an official discourse presented before national and international audiences for the first time. Therefore, *dhimmis* were given an "equal but different" status beside Muslims (Mardin, 1996). However, according to Berkes (1978; 2013a, 2013b), 1856 Hatt-ı Hümayun (The Imperial Reform Edict) was enacted for non-Muslims in return for the 1839 Hatt-ı Şerifi enacted for Muslims, and therefore Muslims and non-Muslims became completely equal before the law, regardless of Islamic *dhimmi* laws. This was followed by the foundation of the Nizami Courts and the enactment of other secular legislation (Bozkurt, 1996).

Throughout these historical developments, the concept of "nation" emerged as the dynamic transition to secularism in Turkey in parallel to the ideological development of the New Ottomans and Young Turks, who are considered the continuation of the New Ottomans, the first intellectual movement in the Ottoman Empire. However, there is a critical difference between them: The New Ottomans took the initiative to fill the gap left by the *ulama* and tried to re-found the basis of legitimacy ignored by the Tanzimat reformists, by depending on religious-legal scholarly traditions of Islam (Findley, 1982). They tried to redefine *asabiyah* in order to hold together the Ottoman society which had begun to disintegrate. In this way, they updated the traditional concept of "country" and presented a new supra-identity as a way to substitute for the lost Muslim umma (Mardin, 1996).

Citizenship and Social Engineering for Nation Building

The implementations of secularism in Turkey were realized through imposing it on social communities state by state. Citizenship education and secularism were the basic dynamics of projects to transform society. In this vein, the perceptions and practices arising from this definition obscured the visibility of religion on the social level and attempted to remove it completely from the public sphere (Gencer, 2000). Kara (2012) examines the process followed by the officials of the Turkish Republic as proceding in three stages:

The first period is between 1919 and 1924, which can also be considered as the continuation of Ottoman modernization in terms of religious policies. The War of Independence had both a pan-Islamist and a pro-caliphal soul and discourse, which revived religious feelings, increased the quantity of publications about religion and consolidated "madrasas." The number and dignity of religious instructors "*mudarris*" and the membership of religiously–based sects increased in educational and legal institutions, foundations, and especially in Parliament. *The second period* is the time of single party rule that can be extended until 1944, even until the 1950 elections. The part of this period up to the end of World War II is troubled and difficult, full of restraints on religious practice, raids, penalties, restrictions and executions. Projects or measures including the abolition of the caliphate, closing "madrasas" and Islamic lodges, deviating religious-charity foundations from their own aims and functions, seriously ignoring religious services and mosques, minimizing religious education, reciting the call to prayer in Turkish, transforming Hagia Sophia into a museum, worshipping in the Turkish language, reading the Qur'an in Turkish, and promoting "Turkish Muslimness" occurred during those years. *The third period* begins with the transition to a multiple-party system arising from postwar conditions. During this period, the strict secular perceptions and regulations were amended and revised; thus, this time may be evaluated as a re-normalization of Turkey in issues regarding religion, as well as in other areas. However, the coup d'état of May 27, 1960, and the following military interventions, including the rise of unqualified politicians and intellectuals, made this normalization process inoperative, and subsequently Turkey could not handle this challenge (Kara, 2012).

With the proclamation of the Republic, all things identified with the past were declared bad, and social life was designed through revolutions. With the military interventions in democratic life in 1960, 1971, 1980 and 1997; we may observe how citizens have been molded through education. Some of revolutionary laws are as follows:

The Law on Unification of Education

According to this law, the individuals in a nation can only be educated in one form. Education in two forms would form two types of individuals. The founders of the Republic in its first years wanted to reconfigure society and considered education as a tool to make this new design sustainable. The enactment of the law on the unification of education in 1924 is the most important step of this project. This law left no opportunity to realize any educational activity without the responsibility of the Ministry of National Education, and all schools were included in the purview of the Ministry of National Education; education with religious and political aims was prohibited and the continuation of the Islamic Sufi and scholarly traditions became impossible. The basis for the scholarly class, who had been raised in the Ottoman madrasas to interact with society, was removed. The statement of Yusuf Ziya Kösemen, Kocaeli Deputy, in the discussions of secularism in the 1947 Republican People's Party Congress defines the type of thinking on which the Law on Unification of Education's implementations were founded (Kara, 2012) as:

Fellows! As you know, in 1924, the Law on Unification of Education, Law number 430 was enacted; this law is in force even today. According to this law, religious schooling, together with religious institutions was passed to the Ministry of National Education. According to this law, this Ministry should deal with the religious and moral education of citizens. However, this important duty was ignored in order to prevent prejudices to our secularity (Proceeding of Seventh Congress of CHP, 1948, 462).

The project of social transformation, which reached its strongest form with the Republic, caused chaos in wide areas since it did not respond to a societal demand, and even was enacted in spite of society. The people with high religious feelings were not in favor of sending their children to schools due to their fear that their children would be educated to be "unbelievers," At the same time, Alevi citizens objected to this implementation by reacting against the compulsory religion courses that were conducted without mentioning "Alawism". On the other hand, non-Muslim citizens objected to the laws that did not allow them to teach their own religions. In the 1950s, as a result of the transition to a multiple-party political system, Imam Hatip schools at elementary and high school levels were opened and they provided the opportunity for religious education as well as a general curriculum. However, in 1997, the military intervened in the administration for the fourth time in a so-called "post-modern coup". Then, the elementary schools were all united under the first three levels of education, closing the Imam Hatip schools' first levels. Moreover, the high school sections of Imam Hatips became four-year vocational high schools. As a result of these changes in education, the graduates of the Imam Hatip schools, like ones from other vocational schools, were restricted in their being able to enter university fields of study other than the faculties of their own areas; faculties of theology for Imam Hatip graduates and in the case of graduates of other vocational schools, higher education in their specializations. In case the graduates of the Imam Hatip schools or other vocational high schools wanted to enter other faculties, their scores on the university entrance exam were cut to a certain extent. This regulation continued in effect until 2011 and the closure of the elementary level in schools continued until 2012. During the same period, Alawism was included in the curriculum of religion courses. Another problem in the relationship between the state and citizenship during this period was caused by the prohibitions on females wearing headscarves. The rights of students and teachers to wear headscarves were only guaranteed in 2013.

As for the teaching profession in Turkey, the elites who embraced the Republican attitude of ignoring the past envisioned in the constitution and its implementation generally did not take up this profession. Since the teaching profession was not perceived in Turkey as a prestigious official duty, it was primarily the cohort at the lower middle class of society who did not comply with the ideology of the state who constituted the teaching staff. This situation can also be considered as an element affecting the following generations' increasingly weak commitment to the ideology and concept of citizenship that were promoted by the early Turkish Republic.

Secular Based Citizenship Education in Turkey

Ever since secularism became an article of the Constitution in Turkey (1937), the relationship of religion with the state, the position of religion before the state, and the limits of religious freedom, have always been debated (Bulaç, 1995). The basic dynamics of the concept of secularism in Turkey can be examined in terms of two main axes of discussion, in spite of the different approaches that have emerged thus far. These axes are the supporters of secularism and its opponents. Since the West established its superiority in the technical and military areas, especially during the Tanzimat era and afterwards, an attitude opposing religion began to emerge as a result of the view observed among the intellectuals of that period i. e. that Islam had prevented development. This view was also accepted in government circles. This attitude was mainly caused by the impulse to rescue the state from its backward position when compared to the West. Gencer (2000) reported the presence of a concern to "rescue the state" during the Nizam-i Cedit, (the New Order), Tanzimat, Constitutional Monarchy, and Republic Periods when efforts to counter the superiority of the West were intensified, and those concerns caused the transition from Islamic Law to positive law. In the historical trajectory from Selim 3rd to Mustafa Reşit Pasha, and from Abdülhamid 2nd to Mustafa Kemal Pasha, the main goal was always to rescue the state with the concern that, "The state will be lost." (Gencer, 2000). This intellectual tradition continued in the Turkish Republic, which was founded on the late-period bureaucratic and intellectual inheritance of the Ottoman Empire. In this period which was based on a concept of a "nation" free from religious content (Köker, 2012), a project of civilizing was to be followed so as to create liberty, modernization was to be followed so as to promote civilizing, and nationalization was to be followed to effect modernization, and secularization was to be followed so as to advance nationalization. In this respect, in parallel with the rise of the modern state from the Tanzimat until the

Republic Period, the transition from Islamic law to secular law was commenced, which finally caused the former to fade from the scene (Gencer, 2000). The first institution to be attacked as a result of Westernization movements was religion. There were views that the superiority of the West resulted from secularism, which triggered the development of secularist views based on nationalization in order to effect a civilizing project, modernization and Westernization.

The expectations of the new regime made the continuation of religion, with its present values and form, impossible for the founders of Republic. However, the role of religion could not be neglected in daily life and the search for how to balance intent and reality required the state to intervene in the religion issue again (Subaşı, 2007). The administrative group of the young Republic who perceived religion to be a threat for the continuity of the state regarded each religiously affiliated action as a political action against the political regime (Berkes, 2013). In addition, they feared that without the control and intervention of the state, religion would turn into a dangerous tool for opposition (Subaşı, 2007), and therefore they were always sensitive to religion and wanted to have control over giving or not giving freedom to religion. The separation of religion from state affairs so that that state and religion would not intervene in each other's scope is in the same vein as the actions undertaken by the Bourgeoisie in the West against the church.

In Turkey, the state took religious authority under its own purview and control instead of leaving it to its own institutional autonomy. According to Berkes (2013), in Turkey, within the frame of the modernization problem, secularization is a broader issue than the mere separation of the authorities of the state and church or compromising between these institutions. Regarding the differentiation of Christianity and Islam, the intervention of Islam in social arrangements like policy, education, judiciary, family life, daily life, etc. is wider in comparison to Christianity. In this regard, social implementation and differences in demands between the two religions resulted in conceptualizations or implementations of secularism that vary from Western understandings. The founders of the Republic were intensely concerned about "the future and sustainability of the state" and this resulted in their distancing themselves from religion and even perceiving it as a threat. Moreover, this situation required the development of policies which assumed that *secular citizens would be good citizens* and their policies were based on measures oriented to this assumption. Therefore, in the Turkish Republic, the state intervened in religious affairs rather than religion intervening in state affairs, it was the state that controlled and inspected religious affairs (Gencer, 2000).

In Turkey, the perception of secularism derived from the French Revolution created an atmosphere where religion was strongly opposed by the religion of the state as in the French case. It was thought that things would be settled in time and that necessarily a tolerant environment would be created. In Turkey, secularism was used in order to exercise power over religion through the state, to decrease the effect of religion on society, and to limit its areas of activity rather than merely separating religious and state affairs while guaranteeing the religious and philosophical beliefs of individuals and groups. Secularity began to be presented as a new belief system and an alternative to religion (Hatemi, 1987; Uludağ, 1995). Within this sense, secularist perceptions and measures were used in order to bring about a new belief system that accepted the dominant belief of "faith in science" instead of Islam (İlhan, 2008; Köker, 2012; Lewis, 1993).

Thus, secularism in Turkey is not the same as in the West. Secularizing measures were applied by state organizations. A separate religious legal entity was not founded; instead, religious affairs were left to the secular state. According to Köker (2012), the reason why Turkey could not solve its problems regarding the consideration and presentation of religion as separate from state affairs and as a belief system related to individual conscience was that Islam is based on the association of religion and the world; and confluence of religion and state. Thus, in order to achieve the principle of secularism in a society where Islam is dominant, religion should be regulated by the state and then the belief that religion and state are conjoined should be changed at the individual level. Thus, the principle of secularization should be directed not at the separation of religion and state, but to the control of religion by the state combined with intellectual reform. Since policy became a phenomenon of domination rather than an administrative process, the ruling/opposition relationship became a struggle to seize/lose control of the state; and therefore the traditional motto "religion would be lost" was replaced by the motto "the state would be lost" and attempts were made to continuously keep Islam under control owing to the fear that it would dominate the state (Gencer, 2000). Berkes (2013) affirms that in the Republican period, there were limitations on religion in three areas within the frame of law. The first one was the impossibility of founding communities based on sects or religious orders. The second one was the impossibility of founding political parties aiming to benefit a certain religious group and the prohibition of religious movements based on political parties. The third limitation was on any actions aiming to even partially change social, economic, politic or legal orders according to religious principles. All were considered crimes based on the perception that this opposed the principle of secularism enshrined in the Constitution.

The disputes about secularism continued with the abolition of the article "The religion of the state is Islam" from the Constitution in 1928 and eventually the addition of the article "Turkey is a secular state" to the Constitution in 1937. Subaşı (2007) defines the image of secularism and relevant measures implemented in

Turkey in the social sphere as a complete flux and reflux, and stresses that Turkish secularism has a sui generis aspect. Scattered secularism does not allow a strong discourse, but only allows prioritizing security, which enables one to understand the directions of Turkish religious policy. For example, there are some uncertainties about the kind of semantic field that religion was related to; under either a single party or a multi-party system, also the policy is vague regarding what it means to leave religion alone. Such ambiguity problematizes not only religious policies but also the educational policies that can be evaluated within this context (Subaşı, 2007). Some attempts were made to impose secular-based nationalism and modernization through measures such as the Unified Education Law, the transition to the Latin alphabet from the Arabic one, setting up community re-education centers, etc. with the aim of raising new generations who would ensure the sustainability of these secular state institutions. However, through those measures, education became an ideological tool of the state throughout the process and especially after the 1930s. In addition, the gap between the cultural codes of the nation and its semantic world prevented the realization of the intended results over the long term. Even though secularism and the measures taken within this context achieved their aims among the dominant group in the state and in its legal measures, they held no value according to the perceptions of most of society. Especially with the transition to a multiple party system, society's eventual turn to alternative sources of power resulted in partial relief with regard to religious freedom and practice in daily life rather than the efficacy of the structural institutions and measures of the state.

Even though this situation is suggested as being secular as stated by the Constitutions of the country, it cannot be ignored that most of Turkish society adopted or wanted to live an Islamic life style. Indeed, many Turkish Muslims felt alienated when they accepted, adopted and obeyed theoretical definitions of being secularized. The definition of citizenship in Turkey was founded on nationalistic identity and general social perceptions were formed in this way, yet these resulted in problems when devout Muslims wanted to employ religious references in regulating their life styles and relationships with the state, since it was impossible for the state to fulfill their demands. A different intent from Western-oriented definitions of "theoretical secularism" was attempted in Turkey through local and original measures, which caused feelings of alienation in most of the society and also created ambiguity in the minds of Muslims. Esed (2002) stressed that most Muslim intellectuals accepted the view that religion should intervene in political life in the modern world. While "secularism" was considered to be synonymous with progressivism, the organization of political processes and economic and social issues according to religion was considered to be "reactionary."

In implementing various legal and regulatory measures on the part of the Turkish state, the sensitivities of devout Muslims and other groups not holding political power were not taken into consideration due to the conditions prevailing during various periods. Similarly, the educational programs organized in schools, or the organs of official or unofficial citizenship education projects did not take these current perceptions into account, all of which served to intensify present problems. Since the proclamation of the Republic, perceptions of secularism could either not be successful or ultimately became problematic in Turkey, since the explanation of what is secularism in Turkey became identified as either irreligious or anti-Islam in the eyes of society. As well there was a dominant perception that the state was continuously involved in all implementations of religion. In addition, the socio-economic background of most teachers was also a salient factor since these teachers were the basis of the educational institutions, which were the main components in ensuring the sustainability of secularism and its relevant institutions.

The pragmatist policy attempted to play on the ambiguity of definitions of secularism but this failed to take into account the reality of the semantic worlds of most Turks, thus leading to a chaotic environment. As a result each faction began to try to oppress the other side over these ambiguous definitions. According to Uludağ (1994), any social institution cannot become completely independent from other social institutions, therefore a complete separation of religious and worldly affairs and making them entirely independent is impossible, since one of them certainly affects or is affected by the other. Within this context, in order to remove the problems in secularism and all of its related social areas, the religion-state relationship should be re-organized in a rational and realistic way, giving consideration to the traditions of society, its historical habits, experiences and beliefs and in addition, the characteristics of the contemporary state.

Conclusion

This chapter has outlined many of the historical reasons for the neglect of citizenship education in modern Turkey. With the advent of the Turkish Republic, it can be said that citizenship education in Turkey aimed at raising good secular citizens. In this historical process, the good citizen became defined as a secular citizen. As part of this process concepts were adapted from other societies and applied to Turkey while neglecting the social, economic and political context of Turkish society. Therefore, citizenship education remained at the rhetorical level imposed by the state but which was not reflected in the behaviors and attitudes of individuals. All sections of society, both secular and pious, tried to use schools and citizenship education as tools to legitimize and sustain their own ideologies and concepts of sovereignty rather than for training good citizens. Within this context, the secular ruling elite prioritized secular citizenship education while the devout prioritized religious education. In both situations, the concept of a universal and comprehensive citizenship education remained weak. The effort of Turkey to become a member of the European Union over the last quarter of century has led to the transformation of the dilemma of secular citizenship education versus religious citizenship education into the discussions of European citizenship versus Turkish citizenship. The disputes over citizenship education in Turkey are likely to continue. There are few comprehensive empirical studies regarding the subject and up to the present it should be stressed that a model of universal citizenship education has not yet been developed in Turkey.

References

An-Na'im, A. A. (2008). *Islam and the Secular State*. Cambridge, MA: Harvard University Press.

Berkes, N. (1978). *Türkiye'de Çağdaşlaşma*. İstanbul: Doğu-Batı Yayınları.

Berkes, N. (2013a). *Türkiye'de çağdaşlaşma*. İstanbul: Yapı Kredi.

Berkes, N. (2013b). *The Development of Secularism in Turkey*. London: Routledge.

Bozkurt, G. (1996). *Türk Kimliği*. Istanbul: Remzi Kitabevi.

Bulaç, A. (1995). *Modernizm, irtica ve sivilleşme*. İstanbul: İz.

Çayır, K. (2011). Turkey's New Citizenship and Democracy Education Course: Search for Democratic Citizenship in a Difference-Blind Polity? *Journal of Social Science Education, 10*(4), (22-30).

Çayır, K., & Gürkaynak, İ. (2008). The state of citizenship education in Turkey: past and present. *Journal of Social Science Education, 6*(2), (50-58).

Esed, M.(2002). *İslam'da yönetim biçimi*. İstanbul: Yöneliş.

Findley, C. V. (1982). *The Acid Test of Ottomanism: The Acceptance of Non-Muslims in the Late Ottoman Bureaucracy*. Princeton University.

Gencer, B. (2000). Türkiye'de laikliğin temel dinamikleri. *Toplum ve Bilim, 84*, (151-171).

Gökalp, Z. (1970). *Türkçülüğün esasları*. Ankara: MEB.

Hatemi, H. (1987). *Batılılaşma*. İstanbul: Bir Yayıncılık.

İlhan, A. (2008). *Hangi laiklik*. İstanbul: Türkiye İş Bankası Kültür Yayınları.

Kara, İ. (2012). *Cumhuriyet Türkiye'sinde Bir Mesele Olarak İslam*. İstanbul: Dergah.

Karal, E. Z. (1998). *Atatürk ve Devrim*. Ankara: Metu Press.

Kili, S. (1969). *Kemalism*. İstanbul: Robert College.

Koçal, A. V. (2012). Bir Hegemonya Aracı Olarak Sekülerleş (tir) me: Tarihsel Bir Perspektiften Türkiye'de Laikliğin Politik Ekonomisi. *Akademik İncelemeler, 7*(2), (107-140).

Köker, L. (2012). *Modernleşme, Kemalizm ve demokrasi*. İstanbul: İletişim.

Lewis, B. (1993). *Islam and the West*. NY: Oxford University Press.

Şerif, M. (1996). *Yeni Osmanlı Düşüncesinin Doğuş*. İstanbul: İletişim.

Ortaylı, İ. (2009). *Osmanlı Toplumunda Aile*. İstanbul: Pan.

Öğün, S. S. (1997). *Politik kültür yazıları: Süreçler, kişiler*. Bursa: Asa.

Subaşı, N. (2007). Türkiye'de laiklik ve din eğitimi: Reel politik güzergâhlar. *Değerler Eğitimi Merkezi Dergisi, 2*, (6-10).

Uludağ, S. (1995). Türk aydını ve kimlik sorunu. In S. Şen (eds.), *Türkiye'de din, devlet, aydın* (315 – 320). İstanbul: Bağlam.

Citizenship Education in Diverse Democracies

How Thick or Thin? How Maximal or Minimal?

Hanan Alexander

Introduction

A key problem in the education of citizens in open, pluralistic, liberal democratic societies concerns the tensions between the character of comprehensive visions of the good that draw upon particular religious, spiritual, moral, and political traditions, on the one hand, and the values and virtues that all citizens need to share in order to create a common civic life together across difference, on the other hand. This problem can be found in liberal democratic states that have or seek ties to particular faith traditions such as Islam, Christianity, or Judaism; secular heritages such as French or possibly Turkish *Laïcité*; national cultures or languages such as German, Polish, Czech, or Lithuanian; or combinations of the above such as modern Hebrew culture and Israeli Zionism. It is especially significant for emerging states in Southeastern Europe with large Muslim majorities, as well as significant landed minorities with alternative ethnic or religious ties that may wish to prepare youngsters for the rights and responsibilities of citizenship in liberal democratic regimes.

In a well-known distinction Michael Walzer situated the particular values of comprehensive visions of the good on a spectrum between thick commitments grounded in local histories, cultures, and languages, on the one hand, and thinner commitments that are shared across the differences of particular faith, moral, and political traditions, on the other (Walzer, 1985). Terence H. McLaughlin situated the concern for the commons along a similarly well-worn distinction that includes commitment to a maximal array of liberal values such as tolerance and mutual respect in contrast to a more minimal and often mechanical subset of these values. (McLaughlin, 1992, 235-50 and 2003, 121-36). In a sense, some of the contours of Walzer's thin political and moral traditions are described by McLaughlin's argument for maximal commitment to shared liberal values. Both reach across difference to define values that citizens in a liberal democracy need to share in common. A difficult question for diverse democratic societies thus concerns how thick we can allow comprehensive visions of the good to become before they eclipse any possibility of a shared civic life. Concomitantly, how extensive we should seek to make the common values that democratic citizens share across difference. McLaughlin offers a useful tool for negotiating these tensions in his further discussion of the burdens and dilemmas of both common and sectoral schooling (McLaughlin, 2003, 121-56).

This chapter is divided into four parts. In the first part I consider the meaning of democracy by situating the discussion of common and comprehensive goods within the context of what John Gray has called the two faces of liberalism, one leaning toward universal toleration, the other toward pluralism. Part two explores the difference between common and comprehensive goods in greater depth via Walzer's distinction between thick and thin moral theories. In the third part I review McLaughlin's distinction between maximal and minimal democratic citizenship along with his discussion of the burdens and dilemmas of common schooling as a mechanism for balancing common and comprehensive goods. The concluding section considers some consequences of this view for citizenship education in diverse democratic societies according to a view that I term the pedagogy of difference. It holds that citizenship education in diverse democracies should initiate youngsters into their own particular heritages while also exposing them to different—even opposing—traditions. In what follows I will add that in addition to these two dimensions of the curriculum, pedagogies of difference should also initiate students into common goods that are agreed upon through a process of dialogue among alternative points of view.

Two Faces of Liberalism

It is useful to begin by distinguishing between two sorts of conceptions of the good – one that advances the beliefs, practices, and interests of a particular culture that may live in proximity to other cultures and another that seeks common ground across different cultures (Alexander, 2001, 41). This distinction can be clarified in light of John Gray's observation that, "Liberalism has always had two faces."

From one side, toleration is the pursuit of an ideal form of life. From the other, it is the search for terms of peace among different ways of life. In the former view, liberal institutions are seen as applications of universal principles. In the latter, they are means to peaceful coexistence. In the first, liberalism is the prescription for a universal regime. In the second, it is a project of coexistence that can be pursued in many regimes.

The philosophies of John Locke and Immanuel Kant exemplify the liberal project of a universal regime, while those of Thomas Hobbes and David Hume express the liberalism of peaceful coexistence. In more recent times, John Rawls and F.A. Hayek have defended the first liberal philosophy, while Isaiah Berlin and Michael Oakeshott are exemplars of the second (Gray, 2002, 2).

Gray calls the politics exemplified by Kant and Locke "universal liberalism" and that exemplified by Berlin and Oakeshott a "theory of modus vivendi." The latter, Gray writes, "is liberal toleration adapted to the historical fact of pluralism." The ethical theory that underpins the search for coexistence among alternative ways of life, therefore, is called "value-pluralism." It entails the idea that "there are many conflicting kinds of human flourishing, some of which cannot be compared in value" (Gray, 2002, 6). According to the liberalism of Kant, Locke, and Rawls, the common beliefs and institutions of a democracy are distinct from particular comprehensive conceptions of the good in that the former are justified according to one account or another of universal reason which is presupposed to be neutral with regard to any parochial life path; whereas the latter are grounded in assumptions of faith or culture that are by no means neutral since they may not be rational and are generally not shared by all members of the democratic community.

According to the liberalism of Hume, Berlin, and Oakeshott, on the other hand, the fact of pluralism precludes the possibility of neutral grounds upon which to create a common life across difference, since any possible account of neutral reason that one might advance is itself a contingent product of history, culture, and language that will prefer one particular way of life over another. There can be no universal principles upon which to base a common life together, therefore, but only a contingent and dynamic set of agreements that may shift and evolve over time as a society of different peoples and traditions lives together and learns from their successes and failures. A vision of the common good on this account has no special epistemic privilege over any other comprehensive vision of the good. Granting such privilege falls prey to what Oakeshott called the fallacy of rationalism in politics or the false idea that rigid techniques of abstract reason can adequately describe the dynamics of human conduct, which are more properly captured in the nuances and intimacies of practical traditions (Oakeshott, 1962, 5-42). What distinguishes these two sorts of goods from one another, then, is not that the one is grounded in universal principals and the other in particular cultures, but rather that the one addresses the problems and predicaments of several faith and cultural communities living together across difference, whereas the other addresses the internal concerns of particular communities in which members share common beliefs, values, and customs.

In an attempt to seek a middle course between these two accounts of liberalism, Rawls referred to what he thought to be an extreme version of the first view as ethical or comprehensive liberalism, since he was aware that the idea of universal toleration limits pluralism by requiring all life choices to follow one or another account of universal reason which becomes the arbiter of what could possibly count as a legitimate concept of the good. In contrast he sought to define a more limited liberal theory, which he called political liberalism. According to this view common beliefs and institutions would be defined only by burdens of judgment that make possible a reasonable public discourse (Rawls, 1993).

Rawls called this discourse "public reason." It required that common civic issues be adjudicated on the basis of reasons shared by all rather than arguments grounded in particular comprehensive goods. Excluding the particular assumptions of comprehensive goods from public discourse, he believed, preserves a robust liberal pluralism by maximizing the freedom to choose private paths regardless of their status vis-à-vis one view of rationality or another. However, as many commentators on Rawls have pointed out, the very idea that adherents to a comprehensive good should leave their most cherished beliefs and values at the door of the public square itself entails a comprehensive vision of the common life; one that prizes among other values public discourse characterized by reasonable neutrality (Callan, 2004; Gutmann & Thompson, 1998; Macedo, 1990; Tomasi, 2000). Political liberalism does not resolve the limitations on pluralism that Rawls set out to address, therefore, but turns out to be yet another comprehensive ethical vision in disguise, one that is concerned with common rather particular goods.

Berlin acknowledged this irredeemable difficulty with universal liberalism well before Rawls's attempt to resolve it in his well-known distinctions between hedgehogs and foxes, on the one hand, and positive and negative liberty, on the other. Berlin followed an obscure fragment from the ancient Greek poet Archilochus by marking two sorts of intellectual types—foxes who know many things and hedgehogs who know one big thing (Berlin, 1953, 3). Societies conceived by foxes encourage citizens to choose among competing paths to human fulfillment, provided they respect the choices of others, whereas hedgehogs assign privilege to those who follow one particular path. Foxes are drawn to a negative concept of freedom, the absence of constraints on, or interference with, a person's actions;

hedgehogs are attracted to positive liberty, the idea of self-mastery, or self-defini-
tion, or control of one's destiny (Berlin, 1969).

Berlin had deep reservations about the latter concept, because of the tendency
among those who advance positive accounts of freedom to distinguish between
one's actual self that acts in the day-to-day world and some occult entity referred
to alternatively as a "true" or "real" or "higher" self, of which a person might not
be fully aware. Thus, it is argued that, although one's empirical self may indeed
feel free, one's true self may actually be enslaved. As Berlin put it so aptly:

> Once I take this view, I am in a position to ignore the actual wishes of men or so-
> cieties, to bully, oppress, torture them in the name, and on behalf, of their `real'
> selves, in the secure knowledge that whatever is the true goal of man (happiness,
> performance of duty, wisdom, a just society, self-fulfillment) must be identical with
> his freedom--the free choice of his `true', albeit often submerged and inarticulate,
> self. (Berlin, 1969, 133)

Berlin leveled this critique not only against the potential authoritarianism inherent in the Counter-Enlightenment Romanticism of such luminaries as G. W. F.
Hegel and his right- and left-leaning intellectual descendants, but also against the
monist moral and political theories of Kant and Locke, who he viewed as nascent
hedgehogs, headstrong about the capacity of one or another account of reason to
negotiate competing ways of life.

The tension between common and comprehensive goods as conceived here,
then, fits squarely within the context of a political theory grounded in value-pluralism, as one way of asking how a modus vivendi that seeks peaceful coexistence
across difference might be constructed in practice through education. This is a
dialectical question of the form, "How is one thing possible given certain other
contradictory or conflicting things?" As noted by Robert Nozick, questions of this
kind require a philosophical explanation that articulates deeper principles that
can remove the apparent conflict and put one's beliefs in alignment (Nozick, 1981,
8).

Two Sorts of Moral Argument

Walzer provided the beginning of such an explanation by distinguishing between
two different interrelated kinds of moral argument, "a way of talking among ourselves, here at home, about the thickness of our own history and culture . . . and
a way of talking to people abroad, across different cultures, about a thinner life

we have in common ... There are the makings of a thin and universalistic morality inside every thick and particular morality" (Walzer, 1985, xi). For this thin universalistic ethic to be sufficiently meaningful to serve as a source for self-determined choices required of democratic citizens, however, it must be embodied in the practices of a local community that displays the features of what Walzer calls moral maximalism: "It will be idiomatic in its language, particularist in its cultural references, and circumstantial in two senses of that word: historically dependent and factually detailed. Its principals and procedures will have been worked out over a long period of time through complex social interactions" (Walzer, 1985, 21). The process as a whole, Walzer continues, "is surely misrepresented when it is described ... as if it had been guided by a single, comprehensive, and universal principle. All such principles are abstractions and simplifications that, when analyzed, reveal their idiomatic, particularist, and circumstantial character" (cf. Oakeshott, 1962).

However, if both common and comprehensive goods are but historically contingent expressions of culture and language, cannot each be conceived on a continuum between thicker and thinner conceptions? The answer is clearly in the affirmative, where the degree of thickness or thinness can be assessed according to the extent to which a version of the good seeks to impose itself as a form of positive liberty on all aspects of life and so is closed off to dialogue with alternative points of view. The alternative, negative liberty, refrains from imposition on others (Berlin, 1969, 118-72). A very thick particular conception of the good would look like an extreme form of ethnic or civic republicanism or religious fundamentalism, whereas a very thick version of the common good across difference, for example one that imposed liberal toleration as a universal ideal, would be tantamount to an extreme form of comprehensive liberalism. As conceptions of the commons thicken, they tolerate increasingly thinner particular ways of life. Conversely, as particular conceptions of the good become thicker, they tolerate thinner approaches to the common good across difference.

Comprehensive liberal states that have a relatively thick conception of the commons, for example, often require particular identities to diminish the extent to which they rely on deeply held beliefs for public purposes. Thus Rawls's conception of public reason permits justification of public policies based only on burdens of judgment shared by all, which precludes particular constituencies from defending their positions based on certain cherished convictions. On this account, a devout Catholic would not be allowed to oppose public support for abortion or same-sex marriage on religious grounds. Conversely, thick republican states will tend to marginalize public expression of customs, languages, or commitments that diverge from the prevailing ethnic, civic, or religious ethos. Even though Hispanics represent a large minority in California, for example, English, not Spanish, remains the primary, if not exclusive, language of public discourse (Alexander, Pinson & Yonah, 2011, 68-256).

An education tied to a comprehensive account of liberalism, in which the principle of universal toleration privileges common over particular goods by granting the former neutrality, would foster rational capacities to make autonomous choices about both personal paths and public policies. However, an education associated with a more pluralistic view of liberalism, in which both common and comprehensive goods are grounded in the dynamic contingencies of history, would seek to cultivate the capacity to participate in active dialogue with those of alternative persuasions in order to nurture a modus vivendi by means of which people of deep difference can life together in peace. For this reason among others William Galston has referred to the first theory as *autonomy* and to the second as *diversity* liberalism (Galston, 1991). But, according to this view, how thick or thin should both the common and comprehensive goods be if an education in these goods is to foster peaceful coexistence?

Two Concepts of Citizenship Education

McLaughlin addressed this question by distinguishing between maximal and minimal concepts of citizenship education, conceived as ends of a continuum, not as a dichotomy. The distinction considers the identities, loyalties, political involvements, and social prerequisites of effective citizens in relation to the common conception of the good across difference in open, pluralistic liberal democracies (McLaughlin, 1992, 50-235; 2008, 36-120). On the maximal side of the continuum, "the citizen must have a consciousness of him or herself as a member of a living community with a shared democratic culture involving obligations and responsibilities as well as rights" (McLaughlin, 2008, 122). On the minimal side, on the other hand, the identity conferred on the individual through citizenship is merely formal or juridical. Loyalties and responsibilities are viewed primarily as local or parochial, involvements are seen as serving interests that are individual or related to a sector, and prerequisites for membership are essentially legal or official.[52]

---

52 For an application of this continuum to Islamic education in liberal democracies see Yusef Waghid, *Conceptions of Islamic Education: Pedagogic Framings* (New York: Peter Lang, 2011).

The more a program in citizenship education leans toward the maximal end of this continuum, then, the greater its emphasis on negotiating shared values dedicated to coexistence across deep difference. Both common and comprehensive goods may be seen, in this view, to be products of dynamic, historically contingent, and often contentious dialogues among incommensurable cultures and traditions, not neutral, static, or universal rational principles; and achieving agreement on common goods of this kind requires a level of dialogue that can only take place among thick particular comprehensive goods. This follows Walzer's analysis quite nicely. However, a more maximal approach to education in citizenship appears to reflect a thicker view of the common goods required for a shared democratic life than Walzer's account might allow.[53] This intensifies the potential conflict between common and comprehensive goods by leaving unresolved such questions as which sort of good is most deserving of primary loyalty and how should conflicts between them be negotiated?

McLaughlin addressed these concerns by distinguishing between the burdens and dilemmas of common and sectoral schooling in diverse liberal democracies (McLaughlin, 2003; 2008, 137-174). He began by constructing a continuum between light and heavy burdens. Toward the light end of this continuum are to be found burdens of unifying aspects of schooling that invoke relatively uncontroversial values reflected in a wide consensus that bridges social divides, whereas on the heavy end are to be found burdens of greater complexity and sophistication that require more sustained argument and deeper understanding (such as the educational role and limitations of personal autonomy or the proper balance between unity and diversity in democratic societies), which according to the nature of the case will be more controversial. Among the burdens associated with common schooling, for example, will be the inclusion of diverse communities representing both majority and minority cultures whereas sectoral schooling will face the burden of teaching common democratic values in institutions that emphasize one particular tradition.

According to McLaughlin, the burdens that can be identified concerning unifying aspects of democratic schooling generate a range of corresponding dilemmas regarding the "diversifying, non-common, or non public" dimensions of education in pluralistic liberal societies. These are dilemmas, not problems or

---

53 In *Reimagining Liberal Education* I referred to this embrace of thick common goods as soft value pluralism. William Galston's harder value pluralism embraces a thinner commons. See W. A. Galston, "Civic Education in the Liberal State." In *Liberalism and the Moral Life*, edited by N. L. Rosenblum, (Cambridge, MA: Harvard Univ. Press, 1989), 89-101, and H. A. Alexander, *Reimagining Liberal Education: Affiliation and Inquiry in Democratic Schooling* (London: Bloomsbury, 2015), ch. 11.

difficulties, since they are often intractable and must be navigated, not resolved, to achieve the trust and support of diverse communities. For example, common schools face dilemmas concerning how to address controversial issues such as abortion and gay rights, about which particular traditions may hold strong opinions, but which are not necessarily resolved among the wider public. Sectoral schools, on the other hand, face concomitant dilemmas concerning how to foster robust affiliation with particular faith communities while at the same time teaching respect for alternative practices and opposing views. If common and comprehensive goods share both a contingent epistemic status and a relative degree of thickness, however, and this point is deserving of emphasis, then separate schooling associated with particular comprehensive goods should carry no fewer burdens or concomitant dilemmas than public schooling associated with common goods. McLaughlin articulated criteria for justifying both common and sectoral schools, therefore, each emphasizing a different side of the tension between common and comprehensive goods, based on balancing fairly heavy burdens with corresponding dilemmas (McLaughlin, 1992, 36-114 and 2003, 98-137; Alexander, Pinson & Yonah, 2011, 256-268).

Consider Israel, a liberal democratic state with a large ethnic majority of around eighty percent Jews and a significant landed minority of approximately twenty percent Palestinian nationals, Muslim and Christian Arabs and Druze.[54] In this case, there is no common system school to speak of, but rather state funded sectoral schools for secular and religious Jews, whose first language is Hebrew, and for Arabs and Druze, whose first language is Arabic. In their analysis of these schools Hanan Alexander, Halleli Pinson, and Yossi Yonah identified a number of burdens and dilemmas of Israeli citizenship education that may be indicative of the tensions faced by other small liberal republics, especially those in which majority and minority cultures espouse conflicting claims about sovereignty and the legitimacy of the state.

The burdens they identified include: (1) *the burden of rival narratives* which concerns open deliberation of a variety of stories concerning the origins and justification of the state; (2) *the burden of cultural misrecognition* which addresses

---

54 Since the Druze community was a persecuted minority in many Muslim societies for centuries, it has developed a strong tradition of loyalty to local national cultures that have offered protection. Syrian Druze identify strongly as Syrians, for example, and Israeli Druze as Israelis. Although Druze culture is Arabic speaking and organized around villages similar to Muslim and Christian culture in the Middle East, not all Druze choose to identify as Arabs. Hence, although an increasing number of Arab citizens of Israel consider themselves to be Palestinian nationals, fewer Druze embrace this identity.

the need to grant appropriate rights and status to both majority and minority cultures; (3) *the burden of socio-economic divides* which promotes policies intended to lessen growing class divisions; (4) *the burden of gender inequality* which considers policies intended to overcome gender bias and promote equality between women and men; (5) *the burden of excess militarism* which relates to the aggression in schools that can be a negative by-product of a citizens army; (6) *the burden of competing interpretations* which relates to the need to explore and validate multiple interpretations of faith traditions such as Judaism, Christianity, and Islam; and (7) *the burden of globalization* in which students are prepared to participate in geopolitical and economic institutions beyond national boundaries.

They also identified the following dilemmas: (1) *the dilemma of universalism versus particularism* which seeks to balance universal claims about justice with local conceptions of the good; (2) *the dilemma of cohesion versus diversity* which seeks to expand social cohesion by expanding the diverse populations included the democratic community while supporting association with robust particular identities; (3) *the dilemma of dialogue versus commitment* which navigates the tension between being open and accepting of the other yet committed to one's inherited or chosen heritage; and (4) *the dilemma of cosmopolitanism versus localism* which promotes simultaneous grounding in both local and international political communities (Alexander, Pinson & Yonah, 2011, 68-264).

Conclusion

The task of maximal citizenship education in diverse democratic societies, then, is to cultivate capacities among students to successfully balance the heavy burdens and concomitant dilemmas of initiation into thick common and comprehensive goods, so as to construct a modus vivendi that promotes peaceful coexistence across deep difference. I call an education in this sort of balancing act the pedagogy of difference (Alexander, 2010, 35-45). Such a pedagogy holds that to embrace the other one must know oneself by becoming intimately familiar with the traditions to which one is heir or with which one chooses to affiliate. But such an intimate knowledge of one's own tradition also requires exposure to the beliefs and practices of others. Hence, there is actually no single pedagogy of difference, but rather a variety of pedagogies each grounded in the traditions of primary identity into which one is to be initiated and the other traditions to which one is also to be exposed.

Elsewhere I have emphasized a variety of characteristics of these sorts of pedagogies, that they adhere to what I have called the conditions of human agency, for example, which include that teachers and learners are to a greater or lesser extent free to make life choices, in possession of sufficient intelligence to understand the relative merit of those choices according to some defensible theory of what it means to be meritorious, and capable of bad choices according to that very theory (Alexander, 2005, 1-18). They are consequently able within reasonable limits to take hold of their destiny and change course, if they so choose. These are the conditions that make possible public dialogue among competing comprehensive goods concerning what beliefs and values to hold in common. I call this sort of dialogue across different moral perspectives, ethical discourse (Alexander, 2005, 44-50 and 2007, 69-343). The particular traditions that embody these comprehensive goods must, therefore, be dynamic, not dogmatic. They are capable of, rather than impervious to, change; open to conversation with rival perspectives and willing to making adjustments to beliefs and practices as a result, not closed and resistant to external influences (Alexander, 2005, 38-109 and 2007, 24-609).

However, in my previous discussions of these pedagogies the emphasis was on exposure to competing comprehensive traditions, such as religious students being exposed to science, Jewish students being exposed to Islam or Christianity, or teaching and learning about both Zionist and Palestinian narratives concerning the establishment of the State of Israel (Alexander, Pinson & Yonah, 2011, 68-256). In the absence of a neutral view from nowhere, I have argued, only exposure to alternative perspectives can make possible the sort of critical attitude required of democratic citizens (Alexander, 2006, 22-205).

The foregoing analysis implies, moreover, that in addition to exposure to rival traditions, maximal citizenship education in diverse democracies also requires initiation into an agreed upon set of thick common values that have emerged from extended dialogue over time, perhaps even generations, which can facilitate coexistence among these very competing views. This suggests a three part curriculum. Beyond initiation into a thick comprehensive tradition of primary identity and exposure to rival perspectives, pedagogies of difference also require education in thick shared values across difference that foster the capacity to navigate disagreement respectfully and seek common ground among competing points of view by engaging the heavy burdens and concomitant dilemmas of both public and separate—common and sectoral—schooling.

References

Alexander, H. A. (2001). *Reclaiming Goodness: Education and the Spiritual Quest*. Notre Dame: University of Notre Dame Press.

Alexander, H. A. (2005). "Education in Ideology." *The Journal of Moral Education* 34, no. 1 (1-18).

Alexander, H. A. (2005). "Human Agency and the Curriculum." *Theory and Research in Education* 3, no. 3.

Alexander, H. A. (2006). "A View from Somewhere: Explaining the Paradigms of Educational Research." *Journal of Philosophy of Education* 40, no. 2 (22-205).

Alexander, H. A. (2007). "What is Common about Common Schooling: Rational Autonomy and Moral Agency in Liberal Democratic Education." *Journal of Philosophy of Education* 41, no. 4 (24-609).

Alexander, H. A. (2010). "Educating Identity: Toward a Pedagogy of Difference." In: Miedema, S. (Ed.). *Religious Education as Encounter: A Tribute to John Hull*. Munster: Waxman.

Alexander, H. A., Pinson, H. & Yonah, Y. (Eds.). (2011). Conclusion to *Citizenship, Education, and Social Conflict: Israeli Political Education in Global Perspective*. New York: Routledge.

Berlin, I. (1953). *The Hedgehog and the Fox: An Essay on Tolstoy's View of History*. New York: Simon and Schuster.

Berlin, I. (1969). *Four Essays on Liberty*. Oxford: Oxford Univ. Press.

Callan, E. (2004). *Creating Citizens: Political Education and Liberal Democracy*. Oxford: Clarendon Press.

Galston, W. A. (1991). *Liberal Purposes: Goods, Virtues, and Diversity in the Liberal State*. Cambridge: Cambridge Univ. Press.

Gray, J. (2002). *Two Faces of Liberalism*. London: New Press.

Gutmann, A. & Thompson, D. (1998). *Democracy and Disagreement*. Cambridge, MA: Harvard Univ. Press.

Macedo, S. (1990). *Liberal Virtues: Citizenship, Virtue, and Community in Liberal Constitutionalism*. Oxford: Oxford Univ. Press.

McLaughlin, T. H. (1992). "The Ethics of Separate Schools." In: Leicester, M. & Taylor, M. J. (Eds.). *Ethics, Ethnicity, and Education*. London: Kogan Page.

McLaughlin, T. H. (1992). "Citizenship, Diversity, and Education: A Philosophical Perspective." *Journal of Moral Education* 21, no. 3.

McLaughlin, T. H. (2003). "The Burdens and Dilemmas of Common Schooling." In: McDonough, K. & Feinberg, W. (Eds.). *Citizenship and Education in Liberal-Democratic Societies*. Oxford: Oxford Univ. Press.

McLaughlin, T. H. (2008). *Liberalism, Education, and Schooling: Essays by T. H. McLaughlin*. St. Andrews Studies in Philosophy and Public Affairs, edited by D. Carr, M. Halstead, and R. Pring. Charlottesville, VA: Imprint Academic.

Nozick, R. (1981). *Philosophical Explanations*. Cambridge, MA: Harvard Univ. Press.

Oakeshott, M. (1962). *Rationalism in Politics*. London: Methuen.

Rawls, J. (1993). *Political Liberalism*. New York: Columbia Univ. Press.

Tomasi, J. (2000). *Liberalism beyond Justice: Citizens, Society, and the Boundaries of Political Theory*. Princeton, NJ: Princeton Univ. Press.

Waghid, Y. (2011). *Conceptions of Islamic Education: Pedagogic Framings*. New York: Peter Lang.

Walzer, M. (1985). *Thick and Thin, Moral Argument at Home and Abroad* Notre Dame: Univ. of Notre Dame Press.

Section Three

Eastern Europe and Russia

To Raise Good Muslims and Good Citizens

The Goals of Religious and Cultural Education for Polish Tatars in the 20ᵗʰ Century

Agata S. Nalborczyk

Introduction – the history of Polish Muslim Tatars before 1918

Polish-Lithuanian Muslim Tatars[55] are one of the traditional Polish minorities. They were the first Muslims to settle within the borders of Poland and Lithuania – countries united since 1385 by the ruler i.e. the king. In the fourteenth century, Tatars came to their new homeland from territories ruled by the Golden Horde which had been an Islamic state since the thirteenth century (Borawski & Dubiński, 1986, 15). First invited to Lithuania as mercenaries, they settled there as political refugees and war captives (Konopacki, 2010, 25f),[56] and since the fifteenth century Tatars settled more systematically near the important political and economic centres (Tyszkiewicz, 2002, 16-17). Some Tatar craftsmen settled in cities, while others served at magnates' courts or as translators of oriental languages (Kryczyński, 2000 [1938], 17). The number of Tatar settlers in Lithuania increased in the subsequent centuries, and it is estimated that during the course of the sixteenth and seventeenth centuries their number reached as many as 25,000 (Sobczak, 1984, 43f). They were settled mostly on the same terms as those before them and lands were given to them in return for their military service in the armed forces (Borawski, 1983, 56-57; Konopacki, 2010, 40-41). Their settlement in

---

55 Tatars are descendants of Mongols who came with the armies of Genghis Khan's descendants, as well as of local Turkic speaking peoples.

56 Lithuania shared borders with the Golden Horde and fought against it to prevent invasions of Lithuanian lands.

the territories of today's Poland started in 1679, when Tatars were granted land by King John III Sobieski in 1679 in Podlachia (Kryczyński 2000 [1938], 27).[57]

Most Polish-Lithuanian Tatars, especially those serving in the army, were direct subordinates of the king without being subject to any local administration. This was one of the means providing them with freedom of religion – they were allowed to practice Islam, erect mosques (Tyszkiewicz, 2008, 155) and raise their children according to the teachings of their own faith (Konopacki, 2010, 33f, 71-72).

Tatars serving in the Lithuanian and Polish army were granted land as fiefdoms in return for their services together with a social status which was in practice similar to that of the local nobility (Zakrzewski, 1988, 574f). In the seventeenth century they officially received all the civil rights of this social class (Borawski and Dubiński, 1986, 85-87; Zakrzewski 1988, 579) and in 1791 finally full political rights were officially granted to them (Bohdanowicz et al., 1997, 14).

As Tatar settlements developed starting from the fourteenth century, various forms of religious life followed, suited to the existing circumstances. From the sixteenth century, local Muslim communities (called *dżemiaty*) functioned wherever there was a concentrated Tatar settlement, mostly around mosques.[58] Imams were elected mostly from among members of the community (Tyszkiewicz, 2008, 155). Until then imams had been brought from the Crimea (Konopacki, 2010, 86), but beginning in the second half of the sixteenth century Polish authorities allowed education of imams inside the country, since Crimea was a hostile state (Sobczak, 1984, 104).

At the end of the eighteenth century, Poland lost its independence and its territories were divided between Russia, Prussia and Austria. The areas inhabited by Lithuanian-Polish Tatars came under Russian rule. This meant that Tatars became subject to Russian legal regulations concerning Muslims (Kryczyński, [1938] 2000, 35). Muslims in Russia enjoyed freedom of religion, the right to erect mosques and to bury their dead in their own cemeteries. Their religious life was regulated by regional spiritual assemblies that were headed by a mufti and in 1831 all Polish-Lithuanian Muslims fell under the jurisdiction of the Tauridae Muslim Spiritual Board in Simferopol, Crimea.[59] Therefore particular Tatar religious

---

57 There are still Muslim communities, mosques and *mizars* (cemeteries) in these villages to this day.

58 At that time there were about 30 mosques within the borders of the Polish-Lithuanian state (Tyszkiewicz, 1986, 286-287).

59 For more details on the Crimean Muftiate see Бойцова, Ганкевич et al. (2009, 136f).

communities lost their autonomy, but local assemblies kept the right to elect an imam (Tyszkiewicz, 2002, 82).

Poland attained independence in 1918 in the aftermath of the First World War after 123 years of partitions. However, the war thinned the number of Tatars in Poland, the majority of whom resettled deep into Russia. Many mosques, houses and cemeteries were demolished during the war, and many villages lost their Tatar character (Kryczyński 2000 [1938], 44).

Despite this great loss to the Tatar minority, Tatars did not shy away from taking an active part in the life of the reborn Polish state. They did, for example, become engaged in educational activities and worked on their own form of civic education, realising the common aims set forth by the Polish state. This article is a presentation of Muslim Tatars in Poland between 1918 and 1939 as citizens who cared about the common fatherland. We also discuss the educational goals, methods and means used by Tatars in raising new generations to be self-aware and loyal citizens of the reborn state.

Polish Tatars 1918-1939 as citizens and Muslims

When Poland regained independence in 1918, nineteen active Muslim communities with five and a half thousand Muslim Tatars found themselves within the new borders of the restored Polish state (Kryczyński, 2000 [1938], 162-163). The Polish parliament introduced a new constitution on the 17th May 1921 and the new legal order started to regulate the life of the Polish society.

Tatars as Polish citizens and their duties towards the State

In the years 1918-1939 Poland was a country inhabited by many ethnicities and people of different denominations, with the ethnic divisions to a high degree corresponding to the religious divisions.[60] The constitution of 17th May 1921 defined

---

60 According to the national census of 1931, Catholic Church adherents constituted the dominant group of 75% of Poland's population, including Roman Catholics (64.8% of the population) and the second largest group of Greek Orthodox Catholics (10.2%). The Orthodox Church encompassed 11.8% of the population and the Evangelical Church 2.6%. Among non-Christian religions Judaism was the most numerous – 9.8%, Muslims and Karaites constituted only small religious communities. The denominational structure corresponded to the ethnic structure. According to the national census of 1921, 98.7% of the Roman Catholics were Polish, and 88% of the Greek Orthodox Cath-

Polish citizens. There were no restrictions in receiving citizenship or enjoying rights connected with it on the grounds of ethnicity, nationality or religion. According to Article 88 of the Constitution all Muslim Tatars were Polish citizens as born from parents with Polish citizenship. According to Art. 96 of the Constitution, all citizens were equal before the law.[61]

The Constitution also defined the duties of Polish citizens. The first duty was "to be loyal to the Republic of Poland" (Art. 89) and "to respect and obey the Constitution of the State and other legal acts" (Art. 90). The next Constitution of 23rd April 1935 defined the same obligation in different words: "Citizens are obliged to be loyal to the State and earnestly fulfil the duties imposed by the State" (Art. 6)

Polish citizens who belonged to religious minorities formally had the same rights as other citizens to abide by the rules of their religion and to be involved in any activity to help its functioning. Art. 110 of the Constitution of 1921 stated:

> Polish citizens belonging to national, religious, or linguistic minorities have the same right as other citizens of founding, supervising, and administering at their own expense, charitable, religious, and social institutions, schools and other educational institutions, and of using freely them in their language, and observing the rules of their religion.

The Constitution of 1935 confirmed this right: "The State guarantees that the citizens are free to pursue their personal values as well as freedom of conscience, speech and association" (Art. 5, point 2). "The State guarantees its citizens the opportunity to develop their personal values as well as the freedom of conscience, speech, and association". It also stated that:

> A citizen's right to have an impact upon public matters shall be measured by his merits and efforts which contribute to the common good. Neither the citizen's background, nor their religion, gender or nationality, can be a reason to limit those rights (Art. 7).

---

olics were Ukrainian. The Orthodox Church included Ukrainians (42.9%), Belorussians (34.1%) and Russians (1.5%). The majority of Evangelical Church adherents were of German origin (59.4%). (Garlicki, 1999, 507).

61   As a result of this regulation, Tatars who had been members of the nobility in the past lost all their privileges.

As we can see, since 1918 Muslim Tatars were equal to other Polish citizens, however, the duties of all citizens and therefore their duties, too, were more directed to loyalty and faithfulness toward the state than it is in modern times.

The legal situation of Tatars as Muslims and religious education

The Simferopol Muftiate was abolished in 1920 when the Soviets seized control over the Crimea. A year later a new Polish constitution of 1921 was adopted, which not only guaranteed freedom of conscience and religion, but also revoked the regulations of the Russian law (Tyszkiewicz, 2002, 141).

The Constitution empowered the state to officially recognize religious denominations by special legal acts, whose content was to be negotiated beforehand with representatives of those denominations. In January 1925 Polish authorities were presented with a document entitled "Provisional Regulations on the Organization of the Church of Muhammad in Poland", which became the basis for a minister's order on temporary recognition of the rules of the Muslim 'church' in Poland. This in turn made it possible to organize an official national Muslim convention that elected Muslim legal representatives.

In 1925, the representatives convened the All-Polish Congress of Delegates of Muslim Communities that established the Muslim Religious Union in the Republic of Poland *(Muzułmański Związek Religijny w Rzeczpospolitej Polskiej* – henceforth MZR), and elected Jakub Szynkiewicz the Mufti (Miśkiewicz, 1990, 35-36, 41f). The MZR statute was approved by the authorities in March 1936. On the 21st of April in the same year the act defining the state's relations with the MZR came into force (Sobczak, 2004, 201). It was by this Act that Islam became officially recognized by the Polish state (Miśkiewicz, 1990, 53-54), and in this respect it is still binding today.[62] The MZR was to be fully independent in managing its internal affairs within the limits of the law and its statute which was ratified by a Cabinet regulation. The government obliged itself to support the Muslim Religious Union financially.

Concerning Islamic religious education, Article 32 of this Act states:

Religious education for young people of Muslim persuasion, in educational institutions whose curriculum applies to young people under the age of 18 and is maintained fully or in part by the State or local government bodies, is, according to the

---

62 Legal acts of that period are still in force, unless repealed by the Sejm, Polish Parliament. For more details see Nalborczyk and Borecki (2011, 350-351).

state regulations, obligatory and to be delivered by teachers nominated by school authorities from amongst persons possessing the qualifications defined by state regulations, and a Mufti's authorisation to teach religion.

It was the Mufti who was responsible for the organisation of Muslim religious education as was stated in Art. 5 point 5 of the statute of the MZR. The Highest Muslim Board was responsible for establishing Islamic schools (Art. 12, point 7). According to Art. 52, any imam could deliver Muslim religious instruction at a public school on the territory of the local Muslim community, all other teachers had to be appointed by the Mufti.

Religious education and citizenship education in public schools

The authorities of reborn Poland introduced free public secular schools, accessible to all children from all social classes, ethnic and religious groups.[63] Citizenship education taught at these schools aimed at bringing up children "as righteous citizens of the mother country" which was one of the goals of the new school system (Mauersberg, 1988,14 ff). In 1928, the Minister of Religious Denominations and Public Enlightenment, Kazimierz Świtalski, said in his speech describing the reform of education, that citizenship education should produce good citizens of the Republic of Poland, ready to serve their home country, ready to work, to perform their duties towards it and ready to fight for it if need be (Araszkiewicz, 1971,12-13).

It was as well a duty of the state to make "accessible also moral guidance and religious consolation to citizens under its immediate care in public institutions, such as educational institutions, barracks, hospitals, prisons, and charitable homes" (Art. 102 of the Constitution of 1921). According to both Constitutions, however, religious instruction was compulsory in schools financed entirely or partly by the state or local authorities. This duty was first stated in the Constitution of 1921:

---

63 For more details concerning the construction of the school system in Poland 1918-1939 see Mauersberg (1988, 16-30).

Within the limits of the elementary school, instruction is compulsory for all citizens of the state (Art. 118)

Instruction in religion is compulsory for all pupils in every educational institution, the curriculum of which includes instruction of youth under eighteen years of age, if the institution is maintained wholly or in part by the state, or by self-governmental bodies. The direction and supervision of religious instruction in schools belongs to the respective religious communities, reserving to the state educational authorities the right of supreme supervision (Art. 120).

These articles of the Constitution were in agreement with another one, describing the right of religious communities to organize their activities and to acquire and possess financial means to maintain them:

Every religious community recognized by the state has the right of organizing collective and public services; (...) it remains in possession and enjoyment of its endowments and funds, and of religious, educational, and charitable institutions." (Art. 113)

Besides the constitutional regulations, the government issued detailed decrees regulating the implementation of the religious instruction in public schools. In the Eastern regions of Poland, inhabited by the majority of the Tatars, religious instruction as a compulsory subject in schools was introduced even before the first Constitution of 1921 by Article 3 of the Order of Provisional Commissioner General of Eastern Lands on school system and education, declared on 11th October 1919.

Following the trends set by the state's political ideology and its attitude to education, the above mentioned document defined the need for religious instruction in schools in the following manner:

Trusting that religious instruction is the best basis for teaching morality, we hereby order that all religions represented in a given school will be taught as a compulsory subject and instruction will be carried out in the respective languages.

In 1931, the Minister of Religious Communities and Public Enlightenment expressed the opinion of the government that religious instruction should help in "the upbringing of brave, creative and selfless citizens on the religious-moral basis" (Araszkiewicz, 1971, 13-14). The Act of 11th March 1932 on the School System defined religious education next to state-citizenship education as complementary factors in raising new generations of patriots (Araszkiewicz, 1971, 14).

The aims of religious and cultural education as defined by the Muslim Tatar community

According to the Constitution of 1921, Polish citizens were obliged to "bring up their children as righteous citizens of the mother country, and to secure for them at least elementary education." (Art. 94). As we can see, one of the most important aims of education and upbringing, so important that it was defined by the Constitution, was to bring up patriots and loyal citizens. The state undertook diverse educational and ideological activities which were meant to facilitate realisation of these aims.

Tatars did not reject the state's aims of citizenship education. On the contrary – they endeavoured to tailor them to the ethnic, religious, and historical character of their community. In the atmosphere of work for the newly re-established state they attempted to find a way to bring up the young generation of Tatars as patriots, conscious of their tradition, history, and religion, but also loyal towards the Polish state. Due to the lack of a tradition of citizenship education it was necessary to establish a new, individual model of the Polish citizen with a Tatar Muslim background.

Tatars themselves defined the aims that were to be realized by all educational activities undertaken by their various institutions established after 1918.

One especially active teacher from one of the junior high schools was Mustafa Gembicki, the author of *Ideology of Polish Tatars* (Pol. *Ideologia polskich Tatarów*) [64] He was also a teacher of Muslim religious education and wrote numerous articles on children's education and upbringing, which were published in Tatar journals. His vision of Tatar community advancement/development was based on their educational accomplishments and drew on the experiences the Tatar community had accumulated since 1918. Its central idea was the purposeful education of the young. Family, as an important segment of every community was to be seen as "the first and an almost sanctified centre from which the whole nation would benefit" (Gembicki, 1938a, 2). Every Tatar family had to realize that it played a part in realizing the idea of national rebirth. Parents' involvement in their children's upbringing and a conscious transmission of cultural values should create a favourable atmosphere which later would be visible in the actions of future generations.

In Gembicki's vision, another group with an educational function was the Tatar intelligentsia organized around academic centres (Warsaw and Vilnius). Their mission was to grasp the complexity of the whole rebirth movement. A group of highly educated Tatars was to become the axis of all educational activities and ini-

---

64 Published in *Życie Tatarskie, 4*, 1938, 2-7.

tiatives – they ought to consciously raise their children to become active members of the community and role models for those young people whose parents were not role models. It was also their task to prepare the didactic ideology, but also to familiarise those less educated with the principles of Islam, its philosophy, ethics and Muslim theology (Gembicki, 1938a, 3-4).

A significant part in the rebirth of Tatar values was also to be played by communities from rural areas. Tatars from small towns, villages and hamlets had always stressed the noble status running through their family histories, which at the same time emphasized their devotion to Poland. Gembicki wrote that they should establish cultural-educational circles which would increase their national consciousness and the understanding of the significance of education for the development of the Tatar community (Gembicki, 1938a, 5). They should be supported in this effort by local Muslim communities.

Particular hope was placed by Gembicki in young married couples who recognized and realized the idea of national rebirth. Their educational potential was seen in the "awakening of the young spirit and thirst for advancement". Spiritual, moral and intellectual awakening was meant to contribute to a general increase in the material culture, which in turn would go on to improve the nation's living conditions and result in the nation's rebirth. In villages, all efforts were aimed at raising the awareness among Tatars of the necessity to improve the level of education.

Religious elements were utilised in the creation of this ideology. And thus the involvement of parents in raising conscious citizens and members of the Tatar nation would result in their receiving the respect of their own children – argued Gembicki, referring to the Prophetic traditions (Hadith) about the importance of the relationship between mother and child (Gembicki, 1938a, 3). Gembicki (1938a, 6) emphasised that "the Qur'an teaches us to learn the good and the true, and supports education and intellectual life". It was Islam that made Tatars virtuous members of this society, fierce warriors and Polish patriots throughout the ages. "There is no virtue or love of the Motherland without God" – wrote Gembicki (1938b, 2).

Shaping an appropriate attitude towards the Polish state was also one of the aims of citizenship education of young Tatars. Gembicki (1938a, 6-7) wrote:

> We have lived in this country for six centuries. We have shared the fate of this country since the times of our ancestors. None of us will voluntarily agree to be buried even in Mecca, Jerusalem, or Constantinople. We wish to die and stay with our ancestors at our humble, but dear little cemeteries, because this country is our Motherland. (…) 'God and Motherland' – these two words tell us as much as they tell the Poles, why we have been created and what our destiny is.

According to Gembicki (1938b, 1) "Man ought to fulfil on earth the duty towards God and Motherland (the state), neighbours, that is the society, towards his family, and himself". "It is our ambition to rise in body and spirit and stand brave protecting our Homeland when we're called upon to do so by the Chief Commander of the Polish Nation and the Ruler of this Country" (Gembicki, 1938a, 7). This illustrates that Gembicki outlined the principles of the Tatar Muslim citizenship education and was conscious of this fact. He wrote: "To raise means to strive towards making one's wards conscious, virtuous, and enlightened citizens" (Gembicki, 1938b, 3).

Mustafa Gembicki wasn't the only one who delineated the aims of cultural-educational activities among Muslim Tatars. Similar subjects were undertaken by other Tatar activists, such as Imam Ali Ismail Woronowicz in *Our social work*, (Tatar Life 1937, 9); *Let us venerate our fathers* (Tatar Life 1938, 9) or Leon Kryczyński in *About the difficulties of social work* (Tatar Life, 1937, 8). All of them recognised the significance of religious matters and Polish-Lithuanian Tatar history in achieving the intended goals of educational activities among young Tatars.

These goals largely coincided with the tasks set for education and upbringing by state authorities at that time as expressed in the above mentioned Article 94 of the Constitution of 1921. The general program of citizenship education in public schools also included religion (mostly Roman Catholicism as the majority religion in Poland) and examples from history (Araszkiewicz, 1971, 13), just as it was prescribed by the Tatars in their manifesto defining the aims of education.

The authorities responsible for education recognized the special needs of Muslim Tatar religious and cultural education in the area of bringing up good and loyal citizens. The evidence of their awareness of the role of the Tatar history in building the identity of Muslim Tatars as citizens of the Polish state is a booklet entitled *Tatarzy w Polsce* (Pol. "Tatars in Poland") published by the Department of Education in Vilnius in 1936. This booklet was a compilation including the history and characteristics of the Muslim Tatar minority and it was published as a supplement to the state's "Dziennik Urzędowy Kuratorium Okręgu Szkolnego Wileńskiego" ("Official Journal of the Vilnius Area Department of Education"). It was supposed to provide help for teachers working in areas with a significant number of Tatars:

> Wishing to take local conditions into consideration when realizing the curriculum, more often than not local teachers will have to cater for their students, members of this nation which has played such a glorious part in the history of our country. (*Tatarzy w Polsce*, 1936, 1)

As a result of their loyalty to the Polish state, Tatars also saw themselves as having a similar role to the one ascribed to them by the authorities – a bridge between the East and the West (Chazbijewicz, 1993, 23f). The Ministry of Foreign Affairs supported contacts between them and Muslim countries, for example, by financing their travels and participation in conferences or conventions (Miśkiewicz, 1990, 139f). Tatars travelling to Muslim countries promoted Polish foreign policy abroad and depicted the Polish state as tolerant and friendly towards Muslims (Chazbijewicz, 1993, 17). Olgierd Najman Mirza Kryczyński after his travel to the Middle East[65] said in his speech during the All-Polish Delegate Convention of Muslim Communities in 1925, "Polish Muslims will be happy if they can be a link between Poland and the world of Islam, likewise if they manage to contribute to make Polish state aspirations a reality" (Kryczyński, 1932, 8).

Another Tatar activist, imam Ali Ismail Woronowicz wrote (1937, 6): "Lofty slogans like 'Tatars are the link between the East and the West', 'Polish Muslim Tatars are the Muslim outpost in Western Europe' are a clear manifestation of what work we need to do for the good of our Reborn Homeland".

The means of fulfilling the goals of raising good Muslims and good citizens

In order to implement the educational goals prescribed by the Polish authorities on one side and by Tatar activists on the other side, Polish Tatars employed different kinds of religious instruction, activities of their organizations, books and periodicals.

The contents used to realize these educational pursuits were to include: religious matters, Polish-Lithuanian Tatar history and traditions of patriotic attitudes towards the Polish state (Wróblewska, 2012, 170).

Islamic religious instruction

Before the 1918, Islamic religious education was mostly provided by imams in mosques. It included instruction in prayer, reading of the Qur'an and Arabic lan-

---

65 Olgierd Najman Mirza Kryczyński was one of the Muslim Tatars sent by the Polish government to the Middle East. In Egypt, he spread the knowledge about the positive attitude of the Polish state toward local Muslims – this information was published by "Al-Ahram" (Miśkiewicz, 1990, 139-140; Chazbijewicz, 1993, 25-26).

guage together with Arabic script (Tyszkiewicz, 2008, 156). However children from families living outside dense Tatar settlement very often did not get any religious education at all beside instructions in how to pray delivered by their parents (Wróblewska, 2012, 18-19). Very often the position of the imam was passed down from father to son, and imams taught their sons only in order to keep the post of imam in the family, because imams enjoyed financial privileges (Konopacki, 2010, 188-190). Higher Islamic education was not provided in the territories inhabited by Polish-Lithuanian Tatars. Before the nineteenth century the most important centre was Turkey, and later, when the Tatars were under Russian rule – Islamic theology was studied by only a few Polish Tatars in Kazan or Symferopol (Tyszkiewicz, 2008, 154).

Religion was what set Tatar Muslims apart culturally, as the foundation of their social norms and values. Therefore, it's no wonder that also after 1918 religion was treated as a very important factor in citizenship education. It was Islam that was presented to the young generations as the source of their spiritual and moral strength and patriotic attitude. The principles important to the Tatar Muslim community and to the Polish state were drawn from the Qur'an as the foundation of the Islamic faith: recognition of what's true and right, supporting education and acquiring knowledge, with the development of intellectual life.

Religious instruction was introduced in the public schools of the territories inhabited by Muslim Tatars in 1919 and after several years new regulations were issued, specifying the form of the instruction in a more detailed way. In the Circular Letter issued by the Ministry of Religious Communities and Public Enlightenment on 5th January 1927, we read:

1. Every public school with at least 12 students of a given faith should provide religious instruction for them in the amount of 2 hours per week. The instruction should be carried out in the local school, or if not possible, in the nearest schools.
2. In towns with more than one public school, for reasons of convenience, all children of the same faith may be gathered for religious instruction in one of the schools.

Even though state law allowed opening denominational schools that taught religious matters beside the prescribed general preparatory subjects, there was little demand for such schools within the Tatar minority. Tatar settlements were dispersed, most of the Tatar families, affected by the war, were impoverished and could not afford to send their children to another city while free education was available in a local public school (Mizgalski, 1998, 104-105). Therefore there were no Islamic schools offering the whole curriculum of primary school. There were only religious schools for children aged between 6 and 8 in every one of the 19 religious communities – one per community (Mizgalski, 1998, 106-107). Consequently, the majority of the Muslim Tatar children attended public schools and received religious education there, mostly in inter-school classes.[66] As was stated above, the Mufti supervised Islamic religious instruction in public schools and appointed teachers. There were also small religious schools for children aged between 6 and 8 in every one of the 19 religious communities (Mizgalski, 1998, 106-107). Islamic religious instruction was also provided in local mosques by Imams and Muezzins or at home by private teachers (Wróblewska, 2012, 52 f).[67] All of these educational institutions also covered a certain amount of knowledge about Tatar history and traditions.

Tatar organizations involved in the transmission of Tatar ideological values

In their efforts to create new generations of Tatars with a strong Muslim Tatar identity and a patriotic attitude towards the Polish state, Polish Tatars also used several religious and cultural organisations functioning on different levels of their society. This was a realization of the directives put forward by Tatar activists and at the same time it harmonized with instructions issued by the state authorities urging to engage these kind of organizations in citizenship education (Araszkiewicz, 1971, 13).

Among such Tatar organizations active between 1918 and 1939 we find:

- Muslim Religious Union (est. 1925) – an all-Polish organization of Polish Muslims, as it was stated before, responsible for the Islamic religious instruction of any kind
- Polish Tatar Association for Culture and Education (Pol. *Związek Kulturalno-Oświatowy Tatarów Rzeczypospolitej Polskiej*) founded in Vilnius in 1926; as part of its activity, its members established the Tatar National Museum (1929), and the Tatar National Archive (1931), both in Vilnius (Tyszkiewicz, 1987,375; Miśkiewicz, 1990, 110-111). The archive played a crucial role in conducting research on the history of the Tatar minority and in preserving Tatar

---

66 For more detalis see: Wróblewska (2012, 61-66).

67 For more details on the course of Islamic religious instruction see: Kryczyński (2000 [1938], 185f).

traditions. It was also an important factor influencing the ethnic revival of this community. An important part of the Association's activities were lectures and public debates as well as the Tatar Library consisting of more than 300 volumes – both books and journals (Miśkiewicz 1990, 107f). There were some small libraries established by local units of the Association as well as local day-rooms for the youth (Miśkiewicz, 1990, 109).

- The Tatar Youth Club (Pol. *Klub Młodzieży Tatarskiej*) established in 1935 by the ZKOTRP was a self-education centre for young people and a place where they could come to take part in celebrations of Muslim holidays (Miśkiewicz, 1990, 116f). Members of the Club visited numerous villages and towns present-ing papers and giving speeches, bringing religious and historical knowledge closer to the people (Wróblewska, 2012, 127f).

- Tatar divisions of the Riflemen's Association (Pol. *tatarskie drużyny Związku Strzeleckiego*) which was a Polish state paramilitary cultural and educational organization created in 1910 in Lviv, were established 1933 in Nowogródek and Słonim; Tatar members of the Riflemen's Association undertook cultural and educational actions to promote civic ideals among young Tatars (Miśkiewicz 1990, 113). The Tatar divisions of the Association were there to unite Muslim youth "wishing to use their energy for military work to the glory of the Home-land and to the good of their compatriots" (Wróblewska, 2012, 160). Tatar youth, members of the Riflemen's Association, showed big interest in Islam, religious education and the history of Tatars. They invited guests delivering lectures on these subjects.

There were other institutions involved in cultural and citizenship education among Tatars as well: the Tatar Youth Day Room established in 1932 with the aim of developing and transmitting Polish Muslim Tatar traditions and artistic groups performing dances, poetry recitations etc. (Miśkiewicz, 1990,108). There were also Tatar balls and receptions organized to celebrate religious festivals, har-vest festivals, the end of the school year, and graduating from Qur'anic lessons (the so-called *lahi*) – these events belonged to the means of raising awareness of their traditions among young Tatars.

Publications and academic activities

Polish Muslim Tatars undertook their own publishing activities in order to spread knowledge about their past and present, traditions and religion. The list of titles published between 1918 and 1939 includes:

- 'Tatar Yearbook' (Pol. "Rocznik Tatarski") est. 1932, a journal academic in character, publishing scholarly articles in 3 issues during the years 1932-1938
- "Tatar Life" (Pol. "Życie Tatarskie") est. 1934, bimonthly "Tatar Life", more popular in character and read mostly by the Tatar community – 69 issues during the years 1934-1939
- "Islamic Review" (Pol. "Przegląd Islamski") published 1930-1931 and 1934-1937; the aim: deepening religious knowledge among the Polish Tatars and delivering information about the modern Muslim world and its past.

Most of these periodicals were financially supported by the Polish authorities (Tyszkiewicz, 1987, 375).

Beside periodicals, books also played a very important role in strengthening Muslim Tatar identity and awakening loyalty towards the Polish state. Historians were especially active in this field. They consciously depicted the aims, scope of subjects and methodology of their research (Wendland, 2013, 104).[68] As examples of such works the following texts could be named: *Tatarzy litewscy. Próba monografii historyczno-etnograficznej* by Stanisław Kryczyński (published 1938) or *Tatarzy litewscy w wojsku polskim w powstaniu 1831* by Leon Kryczyński (published in 1932). Historians focused on the role Tatars had played fighting for Polish independence. They stressed Tatars' patriotism, love for their country and loyalty (Wendland, 2013, 213). Choosing those aspects of history was aimed at validating the Tatar presence in the reborn Poland (Wendland, 2013, 205) but also at promoting a sense of identity among Polish Tatar citizens (Tyszkiewicz, 1987, 381f). Historians' works were used as materials at schools to raise consciousness and produce loyal citizens aware of their traditions and identity.

Conclusions

Polish Tatar Muslims have always been a very active social group in Poland. Ever since they started settling on Lithuanian and Polish lands, their lifestyle and work for their new homeland reshaped their community forever, assigning them a place in the local social structure. They adopted to the new circumstances and changes around them quite skilfully.

When Poland regained independence in 1918, after 123 years of foreign rule, Muslim Tatars as rightful citizens got engaged in working for the good of the reborn motherland. This work involved activities geared towards raising new gen-

---

68 For more details see: Tyszkiewicz (1987, 372f).

erations of young Tatars in the spirit of patriotism and service for the country, i.e. as loyal and aware citizens of the Polish state.

To realise that goal, between 1918 and 1939, Polish Muslim Tatars tried to create a new model of upbringing and education by combining Islamic religious knowledge with Tatar history and Polish cultural values. Both the transmitting of religious issues and the Muslim Tatar tradition aimed at creating a modern Muslim Tatar citizen of the Polish state. Through these efforts, Tatars declared their readiness to take part in the reconstruction of the Polish state and to fight for the country's freedom. This educational model was very effective thanks to a great intensity of activities, a deep involvement and the will of the activists who also recognized the need for creating a new Muslim Tatar identity. In the 1930's, education in the Tatar community was gradually becoming a planned and conscious process as we can see in the example of the educational ideology created among others by Mustafa Gembicki, teacher and Tatar activist. Tatars established several organizations which functioned according to the visions and programs sketched out by Tatar activists. The MZR was responsible for religious issues, and the ZKOTRP for the promotion and dissemination of knowledge about the Tatar past.

These activities were possible partly because of the high level of education among Polish Tatars. The percentage of Tatars with higher education amounted to 14% at that time, while for the whole Polish population this rate was much lower – only 5.1%. (Kryczyński, 1938, 107–108; Tochtermann, 1935, 58).

These aims and efforts made by Muslim Tatars in the field of citizenship education coincided with those defined and implemented by the Polish state. For the Polish government they were proof of a clearly loyal attitude of this religious minority towards the state. The financial and legal support for many Tatar activities in this field can serve as evidence of approval of these efforts by the government which financially supported Tatar periodicals, financed the Islamic religious education in public schools, and officially recognized Islam as a religion in 1936.

Unfortunately, the outbreak of World War II in 1939 stopped the realization of these beneficial initiatives and put an end to these efforts. It caused the destruction of material resources and the dispersal of the Polish Muslim Tatar community.

References

Bohdanowicz, L., Chazbijewicz, S. & Tyszkiewicz, J. (1997). *Tatarzy muzułmanie w Polsce.* Gdańsk: Rocznik Tatarów Polskich.

Бойцова, Е., Ганкевич, В., Муратова, Э. & Хайрединова, З. (2009). *Ислам в Крыму: очерки истории функционирования мусульманских институтов.* Симферополь: Элиньо.

Borawski, P. (1983). Sytuacja prawna ludności tatarskiej Wielkim Księstwie Litewskim (XVI-XVIII w.). *Acta Baltico-Slavica, 15,* (55-76).

Borawski, P. & Dubiński, A. (1986). *Tatarzy polscy, Dzieje, obrzędy, tradycje.* Warszawa: Iskry.

Chazbijewicz S. (1993). Ideologie muzułmanów polskich w latach 1918-1939. *Rocznik Tatarów Polskich, 1,* (15-42).

Garlicki, A. (1999). *Encyklopedia historii Drugiej Rzeczypospolitej.* Warszawa: Wiedza Powszechna.

Gembicki, M. (1938a). Szukajcie a znajdziecie. *Życie Tatarskie, 4,* (1-7).

Gembicki M. (1938b). Wychowanie rodzinne. Rozwinięcie postulatu III ideologii Tatarów polskich. *Życie Tatarskie, 7,* (1-3).

Konopacki, A. (2010). *Życie religijne Tatarów na ziemiach Wielkiego Księstwa Litewskiego w XVI-XIX w.* Warszawa: Wyd. UW.

Kryczyński, O.N.M. (1932). Ruch nacjonalistyczny a Tatarzy litewscy. *Rocznik Tatarski, 1,* (5-20).

Kryczyński, S. (2000 [1938]). *Tatarzy litewscy. Próba monografii historyczno-etnograficznej.* Gdańsk: Rocznik Tatarów Polskich.

Kryczyński, S. (1938). Tatarzy polscy, *Rocznik Ziem Wschodnich,* (106-121).

Mauersberg, S. (1988). *Komu służyła szkoła w Drugiej Rzeczpospolitej? Społeczne uwarunkowania dostępu do oświaty.* Warszawa: Ossolineum.

Mizgalski J. (1998). Oświata wśród Tatarów w Polsce międzywojennej". *Prace Naukowe Wyższej Szkoły Pedagogicznej w Częstochowie. Zeszyty Historyczne, 5,* (101-109).

Nalborczyk, A. S. and Borecki, P. (2011). "Relations between Islam and the state in Poland: the legal position of Polish Muslims", *Islam and Christian-Muslim Relations, 22:3,* (343-359).

Sobczak, J. (2004). Położenie prawne polskich wyznawców islamu. In: Baecker, R. & Kitab, Sh. (Eds.). *Islam a świat* (172-209). Toruń: Mado.

Sobczak, J. (1984). *Położenie prawne ludności tatarskiej w Wielkim Księstwie Litewskim.* Warszawa-Poznań: PWN.

Tatarzy w Polsce. (1936). *Dziennik Urzędowy Kuratorium Okręgu Szkolnego Wileńskiego,* 2 (19), Wilno.

Tochtermann, J.J. (1935) Ilość, rozmieszczenie i struktura zawodowa Tatarów w Polsce , *Wiadomości Geograficzne, 8-10,* (55-60).

Tyszkiewicz, J. (2008). *Tatarzy w Polsce i Europie. Fragmenty dziejów.* Pułtusk: AH.

Tyszkiewicz, J. (2002). *Z historii Tatarów polskich 1794-1944.* Pułtusk: WSH.

Tyszkiewicz, J. (1989). *Tatarzy na Litwie i w Polsce, Studia z dziejów XIII-XVIII w.* Warszawa: PWN.

Tyszkiewicz, J. (1987). Dorobek historyczny Leona i Stanisława Kryczyńskich. In: Taternicki, J. (Ed.). *Środowiska historyczne II Rzeczpospolitej* (371-388). Warszawa: COM SNP.

Wendland, W. (2013). „*Trzy czoła proroków z matki obcej*". *Myśl historyczna Tatarów Polskich w II Rzeczpospolitej*. Kraków: Universitas.

Woronowicz, A.I. (1937). Nasza praca społeczna. *Życie Tatarskie, 9*, (5-6).

Wróblewska, U. (2012). *Oświata Tatarów w Drugiej Rzeczypospolitej*. Warszawa: Semper.

Zakrzewski, A. B. (1998). Czy Tatarzy litewscy rzeczywiście nie byli szlachtą?. *Przegląd Historyczny 79(3)*, (573-580).

The Positions of Muslim scholars in the Volga-Ural Region in the Context of Islamic Ideologies of the 20th and 21st Centuries[69]

Leyla Almazova

Introduction

The areas of modern-day Tatarstan and Bashkortostan have for a long time represented the periphery of the Muslim world. Following Ivan the Terrible's conquest of Kazan and later Russian expansion towards the Ural Mountains, the two completely ceased to be numbered among *Dar al-Islam* lands. The period of Soviet power further distanced the region's populace from the Islamic world. And yet the interesting fact is that despite geographic, historical, cultural, and other differences, the development of Islamic ideologies in these regions resembles those taking place among Muslims all around the world. To exemplify this thesis, we shall examine two time periods – the beginning of the 20th century and the present day.

The process of Islamic modernization at the beginning of the 20th century

The collision of two worlds – the rapidly developing West and the quiescent East, slumbering in its medieval dreams – was marked for the Muslim cultural region by epochal shifts in Weltanschauung, especially in the capitals of Islamic nations and among their enlightened elites. The Muslim community witnessed the emergence within itself of various ideological directions, each of which viewed the paths of so-

---

69 The present article was written in the course of working on a larger project titled "Islamic Intellectual Response to the Challenge of Modernity," with support from the Fulbright Program and the University of Michigan, USA.

cial development from vastly differing positions. Since, in the majority of instances, all issues – political, social, cultural – were examined through the lens of religion, it followed that the main discussion occurred among diverse religious groups.

Toward the end of the 19th century, two main camps made an appearance in the Muslim community: conservatives (or traditionalists) and reformists. There was also a third fraction which was only then acquiring power and which only much later would triumphantly storm through the majority of Muslim nations, beginning with the second decade of the 20th century. We are here referring to the so-called nationalist–secularists who wanted to see nations with Muslim populations developed and consolidated along ethnic lines.

Coming back to the main two trends, it is worth remarking that the phenomenon of traditionalism, according to the classification of William Shepard (Shepard, 1987), is characterized by such features as adherence to *taqlid*,[70] seeking to preserve the powers of the *ulama* and medieval educational traditions, and an unwillingness to change with the passage of time.

Reformism, in turn, may be divided into two types (Knysh, 2011, 398-423): fundamentalist reformers and modernist reformers. The first was "launched in the name of cleansing Islam of 'blameworthy innovations' and restoring its original purity" (Knysh, 2011, 401) without any references to Western ideas, as it did in the cases of 'Abd al-Wahhab (1792) in Arabia and Utiz-Imyani al-Bulgari (1835) (Utiz-Imyani, 2007) in the Volga region. However, towards the turn of the 19th century, the second type of reformism emerged. Defining it is best done through the term "modernization." If modernization is the change, with the passage of time, of all aspects of a life – that is, technological, scientific and institutional progress – then, accordingly, modernism is the ideology that strives to bring consciousness into conformity with the altered living conditions. Through its leaders – Jamal al-Afghani (1897), Muhammad Abduh (1905), Qasim Amin (1908) and others – modernist reformism became the dominant movement among Muslim elites at the beginning of the 20th century. Its characteristics included a theological justification for the idea of free will, the absolutization of the role of reason, calls for revitalization of religion by means of *ijtihad*, and the reinstatement of women's rights. All of this was accompanied by a renewed attention to the text of the Qur'an as a primary source for decision making, and consequently, to a growth in its role in juristic reasoning (*fiqh*). Other significant characteristics of modernist reforms were the liberation of religion from the prejudices and the accumulated layers of later centuries.

---

70 *Taqlid* refers to following the rulings of one of the four recognized legal schools in Sunni Islam.

Turning our attention to the Tatar-Bashkir community at the beginning of the 20th century, we observe the same ideological trends. On the one hand, there were the traditionalists (in Tatar language 'kadimchelar') who did not want to change with the passage of time. Their bastion was the Dīn wa Ma'īshat journal, headed by its editor, Galimetdin Ganislamov and one of its more prolific contributors, Ishmi-Ishan Ishmukhametov (who had studied in Bukhara). Among the ideas they cultivated, we should note their critique of Jadidism (Islamic modernist reform), their preservation of the Bukharan madrasa system of education, their rejection of any European borrowings – theatre, musical evenings, the study of Western and Russian languages – their strict adherence to gender segregation, their apologia for accepting the rulings of the established medieval schools of Islamic law (taqlid), and their preaching of isolationism from the Russian Muslim community (Sardavi, 2004). The traditionalists had their own fairly broad audience, although it is worth noting that after 1905 they had noticeably surrendered their positions, which was especially palpable when it came to the Muslim press and education.

The adherents of modernist reform (in Tatar language islakhchelar[71] or mujaddid[72]) on the other hand, played no less of, and perhaps even a more conspicuous role in the ideological space of that time and place. These included Musa Bigiev (1949), Ziyaetdin Kamali (1942), Zakir Kadyri (1954) – all students of Muhammad Abduh who had received their education from Al-Azhar in Egypt. These were the most famous social activists amongst the Muslim population of Rus-

---

71 "Islah" in Arabic means reform. There was a skeptical attitude to that term in Tatar society: for example Musa Bigiev was strictly against its use. His argument was that Reformation is a totally Western phenomenon that brought the new religion of Protestantism into being. As for Islam – there is not need for the emergence of a new religion, with a new set of beliefs and new forms of rituals. Ziaaddin Kamali on the contrary, embraced that term. For example, on the top of the first page of his book "Dini Tadbirlar" you can read "Islakh kitaphanase" (Reformist Library)

72 Musa Bigiev was called by the honorific title, Mujaddid (renewer), of the age.

sia. Their treatments of leading Islamic concepts such as *ijtihad*,[73] *mujtahid*,[74] *ji-had*,[75] *naskh*,[76] polygamy, *hijab*,[77] and a whole series of other issues, are vital to understanding the pan-Muslim phenomenon of the modernist wing of religious

---

73 *Ijtihad* (diligence, struggle) is the individual religious scholar's study and resolution of questions through the body of legal-theological sources, as well as the system of principles and arguments, methods and examples, employed by him during research into and commentary on the sources. According to tradition, ijtihad came about among Muhammad's supporters while he was still living. As a form of guided activity, ijtihad appeared at the end of the 7th century, when significant disagreements began to appear among the surviving supporters of the Prophet, who were alluding to the famous sayings and deeds of Muhammad. The main goal of ijtihad became the discovery and resolution of questions – new or as yet unsolved by predecessors – in a manner that would simultaneously draw upon Islam and support it.

74 A *mujtahid* (one who evinces diligence, zeal) is a scholar or theologian who has the right to pass independent judgment on important questions of fiqh. Three degrees of *mujtahid* were differentiated according to their respective levels of theological-legal authority: on the level of sharia as a whole, on the level of the *madhhab* (or established legal school), and on a level that dealt with the resolution of separate legal questions. A *faqih* who aspired to the qualifications of a *mujtahid* had to be fluent in Arabic, as well as have mastery of the entire theological-legal body of laws, with all its varying judgments from the main legal schools. Ideally the *faqih* had to know the Qur'an and its interpretations by heart, as well as no less than three thousand hadiths and their commentaries. In addition to this, he was to lead a strict and pious life. As a rule, *faqihs* rarely attained the first or second degree of *ijtihād* during their lifetimes. More often, this degree was bestowed upon them posthumously.

75 *Jihad* (struggle) was initially understood as a struggle to protect and spread Islam. Conceptions that were developed later on, provided the term with a new meaning: a distinction is made between "*jihad* of the heart", or greater jihad (*al-jihad al-akbar*), which referred to the personal moral struggle against the ego (nafs), and lesser jihad, which implied military engagements, and which was aimed at defending Islam from aggression.

76 *Naskh* (abrogation, *an-nasikh wa'l mansukh*) At the foundation of this concept lies the idea that certain commandments in the Quran were intended only for temporary use, and, as circumstances changed, they were either invalidated or replaced with other Qur'anic injunctions during the Prophet's lifetime. However, as the divine word, these commandments went on being read as a part of the Quran. Z. Kamali proposes a new reading of naskh as a universal law of change. (Kamali, 1909, 77–97).

77 *Hijab* (screen, curtain) can refer to a modest garment that covers the body and is worn by a Muslim woman when she goes out in public. Initially, wearing the hijab was prescribed for Muhammad's wives and later for all free Muslim women. There are different forms of the hijab – black or colored, as well as those that conceal the woman from head to toe or those that leave her face and hands visible. Tatar thinkers at the beginning of the 20th century argued with the traditionalists that, on it own, the hijab does not make a woman virtuous. Only a woman's knowledge and education, as well as the

reforms. Like their foreign fellow-thinkers, they preached ideas about the correspondence between Qur'anic tenets and reason: "Religion was created for people, and all of its contents are accessible to human reason. All of the rituals of religious worship from the perspective of reason are explicable, and every detail of Muslim ritualism benefits man. The only two areas that are inaccessible to human mind are the essence of Allah and the afterlife. Everything else, man is fully capable of conceiving with the help of his rational faculty" (Kamali, 2010). These are some of the quotes from the various parts of Ziyaetdin Kamali's *Philosophy of Islam*. Kamali and Bigiev hold the same ideas as their foreign fellow-thinkers about free will, the lofty role of women in society and their sacred status (Musa Bigiev), and the changing significance of the term "Muslim." According to them, a Muslim is not solely one who zealously performs religious rituals, but above all one who truly believes in God and does good deeds.

If the Tatar and Bashkirian modernist reforms were brought to a close by the Bolshevik regime, then their sunset in the foreign East was related to somewhat differing historical events – above all, the fall of the Ottoman empire and the rise of pro-Western, often openly secular regimes in Islamic countries: Turkey, Iran, Egypt, Jordan, Sudan, Pakistan, and some others. While the USSR conducted its struggle against religion, new ideological currents appeared in Muslim countries that were in the hands of pro-Western bourgeoisies. We may count these currents as continuations and developments of Ibn 'Abd al-Wahhab's fundamentalist reform, the main features of which was a return to the "purity" of the Islam of Muhammad's time and its liberation from later, non-Islamic components. Because of this, by the time that the Volga-Ural region returned once again to the arena of ideological debates in the Islamic Ummah, the map of Islamic ideologies had become entirely different.

A brief characterization of modern Islamic trends in the Foreign East

Adeeb Khalid believes that, just as it was a century ago, the most important element in the conceptualization of contemporary Islam is the modern era, which is leading the way to a new understanding of the world with its ambition to classify everything, with its refutation of the supernatural, its belief in science, its formulation of new forms of nationhood and its attendant attributes, and its new

---

corresponding respectful and deferential relation to her on the part of the male section of society would be capable of bringing her to true rectitude. (Bigiev, 2006, 127–256)

forms of informational transfer – at first through print and later through electronic communications. The modern era has sown chaos where habitual order previously reigned; however, it did so without providing various societies with a single trajectory of development. Thus, the modern era in no way requires strictly defined forms of economic development, or clearly established social and cultural patterns of secularization, the rise of democracy, gender equality, etc. (Khalid, 2007, 12). Muslim communities developed their own ideological responses to these challenges of modernity. Over the last 20–30 years, a multitude of religious groups have appeared in the Islamic Umma, all of which variously conceptualize the possible paths of development for Muslim societies. An analysis of the literature from recent years suggests that researchers, in one way or another, have distinguished the following main currents of modern Islam:

Neo-traditionalism, according to William Shepard, is characterized above all by its valuation of local traditions above radical or modernist ones – even non-Islamic values may be highly significant for it. This movement's adherents criticize those who disavow Islam's ancient, adaptive paths of development, since religion always resides within some specific, local, cultural paradigm. They value the depth and complexity of Islamic tradition and the wisdom of Sufi sheiks. El Fadl prefers to call them moderates (El Fadl, 2005, 5), juxtaposing them with puritans; others call them simply followers of traditional Islam (Kurzman, 1998, 6) drawing no difference between the traditionalists of centuries ago and modern believers in the preservation of historical inheritance as an essential part of the Islamic religion.

Fundamentalism, is described as an "intellectual stance that claims to derive political principles from a timeless divine text" [Choueiri, 1990, 9]. Milton-Edwards notes that among its main features are a rejection of Western secularism and reasserting of Muslims' own political structures, institutions and ideas [Milton-Edwards, 2014, 5]. There are some other notions that are used to describe this agenda, for example, Islamism (Khalid), Islamic revivalism (Esposito). According to Adeeb Khalid, Islamism pertains to those who are disillusioned with modernist reforms, which in their opinion have led Islam to a dead end of imitating the West. They see the way out not through bringing Islam into conformity with the modern world, but rather through the building of the modern world according to true Islamic values. With that said, there are those among the Islamists who believe that this goal should be realized through the conquest of political power and the ascendancy of an Islamic state, as well as those who believe that this goal may be attained through the cultivation of personal piety, which should lead to positive changes in society as a whole. Among the representatives authors often list figures uch as Hassan al-Banna, Said Qutb, Abu Ala al-Maududi, Ayatollah Khomeini, al-Zawahiri, etc.

Liberal Islam[78] attempts to assign Western values an Islamic accent, believing that the West's positive achievements are not an inherently Western phenomenon but rather, initially intrinsic to Islam, and should therefore be reinstated, rather than taken from the West. They advocate a separation between religion and the state, in order to protect the former from the latter; they repudiate any forms of coercion in the name of religion and recognize the pluralism of opinion (Knysh, 2011, 457). Among the adherents of Liberal Islam, the most commonly named are Muhammad an-Naim, Abdulkadir Sorush, Rachid Gannouchi, Fazlur Rahman (Kurzman, 2003, 191-203). Some researchers are inclined to call this branch Reformism (Bayoumi, 2010, 79-93); however, this term may refer also to Islamists, since they too propose reforms to the religion by returning it to a state of initial purity and clarity.

Turning to historiography for the problem of classifying modern Islamic religious movements reveals a variety of names and terms, which are fairly arbitrary. Choosing this or that term is always a challenge for the researcher. This author believes that, in order to ameliorate the tangle of terminology, one should use that set of classifications that best applies to the era and society under scrutiny. When doing so, it is necessary to first explain exactly what the author invests in this or that concept. Having done so, most of the disagreements should be resolved.

Main ideological trends amongst Muslims of the Volga-Ural region (The beginning of the 21st century)

The beginning of the religious revival in the USSR is related to Gorbachev's new political course of the 1985-1991 period, when society's attitudes towards religion, and in turn towards Islam, gradually began to change. The 1989 commemoration in Tatarstan and Bashkortostan of 1,100 years since Volga Bulgaria adopted

---

78 There is a whole series of works devoted to this branch of Islam: C. Kurzman, (ed.). (1998). *Liberal Islam: A Sourcebook*. Oxford, England: Oxford University Press; I. M. Abu-Rabi', (2004). *Contemporary Arab Thought: Studies in Post-1967 Arab Intellectual History*. London, England: Pluto Press; L. Binder (1988). *Islamic Liberalism: A Critique of Development Ideologies*. Chicago, IL: University of Chicago Press; C. Kurzman, (2003). Liberal Islam: Prospects and Challenges. In B. Rubin (ed.), *Revolutionaries and Reformers: Contemporary Islamist Movements in the Middle East*, (191–203). Albany, NY: State University of New York Press.

Islam became a reference point for Islamic revival in the region. If in 1985 in Tatarstan there were only 18 operating mosques, today there are more that 1380. In Bashkortostan, towards the end of the 1980s, only 35 mosques remained; today their number approaches 800. The Muslim Religious Board of the Republic of Tatarstan was founded in 1992, headed first by Gabdulla Galiullin (who had studied in Bukhara and Tashkent[79]), then from 1998 by Gusman Iskhakov (educated in Bukhara). That same year the Muslim Religious Board of the Republic of Bashkortostan was also established; its leader became Nurmukhamet Hazrat Nigmatullin (studied in Bukhara). The Central Muslim Spiritual Board of Russia, the successor to the Orenburg Muslim Spiritual Assembly, also operates in Ufa, headed by Talgat Tadzhuddin (educated in Bukhara and Cairo /al-Azhar), who leads approximately 200 parishes in Bashkortostan and another 1,000 in other regions of the Russian Federation. The revival in Muslim educational institutions has likewise undergone a series of stages. Initially, madrasas were opened in increasing numbers (in the mid-90s in Tatarstan there were 20), but not all survived the test of time. Today there are 11 Muslim schools for training religious functionaries operating in Tatarstan. Three of them are universities (Russian Islamic University, The Muhammadiyya Madrasa, the Madrasa of the Millenial Anniversary of the Adoption of Islam). In Bashkortostan there are 5 Muslim schools, one of which is a university (The R. Fakhreddin Russian Islamic University in Ufa).

The Muslim community itself has seen significant changes over the past two decades: though during the wave of religious revival Tatars and Bashkirs filled mosques to the brim on Fridays, various historical, cultural, social, economic, and psychological factors have since then introduced changes in the composition of the congregations. Despite the society's fairly high level of religiosity (79–80% of respondents, ethnic Muslims in Tatarstan and Bashkortostan, referred to themselves as believers (Musina, 2009, 251)), only 4-7% are practicing Muslims. If in the mid-90s, mosque congregants were predominantly seniors – 60 years and older – then today the majority of worshipers are younger – from 18 to 35 years old. Similar trends, albeit with a small delay, may be likewise observed in the Muslim clergy, which is noticeably "getting younger".

Against this socio-religious background, two main ideological camps have formed among Muslims: the Neo-traditionalists, who side with local forms of the

---

79 Before the 1990's the only places where Soviet Muslims could receive religious education were Madrasa Mir-Arab in Bukhara (reopened in 1946) and the Islamic Institute named after Imam Bukhari in Tashkent (founded in 1972). This education was under severe supervision of KGB and curricula included mostly studying Islamic religious rites while paying little of no attention to other aspects of religion such as theology, religious philosophy, etc.

Hanafi school of Islamic Law, and the Fundamentalists, who are the followers of "pure" Islam. Besides these there are other trends with fewer adherents: followers of Liberal Islam, representatives of the "Hizmet" movement of Fethullah Gülen, the so-called "Faizrakhmanists", as well as the Sufi "Suleimanji" movement.

The most privileged position is occupied by the local Neo-traditionalists – Hanafis.[80] The Muslim Religious Board (Muftiate) and the system of professional religious education falls under their influence. We can say the same of the overwhelming number of congregations (with the exception of certain regions in eastern Bashkortostan and the oil producing regions of Tatarstan). The leadership of the Neo-traditional Islam party received its theological education in either Bukhara, or (when it comes to the younger generation) in local schools, supplemented in part with short-term (up to one year) courses abroad.

Their main ideology, which is attractive to the Russian authorities, is the preservation of local Islamic traditions, adapted to the existence of Muslims in multi-ethnic and multi-religious surroundings. And since Islam was for many centuries the main means of preserving Tatar and Bashkir national identity, it follows that today the traditionalists advocate the use of the Tatar language as the language in which Friday services are conducted. The legitimization of the *adat* (local customs, including those that pertain to religious life) in a way that did not contradict sharia, made possible the functioning of many religious rituals that are not proper to Islam in its other areas of proliferation (convocation of Qur'anic *mejlises*, remembrances for the dead, pilgrimages to local sacred places). The historical connection to Central-Asian centres of Muslim scholarship led to the adoption of the Hanafi school of law and the appropriation of Maturidi principles of theological interpretation. Forced to develop under constant Christian missionary pressure, severed from the rest of the Muslim world, and, due to the Soviet experiment, subjected to all the trials of atheistic propaganda, Tatar Islam could not objectively preserve universalistic features.

Among the regional leaders – ideologues of Neo-traditional Islam – we must name – Nurmukhamet Nigmatullin – acting mufti of the Republic of Bashkortostan (RB) and Ildus Faizov – ex-mufti of the Republic of Tatarstan (RT, educated locally), Gabdulkhak Samatov (Samatov, 2006) (deceased 2009, graduated from the Mir-i-Arab Madrasa in Bukhara), Valiulla Yakupov (Yakupov, 2003, 2006 a, 2006 b, 2010) (deceased as a result of an attack in 2012, educated locally), Rustam Batrov (Batrov, 2007) (Moscow Islamic University), Ildar Malakhov (Malakhov,

---

80 The official MRB RT site points out clearly that "MRB RT conducts its religious policy in accordance with the Abu Hanifa school of law". /www.dumrt.ru/

2008)[81] (Mir-i-Arab in Bukhara, and al-Azhar in Cairo) and some others. The sphere of Neo-traditionalist influence is unequivocally the older generation of Muslims, as well as a particular segment of the younger generation – graduates of local and foreign schools who are above all loyal to the older generation and who have found themselves positions in the organizations of spiritual directorates and their subordinate parishes.[82]

Their opponents, the so-called Fundamentalists, have their own point of view on a series of religious issues. On the whole, the local Fundamentalist discourse is quite universalist: ideas about the return to the purity of Islam of the first centuries, and accordingly, an interpretation of divine attributes in the spirit of Ibn Taymiyyah's postulations, a condemnation of religious innovation (visiting "sacred places", *mawlids*, etc.), an adversarial relationship to Sufism and *Kalam*, an adherence to an international language of communication when conducting sermons (in the Russian context, this is Russian). A significant number of Fundamentalists are quite loyal to the authorities; however, the state treats with suspicion these followers of "pure" Islam, though it prefers to act indirectly, through the sanctioned Muslim clergy. They are prevented from leading mosques: so, for example, Shaukat Abubakerov was removed from leading the community at the Aniler Mosque in Kazan, or Ishmurat Khaybullin was forced to leave his position as imam of the Falyak Mosque in Ufa; furthermore, they encounter difficulties finding work. Due to these various persecutions, Fundamentalist leaders are not inclined to advertise their views to the general public. At the same time, through fieldwork, it became possible to establish fruitful contacts with representatives of moderate Fundamentalism– Ishmurat Khaybullin (Khaybullin, 2010) (Al-Azhar University), Ramil Bikbayev (Mecca Islamic University), Shavkat Abubakerov (educated locally, with a residency at the Muslim World League in Mecca), as well as a series of other preachers who are close to these circles (Kamal El-Zant, Ramil Yunusov, Idris Galyautdin). This movement's area of influence is above all the Tatar and Bashkir youth, immigrants from Muslim republics of the CIS and further abroad, for whom the local version of Islam is not habitual. Newly converted Muslims, from the Russians and otherwise historically non-Muslim peoples, likewise choose the Fundamentalist version of Islam, the sermons of which are held in Russian.

---

81 Ildar Malakhov is the editor of the *Risalya* newspaper. Electronic version: http://islam-rb.ru;

82 A vivid example is Ruslan Sayakhov, assistant to the mufti of the Republic of Bashkortostan and graduate of the al-Azhar University.

Yet another current that holds significance for the formation of religious discourse, especially at the beginning of the 2000s, is represented by the Islam of the liberals. Among its representatives we may note Rafael Hakimov (Hakimov, 2010), Aydar Khayrutdinov (Khayrutdinov, 2007), Ayrat Bakhtiyarov (Bakhtiyarov, 2007) (his ideas are nearer to New Age Islam). Despite the large interest that Western researchers and the Western press evince in this phenomenon, the influence of Liberal Islam on the Muslim community is minimal. This is due to a few reasons: none of the Liberal Islamic thinkers had a religious education; they are all, in one way or another, secular scholars who work in the area of the humanities and are not members of Muslim communities in the traditional sense – that is, we should not overestimate the role of this current in the formation of the region's Islamic discourse.

Conclusions

The trends in the development of Islamic society in the Volga-Ural region are quite similar to processes worldwide. If in the beginning of the 20th century the most influential group to oppose official traditionalism was reformist modernism, then by the beginning of the 21st century it is Fundamentalism (whether in its softer or its harder forms) that earns the sympathy of the majority of believers. The reasons for this might consist of the following: adherents of reformist modernism (M. Abduh, R. Rida, M. Iqbal) supposed that gradual progress and appropriation of modern science and Western technologies would gradually obviate the issue of the Islamic World's lagging behind the countries of Europe and America. However, international processes over the course of the 20th century showed that the paths out of the crisis are much more complicated. Economic backwardness has not disappeared to this day, despite the appropriation of Western scientific achievements. Many Muslims are more worried by the threat of losing their Islamic identity, than by the economic backwardness of their countries. The division of society, in connection to this, into 'us' and 'them' activates a feeling of identity, in this case the Islamic one. It is precisely the Fundamentalist interpretations of Islam that proposes a stricter distancing from the 'them', unlike the interpretation of Liberal Islam or local Neo-traditionalism, which are used to operating in a multi-denominational, multicultural society.

A notable fact is that, if the main assortment of ideological currents, in one way or another, exists in basically every place in the world where Muslims live, then state policy towards these groups varies greatly: from supporting different forms of Fundamentalism in the countries of the Persian Gulf, to their strict prohibition, as is the case in most Central Asian countries. Sometimes the popularity of various Islamic currents is in part inversely proportional to the state's religious policy: the more a state supports one current, the less popular it becomes amongst the population, and vice versa.

In the Volga-Ural region, over the course of the two periods we have looked at, the state religious policy towards Islam has a distinct line of succession: the same goals, support methods for allies, and forms of struggle with unwanted elements. In the 21st century, as at the beginning of the 20th, the state is interested in controlling the situation, which is ensured by, on the one hand, law enforcement agencies, and on the other, official organizations of the Muslim clergy – the Muslim Religious Boards. Both then and now, the state is wagering on traditionalism – on those who adhere to the preservation of Islam's local manifestations. The removal in 2011 of Gusman Iskhakov, during whose reign as mufti a whole array of leadership posts was occupied by pro-Fundamentalist imams, and his subsequent replacement with the Neo-traditionalist Ildus Faizov[83], is a classic example of the state meddling in religious institutions, which evokes the Tsarist Administration's mechanism of appointing the mufti in the 18th, 19th, and beginning of the 20th centuries.

Meanwhile, the state's support does not provide the adherents of local neo-traditionalism with popularity or authority among the rank and file Muslims. Despite the fact that the traditionalists have held all of the control levers and powers in the beginning of the 20th century as well as today, their ideological competitors possess certain advantages. Their non-involvement and persecution by the authorities imbue them with moral advantages. In the beginning of the 20th century, the traditionalists' opponents were the reformers-modernists; today, their opponents are various Fundamentalist leaders.

The struggle of ideologies is to a degree the struggle of geopolitical preferences. Local traditions, intertwined with Bukharan educational standards, are common for conservatives from both periods. On the contrary, Istanbul, Cairo, Mecca, and Medina –are the places from which new revivalist ideas emanated. Attempts on the part of the muftiates to forbid or control students' travels abroad after the 1990s, as a rule, have not been effective due to the openness of Russian borders with Muslim countries. The single method of control remains the exemption of graduates of foreign schools from posts in the religious organizations. However,

---

83 After the terrorist murder of Valiulla Yakupov and bombing of his car in 2012, Mufti Ildus Faisov was replaced by Kamil Samigullin (in April, 2013).

even this is not completely effective, since there always remains the opportunity of informal leaders influencing the Muslim community through a system of personal connections. Only through the law enforcement agencies, which persecute the unofficial Muslim leaders and their followers, can the Neo-traditionalist for the time being retain control over the Muslim community. The recent events of July 2012, the murder of the deputy Mufti, Valiulla Yakupov, the most dynamic leader of modern day Tatar Neo-traditionalism, and the attempt on the life of Mufti Ildus Faizov are a testament to the serious blunders in the state's religious policy and the need for its re-examination. As is usual in such cases, there are two ways out: 1) a toughening of measures towards Fundamentalist circles, a consequence of which will be their further intensification of underground work, along with the popularization of their teachings; and 2) a more differentiated approach towards religious dissidents, support for a variety of factions, and the provision of platforms for the expression of the spectrum of opinions for those movements that do operate within the bounds of Russian law. That could make social tensions in religious sphere less painful and lead to pluralism in opinions.

The most important step that the state could take for providing peace and stability in social life would be to work towards economic development and social justice while struggling against corruption at all levels of power. Such measures could lead to high standards of morality throughout the society–the main goal of all religions.

References

Bakhtiyarov, A. (2007). *The Path of Apprehending Through the Heart: From Heart To Heart*. Kazan: Altay-tay.

Batrov, R. (2007). *Instead of Reform*. Nizhny Novgorod: Medina.

Bayoumi, M. (2010). *The God That Failed*. In: Shryock; A. (Ed.) *Islamophobia/Islamophiliu: Beyond the Politics of Enemy and Friend*. (79-93). Bloomington, IN: Indiana University Press.

Bigiev, M. (2006). *Woman in the Light of the Sacred Ayat of the Holy Quran*. Selected Works *(2)*. Kazan: Tatarstan Book Printing House.

El Fadl, K. M. (2005). *The Great Theft: Wrestling Islam from the Extremists*. (336). San Francisco, CA: Harper.

Hakimov, R. (2010). *Djadidizm (Reformed Islam)*. (207). Kazan: Idel-Press.

Kamali, Z. (1910). *Falsafah Islamiah*. (330). Ufa: Sharik Matbagasi.

Kamali, Z. (2010). *Philosophy of Islam* (L. Almazova, Trans. From Old Tatar). Kazan: Tatarstan Book Printing House.

Khalid, A. (2007). *Islam After Communism: Religion and Politics in Central Asia*. (12). Berkley, CA: University of California Press.

Khayrutdinov, A. (2007). *Unknown Islam: The Quran We Do Not Know*. Kazan: Institute of History Printing House.

Khayrutdinov, A. (2009). *Quran: Interpretation Continued*. (92). Kazan: Institute of History Printing House.

Knysh, A. (2011). *Islam in Historical Perspective*. London: Pearson.

Khaybullin, I. A. (2010). *Grammar of the Arabic Language: Brief Version*. Ufa: Salam.

Kurzman C. (Ed.). (1998). *Liberal Islam: A Sourcebook*. (340). Oxford, England: Oxford University Press.

Kurzman, C. (2003). *Liberal Islam: Prospects and Challenges*. In: Rubin, B. (Ed.) *Revolutionaries and Reformers: Contemporary Islamist Movements in the Middle East*. (191-203). Albany, NY: State University of New York Press.

Malakhov, I. (2008). *Sokrovennoe*. Ufa: (Printing house not indicated).

Musina R. N. (2009). Islam and the Problem of Tatar Identity in the Post-Soviet Era. (86-100). *The Denominational Factor in the Tatars' Development*. Kazan: Institute of History Publishing House.

Samatov, G. (2006). *Sharia: Wagaz, Hokem, Fatwa, Jawap-Sawap, Kineshler*. Kazan: Idel-Press.

Sardavi M. (2004). Steel blade against new method. Kazan: Iman.

Shahrour M. (2006). The Divine Text and Pluralism in Muslim Societies. (143-153). In: Kemrava, M. (Ed.). *The New Voices of Islam: Reforming Politics and Modernity: A Reader*. London, UK: I.B. Tauris.

Shepard, W. E. (1987). Islam and Ideology: Towards a Typology. *International Journal of Middle East Studies*, 19(3), (307-335).

Utiz-Imyani A. (2007). *Selected treatises*. Kazan: Tatarstan Book Publishing House.

Yakupov, V. (2003). *Tatarstanda Rasmi Bulmagan Islam*. Kazan: Iman.

Yakupov, V. (2006 a). *Towards a Prophetical Islam*. Kazan: Iman.

Yakupov, V. (2006 b). *Lzhedzhadidism*. Kazan: Iman.

Yakupov, V. (2011). *Islam Today*. Kazan: Iman.

Yunus, R. (2011) *Ramil hazrat Yunus Wagazlere*. Kazan: Akcharlak.

Zant, K. (n.d.). *Tell Me About Faith*. Personal Site: www.kamalzant.ru

Citizenship Education in Russia

Between "Patriotism" and "Spirituality"

Dmitry Shmonin

Current situation and approach to analysis

After the collapse of the USSR in 1991, Russia became much more open to global economic, social, and cultural processes. In the Russian pedagogy of the last decade of the 20th century the processes of the post-Soviet de-ideologization were dominant. Apart from the direct impact of the West, the country has experienced the influence of trends inspired by post-modernist crisis of humanistic ("European") values and new post-secular type of relations between civil society, state, and religion. As a "side effect" of the dismantling of the communist educational system, as well as the utmost openness to the Western influence, the younger generation in Russia developed the ideals and patterns of an individualistic personality free from the traditional moral values and obligations to the society.

Sadly, today, the situation remains unaltered. Mass media, cinema, advertising, and the internet offer youth behavioral patterns and personality development strategies predominantly based on accumulating wealth and success. At the same time, the educational system has largely lost its normative and ideological status.

Speaking of this crisis in education in the perspective of the concept of post-secularism, we rely on recent writings of Jürgen Habermas on theology and social theory, where he has been concerned about the inability of post-modern societies to generate their own values (drawing instead on the heritage of Judeo-Christian values) as the source of social morality and individual ethics. It seems reasonable to listen to Habermas's arguments that modernity no longer implies "the march toward secularism". In a democracy, the secular mentality should be open to the religious influence of believing citizens (Habermas, 2002; Habermas 2005, 339-348; Habermas, 2008).

The rich religious and cultural traditions of Russia, its geo-political status and socio-economic situation, allow us to apply the concept of post-secularism to contemporary Russian society (see the first lines of Habermas' "Notes on a Post-secular Society"). This approach enables us to consider the main issues and prospects of citizenship education in Russia with more clarity.

The challenge: Lack of a collective national idea

Russia, or officially the Russian Federation, is a multiethnic and multidenominational state partly similar to the countries of the Old Europe (we take this term in a political sense) and at the same time – different from them. Definitely, it needs a basic set of value guidelines that would unite this country's citizens of more than 180 nationalities and ethnic groups into a consolidated historical, cultural, and social unity. It should be noted that during the last 20-25 years the country has failed to regenerate or create a sustainable system of collective national values and priorities that are clear to the society. There is a notable lack of principles and regulations for living that could be consciously embraced by the majority of citizens; and also there is no agreement in issues of constructive social behavior and positive guidelines. Nowadays, Russia, and throughout its national history, has been a powerful state, but it has had no general concept that can unify and consolidate its diverse peoples on basic ideas of patriotism and citizenship. This means that, at the moment, there is no common or national ideal for the future.

The influence of religion on education

Through the last decade of the 20th century and the first decade of the 21st century, Russia has seen a steady increase in the influence of religion in society. Mainly, we speak about Eastern Orthodoxy. The second most influential religion in Russia has been Islam, rooted in a number of regions of the country, as well as among an influx of Muslim immigrants. Amid other denominations, one could single out Pentecostals, whose social activity has attracted a significant number of believers. Among the traditional Christian denominations in Russia, the Roman Catholic Church and the Evangelical Lutheran Church, the Armenian Apostolic Church, as well as Buddhist and Jewish communities have not changed dramatically their status and weight in society (Shmonin, 2014).

The Constitution of the Russian Federation (1993) proclaims the state to be secular and explicitly affirms: "No religion may be established as a state or obligatory one" (article 14, paragraph 1). Paragraph 2 of the same article states: "Religious associations shall be separated from the state and shall be equal before the law". In accordance with the provisions of the Constitution, there are no official statistics concerning the number of believers in different religions or/and denominations. However, according to sociological research, among Russian citizens (in per cent of the total population): 64% identify themselves as Orthodox, 1 % belong to other Christian denominations, 6 % proclaim themselves to be Muslims, about 1 % are adherents of other religions including Judaism and Buddhism, and 25% identify themselves as unbelievers (Filina, 2013) .

Speaking of educational institutions, over the 1990s-2000s, traditional religions have significantly reinforced their presence at school. In search of moral and cultural values in place of the lost communist dogmas, significant numbers of teachers have turned to Christianity or Islam depending on their choice of their own roots and the local historical or ethnic background. Religious values and educational programmes based on them have become a comparatively successful alternative to liberal, secular tendencies in education. However, one should point out that over the last 5-7 years, due to closer ties of religious leaders with the federal government and regional authorities as well as the attempts of the state to include Orthodoxy (and to a lesser degree, Islam) in addressing social issues in the absence of, as we mentioned above, any clear shared national idea or ideological framework, we have observed a definite decrease in interest in official religious institutions.

All that relates to school education as well. Federal authorities put emphasis on traditional religions or denominations in education. In 2007 they changed a few passages in article 14, clause 2 of the Russian Federation "Education Law", according to which "bringing up a spiritual and ethical person" was set as a priority.

Here we should make a small terminological clarification. In Russian, the term "spiritual and ethical upbringing" ("*dukhovno-nravstvennoe vospitanie*") sounds specifically spiritual rather than religious. In English it is closer to the adjectives "moral/ethical", but still has a strong association with tradition, traditional culture, and religion. In this way we name theological educational institutions: "*Dukhovnaya seminaria*" (literally, the Spiritual seminary) and "*Dukhovnaya academia*" (literally, the Spiritual academy), but we translate them as "Theological".

On July 21, 2009, during President (in 2008-2012) Dmitry Medvedev's meeting with leaders of the "centralized religious organizations" represented by Patriarch Kirill of Moscow and the heads of Islamic, Jewish and Buddhist denominations in Russia, the concept *traditional religions* was authorized (although, of course, it had been used before). This concept comprehends the above-mentioned four religions or denominations. Soon afterwards another term was introduced in pedagogical practice by the Federal Ministry of Education and Science, that is, "culture-formative religions" (kulturo-obrazujuschie religii), which was used as a synonym that would be more appropriate for the school teachers' vocabulary than "traditional religions". "Traditional" or "culture-formative" religions received the right to be represented as single modules of the "integrative course": "Basics of Religious Cultures and Secular Ethics", intended for the 4th and 5th grades of secondary schools. Let it be noted that the short-list of "culture-formative religions" does not include such Christian denominations as Catholicism and Lutheranism, in spite of their obvious roots in Russian history.

According to aforesaid decisions of 2009, the Federal Ministry launched an experiment in the schools of 19 (later 21) regions of Russia. In accordance with the experimental conditions, parents and children had to make their choice of learning one of four religious traditions. In 2012, after the completion of this experiment, the course "Basics of Religious Cultures and Secular Ethics" was introduced in schools. It allowed school children aged 10-11 and their parents to choose one of the following modules: "Basics of Orthodox culture", "Basics of Islamic culture", "Basics of Buddhist culture", and "Basics of Jewish culture". Other options included "Basics of the World Religions' cultures" and "Basics of Secular Ethics".

The 2012-2013 academic year results clearly depended on local ethnic, geographic and historical features, the policies of regional authorities and some other reasons. Among "denominational" modules, "Orthodoxy" was more popular in the Central Federal District, "Islam" in the North Caucasian and Volga Federal Districts; Jewish culture was chosen by a modest number of learners in the Volga Federal District, and Buddhism was chosen – in the Siberian and Southern Federal Districts. Parents in two North Caucasus republics of Russia made a choice in favor of Islamic culture: in Chechnya - 99% and Ingushetia - 100%.

In general, the results of official monitoring indicate a cautious attitude on the part of parents and teachers to the denominational modules: "Orthodoxy" – 30.4%; "Islam" – 38 %; "Buddhism" and "Judaism" both – less than 1%; alternative modules "World Religions" - 20.6%, and "Secular Ethics" - 44.8% (Filina, 2014).

This data shows that the majority of parents and students chose modules "World Religions" and "Secular ethics" as being the most tolerant, neutral (not denominational) introduction to different religious cultures. In our opinion, however, the choice indicates that parents are looking for the safest option for the child that will facilitate their social and cultural adaptation. In the best case, this "modular" approach leads to a better understanding of the ethnic and religious diversity of the Russian people but does not create a common worldview or set of values, or convey an embracing national consensus.

Search for other ways: "Citizenship and patriotic education"

The complicated, and historically convoluted, interethnic and interdenominational relations, the deficit of absolute, unquestionable values and pervasive moral relativism has become a serious challenge for the federal authorities and the pedagogical community. The awareness of these problems was most notable as the end of the 20th century neared.

Citizenship and patriotic education in Russia's schools and universities is not a current "pedagogical know-how"; the importance of this part of upbringing was proclaimed during all of the Soviet period. In contemporary Russia there were adopted and realized different federal, regional and local plans, conceptions and programmes; the biggest among them: "The patriotic education of the citizens of the Russian Federation for 2001-2005," "The patriotic education of the citizens of the Russian Federation for 2006-2010." The third programme of the same name, designed for 2011-2015, includes a variety of special activities and events funded by the budget and aimed at "shaping the patriotic consciousness of Russia's citizens as a factor in consolidating the nation" (Clause 1 of the Programme "2011-2015").

The new "Federal Education Low", which took effect on September 1, 2013 proclaims (article 3, clause 1): the humanitarian mode of education, priority of the free development of personality, upbringing with mutual respect, citizenship consciousness, patriotism, responsibility, and legal culture. The new educational standard (a highly detailed document published by the Federal Ministry and defining basic parameters of school or university education) introduced in schools in 2014 presupposes a unified course of "The Introduction to the Spiritual and Moral Culture of the Peoples of Russia" that is not divided into denominational modules.

The major burden of these issues falls on the school, on the educators' community, and on teachers themselves, who, being the "purveyors of educational services," are, nevertheless, the ones to influence citizenship education and the spiritual and moral development of students.

As we said above, the idea of a civic nation embracing a system of principal pan-national values is meant to have nothing in common with spiritual and social unification. The unity of the nation is achieved through a value consensus and constant dialogue between diverse social groups, openness to one another, and willingness to cooperatively address national problems, including the upbringing of the new generations of citizens.

The development of the cultures of the peoples of Russia is clearly possible, provided that the country itself exists and develops. Therefore, cultural, ethnic, and religious pluralism is attainable only in the condition of a general pan-national basis for political, social, and economic life and a dialogue of cultures within the country.

Citizenship education and ethical upbringing in schools should be planned. For each stage of education – primary and secondary (including high school) – special plans for upbringing and socializing the pupils should be developed.

We should again emphasize that it is the school as a major socializing institution that carries all the weight of these issues. Interacting with other socializing subjects, the school has to create all the necessary conditions for spiritual, moral, intellectual, social, aesthetic, and in broad sense, human development of young people. According to the main goals, each secondary school should develop its own programme of citizenship upbringing taking into consideration particular ethnic and religious situations. Schools should also provide different out-of-class activities (field trips to museums, theatres, cathedrals and churches of diverse denominations) to implement their programmes. Schools are responsible for ethnic peace, consensus and an atmosphere of tolerance at school.

There are several central points included in citizenship education tasks for schools: a) creating an educational setting that would include the common values of the Russian nation and the peoples of Russia, and of the territorial, regional, and local communities; b) introducing students to the values of a healthy lifestyle, including a responsible attitude to life, lives of other people, nature, and the planet in general; c) introducing young citizens to the values of beauty, harmony, and perfection in the architectural and objective space of the school; d) cooperation with families, parents who participate in school educational and development programmes, with veterans', ecological, national and cultural organizations, and e) with traditional religions (Daniliuk, Kondakov & Tishkov, 2009, 23).

We believe that these complex challenges need a core of traditional values and cooperation with religious organizations. Patriotic upbringing will be sufficiently substantiated if it is based on history and culture, and these are inextricably linked with religion. Citizenship and patriotic education without such bases cannot have a full effect and is insufficient in providing a global, networked perception of the world, given the lack of boundaries and filters on the Internet, which involves young people in a atmosphere of moral relativism, individualism and postmodern critique.

Conclusions

The concept of a post-secular society allows us to describe and discuss the situation in citizenship education and draw conclusions. Traditional religious denominations should be invited to collaborate in the upbringing and socialization of school children and youth. Moreover, they ought to do it, because it is a part of their mission in the world. Religious organizations are able to assure the integrity and stability of public morals. This is particularly characteristic of ethno-centric cultures, with Russia undoubtedly being one of them. Traditional Russian denominations and religious organizations should be pedagogically integrated into the current revival of the public education system. Religious authority and spiritual experience can influence isolated social groups and deter them from pursuing their own unilateral interests. Each particular part of this system, retaining its principles, content, and traditions, should contribute to attaining the general national aim of formulating a consensual ethical worldview for the citizens of Russia.

References

Habermas, J. (2002). *Religion and Rationality: Essays on Reason, God, and Modernity.* Cambridge, Mass.: MIT Press.

Habermas, J. (2005.) *On the Relation between the Secular Liberal State and Religion.* In: The Frankfurt School on Religion: Key Writings by the Major Thinkers. (339-348). New York: Routledge.

Habermas, J. (2008). *Notes on a Post-secular Society.* Sight and Sound 18/06/08. From: http://www.signandsight.com/features/1714.html (Accessed November 10, 2013).

Shmonin, D. *Religion and Education in Contemporary Russia: The Dynamics of Recent Years,* Analysis ISPI, No. 233. (January 2014). From: http://www.ispionline.it/it/pub-blicazione/religion-and-education-contemporary-russia-dynamics-recent-years-9763 (Accessed February 12, 2014).

Filina, O. *Mapping Russia's Religious Landscape.* From: http://indrus.in/articles/2012/09/01/mapping_russias_religious_landscape_17333.html (Accessed November 10, 2013); sociological research of the «Fond obschestvennogo mneniya» [«Public Opinion Foundation»] (http://fom.ru/obshchestvo/10953 (Retrieved 10.11.2013); http://www.orkce.org/sites/default/files/file/mntrng2013.pdf. (Accessed February 04, 2014).

Daniliuk A., Kondakov A. & Tishkov, V. (2009). *Kontseptsija dukhovno-nravstvennogo razvitija y vospitanija lichnosti grazhdanina Rossii* [The concept of spiritual and moral development and education of a citizen of Russia]. Moscow : Prosveschenie.

Section four
North America

Education for Citizenship in Public and Catholic Schools in the United States

Eileen Daily

The founders of the United States of America knew that the democratic nation they were creating could survive only if the people of the nation took their citizenship rights and responsibilities seriously. For more than a century and a half, the American public and private education systems were designed to form good citizens – both relied on some religious education to accomplish this end.

Education is not mentioned in the United States Constitution so authority over education is relegated to the 50 states in their individual sovereignty as long as the states' laws do not violate some other provision of the US Constitution. That said, the United States Congress can create laws affecting the realm of education as long as they relate to a national interest. The No Child Left Behind (NCLB) Act (2002) is one such national educational law. It applies to any school interested in receiving federal funding. It requires states to set standards and conduct annual standardized tests of student learning in reading, writing, mathematics, and science (NCLB, 2002, Sec.1111). NCLB also provides incentive to improve civics education, however it does not require annual testing, and success in civics education is not tied to federal funding (NCLB, 2002, Sec. 2341-2346).

Citizenship education in public schools in the United States is therefore not centrally mandated or controlled. Instead, each state sets its own priorities and outcomes for citizenship education. A survey of the various requirements for public citizenship education would be beyond the scope of this chapter. Instead, we will look at trends in teaching citizenship in the United States without reference to what the teachers surveyed are required to teach.

Control of Catholic school education for citizenship is doubly decentralized in the sense that a) in teaching citizenship as part of a social studies course, a school will abide by the education standards of the state in which it is located and b) there is no central mandate by the United States Conference of Catholic Bishops (USCCB) that Catholic thinking about citizenship must be included in the religion curriculum. That said, the USCCB does provide two particular guidelines for how religion teachers ought to approach citizenship if a school chooses to address it. First, the USCCB provides an outline of the doctrinal elements of a course on Catholic Social Teaching, but it identifies this course as an elective in the overall religion curriculum it recommends (USCCB, 2008). Second, every four years, the USCCB revises and reissues a document called *Forming Consciences for Faithful Citizenship* (2011)

This report relies heavily on two studies. The first is a 2010 study called *High Schools, Civics, and Citizenship* conducted and published by the American Enterprise Institute for Public Policy Research, a non-partisan think tank. Researchers collected data from both public and private high school social studies teachers (Farkas & Duffett, 2010). One hundred and sixty-six Catholic school social studies teachers were included in the survey (Farkas & Duffett, 2010, 39), but there is no way of knowing whether those responding had any knowledge of Catholic Social Teaching. In Catholic schools, Catholic Social Teaching is usually taught in a religion course, not in courses on American government or American history.

The second source of data used is a presentation titled, *Peace and Justice and Young Adult Catholics* (Cidade, 2011). This presentation was compiled by the Center for Applied Research on the Apostolate at Georgetown University (CARA), a center for social science research on Catholicism, from a number of its studies. I have mined the CARA presentation for data related to what young people know about Catholic approaches to citizenship when they leave high school.

Priority Elements of Citizenship Education in the United States

Public and Catholic Schools – Social Studies Teachers

Based on a series of focus groups, the researchers behind *High Schools, Civics, and Citizenship* identified twelve concepts the teachers in the focus groups recognized as important teaching goals in their schools. The researchers then invited social studies teachers in public and private schools to rate the importance of each of the concepts by asking them "How important do you think it should be for your high school to teach students this? Use a one to five scale where five is 'absolutely essential' and one is 'not important at all.'" They then asked the teachers to express "How confident are you that most students from your high school have actually learned this by the time they graduate?" (AEI, 2010, 24) Table 1 communicates the salient results of the survey; the numbers reflect percentages.

Concept	Absolutely Essential	Very Confi- dent	Very and Somewhat Confident Combined
To identify the protections guaranteed by the Bill of Rights[a]	83	24	79
To have good work habits such as being timely, persistent, and hardworking	80	6	50
To embrace the responsibilities of citizenship such as voting and jury duty	78	18	65
To be tolerant of people and groups who are different from themselves	76	19	74
To understand such concepts as federalism, separation of powers, and checks and balances	64	15	69
To be knowledgeable about such periods as the American Founding, the Civil War, and the Cold War	63	15	72
To follow rules and be respectful of authority	60	12	61
To see themselves as global citizens living in an interconnected world	57	9	52
To understand economic principles such as supply and demand and the role of market incentives	50	11	51
To develop habits of community service such as volunteering and raising money for causes	43	14	57
To be activists who challenge the status quo of our political system and seek to remedy injustices	37	5	37
To know facts (e.g., the location of the fifty states) and dates (e.g., Pearl Harbor)	36	7	56

a The "Bill of Rights" is the common name for the first 10 amendments to the United States Constitution (U.S. Const. amend IX). The rights include freedoms of religion, speech, the press, peaceful assembly, to petition the government for redress of grievances, to keep and bear arms, from self-incrimination in a criminal case, from having to house soldiers in one's home, and from excessive bail or cruel and unusual punishments. In addition, it guarantees the rights to due process in court, to a speedy, public trial by an impartial jury of one's peers while represented by counsel and allowed to confront witnesses, not to be tried twice for the same offense, and the right to compensation for property seized.

This section will focus on the first column of numbers. The other two columns will be addressed in the efficacy section that follows. The twelve concepts will henceforth be considered the priorities of the social studies teachers in both public and private schools.

Catholic Schools – Religion Teachers

Catholic Social Teaching is a compilation of Catholic doctrine related to social issues. It is normally organized in seven basic themes:

Life and Dignity of the Human Person. The Catholic Church proclaims that human life is sacred and that the dignity of the human person is the foundation of a moral vision for society.[84]

Call to Family, Community, and Participation. The person is not only sacred, but also social. How we organize our society -- in economics and politics, in law and policy -- directly affects human dignity and the capacity of individuals to grow in community.

Rights and Responsibilities. The Catholic tradition teaches that human dignity can be protected and a healthy community can be achieved only if human rights are protected and responsibilities are met.

Option for the Poor and Vulnerable. A basic moral test is how our most vulnerable members are faring. In a society marred by deepening divisions between rich and poor, our tradition recalls the story of the Last Judgment (Mt 25:31-46) and instructs us to put the needs of the poor and vulnerable first.

The Dignity of Work and the Rights of Workers. The economy must serve people, not the other way around. Work is more than a way to make a living; it is a form of continuing participation in God's creation.[85]

Solidarity. We are one human family whatever our national, racial, ethnic, economic, and ideological differences. We are our brothers and sisters' keepers, wherever they may be. Loving our neighbor has global dimensions in a shrinking world. At the core of the virtue of solidarity is the pursuit of justice and peace.

---

84 All of these are quoted from the USCCB's web site: http://www.usccb.org/beliefs-and-teachings/what-we-believe/catholic-social-teaching/seven-themes-of-catholic-social-teaching.cfm. Accessed October 20, 2013. Hyperlinks embedded in the text on the original site, and some of the texts have been removed.

85 While this includes the right to unionize, it intentionally stops short of a Marxist sense of collective work.

Care for God's Creation. We show our respect for the Creator by our stewardship of creation. ... We are called to protect people and the planet, living our faith in relationship with all of God's creation. This environmental challenge has fundamental moral and ethical dimensions that cannot be ignored. (USCCB, 2014)

If a Catholic school religion department offers an elective course on Catholic Social Teaching, the course will elaborate on these seven themes, exploring their roots in Catholic tradition and their implications in contemporary life (USCCB, 2008, 40-43). In many Catholic schools the religion and social studies teachers will communicate about the overlap between a course in Catholic Social Teaching and a course or series of courses that address citizenship, but this does not always happen. Such communication is largely dependent on the people involved and the structure of the school.

Comparison of Social Studies and Religious Priorities in Citizenship Education

The first comparison worthy of attention is the difference between the contemporary emphasis in social studies courses and the emphasis on citizenship education when the country was founded. The founders of the United States considered the goal of education to be a "coherent worldview for a shared understanding of the common good and the values necessary for democracy" (Cremin, 1980, 482). The authors of *High Schools, Civics, and Citizenship* (2010) note a shift in emphasis in public education in recent decades; the primary aim of education is more for "personal and professional advancement" (2). This is a dramatic change. The founders' emphasis on the common good is more akin to the contemporary Catholic approach to citizenship than is the recent emphasis by social studies teachers on the individual growth of the student.

The similarities between the contemporary social studies priorities and Catholic social teaching include attention to both rights and responsibilities, an acknowledgement of the interconnected world, and attention to the human person, at least as far as the Bill of Rights is concerned.

The subtle differences between the two sets of priorities are significant. In the comparison below, I have paired the Catholic Social Teaching theme with the citizenship aims of social studies teachers to emphasize the similarities. The mapping is not exact. Some of the priorities of social studies teachers appear more than once because some aspects pair better with one principle of Catholic Social Teaching, and other aspects with another. Below each pairing, I highlight the differences between the perspectives.

Catholic Social Teaching	General Citizenship Priorities
Life and Dignity of the Human Person	Many elements of the Bill of Rights –83%[b] (e.g., freedoms related to religion, speech, press, assembly, redress, self-incrimination, cruel and unusual punishment, and rights related to jury trial, compensation for appropriated property, and due process).

b   In the following tables, the percentages listed after each priority indicate the percentage of social studies teachers in both public and private schools who consider the identified learning outcome "absolutely essential" according to Farkas & Duffett (2010).

Each group considers this their most important teaching. The biggest difference is that the Catholic Church holds that this foundational principle of Catholic Social Teaching prohibits abortion and the death penalty, both of which are allowed by the Constitution of the United States.

Catholic Social Teaching	General Citizenship Priorities
Call to Family, Community, and Participation	"To embrace the responsibilities of citizenship such as voting and jury duty" 78% and "To understand such concepts as federalism, separation of powers, and checks and balances" 64%.

The Catholic Church holds that marriage and family are central to the social order and that civil society should uphold and protect that primacy. It also holds that marriage is between one man and one woman. The Constitution of the United States allows homosexual marriage. The Catholic Church says participation in society is a right and a duty, but it does not specify an optimal structure for how a society should govern itself. The social studies teachers emphasize two responsibilities (voting and jury duty) and affirm the importance of federalism, separation of powers, and checks and balances as the structure for civil society that best insures participation by everyone.

Catholic Social Teaching	General Citizenship Priorities
Rights and Responsibilities	The Bill of Rights 83%, responsibilities of citizenship (voting and jury duty) 78%, tolerance of people and groups who are different from themselves 76%, habits of community service (volunteering and raising money for causes) 43%, being activists who challenge the status quo of our political system and seek to remedy injustices 37%

The Catholic Church would disagree with the social studies teachers mostly on issues of emphasis or priority. Catholic Social Teaching emphasizes the responsibilities at least as much as the rights. In addition, Catholics would find, "tolerance" of the other is inadequate as will be fleshed out more fully below. The problem Catholic religion teachers would have with the priorities of building habits of community service and political activism is that fewer than half of the social teachers consider these two lessons to be essential.

Catholic Social Teaching	General Citizenship Priorities
Option for the Poor and Vulnerable	Tolerant of people and groups who are different from themselves 76%, to understand economic principles such as supply and demand and the role of market incentives 50%, habits of community service such as volunteering and raising money for causes 43%, to be activists who challenge the status quo of our political system and seek to remedy injustices 37%

On the topic that the fewest number of social studies teachers thought was important, remedying injustices, the Catholic Church would place a much higher priority. The Church would also object to simply tolerating the poor and vulnerable, but would instead insist on taking active steps to change their circumstances. Likewise, the Catholic Church would challenge the assumption that "economic principles" such as supply and demand are value neutral. The Church would rank community service, volunteering, and raising money for good causes higher than the social studies teachers did, but they would also argue that charity is not enough if injustice continues – they would favor activism for challenging the status quo.

Catholic Social Teaching	General Citizenship Priorities
The Dignity of Work and the Rights of Workers	Good work habits such as being timely, persistent, and hardworking 80%, to follow rules and be respectful of authority 60%, economic principles such as supply and demand and the role of market incentives 50%

The biggest difference in these two positions is the beneficiary of the principle. The Catholic Social Teaching emphasizes the worker. The social studies teachers seem to be emphasizing the economic system, the authority figures, or the employers.

Catholic Social Teaching	General Citizenship Priorities
Solidarity	To be tolerant of people and groups who are different from themselves 76%, To see themselves as global citizens living in an interconnected world 57%

Solidarity is about considering all people to be like one's brothers and sisters. This is a long way from tolerance. Tolerance is about not fighting with each other and allowing the other to be different. Solidarity is about loving each other, which means knowing each other in that difference. The social studies teachers emphasized interconnectedness; the Church would call for active steps to promote the common good in that interconnectedness.

Catholic Social Teaching	General Citizenship Priorities
Care for God's Creation	To see themselves as global citizens living in an interconnected world 57%

Here again, the Catholic Church would argue for an active role in making sure that the planet was well cared for and that that everyone had access to and the advantages of the planet's resources.

Efficacy of Citizenship Education

Public and Private Schools in the Social Studies Curriculum

The authors of *High Schools, Civics, and Citizenship* did not measure learner outcomes; instead they asked teachers how confident they were that the students were learning the twelve most important principles listed above. The percentages of teachers who were "very confident" or "somewhat and very confident" that the students were learning the twelve essential elements of citizenship are noted in Table 1 above.

Consensus has developed in the United States that citizenship education as it is currently practiced is not very effective. The United States Department of Education is responding to the problem by initiating programs, but it falls short of incentivizing improved scores on standardized tests as it does for reading, writing, and mathematics (NCLB, 2002). The U.S. Department of Education recently issued *Advancing Civic Learning and Engagement in Democracy: A Road Map and Call to Action* (2012). As schools come under more and more pressure to improve reading, writing, and mathematics learning, other subjects such as civics, art, and music are sometimes eliminated (1). It also reports that a 2010 study found that only 24% of grade 12 students were proficient in civics and notes that in a 2007 study the United States ranked 139th out of 172 nations in voter participation.

Farkas and Duffett's results suggest that the U.S. Department of Education's conclusions about public schools probably apply to Catholic Schools as well.

Catholic Schools' Religion Curriculum and Catholic Social Teaching

The religion teachers fare no better at successfully communicating the principles of Catholic Social Teaching. A CARA presentation available on the World Wide Web, which seems to have relied on a number of CARA reports, offers bleak data (Cidade, 2011). Catholic young adults aged 18-29 were surveyed; only 23% were "'somewhat' or 'very' familiar" with Catholic social teaching and only 13% were "'somewhat' or 'very' familiar" with the idea of global solidarity (Cidade, 2011, 2). Relying on the same 2007 poll of adults aged 18-29 by CARA and Catholic Relief Services, Cidade (2011, 5) reports:

- Two in three "strongly agree" that every person in the world, regardless of nationality, religion, or ethnicity, is a child of God and has dignity that must be respected.
- More than half (56 percent) "strongly agree" that workers have a right to a living wage and the right to form and join unions. One in four (25 percent) "strongly agree" that an equitable society can be achieved only if special attention is given to the needs of the poor.
- Three in ten (29 percent) "strongly agree" that people in rich countries have an obligation to help those around the globe, not just people in their own communities.
- Just 16 percent "strongly agree" that all human life, from conception to natural death, is sacred and that for this reason, the taking of a life – whether through abortion, the death penalty, or assisted suicide – is wrong.

Two-thirds agreement on the respect for the dignity of all human persons indicates some success in teaching Catholic ethical principles, but the other three bullet points suggest that respondents had little agreement on how that commitment to human dignity should be lived out.

The ideals of United States citizenship (as it was understood by the founders) and Catholic Social Teaching are exemplary models for a peaceful and just world, but in the United States, schools are not very successful at teaching those ideals, nor are the American people very successful at putting them into practice.

Questions for Citizenship Education in the United States

In the fall of 2013, the United States government shut down for several weeks because members of Congress could not reach an agreement on the budget. This does not indicate a "shared understanding of the common good and the values necessary for democracy" (Cremin, 1980, 482). In recent years the divide between understandings of the common good has been growing, making bi-partisan agreement in Congress less and less likely. Is this an effect of the poor outcomes in civics education? Unfortunately, because members of Congress are often held out to young people as models of good citizenship, what young people will learn from Congress is that the inability to agree counts as good citizenship.

One could argue that one of the reasons that citizenship education is no longer effective is that the schools have not educated for a common worldview since the early 1960s. The good side of that is that formerly marginalized groups are not forced to adopt the majority's worldview. But that pluralism also comes at a price. With no common worldview, there is no common language for such concepts as justice and common good. Each of the religious traditions has deep roots for those concepts, but the Catholic experience noted above suggests that religious adherents may not know their religion's logic for justice or serving the common good, so they cannot have an intelligent conversation about such concepts with their neighbors. Will the United States be able to embrace its pluralism and tap into the deep roots of its values so that its democracy will work in the future?

The values being emphasized by social studies teachers today tend to favor corporate and economic interests. One could argue that prioritizing economic health benefits everyone and is thus a good strategy for citizenship, but that argument assumes that individual economic well-being implies that all other aspects of global human life will also thrive. Catholic social teaching would not agree with prioritizing corporate and economic interests.

Migration to the United States is becoming increasingly influential in the Catholic Church. This increase in Catholic plurality could cause more divisions within Catholicism or the migrants' experience of the value of U.S. citizenship could provoke resurgence in the shared appreciation of citizenship and the importance of citizenship education.

Catholic education for citizenship in the United States offers a rich vision for a world of peace and solidarity, but because of the efficacy problems, that vision is not actualized in most of the Catholic population. Any call to the common good that Catholics might be able to issue to their neighbors in the United States goes unspoken by Catholics ignorant of the Church's social teachings and thus it has little influence on the society as a whole.

References

Cidade, M. A. (2011). *Peace and Justice and Young Adult Catholics*. Presentation from: http://www.authorstream.com/Presentation/everydaygrace-1070425-peace-and-justice-young-adult-catholics-cara-presentation-with-no/. (Accessed February 19, 2014).

Cremin, L. A. (1980) *American Education: The National Experience: 1783–1876*. New York, NY: Harper & Row.

Farkas, S. & Duffett, A. M. (2010). *High Schools, Civics, and Citizenship: What Social Studies Teachers Think and Do*. Foreword by Hess, F. M., Schmitt, G. J., Miller, C. & Schuette, J. M. Washington, DC: American Enterprise Institute for Public Policy Research. From: http://www.aei.org/files/2010/09/30/High-Schools-Civics-Citizenship-Full-Report.pdf. (Accessed February 19, 2014).

Gray, M. M. & Cidade, M. A. (2010). *Catholicism on Campus: Stability and Change in Catholic Student Faith by College Type*. Washington, DC: Center for Applied Research in the Apostolate at Georgetown (CARA).

No Child Left Behind (NCLB) Act of 2001, Pub. L. No. 107-110, § 115, Stat. 1425 (2002). From: http://www2.ed.gov/policy/elsec/leg/esea02/index.html. (Accessed February 19, 2014).

United States Conference of Catholic Bishops (USCCB). (2014). Web page on Catholic social teaching. From: http://www.usccb.org/beliefs-and-teachings/what-we-believe/catholic-social-teaching/seven-themes-of-catholic-social-teaching.cfm. (Accessed October 20, 2013).

United States Conference of Catholic Bishops (USCCB). (2011). *Forming Consciences for Faithful Citizenship: A Call to Political Responsibility from the Catholic Bishops of the United States with Introductory Note*. Washington, DC: United States Conference of Catholic Bishops. From: http://www.usccb.org/issues-and-action/faithful-citizenship/upload/forming-consciences-for-faithful-citizenship.pdf (Accessed February 19, 2014).

United States Conference of Catholic Bishops (USCCB). (2008). *Doctrinal Elements of a Curriculum Framework for the Development of Catechetical Materials for Young People of High School Age*. Washington, DC: United States Conference of Catholic Bishops. From: http://www.usccb.org/beliefs-and-teachings/how-we-teach/catechesis/upload/high-school-curriculum-framework.pdf. (Accessed February 19, 2014).

United States Department of Education. (2012). *Advancing Civic Learning and Engagement in Democracy: A Road Map and Call to Action*. Washington, DC: U.S. Department of Education. From: http://www.ed.gov/sites/default/files/road-map-call-to-action.pdf. (Accessed February 19, 2014).

U.S. Constitution Amendments I-X.

Contributions of Religions for Citizenship Education in Canada

A Christian Religious Educator's Perspective

HyeRan Kim-Cragg

Naming Situations: Locating Canada

Canada is a country of immigrants. Under Great Britain's North America Act, the Dominion of Canada was established in 1867. Canada was built at the price of many lives of Aboriginal people. While it is impossible to know exact numbers, it is estimated that 80% of the Aboriginal people living on the Eastern Seaboard from the 18th and the 19th century disappeared, according to Thomas King, a professor of English literature and an educator of Indigenous knowledge and history (2012, 60). Not only did they experience tremendous loss of population, but they also suffered the loss of their cultures and their ways of life that are inseparably connected to their land. When the land was taken away, their identity was torn apart. One of the most horrific episodes in Canadian history related to the Aboriginal people and education is that of the Indian Residential schools. Active from the 1920s throughout the 1960s, although the last school did not close until 1996, the Canadian government ran "residential schools" administered by the Christian churches. This was regarded as education aimed (albeit unintentionally) at cultural genocide, namely, "kill the Indian in the child" as they called it. This colonial legacy, and its past, haunts present day Canadian society.

In the midst of building Canada as a European white nation, many non-European ethnic groups other than Aboriginal people were also discriminated against and disappeared. For example, Chinese people were in Canada as early as the 1860s. They were brought to work on the building of the Canadian railroad, which provided and continues to serve as the bloodline of the body of Canada. Much of their blood was shed in the construction of that bloodline. Though they sacrificed a great deal they still were inhibited from bringing their own families over to join them, let alone being granted citizenship. There was the Chinese head tax, charged to each Chinese person entering Canada who came after the completion of Canadian Pacific Railway, 1885. The reason for charging such a tax was to discourage Chinese people from migrating to Canada. The current Canadian government made an official apology for the wrongs of both the Indian residential schools (2008) and the Chinese head tax (2006). Despite the apology, "Canada is still a colonial society" (People's Citizenship Guide, 2011, 5).

In order to discuss contributions of religions for citizenship education in the Canadian context, we need to name at the outset that Canadian national identity is very much constructed by Eurocentric Christian discourses, demarcated by power and violence. Contesting this white-settler narrative, on the other side of the same coin, we also must claim that Canada was built by and is made up of people of many different races, religions, cultures and languages who continue to inform, form and transform the nation. According to Statistics Canada, by 2031, one-third of the country's population will consist of visible minorities. In Vancouver and Toronto, the biggest cities in Canada, almost 65% of the entire population will be non-white. That does not include the Aboriginal population which is the fastest growing and youngest group in Canada. The so-called ethnic racial and religious minority is soon to become a majority in Canadian society. In the rapidly changing demographics of Canada, it is imperative to dislodge the widely spread deceptive notion of white Canada through critical education that unveils disguised histories. This orients us toward a right path of Canadian citizenship education.

Canada is also well-known as being a nation that is welcoming and hospitable to new immigrants. Yes, it is true that Canada was the first country to create an inclusive immigration and citizenship act, articulating multiculturalism as its official government policy in 1971. However, "this cozy pluralistic notion hides many complicated realities of both the history of immigration and the experience of coming to Canada as an immigrant today," as Nupur Gogia and Bonnie Slade, scholars of equity, sociology and education contend (2011, 7-8). Canadian multiculturalism is advanced under the bilingual framework of English and French, presenting "the original racialized hierarchy of difference and belonging" resulting in "a significant disparity between ethnic minorities and official language minorities with the rights and status each enjoy" (Haque, 2013, 32). Such hierarchy and disparity of systematic inequity raises the following questions: Who is welcoming? Who belongs? Whose language counts as official? These questions need to be addressed in critical inquiries of citizenship education and the roles of religions in it by taking into consideration the impact of education on the integration of young people and their religious and cultural identity formation. The social identity of belonging and being welcoming is constructed in large part due to human migration. Thus, it may be helpful to briefly explore migration as both a context for citizenship education and a cause of identity formation.

Critical Issues of Identity and Belonging in the Context of Migration

Migration is both an ancient and a contemporary human phenomenon. It is a necessity of life. In order to survive and live, any human community, and to some extent, most living creatures, must travel and move. While migration is a necessity of life and has never been absent, it has not always been easy or ended well. Migration creates a contact zone between those who are already living as the inhabitants of a place and those who are moving into the same space. In certain situations, this contact zone becomes a battle zone, resulting in conflicts and leading to violence in some extreme cases (Kwok, 2005).[86]

In this space of contact zones, certain groups who hold the power fit right into the space as the norm, while others feel out of place, even though they are supposed to belong and find security and comfort in that space. Hegemonic normativity is constructed and exercised by the group in dominant power. In his autobiography, Barack Obama unveils this hegemonic normativity that hit him hard, provoking his identity crisis:

> I came across the picture in *Life* magazine of the black man who had tried to peel off his skin…I know that seeing that article was violent for me, an ambush attack… When I got home that night from the embassy library, I went into the bathroom and stood in front of the mirror with all my senses…and wondered if something was wrong with me…My vision had been ultimately altered. On the imported television shows…I noticed that there was nobody like me in the Sears, Roebuck Christmas catalog that Toot and Gramps sent us, and that Santa was a white man (2004, 51-52).

During his age four to six, his family migrated to Indonesia. The library where he saw the picture in *Life* magazine was in the American embassy of Indonesia. That is where he was also celebrating Christmas, as a religious minority, seeing Santa

---

86 Kwok Pui-lan, a renowned postcolonial feminist scholar, a Chinese migrant from Hong Kong, living in the US, sheds light on contact zones as the space of colonial encounters "between people with different and multiple identities. The interaction between two cultures with asymmetry of power is often not voluntary and one-dimensional, but is full of tensions, fractures, and resistance" (43).

Clause who made him feel out of place. He found himself doubly minoritized (religiously and racially), succumbing to this hegemonic normativity. In that early age, Obama might have gone into the "dissonance stage" as a denial and self-depreciating stage ("something wrong with me"), as cross-cultural psychologists Derald Sue and David Sue termed it (1990, 101-102).

In the post-colonial context of encountering others, which foregrounds immigration and citizenship acts, a misrepresentation – the issue of Orientalism – bears worthy attention. Similar to hegemonic normativity at work in young people's identity formation, Orientalism helps to interrogate how certain groups are represented as "the Other" (Said, 1978). Orientalism is well reflected in a new Citizenship guide released by the Canadian state in 2009. Canada is a place where "men and women are equal under the law… [however] Canada's openness and generosity do not extend to barbaric cultural practices that tolerate spousal abuse, 'honour killings,' female genital mutilation, or other gender-based violence" (Study Guide, 2009). In fact, male violence against women and sexual abuse of children are not uncommon in White Canadians' life. Yet, this document seems to suggest that such violence only exists among non-White, non-Christian Canadians by demonizing them as barbaric so as to claim superiority (Anderson, Sharma, & Wright, 2009, 7). Orientalism is at work, making the non-White, non-Christian new Canadians, the Other. However, some scholars wrote back, producing a document called, "The People's (vs. the Government's) Citizenship guide". In the preface they wrote, "this guide is meant to challenge the current government's approach, and instead encourage everyone to question what it means to be a citizen of Canada." While none of the authors in this book are teachers of religions or religious education, their collaborative work finds a kindred spirit in those of us gathered here for the purpose of enhancing citizenship education by making our place (whether it be Europe or North America) more just and more equitable to all, especially those who are "Orientalized", religiously, racially and culturally.

It is time, then, to ask how religions play a part in this endeavor of citizenship education. What are the insights of Christian teachings that may cultivate a community where respect, dignity, and co-dwelling can be experienced and practiced among citizens? The following section of this chapter will try to do just that.

Placing Religions into the Mix: Contributions of Christian Religious Education

Since the Canadian multiculturalism acts (1971), there have been a few attempts to develop and address immigration and citizenship. One of the most recent attempts is called the "Canadian Diversity Model" (Boutilier, 2004). Interestingly, however, this model omits religion as integral to Canadian diversity, which drew the attention of scholars, educators, and policy researchers. They have called into question whether this model has a "secular bias" and such a bias is in itself an example of cultural hegemony or sees religion as a threat to civilized democracy since the events of September 11, 2001. This bias does not reflect or support the changing reality of religious demographics because Christianity, though still holding cultural hegemony, is declining in membership, while Islam is growing to be the largest among the non-Christian religions in Canada.

John Biles and Humera Ibrahim, Canadian policy analysts, note that such a bias may derive from the fear of the unknown (2005, 155, 164). Where does fear come from? It often comes from encountering one who is different from yourself. David Seljak, a Canadian Religious Studies scholar whose work involves the sociology of religion, connects this issue of fear with religious illiteracy reinforced by secularism. He argues that more education on religion would improve religious literacy by reclaiming the public arena of religion which was stolen by the discourse of religious pluralism—namely, in order to recognize other religions, we have banned and removed all religious education from Canadian public school systems. He furthermore contends that such neutral and totalitarian approaches to no-religious education policies in public schools only serves to protect "the dominant Eurocentric culture" thereby sustaining Christian hegemony by default, as norminative, while "preventing the integration of ethnic and religious minorities" (Seljak, 2005, 190). Both fear and religious illiteracy reinforce Orientalism that justifies the othering process of discrimination and exclusion, as discussed above. His point is timely in the most recent debates surrounding the Quebec government's decision to ban people who work in public spaces from wearing religious attire. Public spaces include schools, hospitals, courts, to name just a few, which means, if you are a teacher in a public school, you cannot wear a turban or a scarf (CBC radio, August 29, 2013). This debate evokes critical questions such as: does secular public identity mean non-religious? Given the religious attire that stands out most, this government has decided to ban garments associated with particular religious minorities such as Muslims, Jews, and Sikhs. Are we as a society falling into the danger of sanctioning discrimination against religious minorities?

While the issue of religious minority freedoms and rights are complex, religious literacy, knowing about other religions as well as our own, is one sure way to diminish fear, leading to appreciation and respect for others. This knowing actually often happens in the relationship of encountering others including God. Religious education as "teaching and learning must be grounded in the way that each of us makes meaning in relation to the Holy One," as Christian educators Jack Seymour, Margaret Ann Crain and Joseph Crockett argue (1993, 16).

Encountering the *Other* is the heart beat of many religions including Christianity. One's religious identity as a Christian cannot be formed unless she or he dares to encounter and embrace others, including the Holy One and neighbours. It can be strongly suggested that the practice of encountering others as the practice of hospitality, can cultivate knowing others without fear. This can be regarded as one of the most important contributions of religions for citizenship education. Let me very briefly explain the theological and cultural meanings of hospitality here. Hospitality, as Thomas Reynolds explains, "connotes the surprise arrival of a guest who is accepted and invited inside a home. In the ancient Near Eastern world of the biblical traditions, hospitality emerged as a way of tending to sojourners, travelers requiring refuge and nourishment" (2009, 13). We, who are the members of the house of faith, are called to tend to those who knock on our door in a situation of need with respect. The key to the practice of hospitality is to offer it, willingly and freely, without any condition. This unconditionality teaches us the grace of God, a source of unconditional love, who is revealed through the ones who receive hospitality. Religious educator Siebren Miedema, sharing his learning from Jean-Jacques Surmond, writes:

> on living and learning in the presence of the other...[we] experience transcendence or God's reality [which] is a fruit of the Spirit. This presence of the Spirit comes to light in the encounter of people in ordinary life situations and relations...Within the space of...encounter the partners also experience the Holy.... In Christianity we point here to Jesus...In his life the permanent indwelling of the Spirit of God has come to life in an exemplary way (2013, 238).

Jesus as a refugee at a young age encountered others, absorbing different customs, different languages, and indeed different cultures. He probably witnessed and crossed many contact zones. It is possible to claim that this encounter with others deeply influenced Jesus' own identity and his vocation. Jesus, being indebted to such unconditional hospitality, modeled to us through his life in ministry how to learn from others, especially those being *Othered*, as sinners, outcasts, non-Jews, as well as how to offer hospitality (Kim-Cragg & Choi, 2014, 104-113). He taught his followers that a faithful life can be achieved through encountering others without fear. The practice of hospitality is the most certain way to defeat fear, bias, and prejudices.

Along with the practice of hospitality, another contribution of religions for citizenship education is to live out the vision of the Reign of God. Christian religious education teaches how to behold the eschatological vision of the "Reign of God", enabling us to transcend a current broken reality while imagining a wholesome world, where justice and peace prevail. Education concerned with the theory and the practice of teaching focuses on the ways people learn to negotiate the trajectories of their lives as they search for wisdom about the meaning of life. People's identities shift in this process of negotiation. This meaning of life embedded in people's identity and their relationship is as much theological as paradoxical. We learn to know that we are finite yet our actions shape the future. We live in the world that is broken and imperfect yet we are not confirmed or consumed by it. Writing on Christian faith practices, religious educator Brett Webb-Mitchell calls faith "speech-act-as-gesture" as an utterance that births new realities into being, a gesture that is nothing short of turning one's whole self (mind, body, spirit, will) toward that other reality which transcends our finite present (2003, 106). Christian practice of faith involves fostering an ability for religious communities to create a community beyond what appears to be impossible and to see things that were not seen before. Such practice forms an integral part of religious education by enhancing "appreciation of the power that the religious imagination still holds in public life and the recognition that many will find in it a cure for violence instead of a cause" (Juergensmeyer, 2001, xii).

In sum, Christian religious education with its full potential makes the commitment to learning and unveiling the hidden history—the past that continues to haunt our present life. Knowing the undisclosed history is crucial and critical to citizenship education, as I tried to show in the case of Canada. It reviews and raises a critical awareness of the issue of misrepresentation of Others imparted through the power of othering. It discloses how discrimination and exclusion work, leading to taking steps to stop them through cultivating the practice of hospitality, and learning to encounter others with respect and without fear. It is religious teaching and practice which encourages us to have faith in encountering others as neighbours and not enemies. It is also this teaching and practice that contributes to creating a place, illuminating a glimpse of wholeness, allowing people to taste and see the world that they dream of beyond what can be currently seen and experienced. With that faith and eschatological vision of the Reign of God, creating a just, equitable, respectful, and diverse society may be possible.

Critical Pause: The Issue of Citizenship

It is undeniable that all of us must ensure that those citizens at the margins receive equal and equitable rights in the realms of education, health care, and in every fabric and net of society. It is abundantly clear that we have a long way to go in ensuring these rights. Placing and practicing them fully may take even longer in our schools, hospitals, and other religious and political institutions. However, it may be asked whether the very category of citizenship may justify the neglect and exclusion of those who do not yet or are unable to belong to that category. The answer to the question of who counts is unclear? For who counts as a citizen may depend on who is doing the counting and what is the purpose of counting. The very concept of citizenship exists and rests on various categorizations ranging from "foreigners," "foreign aliens," or "illegal/undocumented migrants" at the bottom of society to "refugees," "temporary workers," "landed immigrants" or "permanent residents" as the next category of the pyramid, of which citizenship sits at the pinnacle. The Canadian scholars who wrote the counter citizenship guide pose a similar question, "Can we create a more equitable and just version of Canadian citizenship? Or should we instead work to challenge ideas of nations, borders, and citizenship and build global alliances?" (People's Guide, 2011, 74)

Let me end my paper with a radical note, by which I mean, true to the etymology of 'radical', going back to the roots, tapping into the Christian traditions that convey ancient wisdom, while offering illuminating new insights for the current and next generations. This is found in the second (or third) century writing of the *Epistle to Diognetus*, which discusses baptized Christians:

in clothing and dwelling places and the rest of life, they demonstrate the amazing and confessedly paradoxical character of the make up of their own citizenship. They are at home in their own countries, but as sojourners... Every country is their homeland and every homeland is a foreign country (1959, 360).

References

Anderson, B., Sharma, N. & Wright, C. (2009). "Editorial: Why No Borders?" *Refuge. 7* (26:2)

Biles, J. & Ibrahim, H. (2005). "Religion and Public Policy: Immigration, Citizenship, and Multiculturalism—Guess Who's Coming to Dinner?" In: Bramadat P. & Seljak, D. (Eds.) *Religion and Ethnicity in Canada.* Toronto: Pearson/Longman.

Boutilier, B. (2004). "The Canadian Diversity Model: A Repertoire in Search of a Framework." *Canadian Policy Research Network* (September). From: http://www.cprn.org/documents/34033_en.pdf (Accessed January 15, 2014).

Gogia, N. & Slade, B. (2011). *About Canada: Immigration.* Halifax: Fernwood.

Haque, E. (2013). "The Bilingual Limits of Canadian Multiculturalism: The Politics of Language and Race." In: Caldwell, L., Leung, C. & Leroux, D. (Eds.) *Critical Inquires: A Reader in Studies of Canada.* Halifax: Fernwood.

Juergensmeyer, M. (2001). *Terror in the Mind of God: The Global Rise of Religious Violence.* Los Angeles: University of California Press.

Kim-Cragg, H. & E. Choi. (2014). *The Encounters: Retelling the Bible from Migration and Intercultural Perspectives.* Trans. L. Kim. Daejeon: Daejanggan (BlackSmith) Publisher.

King, T. (2012). *The Inconvenient Indian: A Curious Account of Native People in North America.* Toronto: Doubleday Canada.

Kwok, P. (2005). *Postcolonial Imagination and Feminist Theology.* Louisville: Westminster/ John Knox.

Landry, B., CBC radio. (August 29, 2013). From: http://www.cbc.ca/asithappens/features/2013/08/29/bernard-landry-quebec-bashing-anglophone-coverage-of-secular-charter/. (Accessed September 4, 2013).

Miedema, S. (2013). "Coming Out Religiously! Religion and Worldview as an Integral Part of the Social and Public Domain". *Religious Education* (108:3).

Obama, B. (2004). *Dreams from My Father: A Story of Race and Inheritance.* New York: Three River Press Said, E. W. (1978). *Orientalism.* New York: Vintage Books.

Reynolds, T. (2009). "A Rooted Openness: Hospitality as Christian 'Conversion to the Other'. *The Ecumenist: A Journal of Theology, Culture, and Society* (46:2) (Spring).

Seljek, D. (2005). "Education, Multiculturalism, and Religion". In: Bramadat P. & Seljak, D. (Eds.) *Religion and Ethnicity in Canada.* Toronto: Pearson/Longman.

Seymour, J., Crain, M. A., & Crockett, J. V. (1993). *Educating Christians: The Intersection of Meaning, Learning, and Vocation.* Nashville: Abingdon.

Sue, Derald & Sue, David (1990). *Counseling the Culturally Different: Theory and Practice.* New York: John Wiley and Sons.

Webb-Mitchell, B. P. (2003). *Christly Gestures: Learning to Be Members of the Body of Christ.* Grand Rapids: Eerdmans.

Epistle to Diognetus 5:4-5. (1959). Greek text in Kirsopp Lake, *The Apostolic Fathers, vol. 2.* London: Heinemann.

People's Citizenship Guide: a response to conservative Canada (2011). Winnipeg: Arbeiter Ring Publishing.

"Study Guide—Discover Canada: The Rights and Responsibilities of Citizenship and The Equality of Women and Men" (2009). From: http://www.cic.gc.ca/english/resources/publications/discover/index.asp. (Accessed January 16, 2014).

Appendix

Messages of Felicitation

Message of Felicitation

László Andor
European Union Commissioner for Employment,
Social Affairs and Inclusion

Ladies and gentlemen,

I am sorry I cannot be with you in Tirana today, but I am glad that I can address you in this way [the communication was through video transmission]. I congratulate the concerned universities on organising this Conference on "Citizenship, Education and Islam in Europe."

First, I would like to stress that the societal and economic integration of people – irrespective of their backgrounds – is at the core of the European Union's values.

Solidarity, respect for fundamental rights and cohesion are those values, which should bring us closer to an inclusive society and through that to a stronger Europe. Let me start with solidarity.

The crisis we are going through at present has increased unemployment, inequality, poverty and social exclusion. However, countries have not been hit uniformly by the consequences of the crisis. The peripheral, southern, countries have weaker macro-economic performances and face major social imbalances. At the same time, we know that negative trends in one country have a spill-over effect in another. Socio-economic disparity and growing interdependence between countries represent an unprecedented challenge for us to act together. For that, there is a clear need for more solidarity between and within the Member States.

In particular, we need to properly address the incomplete character of the European Monetary Union, without any central budget and common growth policy. Among others, addressing problematic developments related to employment and social policies in the EMU will help all countries yield potentials and prevent increasing disparities.

The second value to be mentioned is respect for fundamental rights.

Europe is not just an economic union. It is based on the common endeavor to ensure social progress, such as protection of fundamental rights. The EU guarantees gender equality, free movement of citizens, anti-discrimination and respect for minorities.

Sadly, the recent crisis has generated populist and extremist reactions, which undermine respect for fundamental rights, and often question equal treatment under EU law, in terms of rights and obligations. Some say that our welfare systems are under threat due to migration. However, studies show that migrant workers mitigate skills shortages and labour market bottlenecks, and at the same time safeguard pensions and healthcare protection as the population diminishes and ages.

Regarding the third value, let me turn to cohesion.

When overt racism is replaced by indirect discrimination, migrants and ethnic minorities are often pushed to the margins of society. In such a situation, social and geographic cohesion should be strengthened through a holistic integration policy. This approach consists of social inclusion provisions that not only promote growth but also support equality and diversity.

Access to the labour market and to non-segregated quality education, housing and health services, are vital to ensure inclusion. Furthermore, people should also be empowered from an early age.

In order to take the necessary measures toward this end, public institutions like schools and universities, together with civil society bodies (be they secular or faith-based) play a vital role in Europe. These institutions should provide education for tolerance and diversity in addition to offering academic curricula.

Ladies and gentlemen,

In the EU28, heterogeneity does not lend itself to implement a "one size fits all" European strategy on social inclusion. However, European initiatives can provide necessary direction. Building on them, national--even local--communities can define actions that take account of specific geographical, economic, social, cultural and legal contexts.

Our overarching strategy — Europe 2020 — seeks to achieve smart, sustainable, and inclusive growth, and turn the EU into the sort of Union in which Europeans want to live by 2020.

This is about striking the right balance between macroeconomic, fiscal, employment and social policy. In particular, it aims to increase employment, reduce the number of people living in poverty, and improve the results of our educational systems.

I would like to mention the Social Investment Package that seeks to set out a comprehensive, innovative approach to social policies. It recommends measures to ease the transition from school to the labour market: such as eliminating barriers, including ones arising from discrimination, and fostering skills development.

Investing in targeted youth guarantee schemes is another tool to get young people into the labour market. Based on the Commission's proposal, Member States are called upon to ensure that all young people up to the age of 25 receive a high-quality offer of a job, an apprenticeship, or a traineeship; or the chance to continue their education.

The Youth Guarantee focuses on young people who are neither employed nor in education or training. Unfortunately young people with migrant or ethnic backgrounds are over-represented in this group.

The successful implementation of these initiatives requires that governments work in partnership at all levels with religious, political, and other organisations and agencies in all sectors of society in order to address and overcome the social impact of the economic and financial crisis.

These efforts are complemented by working to promote equality and fight against discrimination through adopting legislation in this respect. The Commission also reports on applying existing European legislation on the subject, namely the Racial Equality Directive; and the Employment Equality Directive which allow for legal actions to be taken if necessary.

What we all stand to gain from the efficient and effective investment in human capital is a stronger social dimension across the board, thanks to collective action to tackle the challenges of unemployment, social exclusion and poverty.

I wish you a fruitful conference!

Message of Felicitation

Ayhan Tekineş

Dean of the Faculty of Humanities,
Beder University

Dear Minister, Chairman of the Austrian Islamic Community, and representatives of the Albanian Religious Communities, and distinguished guests:

Welcome to our conference on the theme of "Citizenship Education and Islam." At Beder University, we are honored to host this conference, which we have organized with the University of Vienna and Tirana University.

I have a distinct memory that my citizenship course (civics course) in elementary school was one of the lessons that I had difficulty in understanding. These lessons were prepared in order to educate individuals to be respectful of laws, devoted to national values and the state, and to pay taxes. Despite some of the aforementioned benefits of this lesson, its normative structure and its peremptory and authoritarian style left negative impressions on me.

Today, the necessity of interaction with different cultures, caused by globalization and social diversity resulting from migration, job relocation, and educational pursuits, has brought citizenship education to the agenda again with the intent of promoting societal peace and tolerance.

Gaining importance within the frame of globalization and accession to the European Union, citizenship education is currently not only limited to teaching political and legal rights, but also includes its universal and cultural dimensions.

Citizenship education can be considered a quest for common values that will assist in preventing disputes among individuals and various groups within society and/or within society at large. The *Second Article of the European Union Agreement* defines common values as being: democracy, freedom, equality, human dignity, the rule of law, and respect for human rights. The educational model that imparts these common values is termed "Democratic Citizenship Education" by the Council of Europe.

"Democratic citizenship education" — which aims to educate individuals to respect humans just because they are human, and also to respect the physical characteristics, moral sensitivities, language, culture, and beliefs of every human—is crucially important for assuring social harmony. Again, within this framework, we observe issues like human rights education and peace education as having increasing importance.

Intercultural dialogue studies are also crucially important in terms of solving problems caused by social diversity and cultural pluralism and providing a peaceful environment for all individuals in a society.

One of the most important elements shaping culture is undoubtedly religion. With the emergence of globalization, areas of dispute might have been expected to decrease, but, on the contrary, belief-based disputes have been observed to increase. A religious education model sensitive to social problems is clearly a requirement in order to prevent religious and sectarian wars.

A religious education which teaches the unifying aspects of religions rather than separating ones, and which deals with current and future problems rather than historical conflicts must incorporate the citizenship issue in its agenda.

The intersection of the social sciences and religion has always been tense. Accurate and sensitive mediation of the relationship between unchanging principles of religion and changeable structures of society is one of the most important duties of religious educators.

In light of this point, it is necessary to discuss the contribution of religious education to citizenship education, which of itself deals with the accordance of a political structure with the society in which individuals live.

It is obvious that today's social and modern life needs to be recognized in order for religious education to help solve the tension between the spiritual quest of individuals and daily life.

Updating religious language in ways that new generations can understand so as to avoid behaviors and attitudes that increase dispute and division is an important duty of religious education.

Another field that religious education should partner with, and contribute to, is emotional education. A religious education model that encourages moral values such as loyalty and self-sacrifice, and is based on empathy and tolerance education, is required.

Religious education can be considered an academic area examining the ways to raise virtuous persons. Being a good citizen is possible through adhering to humanitarian values. Individuals who impart confidence to their society, and who eschew evil actions, are the types of humans described by religion as "*ideal believers.*"

It should be kept in mind that adhering to agreements and fulfilling the needs of both overt and implicit contracts with society and state are religious duties.

Common human values are universal. A concept of universal citizenship does not conflict with religion. Therefore, I want to state my belief that every step, every educational activity, that will be undertaken for protecting humans and avoiding disorders and degenerations in society, rather than protecting the interests of a certain class or race, is important.

In this new period, when the accession of the Albanian State to the European Union is desired, I hope that this conference will make positive contributions to this process.

We will be exceptionally pleased if this conference, held here in Albania, which adopted multiculturalism in full tolerance, makes even a small contribution to social harmony.

I want to thank our rector, Mr. Ferdinand Gjana, for his encouraging support of this conference, my fellow workers for their efforts in preparing this conference, and the Ministry of Foreign Affairs of Austria for its contributions.

In addition, I thank my dear friend, Dr. Ednan Aslan, organizer of this conference series, who has pioneered studies on religion education and who is known for activities in Islamic religious education.

I want to respectfully greet each of you and welcome you all to our conference.

Contributor Biographies

Hanan Alexander is Dean of Students and Professor of Philosophy of Education at the University of Haifa, where he heads the International School and the Center for Jewish Education. A past chair of Haifa's Department of Education, he is also a Senior Research Fellow in the Van Leer Jerusalem Institute. His research interests include political, moral, spiritual, religious, and Jewish education and the philosophy of social research. Alexander has published more than 120 essays in various academic and professional venues, a number of which have been translated into German, Dutch, Chinese, and Hebrew. His books include *Reclaiming Goodness: Education and the Spiritual Quest* (2001), *Ethics and Spirituality in Education: Philosophical, Theological, and Radical Perspectives* (2004), *Citizenship Education and Social Conflict Israeli Political Education in Global Perspective* (2011), and *Commitment, Character, and Citizenship: Religious Schooling in Liberal Democracy* (2102). His new book, *Reimagining Liberal Education: Affiliation and Inquiry in Democratic Schooling*, will appear from Bloomsbury 2015.

Muhamed Ali works as an assistant professor at the faculty of Arts and Social Sciences, in the International University of Sarajevo, where he teaches courses in the area of law and political science. Previously, he served as an assistant professor in the faculty of Islamic Sciences in Skopje, where he taught courses in Islamic Law and the Philosophy of Islamic Law. He actively participates in international conferences and is the author of several articles. He serves as an editorial board member of several journals; *Turkey's Reviewed Academic journal*, the *Journal of Balkan Studies, Albania's Reviewed Academic Journal*, and the *Beder Journal of Humanities* as well as Macedonia's Islamic Community journal, *Hilal*.

Brigit Allenbach, Dr. phil., is a social anthropologist and teaches at the University of Freiburg/CH and at the Zurich University of Teacher Education. She was project leader in the National Research Programme NRP 58 on "Religion, the State, and Society" funded by the Swiss National Science Foundation SNF. Her main areas of interest are migration and transnational studies, diasporas from South East Europe in Switzerland, kinship and gender studies, children and youth studies. Recent publications include: *Muslime in der Schweiz*, ed. (2010), *Jugend, Migration und Religion: interdisziplinäre Perspektiven*, ed. (2011), and "Bairam, Balkanslang, Basketball…: Die vielfältigen Zugehörigkeiten von muslimischen Jugendlichen in der Schweiz" in *Tsantsa* 17: 86-95 (2012).

Leyla Almazova is an Associate Professor in the Department of Regional and Islamic Studies, Institute of International Relations, History and Oriental Studies, at the Kazan Federal University where she teaches courses in Islamic Studies, the Ethno-Religious Situation at the Middle East and the History of Arab-Muslim Philosophy. She has published more than 50 academic works devoted to diverse issues associated with Islam in the Volga-Ural Region. She is the author of a monograph, *The Problem of Man in Tatar Philosophical Thought (end of 19th – beginning of the 20th century)* (2003), a translation from Old Tatar language of Ziya Kamali's treatise, *The Philosophy of Islam* (2010). Currently she is working on another monograph entitled *Current Ideological Debates in Tatar Islam*. Dr. Leyla Almazova was the recipient of a Fulbright Scholarship for the year 2010-2011 at the University of Michigan, USA.

László Andor has been the EU's Commissioner for Employment, Social Affairs and Inclusion since February 2010. Between 2005 and 2010 he represented Hungary, the Czech Republic, Slovakia, and Croatia on the Board of Directors of the European Bank for Reconstruction and Development in London. Previously he was an associate professor at Corvinus University of Budapest and King Sigismund College, the editor of several journals, and advisor to the Hungarian Prime Minister. A Hungarian national, Dr. Andor graduated from the University of Economic Sciences in Budapest in 1989, studied at George Washington University, Washington, D.C., and earned a Master's degree in Development Economics from the University of Manchester in 1993 as a British Council Fellow. He holds a Ph.D. in Economics from the Hungarian Academy of Sciences.

Ednan Aslan is the Chair of Islamic Religious Education in the Centre for Teacher Training and Institute for Islamic Studies at the University of Vienna. Prof. Aslan is chairperson of various working groups on the development of curricula in Germany, Austria, and Southeast Europe and has published extensively on Islamic religious education in Europe. His research focuses on Islamic identity, the future of Islamic theology, and imam-training in Europe. His books include *Islamic Education in Europe* (Böhlau 2009), *Islamic Textbooks and Curricula in Europe* (2011), *The Training of Imams and Teachers for Islamic Education in Europa* (2013), *Islamic Education in Secular Societies* (2013).

Rositsa Atanasova recently finished her law degree at the University of Cambridge after completing a Master's degree in Islamic Studies at the Harvard Divinity School. She is interested in the interaction of Islam with secular legal systems and her graduate work explored the institutional framework of Islamic education in post-communist Bulgaria. As a law student Rositsa specialized in constitutional law, public international law and European human rights law. She has served as the Windsor Fellow at the UK Home Office where she worked in the field of immigration and asylum law.

Eileen Daily M., JD, Ph.D. Assistant Professor of Pastoral Studies at Loyola University Chicago, is a former lawyer turned Catholic religious educator. Her recent work has focused on informal public religious education. She is the author and architect of art/y/fact.Xn, an app for Apple and Android devices that facilitates Christian religious education in the recreational context of art museums.

Juan Galguera Ferreiro is Professor of Law and Religion in the Department of Public Law of the University of A Coruña. He is also Master in International Affairs (Autonomous University of Barcelona) and Master in Journalism (Autonomous University of Madrid-EL PAIS). He served as Deputy Director of Relations with Denominations at the Ministry of Justice of Spain (2006-2010). Prof. Ferreiro is the coordinator of the project "the Arab Spring in Egypt, Libya and Tunisia" financed by the Spanish Ministry of Economy. His research focuses on freedom of expression, freedom of education, freedom of conscience, limits of religious freedom, and relations between churches and State: especially regarding Islam. His books include *Profesores de religión de la enseñanza pública y Constitución Española* (2004), *Relaciones Iglesia-Estado en la II República Española* (2005), *Islam and State in the EU: Imam Training Centres* (2011), *Relaciones Iglesia-Estado en el Franquismo y en la Transición* (2013).

Marcia Hermansen is Director of the Islamic World Studies program at Loyola University Chicago where she teaches courses in Islamic Studies and Religious Studies as a Professor in the Theology Department. Her books include *Muslima*

Theology: The Voices of Muslim Women Theologians (2013), edited with Ednan Aslan, *Shah Wali Allah's Treatises on Islamic Law* (2010) and *The Conclusive Argument from God*, a study and translation (from Arabic) of Shah Wali Allah of Delhi's, *Hujjat Allah al-Baligha* (1996). Dr. Hermansen has also contributed numerous academic articles in the fields of Islamic thought, Sufism, Islam and Muslims in South Asia, Muslims in America, and Women and Gender in Islam.

Doron Kiesel is Professor in the Faculty of Intercultural and International Social Work at the University of Applied Science, Erfurt. He works on issues of migration and integration focusing on the integration of Russian-speaking Jews in Germany since 1990, patterns of integration of ethnic minorities in Germany, and social work in multicultural societies. Since September 2012 he has been Director of Research in the Education Department of the Central Council of Jews in Germany where he also is engaged in the establishment of the Jewish Academy.

HyeRan Kim-Cragg is the Lydia Gruchy Professor of Pastoral Studies at St. Andrew's College in the University of Saskatchewan, Saskatoon, Canada. Her academic interest includes postcolonial studies, feminist theology, anti-racism religious education and intercultural ministry. She has published many articles and essays around identity formation in the globalized post-colonial world. She is the author of *Story and Song: A Postcolonial Interplay between Christian Education and Worship* (2012), and the co-author of Hebrews: *Wisdom Commentaries* (forthcoming). This year she published a co-authored book in Korean *Multicultural Stories Encountered in the Bible* that deals with re-reading the Bible from the perspective of migration as a resource for young people, their parents and teachers.

Mustafa Köylü received his B.A. degree from the Faculty of Theology and an M.A. degree in Religious Education from the Institute of Social Sciences at Ondokuz Mayıs University in 1985, 1989 respectively. He received a D. Miss. from the United Theological Seminary, Dayton, OH in 1997; and a Ph.D. from the Institute of Social Sciences at Ondokuz Mayıs University in Religious Education in 2002 where he is currently professor in Religious Education in the Faculty of Theology. His has published two books in English: *Islam and Its Quest for Peace* (2003) and *Muslim and Christian Reflections on Peace*, ed. (2005), and ten books in Turkish: *Basic Principles of Adult Religious Education* (2000), *Interreligious Dialogue in the Thoughts of Contemporary Christian and Muslim Scholars* (2001), *Religious Communication from Psycho-Social Perspectives* (2003), *Global Moral Education* (2006), *Religious Education according to the Developmental Stages* (2010), *Ethics in* the World Religions (2010), Religious Education, ed. (2012), Contemporary Issues in Religious Education, ed. (2012), Religious Consultation and Religious Services, ed. (2012), and Comparative Religious Education with İbrahim Turan (2014).

Siebren Miedema holds a degree in Education (Philosophy and History of Education) from the University of Groningen, the Netherlands and a degree in Philosophy (Philosophy of the Social Sciences) from the University of Groningen, the Netherlands. He received his Ph.D. in Social Sciences from Leiden University in 1986. He is Professor Emeritus in Educational Foundations in the Department of Research and Theory in Education of the Faculty of Psychology and Education, and Professor Emeritus in Religious Education in the Department of Praxis of the Faculty of Theology, VU University Amsterdam. Recent book publications in English are: *Reaching for the Sky. Religious Education from Christian and Islamic Perspectives.* Ed. With Stella El Bouayadi-van de Wetering, (2012), *Moral Education and Development: A Lifetime Commitment.* ed. (2011), *Religious Education as Encounter. A Tribute to John M. Hull.* ed. (2009), and *Religious Education in a World of Religious Diversity* (2009).

Nadire Mustafi - teaches Islamic religion in secondary schools and lectures at the Muslim Teachers Training College in Vienna. She is General Secretary of the Shura Council which is the principal committee of the Islamic Religious Community in Austria - the IGGiÖ. She is the women's representative for a branch of this body, the Islamic Religious Community in Lower Austria. Her research focuses on Imams as key figures in the process of integration, migration studies, youth research and Islamic religion education.

Agata S. Nalborczyk is Ph.D. in Arabic and Islamic Studies, habilitated Dr. in Religious Studies/ Islamic Studies, Associate Professor at the Department for European Islam Studies, Faculty of Oriental Studies, University of Warsaw. Her research focuses on Islam in Europe (esp. Poland, Central and Eastern Europe), the legal status of European Muslim minorities, Polish-Lithuanian Tatars, gender issues in Islam, Christian-Muslim relations, and the image of Islam and Muslims in Europe. She is a member of the Editorial Board for the series "Annotated Legal Documents on Islam in Europe" (2014), editorial advisor and author for the *Yearbook of Muslims in Europe* (2009-2014), and the author of numerous articles on Islam in Europe published in journals such as *Islam and Christian-Muslim Relations, Global Change, Peace and Security, Islamochristiana, TRANS,* and various edited volumes. She is a member of the Association for the Sociology of Religion and the International Association for the Study of Religion in Eastern and Central

Europe (ISORECEA). Nalborczyk co-authored (2007) the lexicon for journalists "Don't be Afraid of Islam" (in Polish) awarded the International Catholic Union of the Press (UCIP) International Award for Interreligious Dialogue.

Jørgen Nielsen is Hon. Professor of Islamic Studies at the University of Copenhagen, trustee and board member of the International Center for Minority Studies and Intercultural Relations (IMIR) in Sofia, and chairs the Advisory Board of the Erlangen Centre for Islam and Law in Europe at the University of Erlangen-Nurnberg. He has researched and written extensively about Islam in Europe for almost forty years while holding academic positions in Birmingham UK, Damascus, Copenhagen, and Utrecht. He is the executive editor of the *Journal of Muslims in Europe* (Leiden: Brill).

Zeki Saritoprak, Ph.D. is Professor and the Bediüzzaman Said Nursi Chair in Islamic Studies at John Carroll University in Cleveland, Ohio. He holds a Ph.D. in Islamic Theology from the University of Marmara in Turkey. His dissertation, which examines the personification of evil in the Islamic tradition, is entitled *The Antichrist (al-Dajjal) in Islamic Theology* and was published in Turkish in Istanbul in 1992. Professor Saritoprak has also held positions at Harran University in Turkey, Georgetown University, the Catholic University of America, and Berry College in Rome, Georgia and was the founder and former president of the Rumi Forum for Interfaith Dialogue in Washington, DC.

Professor Saritoprak is the author of *Islam's Jesus* (2014) and over thirty academic articles and encyclopedia entries on topics in Islam. He has served as guest editor for issues of the journals *Islam and Christian-Muslim Relations* and *Muslim World*. He is the editor and translator of *Fundamentals of Rumi's Thought: A Mevlevi Sufi Perspective* (2004) and the editor of a critical edition of al-Sarakhsi's *Sifat Ashrat al-Sa'a* (in Arabic; Cairo, 1993). He is currently preparing a book on Islamic spirituality tentatively titled *Islamic Spirituality: Theology and Practice for the Modern World*.

Zekirija Sejdini. Ph.D. Born in Macedonia, Sejdini graduated in 1998 from Marmara University in Istanbul/Turkey in Islamic Theology with a special focus on Islamic Philosophy. He continued his academic studies at the University of Heidelberg in Germany where he received his Ph.D. in Islamic Studies. From 2004 to 2006 he was lecturer at the Protestant College of Higher Education in Ludwigsburg/Germany on "Christian-Islamic Dialogue". In 2004 he moved to Vienna, Austria where he became head of the department for Islamic Religious Education at the Islamic Religious Pedagogical Academy of Vienna and additionally supervisor for Islamic Religious Education in charge of all compulsory and higher education schools of Vienna. In addition, he is a lecturer on Islamic Religious Pedagogy in several Austrian institutions and a lecturer on Islamic Mysticism at the Universities of Vienna and Innsbruck, Tyrolia. Beside his academic positions Sejdini undertakes several responsibilities in the Official Islamic Religious Authority of Austria (IGGiÖ), such as serving as Head of the Shura Council, Member of the High Council, and Spokesperson for the IGGiÖ.

Dmitry Shmonin, Ph.D. (1997), Dr. Sc. in History of Philosophy (2003) is Vice-rector for research at the Russian Christian Academy for the Humanities (St. Petersburg), vice-director of the research programme "Christianity and Islam in contemporary Russia", and Professor of philosophy and history of religious education at the St. Petersburg Orthodox Theological Academy.

Matthias Scharer is the Chair of Catechetics, Religious Education and Didactics of Religion at the Catholic Theology Faculty of the University of Innsbruck. He is a graduate member of the Teaching Staff of the Ruth Cohn Institute International and also educated in Gestalt Therapy and Counselling Supervision. Recently he has supported the implementation of Islamic Religious Education Studies at the University of Innsbruck. His research focuses on Communicative Theology as a new theological culture that includes Interreligious Dialogue and Communication. Communicative Theology has been established in cooperation with Jochen Hilberath (Tübingen) and Brad Hinze (New York) as part of an international and interdisciplinary research group. Together with these two researchers he edits *Communicative Theology – Interdisciplinary Studies* (16 volumes) and with Jochen Hilberath *Kommunikative Theologie* (16 volumes). His books include *Reflections on TCI and Symbolic Interaction* (1986), *Religious Education in School* (1987), *Catechese of Sacraments* (1990; 1999; 2000), *Adult Education* (1995), *Leadership* (2008), *Human Relationship* (2010), and *Communicative Theology* (2003; 2008; 2010; 2012).

Laurentiu D. Tănase holds the Ph.D. from the University of Strasbourg, France; and teaches sociology of religion at the Faculty of Orthodox Theology, University of Bucharest. He was the State Secretary for the Religious Affaires in the Government of Romania (2001-2004) while currently he is a member of the Parliamentary Commission for research on the Communist Period in Romania (CNSAS). He is a member of the International Society for the Sociology of Religion and a member of the French Association of Religious Sociology. He has made many television appearances as an academic authority and is the author of numerous articles and studies on the evolution of the field of religious studies, secularization, globalization and the phenomenon of sects and new religious movements. His publications include *Pluralisation religieuse et société en Roumanie*, ed. (2008).

Ayhan Tekineş graduated from the Faculty of Theology of the University of Marmara and completed his Masters degree at the same university in 1991. In 1997 he received his Ph.D. with a doctoral thesis on "Mushkil al-Hadith". During the period 1994-1998 he worked as a research assistant at Sakarya University, then in 1998 he was appointed as professor at the same university. In March of 2011 Tekineş joined the Faculty of Theology at Fatih University and in October 2011 he was appointed Dean of the Faculty of Humanities at Bedër University, Tirana, Albania.

Selahattin Turan is a professor in the department of educational sciences at Eskisehir Osmangazi University, Turkey. He received his B.A. from Ankara University in 1990; M.A. in 1993 and Ph.D. in 1998 from Ohio State University. Turan joined the Eskisehir Osmangazi University College of Education faculty in 1998. His professional interests are educational policy and leadership, the organizational psychology of organizations, and alternative perspectives in education. He has co-authored many books in educational studies and is the editor of the *Journal of Education and Humanities: Theory and Practice* while serving on the editorial board of the *Turkish Journal of Educational Administration*. He has also published widely in a variety of scholarly journals and presented papers at the annual meetings of many national and international organizations. He is currently the Dean of the College of Education at Eskisehir Osmangazi University and the president-designate of the Economic Cooperation Organization (ECO) Educational Institute in Ankara.

Bibliography

Ackermann, P. (1999). *Politische Bildung*. In: Dagmar, R. & Weißno G. (eds.) Lexikon der politischen Bildung. Didaktik und Schule. Schwalbach/Ts.: Wochenschau-Verl.

Act 26 of November 10th 1992 whereby the Cooperation Agreement between the Spanish State and the Islamic commission of Spain.

Act of 15 July 1912 on the recognition of the followers of Islam according to the Hanafi rite as a religious society. (RGBl 1912/159).

Akarcesmet, S. "Kimse Yok Mu reaches out to Syrians in joint project with UNHCR." *Today's Zaman*, (9 Feb 2014).

Akbulut, A. (1992). *Sahabe devri siyasi hadiselerinin kelami problemlere Etkileri*. Istanbul: Birlesik Yayinlari

Akdağ, B. (2003). Türkiye'de din öğretimi kitaplarında insan hakları problemleri. In: Çotuksöken B., Erzan A. & Silier O. (Eds.). *Ders Kitaplarında İnsan Hakları: Tarama Sonuçları*. (240-263). İstanbul: Tarih Vakfı.

Aktaran, E. (2012). *Worden wie je bent. Kaders voor identiteitsbeleid op de Simon scholen* [Becoming who you are. Frameworks for identity policy at the SIMON schools]. Leusden: SIMON.

Al-'Awwa, M. S. (1989). *Fi al-Nizam al-Siyasi li'l-Dawlah al-Islamiyyah*. Cairo: Dar al-Shuruq.

al-Bukhari, Abu 'Abdillah Muhammad bin Isma'il. (1990). *Al-Sahih*. Edited by Mustafa Dayb al-Bugha. Damascus: Dar Ibn Kathir.

Alexander, H. A. (2001). *Reclaiming Goodness: Education and the Spiritual Quest*. Notre Dame: University of Notre Dame Press.

Alexander, H. A. (2005). "Education in Ideology." *The Journal of Moral Education* 34, no. 1 (1-18).

Alexander, H. A. (2005). "Human Agency and the Curriculum." *Theory and Research in Education* 3, no. 3.

Alexander, H. A. (2006). "A View from Somewhere: Explaining the Paradigms of Educational Research." *Journal of Philosophy of Education* 40, no. 2 (22-205).

Alexander, H. A. (2007). "What is Common about Common Schooling: Rational Autonomy and Moral Agency in Liberal Democratic Education." *Journal of Philosophy of Education* 41, no. 4 (24-609).

Alexander, H. A. (2010). "Educating Identity: Toward a Pedagogy of Difference." In: Miedema, S. (Ed.). *Religious Education as Encounter: A Tribute to John Hull.* Munster: Waxman.

Alexander, H. A., Pinson, H. & Yonah, Y. (Eds.). (2011). Conclusion to *Citizenship, Education, and Social Conflict: Israeli Political Education in Global Perspective.* New York: Routledge.

Allenbach, B. (2011). Made in Switzerland: Politik der Zugehörigkeit und Religion am Beispiel von Secondos aus Südosteuropa. In: Allenbach, B., Goel, U., Hummrich, M. & Weissköppel, C. (Eds.). *Jugend, Migration und Religion. Interdisziplinäre Perspektiven.* (199–224). Zürich/Baden-Baden: Pano/Nomos.

Allenbach, B. (2012). Bairam, Balkanslang, Basketball...: Die vielfältigen Zugehörigkeiten von muslimischen Jugendlichen in der Schweiz. *Tsantsa* 17, (86-95).

Allenbach, B., & Herzig, P. (2010). Der Islam aus der Sicht von Kindern und Jugendlichen. In: Allenbach, B., & Sökefeld, M. (Eds.). *Muslime in der Schweiz.* (296–330). Zürich: Seismo.

Allenbach, B., & Sökefeld, M. (2010). Einleitung. In: Allenbach, B., & Sökefeld, M. (Eds.). *Muslime in der Schweiz.* (9–40). Zürich: Seismo.

Allenbach, B., Herzig, P., & Müller, M. (2010). *Schlussbericht Migration und Religion: Perspektiven von Kindern und Jugendlichen in der Schweiz.* Bern: Nationales Forschungsprogramm NFP 58. From: www.nfp58.ch/files/downloads/SB_Giordano.pdf. (Accessed January 20, 2014).

Al-e Ahmad, J. A. (1982). *Gharbzadegi.* Lexington: Mazda Publisher.

al-Qari, 'Ali bin Sutlan Muhammad. (2002). *Mirqat al-Mafatih Sharh Mishkat al-Masabih.*

al-Tabari, Muhammad bin Jarir. (2000). *Jami' al-Bayan 'an Tafsir Ay al-Qur'an.* Beirut: Mu'assasat al-Risalah.

al-Tayalisi, Sulaiman bin Abi Dawud. (n.d.) *Al-Musnad.* Beirut: Dar al-Ma'rifa.

al-Tirmidhi, Abu 'Isa Muhammad bin 'Isa bin Sawra. (1975). *Al-Jami' al-Sahih.* Edited by Ibrahim 'Atwa 'Awad. Cairo: Maktabat Mustafa al-Babi al-Halabi.

Anderson, B. (2006). *Imagined Communities: Reflections on the Origin and Spread of Nationalism.* (revised ed.). London: Verso.

Anderson, B., Sharma, N. & Wright, C. (2009). "Editorial: Why No Borders?" *Refuge.* 7 (26:2)

An-Na'im, A. A. (2008). *Islam and the Secular State.* Cambridge, MA: Harvard University Press.

Anthias, F. (2009). Translocational belonging, identity and generation: Questions and problems in migration and ethnic studies. *Finnish Journal of Ethnicity and Migration* 4(1), (6–15).

Asad, T. (2003). *Formations of the Secular. Christianity, Islam, Modernity.* Stanford: Stanford University Press.

Aslan, A. (2000). "Dini Cogulculuk Problemine Yeni Blr Yaklasim" [Eine neue Betrachtung der religiösen Pluralität]. *Islami Arastirmalar Dergisi* 4, (17-30).

Aslan, E., Yildiz, E. & Kolb, J. (2014). *Muslimische Alltagspraktiken in Österreich.* From: https://iis.univie.ac.at/fileadmin/user_upload /p_iis/muslimische_alltagspraxis_in_ oesterreich. projektbericht.pdf (Accessed April 14, 2014).

Atay, H. (1983). *Osmanlılarda Yüksek Din Egitim*. İstanbul: Dergah.

Ateş, S. (1989). *Cennet kimsenin tekelinde degildir*. [No one has a monopoly on Paradise]. In: *Islami Arastirmalar, Journal of Islamic Research*. (7-24).

Ayhan, H. (1999a). Cumhuriyet dönemi din eğitimine genel bir bakış. (237-254). Ankara: *Ankara Üniversitesi İlahiyat Fakültesi Dergisi*.

Ayhan. H. (1999b). *Türkiye'de Din Egitimi*. İstanbul: Ifav.

Bade, K. & Troen, I. (Eds.) (1993). *Zuwanderung und Eingliederung von deutschen und Juden aus der früheren Sowjetunion in Deutschland und Israel*. Bonn: Bundeszentrale für politische Bildung.

Bade, K. (2000). *Europa in Bewegung. Migration vom späten 18. Jahrhundert bis zur Gegenwart*. Munich: C.H. Beck Verlag.

Bakhtiyarov, A. (2007). *The Path of Apprehending Through the Heart: From Heart To Heart*. Kazan: Altay-tay.

Balic, S. (2001). *Islam für Europa. Neue Perspektiven einer alten Religion*. Köln-Weimar-Wien.

Balkanski, P. & Zahariev. Z. (1998). *Vavedenie v grazhdanskoto obrazovanie [Introduction to Citizenship Education]*. Sofia: Laska.

Barth, F. (1994). Enduring and emerging issues in the analysis of ethnicity. In: Vermeulen, H., & Govers, C. (Eds.). *The anthropology of ethnicity: Beyond "Ethnic Groups and Boundaries*. (11–32). Amsterdam: Het Spinhuis.

Bar-Yosef, R. (Ed.) (1990). *Family-Absorption-Work. Selected Issues in the Analysis of the Israeli Society*. Jerusalem: The Hebrew University, Department of Sociology.

Bashkësia Fetare Islame. (n.d.) From http://bfi.mk/faqja/ (Retrieved 10 March 2014).

Bashkësia Fetare Islame. (n.d.) From: http://bfi.mk/faqja/?tag=bfi-bojkoton-konferencen-per%20bashkepunim-nderfetar (Retrieved 9 March 2014).

Batrov, R. (2007). *Instead of Reform*. Nizhny Novgorod: Medina.

Bayoumi, M. (2010). *The God That Failed*. In: Shryock; A. (Ed.) *Islamophobia/Islamophilia: Beyond the Politics of Enemy and Friend*. (79-93). Bloomington, IN: Indiana University Press.

Beirut: Dar al-Fikr.

Benavides, G. (1998). Modernity. In: Taylor, M. C. (Ed.). *Critical terms for religious studies*. (186-204). Chicago: University of Chicago Press.

Berger, P. (1971). *La religion dans la conscience moderne*. Paris: Le Centurion.

Bergmann, G. (1988). *Franz Jägerstätter: Ein Leben vom Gewissen entschieden (2 Ausg.)*. (A. Guillet, Eds.) Berlin: Christiana.

Berkes, N. (1978). *Türkiye'de Çağdaşlaşma*. İstanbul: Doğu-Batı Yayınları.

Berkes, N. (2013a). *Türkiye'de çağdaşlaşma*. İstanbul: Yapı Kredi.

Berkes, N. (2013b). *The Development of Secularism in Turkey*. London: Routledge.

Berlin, I. (1953). *The Hedgehog and the Fox: An Essay on Tolstoy's View of History*. New York: Simon and Schuster.

Berlin, I. (1969). *Four Essays on Liberty*. Oxford: Oxford Univ. Press.

Bertram-Troost, G.D., de Roos, S.A. & Miedema, S. (2006). Religious identity development of adolescents in religiously affiliated schools: A theoretical foundation for empirical research. *Journal of Beliefs and Values. 27*, (303-314).

Bigiev, M. (2006). *Woman in the Light of the Sacred Ayat of the Holy Quran*. Selected Works *(2)*. Kazan: Tatarstan Book Printing House.

Biles, J. & Ibrahim, H. (2005). "Religion and Public Policy: Immigration, Citizenship, and Multiculturalism—Guess Who's Coming to Dinner?" In: Bramadat P. & Seljak, D. (Eds.) *Religion and Ethnicity in Canada*. Toronto: Pearson/Longman.

Bilgin, B (2005). Müslüman ülkelerdeki okul kitaplarında hıristiyanlık anlatımı. In: Yılmaz R. (Ed.). *Kültürel Çeşitlilik ve Din*. (331-343). Ankara: Sinemis Yayınları.

Bilgiseven, A. K. (1987). *Egitim Sosyolojisi*. İstanbul: Türk Dünyası Araştırmaları Vakfı Yayınları.

BMUKK. *Bundesgesetzblatt für die Republik Österreich* - BGBl Nr.II 290/2008. From: http://www.bmukk.gv.at/medienpool/17041/lp_vs_hs_ahs_nov_08.pdf. (Accessed December 16, 2014).

BMUKK. *Curriculum for Civic Education*. From: http://www.bmukk.gv.at/medienpool/11857/lp_neu_ahs_05.pdf. (Accessed Februry 16, 2014).

BMUKK. *Grundsatzerlass*. From: http://www.bmukk.gv.at/medienpool/15683/pb_grundsatzerlass.pdf. (Accessed Februry 16, 2014).

BMUKK. *Lehrpläne der AHS Unterstufe*. From: http://www.bmukk.gv.at/medienpool/786/ahs11.pdf. (Accessed February 16, 2014).

Bohdanowicz, L., Chazbijewicz, S. & Tyszkiewicz, J. (1997). *Tatarzy muzułmanie w Polsce*. Gdańsk: Rocznik Tatarów Polskich.

Borawski, P. & Dubiński, A. (1986). *Tatarzy polscy, Dzieje, obrzędy, tradycje*. Warszawa: Iskry.

Borawski, P. (1983). Sytuacja prawna ludności tatarskiej Wielkim Księstwie Litewskim (XVI-XVIII w.). *Acta Baltico-Slavica*, *15*, (55-76).

Boutilier, B. (2004). "The Canadian Diversity Model: A Repertoire in Search of a Framework." *Canadian Policy Research Network* (September). From: http://www.cprn.org/documents/34033_en.pdf (Accessed January 15, 2014).

Bozkurt, G. (1996). *Türk Kimliği*. Istanbul: Remzi Kitabevi.

Brubaker, R. (2007). *Ethnizität ohne Gruppen*. Hamburg: Hamburger Edition.

Bukow, W.D. & Llaryora, R. (1988). *Mitbürger aus der Fremde. Soziogenese ethnischer Minoritäten*. Opladen: Westdeutscher Verlag.

Bukow, W.-D. (1993). *Leben in der multikulturellen Gesellschaft. Die Entstehung kleiner Unternehmer im Umgang mit ethnischen Minderheiten*. Opladen: Westdeutscher Verlag.

Bukow, W.-D., Nikodem, C., Schulze, E. & Yildiz, E. (Eds.) (2001). *Auf dem Weg zur Stadtgesellschaft. Die multikulturelle Stadt zwischen globaler Neuorientierung Restauration*. Opladen: Leske & Budrich.

Bulaç, A. (1995). *Modernizm, irtica ve sivilleşme*. İstanbul: İz.

Bunescu, G. (2004). *Antologia Legilor Învăţământului din România [Anthology of the Laws of Education in Romania]*. Bucureşti: The Institute of Educational Sciences.

Callan, E. (2004). *Creating Citizens: Political Education and Liberal Democracy*. Oxford: Clarendon Press.

Caputo, V. (1995). Anthropology's silent "others": A consideration of some conceptual and methodological issues for the study of youth and children's cultures. In: Amit-Talai, V., & Wulff, H. (Eds.). *Youth culture: A cross-cultural perspective*. (19–42). London: Routledge.

Çayır, K. (2011). Turkey's New Citizenship and Democracy Education Course: Search for Democratic Citizenship in a Difference-Blind Polity? *Journal of Social Science Education, 10*(4), (22-30).

Çayır, K., & Gürkaynak, İ. (2008). The state of citizenship education in Turkey: past and present. *Journal of Social Science Education*, 6(2), (50-58).

Landry, B. CBS radio. (August 29, 2013). From: http://www.cbc.ca/asithappens/features/2013/08/29/bernard-landry-quebec-bashing-anglophone-coverage-of-secular-charter/. (Accessed September 4, 2013).

Cebeci, S. (1999). Cumhuriyet döneminde yüksek din egitimi. (227-235). Ankara: *Ankara Üniversitesi İlahiyat Fakültesi Dergisi*.

Charter of Fundamental Rights of the European Union. *Preamble*. In: *Official Journal of the European Communities*. From: http://www.europarl.europa.eu/charter/pdf/text_en.pdf (Accessed December 18, 2000).

Chazbijewicz S. (1993). Ideologie muzułmanów polskich w latach 1918-1939. *Rocznik Tatarów Polskich, 1*, (15-42).

Christensen, P., & James, A. (2000). Introduction: Researching children and childhood: Cultures of communication. In: Christensen, P., James, A. (Eds.). *Research with children: Perspectives and practices* (1–8). London: Falmer Press.

Cidade, M. A. (2011). *Peace and Justice and Young Adult Catholics*. Presentation from: http://www.authorstream.com/Presentation/everydaygrace-1070425-peace-and-justice-young-adult-catholics-cara-presentation-with-no/. (Accessed February 19, 2014).

Cliteur, P. (2006). Zin en onzin van levensbeschouwelijke vorming [Meaning and nonsense about religious education]. In: S. Miedema (Eds.). *Religie in het onderwijs. Zekerheden en onzekerheden van levensbeschouwelijke vorming* [Religion in education. Certainties and uncertainties of religious education] (33-54). Zoetermeer: Meinema.

Cohen, J. (2002). Zoals het nu gaat, zo kan het niet langer [The current situation should not continue]. *NRC/HB*, January 4.

Cohn, R. C. (1971). Living-Learning Encounters: The Theme-Centered Interactional Method. In: Blank L., Gottsegen G., & Gottsegen M. (Eds.), Confrontations (245-271). New York: Macmillan and London.

Cohn, R. C. (1974). Zur Grundlage des thenezentrierten, interaktionellen Systems: Axiome, Postulate, Hilfsregeln. Gruppendynamik , 3, (150-159).

Cohn, R. C., & Farau, A. (2008). Gelebte Geschichte der Psychotherapie (4. Auflage Ausg.). Stuttgart: Klett-Cotta.

Coles, M. I. (2010): *When hope and history rhyme*. Islam, citizenship and education: building Akhlaq, Adhab and Tahdhib; a discussion paper. [Leicester]: Islam & Citizenship Education Project.

Comisión Islámica de España-CIE-[Islamic Commission of Spain]. From: http://muslim.multiplexor.es/promo/cie.htm. (Accessed January 17, 2011).

Constituția României. (2003). [*Constitution of Romania*]. Monitorul Oficial.

Cooperation Agreement of January 3th 1979. Between the Spanish State and the Holy See, concerning education and cultural affairs (International Treaty).

Cremin, L. A. (1980) *American Education: The National Experience: 1783–1876*. New York, NY: Harper & Row.

Crowley, J. (1999). The politics of belonging: Some theoretical considerations. In: Geddes, A., & Favell, A. (Eds.). *The politics of belonging: Migrants and minorities in contemporary Europe*. (15–41). Aldershot: Ashgate.

Curriculum for Grade 1, approved by the order of the Ministry of Education and Research, no 5350/ 22.11.2004.

Curriculum for Grade 1-12. (2007). *Religion.* Bucharest: The Ministry of Education, Research and Youth.

D'Amato, G. (2010). Die Secondos – Von „tickenden Zeitbomben" zu „Overperformern". In: Ritter, C., Muri, G., & Rogger, B. (Eds.). *Magische Ambivalenz. Identität und Visualität im transkulturellen Raum* (178–185). Zürich: Diaphanes.

Daniliuk A., Kondakov A. & Tishkov, V. (2009). *Kontseptsija dukhovno-nravstvennogo razvitija y vospitanija lichnosti grazhdanina Rossii* [The concept of spiritual and moral development and education of a citizen of Russia]. Moscow : Prosveschenie.

Department for interethnic relations. (2006). *Panorama invatamantului minoritatilor naţionale din Romania in perioada 2003 - 2006, Departamentul pentru relatii inter-etnice.* Bucureşti: Coresi.

Dewey, J. (1897/1972). My Pedagogic Creed. In: J.A. Boydston (Eds.), *John Dewey. The Early Works. Volume 5.* (84-95). Carbondale and Edwardsville: Southern Illinois University Press.

Dewey, J. (1916). *Democracy and Education. An Introduction to the Philosophy of Education.* New York : The Free Press.

Diehm, I. & Radtke, F.O. (1999). *Erziehung und Migration.* Stuttgart: Kohlhammer.

Doedens, F. & Weisse, W. (Eds.) (1997). *Religionsunterricht für alle. Hamburger Perspektiven zur Religionsdidaktik* [Religious education for all. Perspectives on the didactics of religion from Hamburg]. Münster/New York/München/Berlin: Waxmann.

Doğan, R. (1999). *İslamcıların Eğitim Görüşleri ve Ogretim.* Ankara: Bizim Büro Basmevi..

Eisenstadt, S. N. (1987). *Die Transformation der israelischen Gesellschaft.* Frankfurt am Main: Suhrkamp.

EKM Eidgenössische Kommission für Migrationsfragten (2010). *Muslime in der Schweiz. Identitätsprofile, Erwartungen und Einstellungen. Eine Studie der Forschungsgruppe „Islam in der Schweiz" (GRIS).* Bern: EKM.

El Fadl, K. M. (2005). *The Great Theft: Wrestling Islam from the Extremists.* (336). San Francisco, CA: Harper.

Elwert, G. (1990). *Nationalismus und Ethnizität. Über die Bildung von Wir-Gruppen.* Berlin.

Enache, S. (Ed.). (2007). *Educaţia religioasa in şcolile publice.* Targu-Mureş: Pro-Europa.

Endres, J., Tunger-Zanetti, A., Behloul, S., & Baumann, M. (2013). *Jung, muslimisch, schweizerisch. Muslimische Jugendgruppen, islamische Lebensführung und Schweizer Gesellschaft. Ein Forschungsbericht* Luzern: Universität Luzern, Zentrum für Religionsforschung.

Epistle to Diognetus 5:4-5. (1959). Greek text in Kirsopp Lake, *The Apostolic Fathers, vol. 2.* London: Heinemann.

Eppenstein, T. (2004). *Einfalt der Vielfalt? Interkulturelle pädagogische Kompetenz in der Migrationsgesellschaft.* Frankfurt am Main: Cooperative Verlag.

Equality of Women and Men" (2009). From: http://www.cic.gc.ca/english/resources/publications/discover/index.asp. (Accessed January 16, 2014).

Eren, N. (1963). *Turkey Today-and Tomorrow.* New York/London: Praeger Pub.

Esed, M.(2002). *İslam'da yönetim biçimi.* İstanbul: Yöneliş.

Esser, H. (1980). *Aspekte der Wanderungssoziologie. Assimilation und Integration von Wanderern, ethnischen Gruppen und Minderheiten.* Darmstadt: Luchterhand.

Europäische Kommission. (February 2011). *Eurobarometer 74: Die öffentliche Meinung in der Europäischen Union.*

Europäische Kommission. (November 2008). *Eurobarometer 69: 1 Values of Europeans.*
Fabian, J. (1993). Präsenz und Repräsentation. Die Anderen und das anthropologische Schreiben. In: Berg, E., & Fuchs, M. (Eds.). *Kultur, soziale Praxis, Text. Die Krise der ethnographischen Repräsentation* (335–364) Frankfurt/Main: Suhrkamp.
Faist, T. (1997). *Migration und Transfer sozialen Kapitals.* In: Pries, L. *Transnationale Migration.* Baden-Baden: Nomos-Verlag.
Farkas, S. & Duffett, A. M. (2010). *High Schools, Civics, and Citizenship: What Social Studies Teachers Think and Do.* Foreword by Hess, F. M., Schmitt, G. J., Miller, C. & Schuette, J. M. Washington, DC: American Enterprise Institute for Public Policy Research. From: http://www.aei.org/files/2010/09/30/High-Schools-Civics-Citizenship-Full-Report.pdf. (Accessed February 19, 2014).
Fechler, B., Kößler, G. & Liebertz-Groß, T. (Eds.) (2000). *Erziehung nach Auschwitz" in der multikulturellen Gesellschaft.* Weinheim: Juventa Verlag.
Feithen, R. (1985). *Arbeitskräftewanderungen in der Europäischen Gemeinschaft.* Frankfurt am Main, New York: Campus-Verlag.
Ferreiro, J. (2010). "Financing of Minority Religious Societies". In: Michaela Moravčíková (ed.) *Financing of churches and religious societies.* (195-209). Bratislava: Institute for State-Churches Relations.
Ferreiro, J. (2011) "Islamic religious education in Spain". In: Aslan E. (ed.) *Islamic Textbooks and curricula in Europe.* (237-250). Peter Lang: Frankfurt am Main.
Filina, O. *Mapping Russia's Religious Landscape.* From: http://indrus.in/articles/2012/09/01/mapping_russias_religious_landscape_17333.html (Accessed November 10, 2013); sociological research of the «Fond obschestvennogo mneniya» [«Public Opinion Foundation»] (http://fom.ru/obshchestvo/10953 (Retrieved 10.11.2013); http://www.orkce.org/sites/default/files/file/mntrng2013.pdf. (Accessed February 04, 2014).
Findley, C. V. (1982). *The Acid Test of Ottomanism: The Acceptance of Non-Muslims in the Late Ottoman Bureaucracy.* Princeton University.
Forum Politische Bildung: From: http://www.politischebildung.com/?Sel=23 . (Accessed February 16, 2014).
Foster, P. (2007). "The Epistle to Diognetus. Expository Times, 118, (162-168).
Frisina, A. (2010). Young Muslims' everyday tactics and strategies: Resisting Islamophobia, negotiating Italianness, becoming citizens. *Journal of Intercultural Studies.* 31 (557–572).
Galston, W. A. (1991). *Liberal Purposes: Goods, Virtues, and Diversity in the Liberal State.* Cambridge: Cambridge Univ. Press.
Garlan, M. A. (2007). *Ethnopsihologii minoritare in spatiul dobrogean.* Iasi: Lumen.
Garlicki, A. (1999). *Encyklopedia historii Drugiej Rzeczypospolitej.* Warszawa: Wiedza Powszechna.
Gembicki M. (1938b). Wychowanie rodzinne. Rozwinięcie postulatu III ideologii Tatarów polskich. *Życie Tatarskie, 7,* (1-3).
Gembicki, M. (1938a). Szukajcie a znajdziecie. *Życie Tatarskie, 4,* (1-7).
Gencer, B. (2000). Türkiye'de laikliğin temel dinamikleri. *Toplum ve Bilim, 84,* (151-171).
GfK-Austria GmbH. (2009). *Integration in Österreich. Einstellungen, Orientierungen, und Erfahrungen.* From: http://www.bmi.gv.at/cms/BMI_Service/Integrationsstudie.pdf. (Accessed February 16, 2014).
Gocmen, İlkay. "56 TIR ,Kimse Yok Mu' diyen Suriyeliler için yola çıktı." Zaman, (19 Feb. 2014).

Goffman, E. (1974). *Frame analysis: An essay on the organization of experience*. New York: Harper and Row.

Gogia, N. & Slade, B. (2011). *About Canada: Immigration*. Halifax: Fernwood.

Gök, F. (2003). Vatandaşlık ve insan hakları eğitimi ders kitapları. In: Çotuksöken B., Erzan A. & Silier O. (Eds.) *Ders Kitaplarında İnsan Hakları: Tarama Sonuçları*. (158-171). İstanbul: Tarih Vakfı,

Gökalp, Z. (1970). *Türkçülügün esasları*. Ankara: MEB.

Gökalp, Z. (2004). *Türkleşmek, Islamlasmak, Muasırlasma*. İstanbul: Türk Klasikleri.

Gotzmann, A. (2001). *Pluralismus als Gefahr? Jüdische Perspektiven*. In: Malik, J., Rüpke, J. & Makrides, V. (Eds.) *Pluralismus in der europäischen Religionsgeschichte. Religionswissen schaftliche Antrittsvorlesungen*. (35-52). (Europ. Religionsgeschichte, 1). Marburg: Diagonal-Verlag.

Gotzmann, A. (2002). *Eigenheit und Einheit. Modernisierungsdiskurse des deutschen Judentums der Emanzipationszeit*. (Studies in European Judaism, Vol. 2). Leiden, Boston: Brill.

Government Digital Service. From: https://www.gov.uk/life-in-the-uk-test (Accessed February 12, 2014).

Government of the Netherlands. From: http://www.government.nl/issues/integration (Accessed February 12, 2014).

Grand Rapids: Eerdmans.

Gray, J. (2002). *Two Faces of Liberalism*. London: New Press.

Gray, M. M. & Cidade, M. A. (2010). *Catholicism on Campus: Stability and Change in Catholic Student Faith by College Type*. Washington, DC: Center for Applied Research in the Apostolate at Georgetown (CARA).

Gschiegl, S., & Ucakar, K. (2012). *Das politische System Österreichs und die EU (3 Ausg.)*. facultas.wuv.

Gülcan, M. G. (2002). Human rights education in the Turkish educational system. *Human Rights Education and Practice in Turkey in the Process of Candidacy to the EU*. Muzaffer Dartan and Münevver Cebeci, Marmara University European Community Institute (69-81).

Gülen, F. (2012a). *Kuran'da Yahudiler ver Hiristiyanlar* [Juden und Christen im Koran]. From: http://tr.fgulen.com/content/view/11224/3%20%28 (Accessed November 20, 2006; December 05, 2012).

Gülen, F. (2012b). Interview "Islam und Moderne stehen nicht im Widerspruch". *Frankfurtter Allgemeine Zeitung*. (Accessed December 06, 2012.).

Günay Ü., Güngör H. & Ecer A. V. (1997). *Laiklik, Din ve Türkiye*. Ankara: Adım Yayınları.

Gutmann, A. & Thompson, D. (1998). *Democracy and Disagreement*. Cambridge, MA: Harvard Univ. Press.

Gutmann, A. (Ed.) (1993). *Multikulturalismus und die Politik der Anerkennung*. Frankfurt am Main: Fischer Taschenbuch.

Habermas, J. (2002). *Religion and Rationality: Essays on Reason, God, and Modernity*. Cambridge, Mass.: MIT Press.

Habermas, J. (2005.) *On the Relation between the Secular Liberal State and Religion*. In: The Frankfurt School on Religion: Key Writings by the Major Thinkers. (339-348). New York: Routledge.

Habermas, J. (2008). *Notes on a Post-secular Society*. Sight and Sound 18/06/08. From: http://www.signandsight.com/features/1714.html (Accessed November 10, 2013).

Hacohen, D. (Ed.) (1998). *Ingathering of Exiles. Aliya to the Land of Israel. Myth and Reality.* Jerusalem: The Zalman Shazar Center for Jewish History.

Hakimov, R. (2010). *Djadidizm (Reformed Islam).* (207). Kazan: Idel-Press.

Haque, E. (2013). "The Bilingual Limits of Canadian Multiculturalism: The Politics of Language and Race." In: Caldwell, L., Leung, C. & Leroux, D. (Eds.) *Critical Inquires: A Reader in Studies of Canada.* Halifax: Fernwood

Hatemi, H. (1987). *Batılılaşma.* İstanbul: Bir Yayıncılık.

Haydaroğlu, İ. P. (1993). *Osmanlı İmparotorluğunda Yabancı Okullar.* Ankara: Ocak Yayınları.

Heckmann, F. (1992). *Ethnische Minderheiten, Volk und Nation.* Stuttgart: F. Enke.

Herbert, U. (2001). *Geschichte der Ausländerpolitik in Deutschland.* Munich: C.H. Beck Verlag.

Hess, R. (2000). *Juedische Existenz in Deutschland heute: Probleme des Wandels der juedischen Gemeinden in der Bundes republik Deutschland infolge der Zuwanderung russischer Juden nach 1989.* Berlin.

Hilberath, B. J., & Scharer, M. (2012). Kommunikative Theologie: Grundlagen-Erfahrungen-Klärungen. Ostfildern: Matthias-Grünewald.

Holz, K. (2000). *Staatsbürgerschaft: Soziale Differnzierung und politische Inklusion.* Wiesbaden: Westdeutscher Verlag.

Horga, I. (2006). *Religious Education- European approaches and tendencies.* In: Lemeni, A. & Dedu, B. *Învăţământul religios şi teologic în România [The Religious and Theological Education in Romania].* Sibiu: TechnoMedia.

Hoskins, B. L. & Mascherinin, M. (2008). *Measuring Active Citizenship through the Development of a Composite Indicator.* In: Scences+Business Media. Springer: Published online: 12 July 2008.

Howeidi, F. (1985). *Muwatinun, La Dhimmiyun.* Cairo: Dar al-Shuruq.

Humanity In Action Inc. From: http://www.humanityinaction.org/knowledgebase/143-becoming-a-dane-can-danish-ness-be-tested (Accessed February 12, 2014).

Hutchinson, J. & Smith, A.D. (Eds.) (1996). *Ethnicity.* Oxford: University Press.

Ibn Hazm, Abu Muhammad b. Ahmad ben Said Al-Andulusi. [n.d.]. *Al-Muhalla bi'l Asar.* Beirut.

Ibn Kathir, Ismail. (1976). *Al-Sira Al-Nabawiyya.* Edited by Mustafa Abd al-Wahid. Beirut: Dar al-Ma'rifa.

Ibran, N. (2007). *Musulmanii din Romania [Muslims in Romania].* Constanta: Golden Publishing House.

IGGiÖ. *Leitbild.* (2013). From: http://www.derislam.at/?c=content&cssid=IG-Gi%D6&navid=10&par=0 (Accessed January 18, 2013).

İlhan, A. (2008). *Hangi laiklik.* İstanbul: Türkiye İş Bankası Kültür Yayınları.

IMAS International GmbH. (2010). *DER ISLAM IN DEN AUGEN DER BEVÖLKERUNG.* IMAS-Report. From: http://www.imas.at/images/imas-report/2010/06-2010.pdf (Accessed February 16, 2014).

Interview (convorbire), with Mr Yusuf Murat – Great Mufti of Muslims in Romania, at the centre of the Muftyat in Constanta (2008, 2009, 2010, 2013).

Interview (convorbire), with Ms Ene Ulgean – School Inspector, Turk – Tatar minorities, at the Muslim Collegium of Medgidia. (13.02.2008).

Iordachescu, N. (2006). *Masuri legislative referitoare la educatia religioasa si la predarea Religiei dupa 1989 [Legislative measures regarding the Theological education and teaching of Religion after 1989*]. In: Lemeni, A. and Dedu, B. *Învăţământul religios şi teologic în România* [*The Religious and Theological Education in Romania*]. Sibiu: TechnoMedia.

İşler, N. (n.d.). *Din Kültürü ve Ahlak Bilgisi Lise 1.* İstanbul: Meram Yayıncılık.

Isov, M. (2005). *Nai-razlichniat sased: Obrazat na osmantsite (turtsite) i Osmanskata imperia (Turtsia) v uchebnitsite po istoria vav vtorata polovina na 20ti vek* [*The Most Different Neighbor: the Image of Ottomans (Turks) and the Ottoman Empire (Turkey) in Bulgarian History Textbooks in the Second Half of the 20th Century*]. Sofia: IMIR.

Ivanov, I. (2000). *Grazhdansko obrazovanie i interkulturno obrazovanie* [*Citizenship education and intercultural education*]. *Paper presented at the Intercultural Communication and Civic Society Conference.* Sofia, Bulgaria.

Ivanov, I. (2000). *Vaprosi na grazhdanskoto obrazovanie* [*Questions of Citizenship education*]. Shumen: Aksisos.

Jackson, R. (1997). *Religious education: an interpretive approach.* London: Hodder and Stoughton.

Jackson, R. (2004). Intercultural education and recent European pedagogies of religious education. *Intercultural Education.* vol. 15, no. 1, (3-14).

Jackson, R., Miedema, S., Weisse, W. & Willaime, J.P. (Eds.). *Religion and Education in Europe. Developments, Contexts and Debates.* Münster/New York/München/Berlin: Waxmann.

Jägerstätter, F. (2007). Aufzeichnungen 1941 - 1943: Der gesamte Briefwechsel mit Franziska. (E. Putz, Eds.) Graz: Styria Premium.

Joppke, C. (1999). *Immigration and the Nation-State.* Oxford: University Press.

Joppke, C. (2007). 'Beyond national models: Civic integration policies for immigrants in Western Europe', *West European Politics.* vol.30, no.1, (1-22).

Juergensmeyer, M. (2001). *Terror in the Mind of God: The Global Rise of Religious Violence.* Los Angeles: University of California Press.

Kamali, Z. (1910). *Falsafah Islamiah.* (330). Ufa: Sharik Matbagasi.

Kamali, Z. (2010). *Philosophy of Islam* (L. Almazova, Trans. From Old Tatar). Kazan: Tatarstan Book Printing House.

Kämpf, Ph. (2008). *Die „Jugo-Schweiz": Klischees, Provokationen, Visionen.* Zürich: Rüegger.

Kara, İ. (2012). *Cumhuriyet Türkiye'sinde Bir Mesele Olarak İslam.* İstanbul: Dergah.

Karal, E. Z. (1998). *Atatürk ve Devrim.* Ankara: Metu Press.

Kaymakcan, R. (1999). Christianity in Turkish religious education. *Islam and Christian-Muslim Relations,* vol 10, no 3, (279-293).

Kazıcı, Z. (1991). *İslam Müesseseleri Tarihi.* İstanbul: Kayıhan.

Канал 5 [Kanal 5]. (n.d.). From: http://www.kanal5.com.mk/vesti_detail.asp?ID=6457 (Retrieved 9 March 2014).

Kelbecheva, E. (2012) '*The short history of Bulgaria for export'.* In: Nielsen J. (ed.) *Religion, Ethnicity and Contested Nationhood in the Former Ottoman Space.* (233-247). Leiden: Brill.

Khalid, A. (2007). *Islam After Communism: Religion and Politics in Central Asia.* (12). Berkley, CA: University of California Press.

Khaybullin, I. A. (2010). *Grammar of the Arabic Language: Brief Version.* Ufa: Salam.

Khayrutdinov, A. (2007). *Unknown Islam: The Quran We Do Not Know.* Kazan: Institute of History Printing House.

Khayrutdinov, A. (2009). *Quran: Interpretation Continued*. (92). Kazan: Institute of History Printing House.

Kiesel, D. (1996). *Das Dilemma der Differenz. Zur Kritik des Kulturalismus in der interkulturellen Pädagogik*. Frankfurt am Main: Cooperative Verlag.

Kiesel, D., Messerschmidt, A. & Scherr, A. (Eds.) (1998). *Die Erfindung der Fremdheit. Zur Kontroverse um Gleichheit und Differenz im Sozialstaat*. Frankfurt am Main: Brandes und Apsel.

Kili, S. (1969). *Kemalism*. İstanbul: Robert College.

Kim-Cragg, H. & E. Choi. (2014). *The Encounters: Retelling the Bible from Migration and Intercultural Perspectives*. Trans. L. Kim. Daejeon: Daejanggan (BlackSmith) Publisher.

King, T. (2012). *The Inconvenient Indian: A Curious Account of Native People in North America*. Toronto: Doubleday Canada.

Kinsbury, J. A. (1961). Turkey's new constitution. *The Muslim World*. (152-155).

Kızıler, H. & Koçak, N. (2005). *Din Kültürü ve Ahlak Bilgisi Lise 2*. Ankara: İpekyolu Yayıncılık.

Kızıler, H. & Koçak, N. (2005). *Din Kültürü ve Ahlak Bilgisi Lise 3*. Ankara: İpekyolu Yayıncılık.

Knack, S., & Keefer, P. (1997). *Does Social Capital Have an Economic Payoff? A Cross-Country Investigation*. The Quarterly Journal of Economics, 112(4), 1251-1288. doi: 10.1162/003355300555475

Knauth, T. (2007). Religious Education in Germany – a contribution to dialogue or conflict? Historical and contextual analysis of the developments since the 1960s. In: Jackson, R., Miedema, S., Weisse W. & Willaime, J.P. (Eds.), *Religion and Education in Europe. Developments, Contexts and Debates* (243-265). Münster/New York/München/Berlin: Waxmann.

Knauth, T., Jozsa, D-P., Bertram-Troost, G. & Ipgrave, J. (Eds.) (2008). *Encountering Religious Pluralism in School and Society. A Qualitative Study of Teenage Perspectives in Europe*. Münster/New York/München/Berlin: Waxmann.

Knysh, A. (2011). *Islam in Historical Perspective*. London: Pearson.

Koçal, A. V. (2012). Bir Hegemonya Aracı Olarak Sekülerleş (tir) me: Tarihsel Bir Perspektiften Türkiye'de Laikliğin Politik Ekonomisi. *Akademik İncelemeler, 7*(2), (107-140).

Köhler, A. A. (2013). *Die strukturelle Assimilation des Islam in Deutschland*. From: http://islam.de/2579.php (Accessed January 18, 2013).

Köker, L. (2012). *Modernleşme, Kemalizm ve demokrasi*. İstanbul: İletişim.

Konopacki, A. (2010). *Życie religijne Tatarów na ziemiach Wielkiego Księstwa Litewskiego w XVI-XIX w*. Warszawa: Wyd. UW.

Koopmans, R. & Slatham, P. (Eds.) (2000). *Challenging Immigration and Ethnic Relations*. Oxford: University Press.

Koştaş, M. (1999). Türkiye'de laikliğin gelişimi (1920'den günümüze kadar). Ankara: *Ankara Üniversitesi İlahiyat Fakültesi Dergisi*.

Kostovska, T.G. et.al. (2010). *Arsimi qytetar për klasën VIII*. Shkup: Ministria e Arsimit dhe Shkencës e Republikës së Maqedonisë.

Kryczyński, O.N.M. (1932). Ruch nacjonalistyczny a Tatarzy litewscy. *Rocznik Tatarski, 1*, (5-20).

Kryczyński, S. (1938). Tatarzy polscy, *Rocznik Ziem Wschodnich*, (106-121).

Kryczyński, S. (2000 [1938]). *Tatarzy litewscy. Próba monografii historyczno-etnograficznej*. Gdańsk: Rocznik Tatarów Polskich.

Künne, W. (1979). *Die Außenwanderung jugoslawischer Arbeitskräfte*. Königstein, Ts. : Hanstein.

Kurzman C. (Ed.). (1998). *Liberal Islam: A Sourcebook*. (340). Oxford, England: Oxford University Press.

Kurzman, C. (2003). *Liberal Islam: Prospects and Challenges*. In: Rubin, B. (Ed.) *Revolutionaries and Reformers: Contemporary Islamist Movements in the Middle East*. (191–203). Albany, NY: State University of New York Press.

Kwok, P. (2005). *Postcolonial Imagination and Feminist Theology*. Louisville: Westminster/ John Knox.

Kymlicka, W. & Norman, W. (Eds.) (2000). *Citizenship in Diverse Societies*. Oxford: Universuty Press.

Kymlicka, W. (2000). *Politics in the Vernacular. Nationalism, Multiculturalism and Citizenship*. Oxford: University Press.

Lajm Maqedoni Vite. (n.d.) From: http://lajmpress.com/lajme/maqedoni/20338.html (Retrieved 9 March 2014).

Langenheder, W. (1968). *Ansatz zu einer allgemeinen Verhaltenstheorie in den Sozialwissenschaften. Dargestellt und überprüft an Ergebnissen empirischer Untersuchungen über Ursachen von Wanderungen*. Cologne, Opladen: Westdeutscher Verlag.

Lathion, St., & Tunger-Zanetti, A. (2013). Switzerland. In *Yearbook of Muslims in Europe, vol. 5* (pp. 633–647). Leiden: Brill.

Lee, E. (1972). *Eine Theorie der Wanderung*. In: Szell, G. *Regionale Mobilität*. Munich: Nymphenburger Verlagshaus.

Legrand, V. (14. 09 2011). *Islam in Europa und Islamophobie. Treffen des Rates der Europäischen Bischofskonferenzen* (CCEE). From: http://www.comece.org/europeinfos/de/archiv/ausgabe141/article/4171.html (Accessed January 02, 2013).

Lehrpläne der IGGiÖ in Österreich. From: http://www.schulamt-islam.at/index.php?option=com_content &view=article&id=22&Itemid=34 (Accessed April 14, 2014).

Lehrpläne von Bayern. From: http://www.izir.de/images/docs/ Islam unterricht_HS.pdf (Accessed October 14, 2013).

Leirvik, O. (2004) Religious education, communial identity and national politics in the Muslim world. *British Journal of Religious Education*, vol 26, no, 3, (223-236).

Lewis, B. (1968). *The Emergence of Modern Turkey*. 2nd. London: Oxford University Press, 1968.

Lewis, B. (1988). *The Political Language of Islam*. Chicago: University of Chicago Press.

Lewis, B. (1993). *Islam and the West*. NY: Oxford University Press.

Lister, R. (2007). *Gendering Citizenship in Western Europe. New challenges for citizenship research in a cross-national context*. Bristol: The Policy Press.

Luckman, T. (2003). "Transformations of Religion and Morality in Modern Europe". In: *Social Compass*, vol. 50 (3).

M.E.B. Komisyon. (2000). *İlköğretim Din Kültürü ve Ahlak Bilgisi Dersi Öğretim Programı*. İstanbul: M.E.B.

M.E.B. Komisyon. (2005a). *İlköğretim Din Kültürü ve Ahlak Bilgisi 6*, İstanbul: M.E.B.

M.E.B. Komisyon. (2005b). *İlköğretim Din Kültürü ve Ahlak Bilgisi 7*, İstanbul: M.E.B.

M.E.B. Komisyon. (2005c). *İlköğretim Din Kültürü ve Ahlak Bilgisi 8*, İstanbul: M.E.B.

M.E.B. Komisyon. (2005d). *Orta Öğretim Din Kültürü ve Ahlak Bilgisi Dersi (9. 10. 11 ve 12. sınıflar) Öğretim Programı*, İstanbul: M.E.B.

Macedo, S. (1990). *Liberal Virtues: Citizenship, Virtue, and Community in Liberal Constitutionalism*. Oxford: Oxford Univ. Press.

Mackert, J. (1999). *Kampf um Zugehörigkeit: Nationale Staatsbürgerschaft als Modus sozialer Schliessung*. Opladen: Westdeutscher Verlag.

Malakhov, I. (2008). *Sokrovennoe*. Ufa: (Printing house not indicated).

Mardin, Ş. (1982). Turkey: Islam and modernization. In: Caldarola C. (ed.) *Religions and Societies: Asia and Middle East*. Berlin/New York: Mouton.

Marik-Lebeck, S. (2010). *Die muslimische Bevölkerung Österreichs: Bestand und Veränderung 2001-2009*. In: Janda, A. & Vogl, M. (Eds.). Islam in Österreich. (7). Wien: Österreichscher Integrationsfonds.

Matzdorf, P., & Cohn, R. C. (1992). Das Konzept der Themenzentrierten Interaktion. In: L. C., & S. R. (Eds.), TZI. Pädagogisch-therapeutische Gruppenarbeit nach Ruth C. Cohn (39-92). Stuttgart: Klett-Cotta.

Mauersberg, S. (1988). *Komu służyła szkoła w Drugiej Rzeczpospolitej? Społeczne uwarunkowania dostępu do oświaty*. Warszawa: Ossolineum.

Mautner, M., Sagi, A. & Shamir, R. (Eds.) (1998). *Multiculturalism in a Democratic and Jewish State*. Tel Aviv: Ramot.

Mazilu, R. (April 9, 2006). "cetatenia europeana". In: rev. *Cadran politic – revista de analiza si informare politica*. From: www.cadranpolitic.ro (Accessed October 17, 2013).

McGuire, M. B. (2008). *Lived religion: Faith and practice in everyday life*. New York: Oxford University Press.

McLaughlin, T. H. (1992). "Citizenship, Diversity, and Education: A Philosophical Perspective." *Journal of Moral Education* 21, no. 3.

McLaughlin, T. H. (1992). "The Ethics of Separate Schools." In: Leicester, M. & Taylor, M. J. (Eds.). *Ethics, Ethnicity, and Education*. London: Kogan Page.

McLaughlin, T. H. (2003). "The Burdens and Dilemmas of Common Schooling." In: McDonough, K. & Feinberg, W. (Eds.). *Citizenship and Education in Liberal-Democratic Societies*. Oxford: Oxford Univ. Press.

McLaughlin, T. H. (2008). *Liberalism, Education, and Schooling: Essays by T. H. McLaughlin*. St. Andrews Studies in Philosophy and Public Affairs, edited by D. Carr, M. Halstead, and R. Pring. Charlottesville, VA: Imprint Academic.

McLaughlin, T.H. (1992). Citizenship, Diversity and Education : A Philosophical Perspective. *Journal of Moral Education*, 21, (235-250).

Meaning, Learning, and Vocation. Nashville: Abingdon.

Medreseja Isa Beu. (n.d.) From: http://www.medreseja-isabeu.com/reth-medreses/ (Retrieved 9 March 2014).

Meulemann, H. (1996). *Werte und Wertewandel. Zur Identität einer geteilten und wieder vereinten Nation*. Weinheim u.a.: Juventa-Verlag.

Miedema, S. & ter Avest, I. (2011). In the Flow to Maximal Interreligious Citizenship Education. *Religious Education*. 106, (410-424).

Miedema, S. (2000). The Need for Multi-Religious Schools. *Religious Education*. 95, (285-298).

Miedema, S. (2003). *De onmogelijke mogelijkheid van levensbeschouwelijke opvoeding* [The impossible possibility of worldview education]. Amsterdam: VU University Press.

Miedema, S. (2006). Educating for Religious Citizenship. Religious Education as Identity Formation. In: De Souza, M., Engebretson, K., Durka ,G., Jackson, R. & McGrady, A.

(Eds.) *International Handbook of the Religious, Spiritual and Moral Dimensions of Education. Vol. I and II.* (965-974). Dordrecht: Springer.

Miedema, S. (2007). Contexts, Debates and Perspectives of Religion in Education in Europe. A Comparative Analysis. In: Jackson, R., S. Miedema, W. Weisse & J.P. Willaime (Eds.), *Religion and Education in Europe. Developments, Contexts and Debates.* (267-283). Münster/New York/München/Berlin: Waxmann.

Miedema, S. (2012). *Levensbeschouwelijke vorming in een (post-)seculiere tijd* [Worldview education in a (post-)secular age]. Amsterdam: VU University Press.

Miedema, S. (2013). "Coming Out Religiously! Religion and Worldview as an Integral Part of the Social and Public Domain". Religious Education (108:3).

Miedema, S., & Bertram-Troost, G.D. (2008). Democratic Citizenship and Religious Education: Challenges and Perspectives for Schools in the Netherlands. *British Journal of Religious Education. 30,* (123-132).

Miles, R. (1992). Einwanderung nach Grossbritannien – eine historische Betrachtung. In: Institut für Migrations- und Rassismusforschung (Ed.) *Rassismus und Migration in Europa.* (268–270). Hamburg: Argument.

Ministerio del Interior [Ministry of the Interior]. From: http://www.mir.es/. (Accessed February 2, 2014).

Ministry of Education and Science. From: http://www.mon.bg/?go=page&pageId=1&subpageId=28 (Accessed February 12, 2014).

Ministry of Education and Science. From: http://www.mon.bg/?go=page&pageId=13&subpageId=177 (Accessed February 12, 2014).

Ministry of Education and Sinece. From: http://www.mon.bg/?go=page&pageId=1&subpageId=25 (Accessed February 11, 2014).

Mizgalski J. (1998). Oświata wśród Tatarów w Polsce międzywojennej". *Prace Naukowe Wyższej Szkoły Pedagogicznej w Częstochowie. Zeszyty Historyczne, 5,* (101-109).

Moravcikova, M. & Lojda, M. (Eds.). (2005). *Islam in Europe.* Bratislava.

Müller, M. (2013). *Migration und Religion: Junge hinduistische und muslimische Männer in der Schweiz.* Wiesbaden: Springer VS.

Müller-Schneider, T. (2000). *Zuwanderung in westlichen Gesellschaften.* Opladen: Leske & Budrich.

Muhammad 'Ali Ibn Muhammad Ibn 'Allan. (2004). *Delil al-Falihin li Turuq Riyad al-Salihin.* Beirut: Dar al-Ma'rifa.

Musina R. N. (2009). Islam and the Problem of Tatar Identity in the Post-Soviet Era. (86-100). *The Denominational Factor in the Tatars' Development.* Kazan: Institute of History Publishing House.

Nalborczyk, A. S. and Borecki, P. (2011). "Relations between Islam and the state in Poland: the legal position of Polish Muslims", *Islam and Christian-Muslim Relations, 22:3,* (343-359).

Nasr, S. H. (1989). *Knowledge and the Sacred.* Albany New York: State University of New York Press

Newman, K. J. (1986). *Pakistan unter Ayub Khan und Zia-ul-Haq.* Köln: Weltforum Verlag.

Nicht veröffentlichte Interviews der Forschungsgruppe "Imame in Österreich". From: http://imameoesterreich.univie.ac.at/ (Accessed May 04, 2014b).

Nicht veröffentlichte Interviews mit den muslimischen Privatschulen in Wien. From: http://citizenshipeducation. univie.ac.at/ (Accessed April 21, 2014).

Nielsen, J. S. et al (Eds.) (2013). *Yearbook of Muslims in Europe.* vol. 5, Leiden: Brill.

No Child Left Behind (NCLB) Act of 2001, Pub. L. No. 107-110, § 115, Stat. 1425 (2002). From: http://www2.ed.gov/policy/elsec/leg/esea02/index.html. (Accessed February 19, 2014).

Norton, J. D. (1988). *The Turks and Islam.* In: Sutherland S. et al (Eds.) *The World's Religions.* (390-408). Boston: G. K.: Hall and Co.

Nozick, R. (1981). *Philosophical Explanations.* Cambridge, MA: Harvard Univ. Press.

Nursi, Bediüzzaman Said. (1976). *Mektubat.* Istanbul: Sozler Yayinevi.

Nyrop, R. F. (1973). *Area Handbook for the Republic of Turkey.* 2nd Washington D. C.

Oakeshott, M. (1962). *Rationalism in Politics.* London: Methuen.

Obama, B. (2004). *Dreams from My Father: A Story of Race and Inheritance.* New York: Three River Press Said, E. W. (1978). *Orientalism.* New York: Vintage Books.

Observatorio del Pluralismo religioso en España". From: http://www.observatorioreligion. es/directorio-lugares-de-culto/ (Accessed February 3 2014).

Öğün, S. S. (1997). *Politik kültür yazıları: Süreçler, kişiler.* Bursa: Asa.

Organic Act 1/2002. March 22nd, on the right of Association.

Organic Act 2/2006 of Education of May 3th.

Organic Act 8/2013 for the Improvement of the Educational System, of December 9th.

Organization for Economic Co-operation and Development (OECD). From: http://www. oecd.org/pisa/pisaproducts/46619703.pdf (Accessed February 12, 2014).

Ortaylı, İ. (2009). *Osmanlı Toplumunda Aile.* İstanbul: Pan.

Osman, N. S. (2007). *Tatars from Dobrogea.* In: *Karadeniz [The Black Sea],* the tatar comunity newspaper, no. 177/December.

Overall curriculum Part 1. From: Official Web site of the Office of Education of the Islamic Religious Community in Austria: http://schulamt-islam.at/images/stories/lehrplaene/gesamt_1-99.pdf (Accessed January 30, 2014).

Overall curriculum Part 2. From: Official Web site of the Office of Education of the Islamic Religious Community in Austria: http://schulamt-islam.at/images/stories/lehrplaene/gesamt_100-195.pdf (Accessed January 30, 2014).

Özdalga, E. (1992). On Islamic revivalism and radicalism in Turkey. In: Reimer J. (Ed.) *The Influence on the Frankfurt School on Contemporary Theology.* (331-342). Lewiston: The Edwin Mellen Press.

Paideia Foundation. From: http://www.paideiafoundation.org/ssp.php?page=18 (Accessed February 10, 2014)

Pajevic, A. (2006). *Daham statt Islam.* Der Tagesspiegel. From: http://www.tagesspiegel.de/politik/international/oesterreich-daham-statt-islam/757274.html. (Accessed February 15, 2014).

Pelinka, A. (1979). *Zur Strategie der politischen Bildung in Österreich.* ÖZP 1979/1 (67-90).

People's Citizenship Guide: a response to conservative Canada (2011). Winnipeg: Arbeiter Ring Publishing.

Peres, Y. (1985). *Ethnic Relations in Israel.* Tel Aviv: Sifriyat Hapoalim.

Pew Research Religion and Public Life Project. *"The Future of the Global Muslim Population: Regional Europe."* From: http://www.pewforum.org/2011/01/27/future-of-the-global-muslim-population-regional-europe/. (Accessed January 27, 2011). Publishing.

Putz, E. (2007). Franz Jägerstätter - Martyr: A Shinig Example in Cark Times. (S. L. Episcopal Chair of the Diocese of Linz, Eds., & C. L. Danner, Übers.) Franz Steinmassl.

Ramadan, T. (2001). *Muslime in Europa.* Marburg, Germany: MSV.

Ramadani, N. (2010). *Etika e religjioneve për klasën e pestë*. Shkup: Ministria e Arsimit dhe Shkencës e Republikës së Maqedonisë.

Rawls, J. (1993). *Political Liberalism*. New York: Columbia Univ. Press.

Rawls, J. (1993). *Political Liberalism*. New York: Columbia University Press.

Red Squirrel Publishing. From: http://lifeintheuk.net/index.php/news/polish_score_top_marks_in_britishness_test/, (Accessed February 12, 2014).

Reed, H. A. (1954). Revival of Islam in secular Turkey. *The Middle East Journal*. (267-282). vol. 8, pt 3.

Registro de Entidades Religiosas del Minisaterio de Justicia". From: http://maper.mjusticia. gob.es/Maper/RER.action#bloqueBuscadorProcesos (Accessed February 3, 2014).

Reynolds, T. (2009). "A Rooted Openness: Hospitality as Christian 'Conversion to the Other'.

Samatov, G. (2006). *Sharia: Wagaz, Hokem, Fatwa, Jawap-Sawap, Kineshler*. Kazan: Idel-Press.

Sardavi M. (2004). Steel blade against new method. Kazan: Iman.

Saritoprak, Z. "Said Nursi on Muslim–Christian Relations Leading to World Peace."*Islam and Christian–Muslim Relations*, Vol. 19, No. 1 (25–37). (January 2008).

Scharer, M., & Hilberath, B. J. (2003). Kommunikative Theologie. Eine Grundlegung (2 Ausg., Bd. 1). Mainz: Matthias-Grünewald-Verlag.

Scharer, M., & Hilberath, B. J. (2008). The Practice of Communicative Theology. Introduction to a New Theological Culture. New York: The Crossroad Publishing Company.

Schiffauer, W. (2004). Vom Exil- zum Diaspora-Islam. Muslimische Identitäten in Europa. *Soziale Welt 55(4)*, (347–368).

Schoeps, J., Jasper, W. & Vogt, B. (1996). *Russische Juden in Deutschland. Integration und Selbstbehauptung in einem fremden Land*. Weinheim: Beltz, Athenäum.

Schoeps, J., Jasper, W. & Vogt, B. (1999). *Ein neues Judentum in Deutschland? Fremd und Eigenbilder der russischjüdischen Einwanderer*. Potsdam: Verlag für Berlin-Brandenburg.

Schweizerischer Bundesrat (2013). *Bericht des Bundesrates über die Situation der Muslime in der Schweiz*. From: http://www.ejpd.admin.ch/content/dam/data/pressemitteilung/2013/2013-05-08/ber-d.pdf. (Accessed January 20, 2014).

Sedgwick, M. (2013). 'Something Varied in the State of Denmark: Neo-nationalism, Anti-Islamic Activism, and Street-level Thuggery'. *Politics, Religion and Ideology*. vol. 14, (208-233).

Seljek, D. (2005). "Education, Multiculturalism, and Religion". In: Bramadat P. & Seljak, D. (Eds.) *Religion and Ethnicity in Canada*. Toronto: Pearson/Longman.

Şerif, M. (1996). *Yeni Osmanlı Düşüncesinin Doğuş*. İstanbul: İletişim.

Seymour, J., Crain, M. A., & Crockett, J. V. (1993). *Educating Christians: The Intersection of*

Shahrour M. (2006). The Divine Text and Pluralism in Muslim Societies. (143-153). In: Kemrava, M. (Ed.). *The New Voices of Islam: Reforming Politics and Modernity: A Reader*. London, UK: I.B. Tauris.

Shaw S. J. & Kural E. (1977). *History of the Ottoman Empire and Modern Turkey*. vol. II, Cambridge: Cambridge University Press.

Shepard, W. E. (1987). Islam and Ideology: Towards a Typology. *International Journal of Middle East Studies*, 19(3), (307–335).

Shmonin, D. *Religion and Education in Contemporary Russia: The Dynamics of Recent Years*, Analysis ISPI, No. 233. (January 2014). From: http://www.ispionline.it/it/pub-blicazione/religion-and-education-contemporary-russia-dynamics-recent-years-9763 (Accessed February 12, 2014).

Shotarovska, B. et.al. (2010). *Njohja me religjionet për klasën V.* Shkup: Ministria e Arsimit dhe Shkencës e Republikës së Maqedonisë.

Sobczak, J. (1984). *Położenie prawne ludności tatarskiej w Wielkim Księstwie Litewskim.* Warszawa-Poznań: PWN.

Sobczak, J. (2004). Położenie prawne polskich wyznawców islamu. In: Baecker, R. & Kitab, Sh. (Eds.). *Islam a świat* (172-209). Toruń: Mado.

Spanish Constitution 1978.

Spülbeck, S. (1997). *Ordnung und Angst. Russische Juden aus der. Sicht eines ostdeutschen Dorfes nach der Wende.* Frankfurt am Main, New York: Campus.

Stromberg, C. (2001). *Akkulturation russischer Juden in Deutschland und Israel: Wertekongruenz und Wohlbefinden.* Lengerich: Pabst.

Study Guide—Discover Canada: The Rights and Responsibilities of Citizenship and The

Subaşı, N. (2007). Türkiye'de laiklik ve din eğitimi: Reel politik güzergâhlar. *Değerler Eğitimi Merkezi Dergisi, 2,* (6-10).

Sue, Derald & Sue, David (1990). *Counseling the Culturally Different: Theory and Practice.* New York: John Wiley and Sons.

Szyliowich, J. S. (1973). *Education and Modernization in the Middle East.* Ithaca and London: Cornell University Press.

Talos, E., & Neugebauer, W. (Eds.). (2012). *Austrofaschismus. Politi - Ökonomie - Kultur 1933 - 1938.* Wien: Lit Verlag.

Tanase, L. D. (2008). *Pluralisation religieuse et société en Roumanie.* Bern: Peter Lang.

Tanase, L. D. (2009). "Study regarding the Muslim community and the Islamic education in Romania". In: Aslan, E. (Ed.) *Islamic education in Europe.* (367-402). Bölau: Wien.

Tatarzy w Polsce. (1936). *Dziennik Urzędowy Kuratorium Okręgu Szkolnego Wileńskiego, 2* (19), Wilno.

Taylor, Ch. (2007). *A Secular Age.* Cambridge, MA/London, England: The Belknap Press of Harvard University Press.

M.E.B. (1990) Tebliğler Dergisi: 553.

M.E.B. (2000) Tebliğler Dergisi: 2517.

Temkov, K. (2010). *Etika për klasën VI.* Shkup Ministria e Arsimit dhe Shkencës e Republikës së Maqedonisë.

Ter Avest, I. (2003). *Kinderen en God, verteld in verhalen* [Children and God, told in Stories]. Zoetermeer: Boekencentrum.

Ter Avest, I. (2009). Dutch children and their 'God': the development of the 'God' concept among indigenous and immigrant children in the Netherlands. *British Journal of Religious Education. 31,* (251-262).

The Copenhagen Post. From: http://cphpost.dk/news/new-citizenship-tests-still-not-ready.4662.html (Accessed February 12, 2014).

The Ecumenist: A Journal of Theology, Culture, and Society (46:2) (Spring).

The Federal Law of 13 July 1949 concerning religious instruction in schools. (RelUG; BGBl.190/1949).

the Social and Public Domain". *Religious Education* (108:3).

Tiedemann, B. (2007). *Menschenwürde als Rechtsbegriff: eine philosophische Klärung.* Berlin: BWV.

Timis, V. (2006). "Religious Education within the Curricular area of Man and Society". In: Lemeni, A. & Dedu, B. *The Religious and Theological Education in Romania*. Sibiu: TechnoMedia.

Tochtermann, J.J. (1935) Ilość, rozmieszczenie i struktura zawodowa Tatarów w Polsce , *Wiadomości Geograficzne, 8-10*, (55-60).

Todorov, T. (1996). *Abenteuer des Zusammenlebens. Versuch einer allgemeinen Anthropologie*. Berlin: Wagenbach.

Tomasi, J. (2000). *Liberalism beyond Justice: Citizens, Society, and the Boundaries of Political Theory*. Princeton, NJ: Princeton Univ. Press.

Topcuoglu, A.A. (2012). "Modern hukuk ve Islam'da vatandaslik kavraminin hukuki temeli". In: *Gazi Üniversitesi Hukuk Fakültesi Dergisi* C. XVI, Y. 2012, No. 3.

Topic Overview 1 class. (n.d.). From: Official Web site of the Office of Education of the Islamic Religious Community in Austria: http://schulamt-islam.at/images/stories/lehrplaene/klasse1.pdf (Accessed January 30, 2014).

Treibel, A. (1999). *Migration in modernen Gesellschaften*. Weinheim: Juventa.

Tyszkiewicz, J. (1987). Dorobek historyczny Leona i Stanisława Kryczyńskich. In: Taternicki, J. (Ed.). *Środowiska historyczne II Rzeczpospolitej* (371-388). Warszawa: COM SNP.

Tyszkiewicz, J. (1989). *Tatarzy na Litwie i w Polsce, Studia z dziejów XIII-XVIII w.* Warszawa: PWN.

Tyszkiewicz, J. (2002). *Z historii Tatarów polskich 1794-1944*. Pułtusk: WSH.

Tyszkiewicz, J. (2008). *Tatarzy w Polsce i Europie. Fragmenty dziejów*. Pułtusk: AH.

U.S. Const. Amend I-X. U.S. Constitution, Amendments I-X.

Ugrinoski, K. et.al. (2009). *Arsimi qytetar për klasën VII në arsimin fillor tetëvjeçar*. Shkup Ministria e Arsimit dhe Shkencës e Republikës së Maqedonisë.

Uludağ, S. (1995). Türk aydını ve kimlik sorunu. In S. Şen (eds.), Türkiye'de din, devlet, aydın (315 – 320). İstanbul: Bağlam.

United States Conference of Catholic Bishops (USCCB). (2008). *Doctrinal Elements of a Curriculum Framework for the Development of Catechetical Materials for Young People of High School Age*. Washington, DC: United States Conference of Catholic Bishops. From: http://www.usccb.org/beliefs-and-teachings/how-we-teach/catechesis/upload/high-school-curriculum-framework.pdf. (Accessed February 19, 2014).

United States Conference of Catholic Bishops (USCCB). (2011). *Forming Consciences for Faithful Citizenship: A Call to Political Responsibility from the Catholic Bishops of the United States with Introductory Note*. Washington, DC: United States Conference of Catholic Bishops. From: http://www.usccb.org/issues-and-action/faithful-citizenship/upload/forming-consciences-for-faithful-citizenship.pdf (Accessed February 19, 2014).

United States Conference of Catholic Bishops (USCCB). (2014). Web page on Catholic social teaching. From: http://www.usccb.org/beliefs-and-teachings/what-we-believe/catholic-social-teaching/seven-themes-of-catholic-social-teaching.cfm. (Accessed October 20, 2013).

United States Department of Education. (2012). *Advancing Civic Learning and Engagement in Democracy: A Road Map and Call to Action*. Washington, DC: U.S. Department of Education. From: http://www.ed.gov/sites/default/files/road-map-call-to-action.pdf. (Accessed February 19, 2014).

Utiz-Imyani A. (2007). *Selected treatises*. Kazan: Tatarstan Book Publishing House.

Valchev, R. (2004). *Interaktivni metodi i grazhdansko obrazovanie [Interactive methods and citizenship education]*. Sofia: Open Education Center.

Valchev, R. (2005). *Kniga za uchidelya* [*A Handbook for the Teacher*]. Sofia: Open Education Center.

Valchev, R. (UNESCO) (2006). *Education, Intercultural Dialogue and the Development of Democratic Attitudes: the Reality and Perspectives - the perspectives from South-Eastern Europe, Dialogue among Civilizations*. Paris.

Valk, P., Bertram-Troost, G., Friederici, M. & Béraud, C. (Eds.) (2009). *Teenagers' Perspectives on the Role of Religion in their Lives, Schools and Societies. A European Quantitative Study*. Münster/New York/München/Berlin: Waxmann.

Van der Kooij, J.C. , de Ruyter, D.J. & Miedema S. (2013). "Worldview": the meaning of the concept and the impact on Religious Education. *Religious Education. 108,* (210-228).

Waghid, Y. (2011). *Conceptions of Islamic Education: Pedagogic Framings*. New York: Peter Lang.

Walzer, M. (1985). *Thick and Thin, Moral Argument at Home and Abroad* Notre Dame: Univ. of Notre Dame Press.

Wardekker, W.L. & Miedema, S. (2001). Identity, Cultural Change and Religious. *Education. British Journal of Religious Education. 2,* (76-87).

Wax, R. H. (1971). *Doing fieldwork: Warnings and advice*. Chicago: The University of Chicago Press.

Webb-Mitchell, B. P. (2003). *Christly Gestures: Learning to Be Members of the Body of Christ*.

Wellhausen, J. (1889). *Skizzen und Vorarbeiten*. Berlin: Georg Reimer.

Wendland, W. (2013). „*Trzy czoła proroków z matki obcej". Myśl historyczna Tatarów Polskich w II Rzeczpospolitej*. Kraków: Universitas.

Wenninger, F., & Dreidemy, L. (Eds.). (2013). Das Dollfuß/Schuschnigg-Regime 1933-1938. *Vermessungen eines Forschungsfeldes*. Wien: Böhlau.

Wikipedia (2011). Wort des Jahres. From: http://de.wikipedia.org/wiki/Wort_des_Jahres. (Accessed July 28, 2012).

Wikipedia. From: http://en.wikipedia.org/wiki/Active_citizenship, (Accessed February 17, 2014).

Williams, K., Hinge, H. & Persson, B. L. (2008). *Religion and Citizenship Education in Europe*. London: CICE.

Woronowicz, A.I. (1937). Nasza praca społeczna. *Życie Tatarskie, 9,* (5-6).

Wróblewska, U. (2012). *Oświata Tatarów w Drugiej Rzeczypospolitej*. Warszawa: Semper.

www.culte.ro – *State Secretariat for the Religious Affaires* - Governmental organism within the Ministry of Culture and Cults, (*Secretariatul de Stat pentru Culte* – Organism guvernamental în componenţa Ministerului Culturii şi Cultelor).

www.dri.gov.ro - the *Department of inter-ethnic relationships (DIR)* is a governmental institution founded in 2001 and its aim is '*to be one of the main factors to promote good inter-ethnic relations, pluralism and diversity*' The department is subordinated to the Prime Minister and is coordinated by a Secretary of State. www.edu.ro – *Ministry of National Education, Research and Youth, (Ministerul Educaţiei Nationale).*

www.muftiyat.ro - the official website of the Mufti at of the Muslim community in Romania

www.tatar.ro – the official website of the Tatar community in Romania

www.udtr.ro - Romanian, Democratic Turkish Union.

Yakupov, V. (2003). *Tatarstanda Rasmi Bulmagan Islam*. Kazan: Iman.

Yakupov, V. (2006 a). *Towards a Prophetical Islam*. Kazan: Iman.

Yakupov, V. (2006 b). *Lzhedzhadidism*. Kazan: Iman.

Yakupov, V. (2011). *Islam Today*. Kazan: Iman.

Yunus, R. (2011) *Ramil hazrat Yunus Wagazlere*. Kazan: Akcharlak.

Yuval-Davis, N. (2011). *The politics of belonging. Intersectional contestations*. London: Sage.

Yuval-Davis, N., Kannabiran, K., & Vieten, U. M. (2006). Introduction: Situating contemporary politics of belonging. In: Yuval-Davis, N., Kannabiran, K., & Vieten, U. M. (Eds.). *Situating contemporary politics of belonging.* (1-14). London: Sage.

Zakrzewski, A. B. (1998). Czy Tatarzy litewscy rzeczywiście nie byli szlachtą?. *Przegląd Historyczny 79(3)*, (573-580).

Zant, K. (n.d.). *Tell Me About Faith*. Personal Site: www.kamalzant.ru

Zehnpfennig, B. (2011). Adolf Hitler: Mein Kampf. Studienkommentar. Stuttgart: UTB.

Zentrum polis. From: http://www.politik-lernen.at/ (Accessed February 16, 2014).

ZRD. *www.islam.de*. (15.09.2009). From: http://zentralrat.de/3035.php (Accessed January 10, 2013).

Zucconi, C. G. (2011). Christus oder Hitler?: Das Leben des seligen Franz Jägerstätter. Würzburg. Echter.

Бойцова, Е., Ганкевич, В., Муратова, Э. & Хайрединова, З. (2009). *Ислам в Крыму: очерки истории функционирования мусульманских институтов*. Симферополь: Элиньо.

Министерство за култура [Ministry of Culture]. (30.04.2013) From: http://www.kultura.gov.mk/index.php/odnosi-so-javnost/soopstenija/933-treta-svetska-konferencija-za-megjureligiski-i%20megjucivilizaciskidijalog (Retrieved 8 March 2014)

Република Online [Republic Online]. (08.05.2013). From: http://republika.mk/?p=64376 (Retrieved 9 March 2014).